TAKING LIBERTIES

SUSAN N. HERMAN

TAKING
LIBERTIES

The War on Terror
and the Erosion
of American Democracy

To Mike Gaynier,
With gratitude for
your support of the ACLU
and our liberty.

Best,
Susan Herman

OXFORD
UNIVERSITY PRESS

OXFORD

UNIVERSITY PRESS

Oxford University Press, Inc., publishes works that further
Oxford University's objective of excellence
in research, scholarship, and education.

Oxford   New York
Auckland   Cape Town   Dar es Salaam   Hong Kong   Karachi
Kuala Lumpur   Madrid   Melbourne   Mexico City   Nairobi
New Delhi   Shanghai   Taipei   Toronto

With offices in
Argentina   Austria   Brazil   Chile   Czech Republic   France   Greece
Guatemala   Hungary   Italy   Japan   Poland   Portugal   Singapore
South Korea   Switzerland   Thailand   Turkey   Ukraine   Vietnam

Published by Oxford University Press, Inc.
198 Madison Avenue, New York, NY 10016

www.oup.com

Oxford is a registered trademark of Oxford University Press

Library of Congress Cataloging-in-Publication Data
Herman, Susan N.
Taking liberties : the war on terror and the erosion of american democracy / Susan Herman.
    p.   cm.
Includes bibliographical references and index.
ISBN 978-0-19-978254-3 (hardback)
1. Terrorism—Prevention—Law and legislation—United States. 2. Internal security—United States.
3. Detention of persons—United States. 4. Electronic surveillance—United States.
5. Civil rights—United States. 6. War and emergency powers—United States.
7. War on Terrorism, 2001–2009. I. Title.
KF9430.H47   2011
344.7305'32517—dc23   2011016285

9 8 7 6 5 4 3 2

Printed in the United States of America
on acid-free paper

To Paul, who was with me every step of the way,

with love.

Contents

Acknowledgments

MY HEARTFELT THANKS to my readers and sources, without whom this book truly would not have been possible: Liz Brandt, Nusrat Choudhury, George Christian, Ralph Fertig, Paul Gangsei, David Gangsei, Erica Herman Gangsei, Lee Gelernt, Melissa Goodman, George Herman, Jameel Jaffer, Abdullah al-Kidd, Lindy Laub, Mary Lieberman, Michael Madow, Christopher Man, Brandon Mayfield, Nick Merrill, David Nevin, Roya Rahmani, Paul Rashkind, Anthony Romero, Ali Safavi, Erich Scherfen, Steve Shapiro, Jay Stanley, Rubina Tareen, Nelson Tebbe, Jennifer Turner, Vic Walczak, and Ben Wizner.

For their invaluable research assistance and support, I am grateful to Emily Powers, Anita Aboagye-Agyeman, Allison Lack, Tia Clinton, and Ateqah Khaki, and for their commitment to this project and wise advice, I thank my agent, Sydelle Kramer, and my editor, Dave McBride.

For academic support and early encouragement, I thank my colleagues and faculty workshop members at Brooklyn, Cornell, and NYU Law Schools, and the Brooklyn Law School research stipend program. Thanks also to Professor Theodore Ruger.

I also want to thank and acknowledge the perceptive early critics of the Patriot Act, including Rachel King, whose work at the ACLU served as a template for all who followed, and Russell Feingold, the only senator to vote against the Patriot Act.

TAKING LIBERTIES

Introduction

A N ACQUAINTANCE, KNOWING of my position as president of the American Civil Liberties Union, asked me to tell her what the ACLU was doing these days. "But don't tell me about that Guantánamo stuff," she said. "I'm so sick of hearing about that. Why should I care about those people when they're not even Americans?" I started to explain that the Patriot Act and other post-9/11 antiterrorism measures do affect Americans, including her, but she waved me off, insisting that all of that had nothing to do with her.

This woman is not alone is assuming that the War on Terror does not affect law-abiding Americans, or even that all "that Patriot Act stuff" ended when George W. Bush left the White House. But she is wrong. Her own rights and those of many other ordinary Americans—and even the democracy she takes for granted—are compromised by antiterrorism strategies unleashed after September 11, 2001. She could be one of the hundreds of thousands of innocent Americans the FBI has been spying on using the broad net of the Patriot Act and supplemental powers; her banker and her stockbroker, among many others, have collected financial and other personal data about her to lodge in government databanks, ready to trigger an investigation of her if the government happens to connect some dot of information to her dots (even if she's done nothing wrong); her computer geek neighbor might be one of the innumerable telecommunications workers and librarians whom the FBI has conscripted to gather information on hundreds of thousands of occasions, perhaps about her friends or acquaintances—and then ordered not to tell anyone anything about their experience on pain of criminal prosecution; her nephew could be the computer studies student prosecuted for providing "material support to terrorists" (a crime punishable by up to fifteen years, imprisonment) because he served as webmaster for a website posting links to other people's hateful comments; her son could be the college student detained and interrogated for packing his Arabic-English flash cards to study during a plane flight; she could find herself unable to complete an important business or personal trip because her name was incorrectly placed on a No Fly list, or simply because she has a common name, like "T. Kennedy"; her favorite charity could be shut down for years or even permanently because a government bureaucrat once decided to investigate it even if the investigation went nowhere; her generous contribution toward humanitarian relief might be sitting in government escrow for years instead of reaching the intended recipients or being returned to her; her doctor's assistant could be the young Kashmiri-American who was stopped and searched in the New York City subways on twenty-one separate occasions even though the odds of the same person being selected for a "random" search that often are 1 in 165 million. She might not know the Americans whose lives were seriously derailed because government agents mistakenly identified them as terrorists—like the Oregon lawyer who was falsely suspected of involvement with terrorist incidents in Spain due to an incorrect identification of his fingerprint, or the former University of Idaho football player who was arrested on the pretext that he was needed as a "material witness" although he was never asked to testify—but post-9/11 policies have also fostered devastating mistakes like these.

All of these things have happened; all of these things can keep happening. Should we be willing to tolerate this level of surveillance, intrusion, and potential error because these efforts are helping to keep us safe? The beginning of the second post-9/11 decade is a good time to start a serious reevaluation of our approaches to fighting terrorism and to expose and question some underlying assumptions that may not be serving us well. The War on Terror decade has generated a powerful frame for evaluating government antiterrorism strategies, based on three assumptions: (1) terrorism is an exceptional threat; (2) we need to adapt by giving up rights in order to be safe; and (3) our strategies for combating terrorism have to remain secret so we just have to trust the president, who is best able to operate in secrecy, to decide what rights we need to give up. This fear-inflected frame is the very antithesis of constitutional democracy. The time has come to rattle this frame and return to first principles in reevaluating our course.

In this book, I will not be talking about "that Guantánamo stuff." Many other books, articles, and nationwide conversations have agonized about the legality, constitutionality, and morality of the detention and interrogation policies 9/11 tempted us to use against suspected terrorists. Many scholars and pundits have also criticized the Bush/Cheney Administration up, down, and sideways for its responses to 9/11. This book is about us and it is about now. A decade is a long enough time to allow us to step back and try to look at the whole picture of the costs and benefits of strategies that were forged during the panicky days right after 9/11. The death of Osama bin Laden in some respects ended an emotional chapter, perhaps freeing us to view the costs and benefits of our antiterrorism strategies with a calmer eye. And more than halfway through Barack Obama's term is a good time to disentangle the criticisms of George W. Bush's policies, many of which are still with us, from the more personal criticisms of his presidency itself.

It is not surprising that in the weeks immediately following 9/11, the president and Congress reacted by creating dragnets of all kinds aimed at investigating and preventing any possible recurrences. They did not know whether there were terrorist sleeper cells embedded around the country, how the hijackers had financed their activities, or how Al Qaeda could be neutralized, but they wanted to find out as much as possible in all these areas and to be able to take any action that might be productive. A frightened country demanded protection as well as comfort. So the country's leaders improvised and adopted a wide variety of emergency measures that could imaginably discover or thwart terrorists. The prevailing idea at the time was that we should take aggressive preventive action even if we didn't have evidence that a particular action would actually enhance our safety, as long as there was some chance that it might do so. This attitude was epitomized by Vice President Dick Cheney's "1 percent doctrine": "If there's a 1% chance that Pakistani scientists are helping al-Qaeda build or develop a nuclear weapon, we have to treat it as a certainty in terms of our response. It's not about our analysis . . . It's about our response."[1]

Congress's chief contribution was the USA PATRIOT Act, a rather labored acronym for an act actually entitled "Uniting and Strengthening America by Providing Appropriate Tools Required to Intercept and Obstruct Terrorism Act of 2001."[2] This Act was passed a mere six weeks after 9/11, without any meaningful deliberations or hearings. In retrospect, the assertion that Congress already knew exactly what tools were required to obstruct terrorism sounds like fear-induced swagger. The contents of the Act matched its over-confident title. In hundreds of provisions amending previous laws, the Patriot Act empowered administration officials to spy on anyone, including Americans, with less basis for suspicion and less judicial review; it stretched and repurposed criminal laws by allowing prosecution for "material support" of terrorism even if the person prosecuted did not have any intention of supporting terrorists; it exposed business records, including medical, educational, and library records, to easy capture by government agents in several different ways; and it expanded the reach of the Foreign Intelligence Surveillance Act, initially designed to keep track of Soviet spies, to more easily cover spying on

Americans. Many of these provisions threatened privacy; the freedoms of speech, association, and religion; due process; and equality, but supporters declared that although this was unfortunate, it was necessary—we have to give up some of our rights in order to be safe. Only one senator, Russell Feingold, voted against the Patriot Act and introduced measures to hone its provisions, questioning the widespread assumption that security and liberty were contestants in a zero-sum game.[3] President Bush provided dragnets of his own, like a declaration of emergency under which he abruptly seized the assets of a number of American charities, and the creation of a highly secret "President's Surveillance Program" under which the National Security Agency conducted surveillance of countless numbers of Americans, in defiance of the law in existence at the time. Bush and Cheney were as willing to dispense with the Constitution's checks and balances as its rights for the sake of combating terrorism, and so the administration repeatedly tried to minimize the role of Congress and the courts—and the American people themselves—in formulating or reviewing antiterrorism strategies.

It is understandable if some of those immediate reactions were overreactions. There are many reasons to be skeptical of the decisions made in the fog of 9/11. First, the course of many of our antiterrorism strategies was set before anyone had a chance to study the events of 9/11, so antidotes were being prepared before the disease had been diagnosed. Second, decisions made in the grip of fear are not likely to be balanced. Third, strategies that may have seemed plausible as emergency measures in the fall of 2001 could prove, over time, to be inefficient, too costly (in terms of rights or resources), or even counterproductive. Finally, short-term emergency sacrifices of rights can be regarded as a break in our usual patterns. Continuing into a second decade and beyond, these emergency measures stop being temporary exceptions and become part of who we are: the New Normal. For these reasons, the 9/11 Commission, which actually did study the causes and consequences of 9/11, recommended that the executive branch be required to bear the burden of showing why extraordinary powers conferred after 9/11 should be retained.[4]

But our approach to counterterrorism strategies has not changed appreciably during the past decade, despite the fact that a new president occupied the White House. President Barack Obama inherited the weapons and infrastructure of Bush's War on Terror, along with government employees who had been engaged in the campaigns, and much of the litigation brought to challenge the constitutionality of actions like those listed above. Obama's rhetoric has certainly been different. He has expressed skepticism about the misleading "war" metaphor and promised his allegiance to constitutional values. In his inaugural address he declared, "We reject as false the choice between our safety and our ideals."[5] And he has disavowed some Bush-era tactics. His first executive orders promised to close Guantánamo, to impose limits on harsh interrogation techniques, and to put democracy back on track by increasing the transparency of government.

Nevertheless, the Obama Administration has explicitly endorsed or just continued to employ most of the Bush/Cheney post-9/11 strategies when it comes to the rights of ordinary Americans to be free from unfair prosecutions and excessive government spying. Obama's Solicitor General and Supreme Court choice Elena Kagan, for example, told the Supreme Court that a Patriot Act–enhanced provision criminalizing the provision of "material support" to terrorists could properly be applied to prosecute people who try to persuade terrorist groups *not* to commit acts of terrorism, or even to lawyers filing briefs on behalf of groups the government believes have ties with terrorism.[6] Obama might never actually prosecute humanitarians or lawyers, but he does want to retain the dragnet power to do so. Candidate Obama denounced the use of National Security Letters to gather information about innocent Americans without any court order, but the Obama Administration has asked Congress to expand the reach of this power.[7] Senator Obama voted in favor of the institutionalization of an expanded version of Bush's National Security Agency warrantless spying program, and in favor of granting immunity to the telecommunications providers who cooperated with that program even while it was plainly illegal. Consistently with those positions, the Obama Administration has defended the constitutionality of that controversial program. Although President Obama has expressed a greater willingness to share power with Congress, he sometimes echoes at least some of Bush's antipathy to meaningful congressional oversight. Obama threatened, for example, to veto a version of the 2010 intelligence authorization bill in which congressional Democrats provided for increased oversight of intelligence agencies.[8] And Obama's Justice Department has continued the Bush effort to sideline the courts by any means imaginable. His lawyers, for the most part, stick to the Bush lawyers' script. They employ the same extreme procedural arguments, including the state secrets privilege and claims of immunity, to tell the courts that they should not even think about finding executive actions like sprawling surveillance programs unconstitutional, or finding Bush-era government officials accountable for illegal actions.

The Obama Administration seems, at least at times, to agree with the Just Trust Us philosophy that unilateral executive power is acceptable—as long as the people wielding that power act in good faith. President Obama and his appointees no longer object as strongly to unilateral executive power as candidate Obama did, because they believe that they truly are trustworthy. Attorney General Eric Holder, for example, issued a much heralded revised policy on use of the state secrets privilege.[9] In the extreme form employed by the Bush Administration, this claim of privilege asserted that the executive branch rather than the courts should get to decide which cases the courts must dismiss if the executive branch says that the very act of litigating a claim would compromise national security. Bush lawyers had argued, for instance, that the president's surveillance program was too secret even to be reviewed by the courts, as was the "extraordinary rendition" program that led to people being kidnapped and sent to other countries where they were locked in black holes and tortured. Holder earnestly announced that his state secrets policy would be different—*he* would only claim the privilege where it really is necessary. But he still reserved the option of not showing the courts the documents on which his assessment is based.[10] Just trust *us*. We're different.

The Holder state secrets policy itself is not substantively different from his predecessors' policy and, given that the whole point of these privilege claims is to prevent issues from being openly discussed, we are unlikely ever to be able to evaluate whether Holder's application of that policy will indeed be different. The Holder Justice Department clearly understands the dangers of unilateral executive power exercised in secret—the policy announces that the state secrets privilege will not be used to cover up mistakes—but expects us to be reassured by a solemn insistence that, unlike their predecessors, *these* lawyers will not succumb to those dangers. Plato, in *The Republic*, uses the myth of Gyges, who discovers a ring that renders him invisible, to discuss the temptation of those who believe their actions are invisible to disregard the limits of the law.[11] It is unrealistic to believe that people who have undertaken a noble mission—to safeguard the American people—will police their means of pursuing that mission effectively if they also believe that they will not be accountable for their actions. That is why the Constitution establishes an elaborate system of checks and balances to provide accountability. But wielding the state secrets privilege, invisible government actors claim the power to decide for themselves when and if they will give up their cloak of invisibility. Thus, in a case involving eavesdropping without a warrant, Obama Administration lawyers who were urging the court to dismiss the case on the basis of the state secrets privilege acknowledged that secrecy can indeed provide a cover for government misconduct. So the lawyers addressed this problem by promising the court that the government (under Bush as well as Obama) really had not committed any misconduct. And they continued to conceal documents that might have shed light on whether or not that assertion was accurate.[12]

It is certainly true that, in some respects, the Obama Administration has used its weaponry more sparingly and with more circumspection. Bush-era officials, for example, denied Swiss Islamic scholar Tariq Ramadan a visa to enter the United States, preventing him from accepting a teaching position at Notre Dame. Their justification changed so abruptly (Did he preach or endorse terrorism? Had he contributed to an Islamic charity with alleged ties to terrorism?) and matched the actual facts so poorly (Ramadan styles himself as an anti-jihad Islamic reformer) that it began to seem obvious that this was an ideological exclusion—a McCarthy-like attempt to keep prickly ideas out of the country. Obama lawyers initially defended this exclusion in court, but the issue was mooted when Secretary of State Hillary Clinton issued Ramadan his visa. While other scholars shared Ramadan's fate under the Bush Administration, the Obama Administration does not seem to be trying to fence out ideas. During the Bush era, antiwar activists frequently complained that they were being subjected to special surveillance, harassment, or other retaliation because they expressed their dissenting views in ways that are supposed to be protected by the First Amendment.[13] Comparable complaints about misuse of anti-terrorism powers against dissenters or political opponents have not been leveled against the Obama Administration.[14]

It is still too early to assess to what extent the Obama Administration will manage to avoid the mistakes and abuses of Bush Administration officials in implementing antiterrorism laws—like the prosecution of a University of Idaho graduate student for posting links on a website, or the FBI's persecution of Oregon lawyer Brandon Mayfield, who was suspected of involvement in the Madrid train bombing even after it should have been apparent that he was completely innocent. But tools as powerful as those in the post-9/11 arsenal are dangerous no matter who wields them. Dragnets, especially when used in secret, will sweep in people who are not the intended targets—people who are innocent but who suffer collateral damage. When broad discretionary powers are delegated to thousands of government agents, it is inevitable that there will be serious lapses of judgment somewhere along the chain. George W. Bush did not tell the FBI to arrest Brandon Mayfield. And not every Transportation Security

Administration (TSA) or FBI agent will exercise discretion in the same way Barack Obama or Eric Holder would.

Furthermore, many of the Patriot Act–enhanced statutes do harm even when they are not called into play. Dragnet laws that make it possible to prosecute other webmasters, or to prosecute humanitarians who come too close to members of a designated "terrorist" group while they are distributing aid, abridge our First Amendment rights by their very existence. They cause people to think twice about whether to engage in speech or association that might draw unwanted government attention or suspicion. Laws that threaten nonprofit charities and foundations with the possibility of being blacklisted and having their assets unceremoniously seized, on the basis of secret hearsay evidence, discourage people from exercising their First Amendment right to choose their associations and to fulfill their religious obligations by contributing to charities of their choice. Overbroad surveillance laws deter people from speaking freely on international calls, even if they are talking to their attorney or an investigative journalist, making it difficult for lawyers and reporters to do their jobs. Laws that require schools, hospitals, and libraries to turn over sensitive records to the government undermine relationships of trust and cause people to think twice before sharing information that might be needed to help them.

The immediate emergency after 9/11 was to apprehend and neutralize members of Al Qaeda. But the War on Al Qaeda quickly morphed into a generalized War on Terror. Many Patriot Act and other tools that may have seemed acceptable approaches to dismantling Al Qaeda and its direct threat to Americans on American soil are not actually limited to that goal. The emergency-inspired antiterrorism laws I will describe apply in full force to dozens of other government-designated "terrorist" groups, ranging from Hamas to Turkish Kurds to pro-democracy activists in Iran. And some of the post-9/11 expanded powers have already been prey to mission creep. Patriot Act–authorized "sneak and peek" warrants, dispensing with notice that one's premises have been searched, were used 763 times in fiscal year 2008, but only 3 of those cases involved terrorism investigations.[15] When a Patriot Act anti-money-laundering provision was used to investigate the owner of a Las Vegas strip club for bribery, Nevada Senator Harry Reid remarked: "The law was intended for activities related to terrorism and not to naked women."[16] Once we become accustomed to lowering our baselines—of what counts as an acceptable level of surveillance, or a tolerable criminal law, for example—it is all too easy for us to endorse the use of increasingly familiar tools against anyone, not just a suspected terrorist, but a tax evader or a racketeer. And the Constitution is downsized another notch to accommodate another law enforcement strategy.

Legal historian Geoffrey Stone reminds us that Americans have, in the past, overreacted during times of war or crisis—our shameful treatment of West Coast Japanese-Americans during World War II, our war on an ideology during the McCarthy era—but observes that after the emergency ends, we generally regret what we have done and are able to regain our balance.[17] But when does the emergency of terrorism end? Unlike a conventional war, the "War on Terror" has no natural end point. As Barack Obama has recognized, terrorism is a tactic. We cannot end this metaphorical war by signing a peace treaty with Al Qaeda and dozens of other groups we list as terrorists. Are we willing to countenance a second decade of emergency reactions that are more costly to our rights and to our democracy than most Americans realize? The time has come to decide whether these weapons are truly consistent with our Constitution's foundational principles, rather than just trusting that the current president will use them more wisely than his predecessor. As Justice Robert Jackson so memorably said in the *Korematsu* case, dissenting from the Supreme Court ruling allowing over 100,000 loyal Japanese-Americans to be removed from their homes because the government said it was impossible to distinguish a few disloyal individuals, once we opportunistically revise a constitutional principle, "[t]he principle then lies about like a loaded weapon, ready for the hand of any authority that can bring forward a plausible claim of an urgent need. Every repetition imbeds that principle more deeply in our law and thinking and expands it to new purposes."[18]

Those who trust Barack Obama more than they trusted George W. Bush should bear in mind that there will be other presidents after Obama. The level of trust in a particular administration can indeed affect the extent to which people will fear being arrested or investigated for exercising their rights. But future presidents will inherit the Bush-era arsenal of weapons unless we persuade Obama and Congress to disarm or retrofit some of the undesirable ones now, and those presidents may be less sensitive to constitutional values than a former Constitutional Law professor.

Whatever one's personal views of Barack Obama, it seems surprising that at a time when, according to public opinion polls,[19] three-quarters of the American people distrust the federal government, we are willing to trust that same government to strike the right balance between our cherished constitutional rights—indeed, our democracy itself—and national security. Why is this so? One reason is certainly that most Americans do underestimate the costs of our antiterrorism programs—in privacy, liberty, fairness, and equality as well as in resources. This is partly because so many of those costs are invisible behind the wall of secrecy; because the laws involved are dauntingly complex and hard to comprehend; and because it is difficult to put together a complete picture just based on periodic news stories about particular incidents or debates. I am writing this book to offer a more complete and coherent account of those costs.

A second reason there has not been more resistance is undoubtedly that many Americans believe that these laws and policies will not cause them much inconvenience if they are not Muslims or Arabs. As the following chapters will show, many of our post-9/11 strategies do have a significant impact or potential impact on a large number of people regardless of their religion or ethnic origin. But it is true that the most substantial costs of our antiterrorism campaign have fallen on Muslims and Arabs, whether they are American citizens or not. Muslim-Americans are more susceptible to being prosecuted even if they are innocent, to being prevented from returning to their homes in the United States because they are incomprehensibly included on a No Fly list, to having their banks inexplicably decide to close their accounts, or to having their legitimate charities put out of business.

Muslim-Americans are Americans, even if their names or religious practices seem unfamiliar to many, and they have the same constitutional rights as all other Americans. But as shown by the recent controversy over the New York City mosque planned for a site near the World Trade Center, Muslims are readily stereotyped as terrorists or potential terrorists because the 9/11 hijackers were Muslims. Rationally, everyone should know that the vast majority of the millions of Muslims in the United States are law-abiding people who have nothing to do with terrorism. Rationally, everyone should understand that targeting all Muslims, or any Muslim who happens to be within sight, is a remarkably ineffective and probably counterproductive way to fight terrorism. But emotionally, many Americans are suspicious of Muslims generally and so are willing to countenance treating any or all Muslims as suspect.[20] This stereotyping is unjustifiable and un-American. Earlier waves of immigrants, whether Irish, Italian, or Jewish, also met hostility and discrimination. During the post–World War I Palmer Raids, thousands of Russian and Eastern European immigrants were arrested, prosecuted, deported, and sometimes abused because Attorney General Mitchell Palmer thought that because some anarchists were immigrants, it was logical to assume that any immigrant (people whom he described as looking "sly and crafty") might be an anarchist.[21] We should be able to learn from our history that when we assume guilt by association, when we target groups of people because of their religion or ethnicity, no good is accomplished and we are later ashamed. The Equal Protection Clause of the Fourteenth Amendment, added to the Constitution after the Civil War to prevent the freed slaves from being abused because of their race, embodies our commitment to treating every person as an individual rather than solely as a member of a racial, ethnic, or religious group. The American tradition of tolerance goes back to the original framers of the Constitution in the eighteenth century. Benjamin Franklin, for example, writing in his autobiography about the nonsectarian nature of a church in Philadelphia, said that "even if the Mufti of Constantinople were to send a missionary to preach Mohammedanism to us, he would find a pulpit at his service."[22]

An additional reason we have been just trusting the president is that the last ten years have inculcated in many Americans a sense that we cannot know enough to make the policy decisions about how much surveillance is too much or whether particular security programs work. While it is certainly true that the rigors of secrecy make it difficult for us to assess what benefits we may be getting from broad material support laws, wholesale surveillance, or massive data banking, for example, there is no good reason why the American people cannot be included in the decision-making process to a greater degree than we have been so far. We, the people, have been excluded by excessive claims of secrecy and infantilized by the Just Trust Us approach. The other side of the Just Trust the Government coin is distrust of the American people. In the chapters to follow, I will document how antiterrorism laws are built on lack of faith in the American people, with our leaders positing that we can't be trusted to evaluate hateful ideas for ourselves, that we can't be trusted to talk to a terrorist, that we can't be trusted to form our own opinions about the wisdom of antiterrorism measures. This is not American democracy.

Some might contend that we accept this diminished, antidemocratic role because Americans have become generally disengaged and passive and do not expect to be able to control the government. If this is true, it is a dangerous pattern and one that we, like many of the people I will describe in the book, should resist vigorously. In addition to fighting apathy, we also battle powerful psychological forces when we confront the question of what to do about terrorism and rights. Fear of terrorism makes it difficult for us to be rational and easy for us to hope that the government actually does know better than we ever could how to protect us. And so we may not really want to learn that the government's promises to keep us safe are inflated or that particular tools vaunted for their ability to obliterate terrorism don't amount to much more than dearly bought magic beans.

Because we prefer, or maybe even need to believe that we can buy security by squandering our liberty, contrary information may bounce right off of us. Linguist George Lakoff tells us that a frame on an issue, once embedded, can trump facts.[23] The War on Terror frame has us start with the assumption that we are unsafe unless we give up some of our rights and, conversely, that giving up some of our rights is likely to make us safer. Beginning with that premise, people have been willing to trust the New York City Police Department, for example, when it declares that random searches of backpacks in the subway will deter terrorists. We want it to be true, and so perhaps we, like the court finding the program to be constitutional, don't want to ask too many hard questions. Will this program really prevent terrorism if any terrorist can simply walk away and enter the subway at a different stop? Shouldn't we be concerned if it seems that the program, despite contrary assurances, involves racial profiling of people with brown skin who look Muslim or Arab? I have heard people say that they don't actually think the New York City subway search program is an effective way to prevent terrorism, but it still makes them feel safer. After a decade of watching antiterrorism measures being instituted and listening to assurances that they are effective—usually with little or no evidence offered to back up those assertions, on the excuse that both our successes and failures must be kept secret—are we willing to ask hard questions about whether those programs are really effective, cost-effective, or counterproductive? Or are we so anxious that we will accept placebos, even if they have serious side effects? Are we willing to play our intended role in a constitutional democracy, or do we prefer to let the president decide what's best for us?

Democratic distrust is not ad hominem. It extends equally to George W. Bush, Barack Obama, and every one of their successors. The Constitution is a very distrustful document. Under its hydraulic system of checks and balances, presidents are rarely allowed to make important decisions—like appointing a Supreme Court Justice, entering a treaty, or declaring war—without participation by Congress. The courts then provide an essential check if the president and Congress are not respectful enough of our rights. But during most of the War on Terror decade, Congress has remained passive, letting the president make too many key decisions unilaterally and allowing the executive agencies to police themselves. As the examples I will give clearly show, this is a mistake, just as the Constitution predicted. Discretionary powers exercised in secret, without sufficient oversight, are easily subject to abuse and, as I will document, have in fact been extensively abused.

And the courts have allowed themselves to be muzzled, an even graver mistake. In fact, the courts have actively collaborated in keeping themselves from speaking out on behalf of our rights. Although the Supreme Court decided a series of historic cases questioning the president's and then Congress's detention policies ("that Guantánamo stuff"), the Court simply declined to hear case after case where Americans complained that our own rights are being compromised by excessive secrecy and overzealous antiterrorism strategies—the issues I will be discussing in this book. The lower federal courts have hidden behind a dizzying array of procedural excuses for refusing to consider constitutional claims about issues affecting us. A number of courts have declared that no one has standing—that is, the right to bring a lawsuit—to challenge eavesdropping programs unless they can prove that the government has been listening to their own telephone calls or intercepting their own e-mails. This is a true Catch-22, when the whole point of secret surveillance is that the target is unaware of being the target. Accepting this definition of standing amounts to benching the courts. Executive branch demands for secrecy have compromised litigation in many cases and wholly precluded it in others, as courts have accepted radical standing, governmental immunity, and state secrets privilege arguments. Courts have allowed the government to conceal key documents from the lawyers on the other side and sometimes from the court itself, and even conspired to keep the very existence of entire cases a secret. The Supreme Court refused to decide any case about the domestic impact of antiterrorism strategies until 2010. And then, in the case of *Holder v. Humanitarian Law Project*,[24] the Court essentially just deferred to the government's assertions that the dragnet law in question (a broad material support law) was useful enough to warrant elbowing the First Amendment out of the way.

This book will show how ordinary Americans have been affected by the War on Terror by having our own rights and privacy compromised, by being deterred from exercising our collective right to free speech and association, and by having our democracy skewed. Aspects of a number of these stories may be familiar to some from news accounts over the years. But it is critical to put together the pieces of this puzzle to see the full picture and to observe the themes that emerge: the pitfalls of excessive secrecy, the consequences of abdication by Congress and the courts, and the enduring wisdom of the Constitution's prescribed methods for protecting our rights. It should also be noted that these stories are only the tip of an iceberg of consequences. I will discuss, for example, six people—four librarians and two Internet service providers—who challenged a particular form of surveillance called the National Security Letter. Hundreds of thousands of National Security Letter requests have been served since 9/11 but, because of draconian gag orders built right into the statute, the public only knows the stories of these six intrepid individuals. The people involved in the hundreds of thousands of other instances apparently caved in to the government's demands to turn over sensitive records about their clients or patrons without any court order and never to mention the experience to anyone, and so we don't know what they might have to say. Secrecy prevents us from fully assessing costs—as well as benefits—and also means that we often cannot see the features of the people adversely affected by our policies, even when we know they exist. The stories that can be told and woven together at this point are not a complete history, but they are troubling enough to cause concern and to help us visualize what else might be behind the curtain.

I also want to stress that many of the people whose stories I will tell are not just victims. In a decade when all three branches of government failed to safeguard our constitutional values, ordinary Americans—librarians like George Christian of Library Connection of Connecticut, Internet service providers like Brewster Kahle of the Internet Archive and another patriotic litigant who spent over six years identifiable only as John Doe, as well as military leaders, social workers, journalists, administration officials who made the difficult decision to share their concerns about runaway programs with reporters, even local governments—rose up to do the job the Constitution expects "the people" to do—to be the government and to defend our constitutional birthright.

My interest is not in flogging the Bush Administration for its errors or indulging in *schadenfreude*. My focus is primarily on powers and potential problems that are still in play as I write. Unlike Andrew Bacevich[25] and some others who have written damning critiques of the Bush Administration's War on Terror, I do not seek to portray 9/11 as a convenient excuse for people who wanted to aggrandize executive power for their own selfish reasons. There are many other reasons why presidents and government officials of good faith who do believe in constitutional values are willing to seek overinflated executive powers when it comes to national security. It is these natural pressures I am interested in exploring, rather than engaging in ad hominem attacks.

Several caveats: First, I do not claim to be an expert on how to defeat terrorism. After more than three decades of studying, teaching, and writing about the Constitution and more than two decades working closely with the ACLU, I think I can claim some expertise on the subject of civil liberties. My perspective is from the civil liberties side of the scale, but that doesn't mean I do not understand that these issues can look different from the point of view of the president and Congress, as we hold them responsible for our protection and blame them if they fail. If my views tilt toward the civil liberties side of the balance, I hope to counteract the constant pressure on our elected officials to tilt to the other side and look to short-term pragmatism (including the results of the next election) rather than to our long-term values. It is not my purpose—or within my competence—to judge which antiterrorism techniques are or are not effective, but I will point out places where experts seem to question our current assumptions about what is effective, because these are the very places where the judgment of the American people should be invited. I am not prescribing any specific antiterrorism program, but I am inviting all Americans to play a more significant role in the process of deciding whether we need to correct our course. My criticism is primarily skepticism, and my goal is primarily the central goal of the Constitution: to make sure that important policy decisions are made by the right decision-makers.

Second, although I am proud to serve as president of the ACLU and I rely heavily on the admirable work of ACLU lawyers and staff members both in information gathering and analysis, this book is intended to reflect my own views, which are not necessarily those of the ACLU in all respects. But with the ACLU, I believe that the constitutional concerns I raise go beyond partisan politics. There are many areas where libertarians and civil libertarians share concerns about excessive secrecy, excessive surveillance, and unconstrained government power. Conservatives like Bruce Fein[26] agree with people to their left on the political spectrum, like Anthony Lewis,[27] that during the War on Terror decade we have lost our balance and jeopardized our constitutional heritage. The heroes I will describe, those who stood up for constitutional rights and American tradition, include Democrats like Russell Feingold, the sole opponent of the Patriot Act in the Senate, and also libertarians like Ron Paul, who has fought intrusive security measures like bodyscanners at the airport,[28] and whose supporters formed a group to oppose the reelection of any members of

Congress, no matter what their party, who voted to confer immunity on the telecommunications companies that had collaborated with the Bush Administration's illegal surveillance program.[29] Steven Bierfeldt, Development Director of the Campaign for Liberty, an outgrowth of Ron Paul's presidential campaign, became an ACLU client when he was detained at the St. Louis Airport because he was traveling with a quantity of cash connected with his work.[30] Like the ACLU, the Cato Institute has consistently critiqued government overreaching in antiterrorism efforts as unconstitutional and ineffective. In a foresightful 2002 Cato article called "Breaking the Vicious Cycle: Preserving Our Liberties While Fighting Terrorism,"[31] Timothy Lynch argued that lawmakers have developed a destructive pattern of restricting additional civil liberties after every terrorist incident without ever stopping to examine whether earlier hastily adopted restrictions have proved to be effective. "We can either retain our freedom," the article said, "or we can throw it away in an attempt to make ourselves safe." A 2010 book edited by Cato staff, entitled *Terrorizing Ourselves: Why U.S. Counterterrorism Policy Is Failing and How to Fix It*,[32] updates and elaborates on the concerns raised in that article, arguing that politicians are manipulating fear for political purposes and that we are defeating ourselves by succumbing to fantasies about the nature of and cures for terrorism.

One book cannot examine all facets of the issues I raise. Because I am focusing on the rights of Americans, I will not examine the particular impact of antiterrorism measures on non-Americans, an important topic eloquently discussed by David Cole.[33] And because admirable books, including Geoffrey Stone's, examine our history of respect for civil liberties in times of emergency or war, I will not try to repeat that work by spending any significant amount of space on historical context.

What I do aim to do is to correct the lack of balance in our perceptions of the War on Terror by showing how innocent Americans have been prosecuted, incarcerated, blacklisted, watchlisted, conscripted as antiterrorism agents, spied on, and gagged. Part I, "Dragnets and Watchlists," will describe post-9/11 measures, starting with material support laws, that have a substantial effect on First Amendment rights of free speech, free association, and free exercise of religion, as well as on due process and equality. In addition to criminalizing and deterring protected speech, these laws deprive those charged of due process, minimize the role of juries, threaten humanitarians with prosecution for providing aid in troubled parts of the world or even, paradoxically enough, for trying to talk terrorist groups into abandoning their violent tactics. Among those already affected by prosecution under these elastic material support laws, as I will describe, are the Idaho webmaster already mentioned, and an Iranian woman who was granted asylum in the United States after she had been brutally punished for supporting a pro-democracy group in Iran and then found herself prosecuted by the United States for supporting the same group. Next, I will discuss the presidential emergency program allowing the government to seize a charity's assets, with no notice or hearing, which turned into a campaign against Muslim charities, an attack on the freedom of religion, and a serious threat to other nonprofits—all based on a declaration of an emergency now going into its second decade. The first section will conclude with a discussion of security systems, including watchlists used at the airport and by "financial institutions," and then an examination of how businesses have been enlisted as antiterrorism enforcers and data collectors for government databanks.

Part II, "Surveillance and Secrecy," will describe the damage post-9/11 surveillance measures have done to privacy and to essential principles of the Fourth Amendment, our constitutional protection against unreasonable searches and seizures. This section will tell the story of Brandon Mayfield, the American citizen living in Oregon who was ensnared by the Foreign Intelligence Surveillance Act, and the stories of businesses, librarians, and Internet service providers who tried to protect their customers' and patrons' records and found that during the War on Terror decade they had to fight just to get to talk to Congress or a court about whether their constitutional rights were being violated. Finally, I will explore the dramatic story of how President Bush tried to keep either Congress or the courts from reviewing the wisdom and constitutionality of a massive eavesdropping program involving the National Security Agency, and how Congress and President Obama have followed suit.

Part III, "American Democracy," will discuss what we can learn from the failure of all three branches of the federal government to protect constitutional rights during the War on Terror decade. Any president— Bush, Obama, Lincoln, or Roosevelt—will be tempted to err on the side of choosing dragnets and secrecy. Congress has learned something about the importance of oversight in the past decade but is still unlikely to act as a needed check on presidential power. The courts, with a few notable exceptions, have failed to play their expected role of pushing back against governmental programs that compromise rights and democracy. This section will also discuss the impact of secrecy on the courts, and on our First Amendment right of access to judicial proceedings. In conclusion, I will ask what we can learn from our own history and from other countries in recharting our course—by examining not just what mistakes we have made, but how in the past we or our counterparts have succeeded or failed in changing course after straying because of perceived emergencies. My conclusion comments on the Constitution's multiple strategies for self-preservation, including a wide range of both familiar and lesser known rights, checks and balances, and even the structures of federalism. And the foremost and ultimate protection of our democracy is what the Preamble's opening describes as the real government of the United States: ordinary Americans.

I.

DRAGNETS
AND WATCHLISTS

1.

The Webmaster and the Football Player

They were doing things I didn't ever think government agents would do.—Liz Brandt, University of Idaho Law School (2010)

What angers me most is that these are resources that could be spent pursuing real bad guys.—David Manners, former CIA station chief for Jordan (2004)

The part that surprised me was when I read the First Amendment instructions.—John Steger, Idaho juror (2004)

JOHN STEGER, a retired Idaho forest worker, did not expect that he would be sitting in judgment on the Patriot Act or on the First Amendment when he was called for jury duty in April 2004. The case he was assigned to hear was a criminal prosecution against Sami Omar al-Hussayen, a thirty-four-year-old University of Idaho doctoral student whose Saudi name and origins must have seemed exotic in Idaho, a highly conservative state where Arabs make up less than two-tenths of 1 percent of the population.

Sami, who was in the country on a student visa, had been living in Moscow, Idaho (population about 20,000), for five years, along with his wife, Maha, and their three young boys while he worked toward his degree in computer studies. As a Muslim student leader, Sami had led a candlelight vigil on the Idaho campus shortly after 9/11, condemning the attacks as an affront to Islam. His neighbors knew him as a gentle man, the last person anyone would suspect of terrorist sympathies. But Sami was on trial for providing "material support" to terrorists because he volunteered as a webmaster for the Islamic Assembly of North America, a Michigan-based organization, among other groups. The Islamic Assembly described its websites as designed to "[s]pread the correct knowledge of Islam; [and] [w]iden the horizons and understanding . . . among Muslims concerning different Islamic contemporary issues."[1] To serve this educational mission, Sami had set up links so that people could look at a wide variety of sources firsthand, including some anti-American speeches, articles, and "fatwas" (interpretations of Islamic law by Muslim clerics) that advocated criminal activity and suicide operations. Sami said that he didn't himself know what all the sources said, as he did not read them all—he was just posting links, like a journalist reporting what others have said.

Why had the government focused on Sami? One of the Bush Administration's immediate post-9/11 ideas about how to prevent terrorism was to disrupt terrorism-financing networks. Sections of the Patriot Act and a September 2001 Executive Order aimed to starve terrorists by going after the donors and networks that supported them. Suspecting that terrorism-financing networks existed within the United States—there was talk of a pipeline of money flowing from Brooklyn mosques to Al Qaeda—government agents set out to discover who was running those networks. It was certainly no coincidence that Sami was a Muslim and worked with an Islamic charity. Islamic charities were a prime focus of the government's attention. But although, as chapter 3 will recount, many other Muslim charities were put on government watchlists or simply put out of business, the Islamic Assembly was not on any watchlist. Other Patriot Act provisions allowed the government to study Sami's banking records, and so the FBI also learned that he had made substantial contributions to Islamic charities.[2] Of course, giving generously to charity is a religious obligation for all faithful Muslims, just as it is for observant Catholics and Jews.

As it turned out, the agents were looking too hard. The FBI misinterpreted various facts as conforming to their theory that Sami was a terrorist mastermind. For example, investigators hypothesized that Sami's studies were really just a cover for his coming to the United States to raise money for terrorists. As support for this suspicion, they pointed to the fact that he had switched dissertation advisors in the middle of the school year—an unusual thing to do and a sign, they concluded, that he was stalling and that his dissertation was fictitious. But the actual reason Sami switched advisors was that his initial advisor was battling cancer. He found a new advisor so that he could finish his dissertation on schedule. Sami, a serious student who was maintaining a 3.8 average, was only a few months from completing his dissertation when the FBI entered his life.

Having focused on Sami, the government agents pulled out all the stops to come up with evidence to support their theory. Using yet another Patriot Act expansion of authority, they got the Foreign Intelligence Surveillance

Court to let them tap Sami's phone and to review his e-mails—even though they did not have probable cause to believe that he had committed any crime. Over the course of a year, they intercepted about 10,000 telephone calls and 20,000 e-mails involving Sami, his wife, and his family. In this context too, agents misinterpreted innocuous information, perhaps due to mistranslations. For instance, during one telephone conversation, Maha told a friend of her delight on discovering that a Kraft cheese product her children had enjoyed in Saudi Arabia was also available in Idaho. This comment was taken as evidencing an anti-American attitude—that the only thing she liked about America was Kraft cheese.

Despite the mountain of information the FBI gathered about Sami, they evidently did not come up with any concrete evidence to show that the organizations with which Sami was associated were financing terrorism or that Sami approved of terrorism—no less supported it. Therefore, when Sami was arrested, he was not arrested on terrorism or even material support charges. He was arrested for immigration fraud, charged with lying on his student visa forms. According to the government, Sami lied in saying that he had come to the United States "for the sole purpose of" study and not to work—a promise they said was violated by his webmaster duties. Second, the government alleged that Sami had not complied with a post-9/11 requirement that men[3] entering the country provide the government with a list of organizations to which they belong or which they support[4] because he had not listed the Islamic Assembly. According to Sami's lawyers, this was the first time anyone had ever been charged with a crime for not telling the government about their volunteer charity work.

Sami's arrest in February 2003 sent shock waves through the university town. As many as a hundred federal, state, and local officials stormed the Idaho campus at 4:00 A.M., wearing flak jackets and brandishing large weapons. One frightened child in a family housing unit next to Sami's, on seeing the swarm of armed agents, screamed, "Mommy, the war is starting!" Idaho, founded as a land-grant school, attracted students from the Middle East and developing nations who came to acquire skills in areas like agriculture and engineering, and so there were some 175 to 200 Arab students enrolled at that time. In addition to waking Sami and his family, agents rang the doorbells of all of the other Arab students at Idaho—referring to them as Sami's "associates"—to question them about whether they knew anything about terrorism or terrorism financing. This started at about 5:00 A.M. and continued until all had been questioned. These students reported being threatened with jail or deportation if they refused to answer questions; one reported being interrogated for seven hours. Dragnet interrogation of Arabs and Muslims was one technique the FBI adopted after 9/11, questioning thousands of people who were not actually suspected of anything—except of possibly knowing other Arabs and Muslims.[5] Immigration status—these students were dependent on their student visas—was a useful lever for getting people to submit to questioning they otherwise would have had a right to decline.

No one other than Sami was charged with anything. Liz Brandt, a member of the faculty at Idaho's law school who found herself enlisting lawyers for the interrogated students to consult, recalls that the event was promoted to the media as the successful discovery of a sleeper cell in Idaho. Attorney General John Ashcroft fed that impression, describing Sami as part of a "terrorist threat to Americans that is fanatical, and it is fierce."[6] People who did not know Sami, Brandt says, tended to trust the government and to assume that Sami "must have done something really wrong." But, she adds, people who knew Sami never believed that he could be guilty of supporting terrorism. "When I heard the charges, I thought, this just can't be. It was like a War of the Worlds hoax."

The prosecutors argued that Sami was so dangerous that he should be denied bail pending his trial. But the federal magistrate judge who reviewed their arguments was not persuaded. Sami, who had been living a peaceful life with his family, did not seem likely to flee. The entire family was completely integrated into the community. The boys, ages nine, six, and three at the time, attended local schools and played soccer and skateboarded with neighboring children. Sami worked with food banks and an organization supporting military families. Maha had developed close friends. (After Sami's arrest, the community formed a "protective shell" around the family, says Liz Brandt. Maha did not know how to drive, so neighbors regularly took her to the supermarket, for example, and everyone worked hard to soothe the children, who were traumatized by their experience and by seeing their father in jail.)

The magistrate judge ordered that Sami be allowed to await the trial at home. Instead of releasing him, however, the government tried another tack. The day after the federal magistrate judge ordered him freed, the government asked an immigration court judge to order that Sami be deported (on the theory that he was working in addition to studying) and to lock him up until his deportation. The immigration judge agreed, ordering that Sami be held pending his deportation and so Sami spent seventeen months incarcerated, in solitary confinement, locked in his cell for twenty-three hours a day while awaiting his trial. Immigration charges were also brought against Maha, whose immigration status was dependent on Sami's. As bewildered and shocked as Sami was by the charges against him, he told his lawyer, "They can do whatever they want with me. They can put me in prison for the rest of my life, but not my wife and children." Maha agreed to "voluntarily" return to Saudi Arabia in exchange for the government's agreement not to lock her up too. In November 2003, she was given three months to leave the country. This agreement was designed to allow her to remain in the country during Sami's trial. But when the trial was later postponed for several months, the government refused to allow Maha and the children an extension. Sami therefore had to face the rest of his time in jail and the ordeal of a nine-week felony trial without his family. He occupied himself in jail by working on his dissertation, still hoping that he would be able to complete his degree.

Over a year after Sami's arrest, the government decided that it had enough evidence to add terrorism-related charges—based on the material support laws—to the immigration charges. The indictment now alleged that the website Sami worked on encouraged contributions to Hamas, a Palestinian group blacklisted as a "foreign terrorist organization."[7] (The government's theory about which terrorists Sami was supporting shifted more than once, from Al Qaeda to Hamas to Chechnyan rebels.) Using the broad net of the Patriot Act, the government charged Sami with the crime of providing "expert advice or assistance" to terrorists.[8] Sami did have expertise in computer studies. But had he actually provided material support to Hamas or any other terrorists? The government's view was that all the jury needed to believe to convict Sami was that he had used his expert skills as a webmaster in a manner that would enable people to encounter hateful ideas, perhaps be persuaded, and perhaps then offer their support. The potential sentence Sami faced was up to fifteen years on each of three terrorism-related charges, and up to twenty-five years on each immigration fraud charge.

In an opening statement at trial, prosecutor Kim Lindquist told the jury that Sami was supporting terrorists in Israel, Chechnya, and other locations through a network of websites used to recruit terrorists, to raise money, and to spread incendiary rhetoric. Juror John Steger's first reaction: "When he got done, I thought, this guy's going to be in jail for life."

As Sami's lawyer, David Nevin, pointed out, however, the government's theory was so broad that it ran up against the Constitution's guarantee of freedom of speech. The First Amendment had been interpreted to prohibit prosecuting people for advocating ideas unless their advocacy is intended to and is likely to incite imminent unlawful action—the so-called *Brandenburg* doctrine.[9] If Sami could be found guilty of a crime for posting fatwas on a website, Nevin argued, CNN could also be found guilty for airing speeches by Osama bin Laden.[10] Ironically, an Israeli terrorism expert who served as a prosecution witness testified at the trial that he himself had posted much of the very same material on his own website,[11] as had the BBC on its website. A lot of people were interested in knowing how jihadists explained themselves. Nevin asked the judge to dismiss the prosecution on the ground that it violated the First Amendment. The judge denied the motion, saying that an opinion explaining this decision would follow. No opinion ever followed.

Material Support of Terrorism

The law that was used against Sami had become progressively more hostile to First Amendment values. The first material support law, enacted in 1994,[12] made it a crime to give terrorists concrete assistance like weapons or cash. That statute contained several critical exceptions: (1) people could not be prosecuted for humanitarian assistance, like providing medical care, to someone "not directly involved in such violations"; and (2) investigations could not be initiated on the basis of "activities protected by the First Amendment, including expressions of support or the provision of financial support for the nonviolent political, religious, philosophical, or ideological goals or beliefs of any person or group."[13] If someone supported a group that engaged in both terrorist and nonterrorist activities—like running a nursery school—the prosecution could only get a conviction by showing that the accused intended to support terrorism and that there was an actual connection between the donation and terrorist activities. And people could not be targeted on the basis of their religion or their associations.

Looking back, that was the legislative equivalent of a baby step. The first major expansion of this material support statute was signed into law by President Bill Clinton in 1996 as part of the Antiterrorism and Effective Death Penalty Act of 1996—a response to the Oklahoma City bombing. This revision spared prosecutors the burden of showing intent to promote terrorism and of showing how terrorist organizations actually used donations, on the theory that money was fungible.[14] If a terrorist did not have to pay for medical treatment, the theory went, the money saved could be used to buy bombs. The provision guaranteeing special protection for First

Amendment activities was eliminated. These revisions made it considerably easier to get convictions but left less space for freedom of speech.

Five years later, the Patriot Act expanded the definition of material support to include any form of "expert advice or assistance"—spreading the dragnet wider and making the prosecutor's job that much easier.[15] "Expert advice or assistance" covers some acts that should certainly be criminal and in fact already were under other laws, like teaching terrorists to make bombs. But this term is so vague and open-ended that it has obvious potential for also capturing other kinds of conduct, including humanitarian aid. A doctor who provides medical treatment to a terrorist would seem to fit that description—or maybe a computer whiz. The statute contained no definition of "expert advice or assistance" at the time, so it was hard to tell what the limits of this concept might be, if there were any at all. Sami's prosecution was the first occasion on which the government relied on the Patriot Act's "expert advice or assistance" provision.

Throughout nine weeks of testimony and arguments, John Steger and his fellow jurors—three other men and eight women, including a banker, a PhD in education, and the owner of a lumberyard—didn't hear any evidence that seemed to them to substantiate the material support charges. "There was not a word spoken that indicated he supported terrorism," said John. The prosecution claimed that the charity's website featured links to other websites inviting donations to organizations like Hamas; the defense explained that those links had once existed but had been removed before Sami became webmaster. The prosecutor argued that it did not matter under the law whether or not Sami intended to aid terrorists as long as he knew that the website he worked on solicited donations, but there was no evidence to support that contention either. The prosecutor also argued, correctly, that the material support law did not require the government to show that anyone had clicked on a link leading to Hamas or had actually made a donation to a terrorist organization. This case could be brought only because the government did not have to prove very much at all under the post–Patriot Act material support laws.[16] But the jury found that the prosecution's proof did not even meet that low standard.

The jurors came to understand that this trial was not just about terrorism but also about the First Amendment. "We talked," John said, "about that we weren't going to step on anybody's rights to hold the opinion they had." As the jurors learned or rediscovered, First Amendment law protects the right to read or to voice hateful opinions—and it applies to everyone lawfully in the country, not just to citizens. Many of the rights the Constitution guarantees are, like the First Amendment, general limitations on what the government can do. Others, like the Due Process Clause, apply to all "persons" or all those accused of a crime and so cover citizens and noncitizens alike. Very few constitutional protections (like the Fourteenth Amendment's hard-to-define "privileges and immunities") are reserved only for citizens.

United States citizens are, of course, just as subject to the material support laws as Sami al-Hussayen. Even if the prosecution's theory in the *al-Hussayen* case does not seem to threaten the average American with prosecution, it threatens our shared fundamental rights. The attempt to build a wall between the American people and hateful ideas is inherently inconsistent with one of the First Amendment's core ideas. The First Amendment represents a commitment to trusting Americans, in this instance to confront the marketplace of ideas without having the government prescreen those ideas for us. The patronizing notion that the government should remove potentially dangerous ideas from the marketplace misconceives the Constitution's underlying view of the relationship of the government and the individual. The material support law, read as broadly as it was in this case, transfers immense power to the government to control ideas and disempowers the people.

Choosing constitutional principle over a fear-driven conviction, this Idaho jury of ordinary Americans took only two or three hours—after a nine-week trial—to agree to acquit Sami on all of the terrorism-related charges. They were not deterred by the fact that Sami was a Saudi citizen also charged with immigration fraud. The jurors debated the alleged immigration violations separately, finding those charges much more difficult. Whether Sami's statements on the immigration forms were intentionally misleading and whether the forms themselves were unclear were hot topics of debate among the jurors for six days in a discussion so intense that some jurors were reduced to tears. The jury voted to acquit Sami on three of the immigration charges but was unable to reach consensus on the other eight.

Is this a *Twelve Angry Men* happy ending? Sami's life was ravaged notwithstanding the decisive acquittals on the material support charges. He had been locked up and held in solitary confinement for seventeen months and his family was forced to return to Saudi Arabia without him. The fact that the jury had deadlocked on eight of the immigration charges meant that the government could retry him on those charges. With that prospect hanging over his head, Sami decided to drop his appeal from the immigration court's deportation order and return to Saudi Arabia to rejoin his family. And although he had escaped conviction under the dragnet material support law, this law remained available to ensnare other law-abiding people—including American citizens—and to cast a shadow on our First Amendment rights.

From the government's point of view, it is easy to understand why broad laws like this one can seem desirable. The material support laws are designed to enable criminal prosecutions in situations where the government does not have proof that someone they suspect is a terrorist, or has conspired with terrorists, or is attempting to help terrorists. This expanded dragnet might conceivably catch an actual terrorist who could not otherwise be caught, although we have no way to estimate the likelihood of that happening. But what about the costs—the collateral damage to individual people, to the First Amendment, and to our concept of our relationship to our government—when these laws can capture the innocent and intimidate everyone else?

The desire to wield this broad a net, regardless of how great the potential costs might be, is typical of the Just Trust Us philosophy prevalent after 9/11. We are asked to assume that prosecutors won't use the net against the wrong people and so the costs of this strategy can be controlled. But that optimistic assumption, as Sami's case shows, doesn't always work out so well in practice. Investigators are not immune to wishful thinking, no matter who is president. The investigators in Sami's case wanted so much to find and disrupt a terrorist-financing network that they did not seem to notice that they were molding the facts in a procrustean fashion—or that their theory of the case was a severe threat to First Amendment values. And so they made a serious mistake in this case. But even if prosecutors were superhumanly able to make only the wisest choices in deciding whom to charge, the very existence of this statute stifles free speech. Why would other students or computer experts agree to help run a chat room or post controversial materials if the result could be criminal prosecution? Will people become fearful that informing themselves by reading the ravings of terrorists, or associating themselves with any Islamic charity no matter how legitimate that charity is, might leave them in Sami's position—a focus of the government's attention even if they have not done anything other than add to a conversation? What if the next jury isn't as thoughtful as John Steger and his neighbors?

The government got this one wrong but these Idaho jurors, with this trial as their crash course in First Amendment law and values, stood up to defend the Constitution. Ultimately, the Constitution itself gets the credit for providing the fail-safe of jury trials. In Article III of the Constitution as well as in the Sixth Amendment, the framers expressed their trust in the American people by empowering us to protect our rights by deciding whether someone the government has charged with a crime should be convicted. We are not told to just trust the government; we are asked to think for ourselves. As the Constitution's Preamble promises, we *are* the government. John Steger and his fellow jurors vindicated the Constitution's faith in the American people. They resisted any urge they might have had to lock up Sami al-Hussayen just in case the government's suspicions about him were right after all despite the lack of evidence— a victory for due process; they resisted the idea that a person can be prosecuted for making hateful ideas accessible to others—a victory for the First Amendment; and they resisted lowering their due process and First Amendment standards because Sami was an Arab, a Muslim, and a foreigner—a victory for the guarantee of equal protection of the laws. But the expanded material support law still remains available for use or misuse on other occasions.

Sami is back in Saudi Arabia, teaching at a university and continuing his computer work. Profoundly affected by these events, he is still trying to reconcile his own experience with his lifelong belief that the United States stands for what is good and right. As for the residents of Moscow, Idaho, Liz Brandt says that watching these events unfold brought the liberals and libertarians of that community together. The liberals were already suspicious of the Patriot Act, which, she says, made this all possible because it did not provide enough protection against the government "running amok." To the libertarians, she says, the vision of armed federal agents in flak jackets occupying the Idaho campus due to a mistake, and then not backing off even as their case fell apart, was chilling. "This just looked like huge government, because it was."

The Football Player

Another consequence of the misguided prosecution of Sami al-Hussayen was that it derailed the life of an American citizen who was no guiltier than Sami of helping terrorists but never got the chance to be exonerated by a jury. Sami's acquittal did not undo the damage that his prosecution brought to himself, to his wife and children, or to a young man he had met at Idaho.

Lavoni T. Kidd was born in Wichita, Kansas, and attended the University of Idaho, where he was a star running back on the football team, the Vandals, leading the team in rushing in 1995.[17] ("They had plays designed just for me.") Both his parents were also American-born citizens—his father worked as a corrections officer and his mother at IBM. His grandfather was a Pentecostal minister. Lavoni's Idaho football coach was a very important person in his life. ("John L. Smith taught me to be a man. I still hear his voice in my head all the time.") Another critical development during his college years was that he studied religion and found the one religion that he felt fulfilled him spiritually. He converted to Islam, changing his name to Abdullah al-Kidd. His grandfather, although far from pleased that his grandson had not decided on the church, was nevertheless glad that he found a role for prayer in his life. Other members of the African-American Kidd family might have related this conversion to the famous decision of another athlete, boxer Cassius Clay, to convert to Islam and change his name to Muhammad Ali.

Serious about his newfound religion, Abdullah was delighted to receive a scholarship from a Saudi university to study Arabic and Islamic law in the spring of 2003. He planned to fly to Saudi Arabia on March 16 to begin work on his doctorate in Islamic studies. Instead he was dramatically arrested at the ticket counter at Dulles International Airport, handcuffed, and interrogated. He was taken into custody and moved, in painfully restrictive shackles, from Virginia to Oklahoma and then to Idaho by way of Arizona and Wyoming. He was locked up in high-security prisons where he was strip searched, rarely allowed to leave his cell, denied showers, denied visits by his family, and barely able to sleep under the bright lights that shone twenty-four hours a day. "It was the most horrible, disgraceful, degrading moment of my life," he says. "I was treated worse than murderers."[18] After sixteen days of this nightmarish ordeal he was finally released from custody, but on the condition that he surrender his passport, confine his domestic travel to four states, move in with his in-laws in Nevada, meet with a probation officer regularly, and agree to home visits. Desperate for work, he took a job moving furniture. After living under these trying conditions for fifteen months, Abdullah had lost his scholarship, his wife, and his patience. He was unable to find a steady job because, in his words, he was "treated like a felon." He began to suffer heart palpitations and insomnia.

Why was he arrested? Not because he was charged with any crime. The Fourth Amendment, which prohibits unreasonable searches and seizures, prohibits arrests unless they are backed by probable cause to believe that a suspect has committed a crime. Evidently, no one dared to claim that probable cause existed in this case—even under the lenient material support laws—and as an American citizen, Abdullah was not subject to immigration laws and so the government could not fall back on the pretext used in Sami al-Hussayen's case. So the government resorted to a different pretext, arresting Abdullah as a material witness on the theory that he had known Sami al-Hussayen at Idaho and that the government needed his testimony at Sami's trial. The application for a material witness arrest warrant alleged that Abdullah had met with Sami al-Hussayen's "associates"—that is, other Arab students at Idaho—that he had contact with the same Islamic charity featured in Sami's prosecution, and that at one point he had been involved in a financial transaction with Sami. The affidavit did not say just what evidence the prosecutors thought Abdullah might be able to offer at Sami's trial. In fact, he was never called as a witness in any proceeding. After Sami's trial, an FBI supervisor in Spokane told a reporter that government agents thought that Abdullah had information relevant to one of the immigration charges—not a terrorism or terrorism-financing charge, but the charge that Sami had violated the terms of his visa by working. The prosecutors, the supervisor said, had intended to call him as a witness but then changed their minds for strategic reasons.[19]

The explanation that Abdullah was arrested because he had information about a routine immigration violation is impossible to square with the severity of his treatment—he was treated as a high-security prisoner, and kept in a cell in Alexandria, Virginia, that he was told had housed John Walker Lindh and Zacharias Moussaoui, both of whom are serving lengthy sentences for terrorism-related offenses. The same FBI supervisor also described "red flags" that led the FBI to be suspicious of Abdullah himself—like the nature of some books and tapes about Islam that he had possessed or sold. And FBI Director Robert Mueller, reporting to Congress on successful antiterrorism efforts, listed Abdullah as one of five suspected terrorists in custody.[20] The other four were charged with crimes; Abdullah never was. Perhaps Abdullah al-Kidd was deemed guilty by association with ideas, as Sami was; perhaps he was deemed guilty because of his association with Sami, who wasn't even guilty.

The material witness statute[21] was designed to ensure that key witnesses who are about to flee the jurisdiction will be available to testify at a trial. But in the heat of the hunt for terrorists in the fall of 2001, that statute was pressed into service and used as a pretext in this and dozens of other cases to lock people up on the basis of hunches, biases, and flimsy evidence. Jose Padilla, the alleged "dirty bomber" apprehended at O'Hare airport, had been arrested as a material witness before he was declared to be an enemy combatant and then finally prosecuted and convicted of the crime of conspiracy to provide support to terrorists. One early target of the newly expansive use of material witness laws, the unluckily named Osama Awadallah, was ostensibly being held—under brutal conditions[22]—so that he could testify before a grand jury and tell them what he knew about terrorism. The District Court agreed with Awadallah's argument that the statute was never intended to allow locking up people at length so that they could testify before grand juries, which can meet for many months on end. But New York's Second Circuit Court of Appeals disagreed, allowing the material witness statute to be used expansively (although stopping short of authorizing pretextual detentions), and the Supreme Court declined to review that decision.[23] Of approximately seventy people detained as material witnesses in terrorism cases, over half were never called to testify at all.[24] The cooptation of this statute as a preventive detention tool is typical of the improvisatory mind-set of the fall of 2001—addressing what was viewed as an emergency situation by adapting laws intended for other purposes without seeking actual legislative changes. Congress did not design the material witness statute as a preventive detention dragnet, but it has been used in that manner and Congress has not reacted to disavow this executive branch retrofitting of the law. The Attorney General had resorted to this form of self-help because Congress had refused to authorize the arrest or detention of United States citizens without probable cause. During the Patriot Act debates, Congress had been willing to allow preventive detention only of *non*citizens for a maximum of one week before the government would be required to show probable cause for an arrest.[25]

The agents who stretched the material witness statute to capture Abdullah al-Kidd also stretched some facts. The affidavit the government filed to apply for a material witness arrest warrant said, "Kidd is scheduled to take a one-way, first class flight (costing approximately $5,000) to Saudi Arabia on Sunday March 16, 2003, at approximately 6:00 EST. . . . It is believed that if al-Kidd travels to Saudi Arabia, the United States Government will be unable to secure his presence at trial via subpoena."[26] But what was said to have been a suspiciously expensive one-way airline ticket was actually a round-trip coach ticket that cost one-third as much—$1,700. And the affidavit did not mention that Abdullah al-Kidd was a native-born American citizen, that he had a wife and two children living in the United States, that he had voluntarily cooperated with the FBI on a number of previous occasions when agents had asked to interview him (he even offered to teach classes to help the agents understand Islam), and that no one had ever told him that his travel abroad might present a problem because his testimony might be needed. There is no need to incarcerate a potential witness if that witness is willing to testify and the material witness statute itself only applies to people who are unavailable. At a court appearance in Virginia the day after his arrest, Abdullah told the judge that he would have cooperated and turned himself in if he had been told that a warrant was being issued—but that didn't happen. He then asked the court if his testimony in Idaho could be expedited so he could get on with his life—but that didn't happen either.

Abudullah al-Kidd may never have testified at Sami's trial, but he is still hoping, years later, that he will be able to testify at the trial of a lawsuit he brought against Attorney General John Ashcroft. The suit alleges that Ashcroft was one of the chief architects of the policy of pretextual misuse of the material witness statute to detain people if no other grounds could be established. He argues that Ashcroft's policies unconstitutionally created an end run around necessary Fourth Amendment protections. His lawyer, Lee Gelernt of the ACLU, says, "Deciding to sue the federal government in a 9/11 case takes a lot of courage and I have seen that in Abdullah over the past five years. I have also seen how much he not only wants to vindicate his own rights, but to ensure that no other person in the future is subjected to what he endured."

The Bush and then Obama Justice Departments responded that the Attorney General should be immune from any lawsuit on this subject. The full Ninth Circuit Court of Appeals (which sits in California but covers other states including Idaho), just about evenly divided, voted to deny Ashcroft's request for dismissal and to allow the case to proceed.[27] The Obama Administration then asked the Supreme Court to review that decision, insisting that the case should be dismissed. Like their Bush-era predecessors, the Obama lawyers are demanding discretion to decide when and for what purposes to use the material witness statute and do not want anyone to hold them accountable for their decisions. "One aspect of this long litigation that has been frustrating is the degree to which the positions of the Bush and Obama Administrations are virtually identical," says Gelernt. The Supreme Court agreed to take the case[28] and heard argument on March 2, 2011. The Court has not yet reached a decision as this book goes to press. If the cases discussed in chapter 11 give any indication of the Court's attitude, it will be surprising indeed if a majority of the Justices agrees to let al-Kidd's lawsuit proceed rather than finding the Attorney General immune.

The Material Support and Material Witness Dragnets

The prosecutors' view in Sami's case was that they knew better than the First Amendment; in Abdullah's case, they thought they knew better than the Fourth Amendment. Both Sami and Abdullah were caught in dragnet statutes broad enough to allow their use for preventive detention—to lock up people whom the government does not have enough evidence to prosecute but who are regarded as suspicious primarily on the basis of their associations[29] and their religion. This should be unconstitutional, but the courts, as will be described in the next chapter, have upheld broad interpretations of the material support laws, just as the Second Circuit upheld a broad interpretation of the material witness law. This is why Sami had to rely on a jury—as did many others, including Americans, who were accused of material support. The elastic material support laws, although they had rarely been used pre-9/11, quickly became one of the most popular tools for prosecutors in terrorism cases.[30] The Patriot Act's expansion of material support laws was part of a repurposing of the criminal law to prevent terrorism, rather than to punish acts that have occurred. This attempt to shift the criminal law to a "prevention paradigm"[31] has created innumerable due process problems. Prediction is a far more unreliable basis for punishment[32] than proof that someone has actually committed a terrorist act, or attempted or conspired to aid terrorists (all of which are crimes under pre–Patriot Act law). But an expansion that may seem plausible in the abstract may look different seen up close. The conviction rate on the kind of material support charge brought against Sami is surprisingly low, suggesting that other juries may share the skepticism of John Steger and his colleagues about these attempts to condemn people for remote or speculative connections with terrorism.[33] According to one study, only about a third of material support charges under these statutes resulted in convictions, although about half of the cases in which those charges were brought resulted in a conviction on another charge.[34] Although material support charges were the top charges in 162 federal prosecutions brought between 2001 and 2006, they were the top charge in convictions in only eight cases during that period.[35]

Sami's case reflects another popular approach prosecutors use when they suspect noncitizens but lack sufficient evidence to bring a terrorism-related charge: using immigration law in the same opportunistic manner prosecutors used tax law against Al Capone.[36] The number of immigration prosecutions has skyrocketed since 9/11 under both Bush and Obama.[37] But studies show that the number of prosecutions considered to be terrorism prosecutions has steadily declined each year since 2002.[38] Perhaps prosecutors have gradually realized that bringing a large number of prosecutions will not make us any safer if the wrong people are being prosecuted.[39] Some would like to attribute the fact that there has been no major terrorist attack recently to the success of our post-9/11 enforcement strategies, like aggressive use of broad material support laws. A September 2009 report of the Transactional Records Access Clearinghouse (TRAC), which studies criminal prosecution data, responded:

> [T]he picture that emerges from TRAC's examination of extensive government records—agencies continuing to waste their time on investigations that go nowhere, prosecutions that ultimately result in minimal sentences—strongly suggests that this may not be the case. Whatever the ultimate judgment on the broader question, there can be little doubt that the unfocused, wandering and erratic federal effort, revealed by TRAC's careful review of hundreds of thousands of records, could be significantly improved.[40]

The 9/11 Commission staff noted another obvious problem with the breadth of the material support dragnet—the strong potential for religious profiling in prosecutions that are not based on hard evidence.[41] The idea that vague laws invite discriminatory treatment of Muslims finds confirmation in the experience of Sami al-Hussayen. It seems that federal agents were apt to view innocuous facts as damning because the conclusion that Sami was another Osama bin Laden conformed to a stereotype of Saudi Muslims, and the facts were interpreted to fit that conclusion.

The same can certainly be said of the material witness laws—they invite discriminatory as well as pretextual use. Yet Obama Administration lawyers continued to argue against Abdullah al-Kidd's lawsuit because they too evidently wanted the option of employing this kind of preventive detention. They trust themselves to avoid religious profiling and to avoid First Amendment–hostile prosecutions like Sami's. And so they argue to keep these weapons loaded.

2.

"Foreign Terrorist Organizations," Humanitarians, and the First Amendment

We've come to love our fears more than our freedoms.—Rep.
Dennis Kucinich (2010)
The vague language of the [material support] law leaves us won-
dering if we will be prosecuted for our work to promote peace and
freedom. —Former President Jimmy Carter (2010)

The Iranian Democrat

Roya Rahmani is the pseudonym of an Iranian refugee who is terrified that her family and friends in Iran will suffer retaliation if her actual identity were to become known. Iran treated her as a criminal for supporting an Iranian pro-democracy movement—and so has the United States of America.[1]

Roya was seventeen years old when the Shah of Iran was deposed, thanks in part to the work of a group known as the PMOI (People's Mujahedin Organization of Iran—also sometimes called the MEK), whose members Roya regarded as heroes. Like her compatriots, she hoped that life in Iran would get better. Instead, within a few years, the new regime shut down the universities, the newspapers, and all channels of political protest. Roya had expected to study at a university like other members of her family, but that was no longer a possibility. So she decided to support the PMOI, which continued to protest the repressive measures of the Ayatollahs. Her determination to fight for democracy did not waver even when people delivering the PMOI's newspaper began to suffer attacks and when supporters were jailed, tortured, and even executed. The choice, she says, was "to surrender to the religious theocracy or to fight, as we had against the Shah." "I was inspired by their heroism," she says, "and I thought, give me freedom or give me death." She was also impressed by the fact that even as the government's crackdown became increasingly brutal, the PMOI remained committed to a peaceful struggle for regime change. She attended rallies and worked to educate other Iranians. But then her brother was arrested and executed. And then she herself was arrested and jailed—for the crime of "waging war on God." "I still get shivers through my body when I think about those years," she says. For three and a half years in jail, she suffered psychological and physical brutality, having the soles of her feet and legs flogged until she could not walk. She heard the screams of other prisoners and had difficulty sleeping in cells so crowded that it was not even possible to sit down. Women, she says, were regarded as "fair game."

When she was finally released, Roya was unable to get a permanent job in Iran because she was still viewed as an enemy of the state. So she made the difficult decision to leave Iran for a neighboring country. But she found that even outside Iran she was threatened and so in 1998 she decided to immigrate to the United States. Because of her excruciating experiences and very credible fear of continuing persecution, the United States granted her political asylum.

Life in exile was hard. "Not a day goes by without my thinking about the repression, shortages, and other horrors my family and friends in Iran still suffer," she says. And so when she settled in Los Angeles, Roya became involved with the Iranian community there and continued to work to promote democracy in Iran through rallies and educational events. She also raised funds for other refugees who had fled Iran and had no means of support, through an organization called the Committee for Human Rights.

In February 2001, after having been in the United States for about twenty months, Roya was in a Starbucks in Los Angeles when, to her utter shock and horror, FBI agents arrested her. The charge? Providing material support to the PMOI, which the government linked with the Committee for Human Rights. "This time I was being persecuted by a very different government for providing material support to the same group."

This prosecution was made possible because the State Department had designated the PMOI as a "foreign terrorist organization" and therefore the prosecutors only needed to prove that Roya supported the organization in question. They did not need to prove that she had any intention of supporting terrorist activity. (Such proof evidently would not have been possible. Transcripts of conversations with Roya show that when undercover informants asked her if she was interested in supporting armed struggle, she insisted that she was only interested in providing humanitarian aid to refugees.) Did the prosecutors have to prove that her contributions actually supported terrorist activity? No. Did the prosecutors need to prove that the PMOI actually was a terrorist group? No. They only needed to prove that the group had been designated and, under the later version of the material support law, that Roya was aware that the PMOI was on the government's blacklist. ("We had no clue that what we were doing was illegal," says Roya. "I had never even gotten a parking ticket.")

What evidence did the Secretary of State have that the PMOI was a terrorist group? We don't know, because such designations take place behind closed doors and can be based on hearsay evidence—like self-serving allegations made by Iranian government officials who regard the PMOI as a threat to their own hegemony. The PMOI's stipulated mission, to promote a transition from Iran's current fundamentalist regime to a secular democratic government, would seem to be consistent with United States foreign policy. But evidently President Bill Clinton's State Department was more interested in 1997 (when the designation was first made) in the possibility of rapprochement with the Iranian government than in backing a pro-democracy movement, and Iran demanded condemnation of its leading political opponent as a condition of any thaw in relations.[2]

The statute allows a "foreign terrorist organization" to challenge its designation (assuming the organization has read about the designation in the Federal Register and acts within the strict time limits prescribed).[3] The PMOI had tried challenging its designation in the United States courts, but the standard of review under the statute is minimal. The reviewing court is not allowed to consider whether the material relied upon was accurate, but only whether there was "substantial support" for the designation. So, not surprisingly, the PMOI's designation was upheld.[4] The courts are traditionally extremely deferential about matters of foreign policy. And as a foreign organization the PMOI does not have constitutional rights but only the limited procedural rights the statute confers.

But Roya and her codefendants, some of whom are American citizens, do have constitutional rights, including the right to due process. Because it was no defense under the statute that they had only worked to provide humanitarian relief and did not intend to support terrorism, Roya and her codefendants wanted to defend themselves by arguing that the designation was wrong. In their view, the PMOI simply was not a terrorist organization: the PMOI disavowed the strategy of targeting innocent people to make a political point. But the Ninth Circuit Court of Appeals, in California, ruled in 2005 that Roya and her colleagues were not allowed to raise that defense either.[5] Because the process of designation was secret, the court said, the designation could not be challenged even by someone whose freedom hinged on this decision. Right or wrong, as far as Roya and her codefendants were concerned, the designation was conclusive.

"My view of the American justice system when I came to this country was very different from what I learned about," Roya says. "I had come to a country championed as the leader of the free world." While the United States courts refused to allow her to question the designation of the PMOI, courts in the UK and the European Union ruled that the organization is not in fact a terrorist group and required that it be removed from watchlists within their jurisdictions.[6]

Barack Obama took office while Roya's prosecution was still pending. She might have hoped that the new administration would resolve her Kafkaesque dilemma, but as she listened to Obama's inaugural address, she heard him express his desire to reach out to the mullahs in Iran and her heart sank. The prosecution continued unabated. Prevented from defending herself against the charges, she resigned herself to entering a conditional guilty plea in April 2009. Her lawyers are still planning an appeal on constitutional grounds—including a First Amendment argument that her fundraising and educational activities were nothing more than traditional political speech and so the material support statute cannot constitutionally apply to her.

Because the designation process takes place in secret, it is difficult to evaluate the United States government's conclusions about the PMOI. We can't know what the designation was based on. But even if the branding of this particular group as dangerous was based on reliable information, the important point here is that given the peremptory and secret nature of the process, such designations can be wrong and someone in Roya's position could serve a lengthy sentence on the basis of a misunderstanding, or on raw politics. The government's identification of groups as connected with terrorism has indeed been far from infallible, as the next chapter will show. I don't know if Roya was right about this organization or if she could have convinced a jury that the State Department had misunderstood the nature of the PMOI, or was using her as a political pawn. But due process requires that she be given a chance to do so because that is only fair—and not just for her sake, but for ours. As the trial of Sami al-Hussayen shows, the constitutional right to trial by jury serves as an indispensable check on government decisions about who should be punished. Safeguards are especially critical with respect to decisions made behind closed doors, because there is otherwise so little accountability. This material support law as now structured gives juries almost nothing to decide. By design, the law forces us to just trust the government to designate selected organizations, sometimes for political reasons (the PMOI but not the PLO or the IRA) and then to select people to punish for their association with those organizations. By offering the government a shortcut to conviction that bypasses key questions of personal culpability, this material support law prevents the American people from playing any meaningful role in evaluating whether it is fair to punish even well-intentioned support of selectively designated organizations.

The blacklist material support approach is based on the theory that certain organizations should be made "radioactive" so that they will not have any resources with which to do harm. This theory may well have seemed like a good idea in the fall of 2001, but experts differ as to whether it is actually the wisest approach to every insurgent group. The statute's approach minimizes the significance of the fact that organizations are often multifaceted. What if the PMOI did employ a variety of strategies for promoting the goal of regime change in Iran, some violent and some nonviolent, just as the African National Congress (ANC) did in opposing the apartheid regime in South Africa? Roya thinks the comparison between the PMOI and the ANC is quite apt. Would an American jury, if asked, have been willing to convict Nelson Mandela of an American crime for his material support of the ANC? Of course Iran has an interest in preventing its insurgents from seeking regime change through violent or even peaceful means. But if the United States wants to use domestic criminal sanctions against those who support foreign organizations, the Constitution's jury trial provisions are supposed to give the American people an essential role to play in that decision. Through our representative jurors, we would then have the ability to distinguish between people who give weapons to Al Qaeda and people who make donations to democracy-promoting organizations like the PMOI or ANC, regardless of whether those organizations have checkered records in their own countries. As matters now stand, we are excluded while all the key decisions are made behind closed doors. The other side of the "Just Trust the Government" coin, once again, is minimization of the role of the American people and of democracy itself.

As Roya's case also reminds us, the War on Terror has been conceived as being far broader than a war on Al Qaeda and related anti-American groups. The dragnet material support laws not only can be but have been used against Americans, citizens and noncitizens alike, whose crime is supporting regime change and democracy in Iran. "When I came to the United States," Roya says, "I thought, I will be the voice of those who can't have their voices heard. But for the past ten years I have been silenced. It seems that I have moved from one prison to another prison." It remains to be seen whether the metaphorical American "prison" she describes will become another actual prison.

Peacemakers and Humanitarians

Another group designated as a "foreign terrorist organization" is the Kurdistan Workers Party, also known as the PKK. This group opposes the Turkish government's treatment of Kurds, including, for example, what supporters characterize as systematic repression of Kurdish identity and the jailing of Kurdish children who attended protest demonstrations.

Ralph Fertig, a professor at the University of Southern California and retired judge, is a lifelong activist dedicated to nonviolence who has gotten to know some Kurdish advocates well. Ralph became involved with the Humanitarian Law Project because he wanted to offer his professional skills to try to persuade national forces to extend human rights to subject populations and to persuade insurgent groups, like the PKK, to use peaceful dispute resolution methods to achieve their goals rather than resort to terrorism and violence. He has campaigned on behalf of the rights of Kurds in Turkey with members of Congress and in the United Nations Commission on Human Rights, and he has conducted training sessions with Kurds from Turkey to teach and encourage them to take their grievances against the Turkish government to the U.N. Ralph says that the Kurdish advocates with whom he works do not disclose whether or not they are members of the PKK for fear of severe punishment or even summary execution.

When the Secretary of State designated the PKK as a "foreign terrorist organization" in 1997, Ralph and his colleagues worried about the consequences of this designation to their organization. Might their work now be subject to the vague language of the 1996 law, which had expanded the reach of the material support statute by eliminating the exemption for humanitarians who provide what might be considered to be "services," "personnel," or "training" to any group designated as a foreign terrorist organization? Might they be prosecuted? Could they honestly reassure people who wanted to work with them or donate money that they were not opening themselves to prosecution, or would they lose supporters?

Ralph and his colleagues, along with an organization working with another "foreign terrorist" designated group—the Sri Lankan LTTE,[7] decided to seek help from the courts, with the assistance of lawyers at the Center for Constitutional Rights. In 1998, they brought a lawsuit arguing that some of the 1996 law's vague provisions violated their First Amendment rights of freedom of speech and freedom of association as well as their right to due process. The case was wending its way through the California federal courts, with some success, when matters got worse. The Patriot Act further stretched the definition of material support to include supplying "expert advice or assistance" to any designated terrorist group—the elastic provision used to prosecute Sami al-Hussayen. So the Humanitarian Law Project (HLP) geared up again and, in another round of litigation, challenged this new provision which seemed even more likely to jeopardize their mission. The federal district court in California again agreed with HLP that parts of the statute were unconstitutional.[8] Then, in 2004,[9] Congress made several changes to clarify the material support law. Although Congress did not add an intent requirement of the sort that could have helped Roya Rahmani, Congress did prohibit convicting someone for supporting a "foreign terrorist organization" if that person did not know the group in question had been blacklisted.[10] Some of the other 2004 clarifications were less helpful to HLP. The new law, for example, provided a definition of "expert advice or assistance" as "advice or assistance derived from scientific, technical or other specialized knowledge"[11]—a definition that doesn't seem any narrower or clearer. After eleven years of protracted and complex litigation, the Ninth Circuit Court of Appeals parsed all the group's accumulated claims under the current statutes, upholding some of the challenged provisions but finding that others were indeed unconstitutionally vague.[12] The Court of Appeals regarded general words like "training" or "expert advice or assistance" based on "other specialized knowledge" as terms that would leave a reasonable person in doubt about whether activities like HLPs were illegal. And so that court ruled that the government was not allowed to prosecute Ralph and his colleagues for talking to terrorists.

By this time, the Obama Administration had taken over. But that did not change the government's stance in this case, any more than it had in the *al-Kidd* case. The new administration asked the Supreme Court to review the Court of Appeals decision in the case, now retitled *Holder v. Humanitarian Law Project*.[13] The Supreme Court, which had been resolutely refusing to review all other decisions about the impact of antiterrorism measures on our constitutional rights (as will be explained in chapter 11), agreed to hear this one. At the argument, Obama's then-Solicitor General, Elena Kagan, reiterated arguments that her Bush-era predecessors had made in the courts below. Yes, the government needs a dragnet this broad, she argued. Activities like Ralph Fertig's—teaching terrorists how to stop being terrorists—are not distinguishable from activities like Roya Rahmani's—contributing money to a branch of a designated group— because the benign intent of a person providing any form of "material support" doesn't matter. "Expert advice" does include counseling on how to use dispute resolution methods because familiarity with these methods is a form of expertise. And the law makes no exceptions for peacemakers—or even for lawyers who associate themselves with a designated group. In response to questions from several Justices, Kagan said that the expanded material support law could indeed be used to prosecute lawyers for filing a brief on behalf of a "foreign terrorist organization."[14]

The Supreme Court, disagreeing with the Court of Appeals, thought the material support law's provisions left no doubt about whether the Humanitarian Law Project's activities were covered—they were, said the Court, because the group's members contributed valuable specialized knowledge about dispute resolution and lobbying methods. The Court recognized that applying the statute in these circumstances would ban speech: "Plaintiffs want to speak to the PKK and the LTTE, and whether they may do so under [the material support law] depends on what they say."[15] A majority of the Court, in an opinion written by Chief Justice John Roberts, ruled against the plaintiffs' First Amendment claim, however, deciding that prosecuting HLP for its speech would not violate the Constitution. In reaching this conclusion, Roberts relied on two government arguments, neither of which had much empirical support. First, the Court was willing to apply the "money is fungible" theory to this very different form of "contribution." If the PKK accepts a contribution of training in lobbying skills, the Court reasoned, that group could then spend its financial resources elsewhere. Furthermore, the Court said, the PKK could abuse the skills in question to promote terrorist goals—by cynically engaging in peaceful negotiations in order to buy time to regroup and lull their opponents into complacency, for example.[16] The second argument the Court accepted was even more all-encompassing, although equally unsupported by actual evidence: HLP's working with a terrorist group in this manner could lend the group legitimacy and thus help it to gain support for its illicit purposes.

These arguments are not wholly implausible, but they do not satisfy the traditional heavy burden the government is required to shoulder in order to restrict speech. Under previously established First Amendment law, the government was supposed to have the burden of showing that this prohibition of speech was necessary to serve the compelling purpose of preventing terrorism. It is certainly highly debatable whether the strategy of making a group like PKK radioactive is "necessary" to prevent terrorism, or indeed whether it is effective. Author and antiterrorism expert Jessica Stern, a member of the Council on Foreign Relations, has advanced terrorism studies enormously by talking with Christian, Jewish, and Muslim terrorists to try to understand them instead of trying to guess what makes them tick from afar.[17] And Ralph Fertig believed, certainly not unreasonably, that it would reduce the evil of terrorism if terrorists could be dissuaded from violence. The First Amendment is supposed to put a heavy thumb on the scale, allowing Americans to speak unless it is not reasonably debatable that our speech will cause imminent harm. But six Justices, professing the judiciary's incompetence to choose among strategies for fighting terrorism, announced that they were going to defer to the judgment of the political branches. The majority said, "At bottom, plaintiffs simply disagree with the considered judgment of Congress and the Executive."[18]

The whole point of the First Amendment is that Americans are entitled to disagree with Congress as well as the Executive when it comes to speech. As Justice Stephen Breyer pointed out in his dissent, it is not at all clear that Congress actually was as dismissive of free speech values in this instance as the Court was. The legislative history the majority interpreted as showing that Congress intended the material support law to go this far dated from 1996—before some of the current expansions—and quite clearly referred only to harmful or truly fungible contributions like weapons or money.[19] And Congress included a provision in its otherwise sweeping law saying, "Nothing in this section shall be construed or applied so as to abridge the exercise of rights guaranteed under the First Amendment to the Constitution of the United States."[20] So Congress tried to defer to the First Amendment, but the Court, instead of exercising independent judgment to give the First Amendment breathing space, reduced that breathing space by deferring to the executive branch's broad interpretation of the statute. The Court justified its deference by noting that the Justices do not begin each day with terrorism briefings.[21] But that is exactly why the Constitution created a politically insulated judiciary that could maintain an independent point of view in applying First

Amendment principles. The Supreme Court played that role of objective arbiter in the Guantánamo cases, but not here.

In deciding to just trust Congress instead of the Constitution, the Court stifled the Humanitarian Law Project as well as many others who now must fear prosecution and think hard about whether to abandon all kinds of work involving communication with people who might belong to designated groups. For one thing, it is difficult to tell what might count as a contribution of expertise. At the oral argument, Justice Sonia Sotomayor called attention to the breadth of this concept by inquiring whether it would violate the material support law to teach a member of a "foreign terrorist organization" to play the harmonica.[22] David Cole, HLP's lawyer, asked rhetorically if the *New York Times* could be prosecuted under this statute for accepting, editing, and publishing an op-ed by Hamas leaders, as it has done.[23] Among the organizations and people who took this case so personally that they joined amicus briefs urging the Court to uphold our First Amendment traditions was former President Jimmy Carter, whose Carter Center works with insurgent groups whose participation is essential in trying to ensure fair elections in places like Lebanon. Carter told the Court that this statute threatens his mission. To further the goal of promoting peace in the Middle East, the Carter Center had planned a student parliament on peaceful conflict resolution for Palestinians and Israelis that would entail working with members of Hamas, a designated organization, for example.[24] Does the Carter Center now have to compromise its effectiveness by trimming its sails to stay far away from any designated group? Human Rights Watch, which investigates human rights abuses, including abuses by insurgent groups, joined the Carter Center and an organization called Christian Peacemaker Teams in the ACLU's amicus brief. Would it now be a crime for investigators to do anything more than listen to tales of human rights abuses? May they not try, for example, to persuade a terrorist group not to impress children into its ranks, or simply share educational information about human rights norms?[25] Even if "expert" investigators are scrupulous in trying to toe the spot where they think the line is, might they find themselves visited by the FBI—perhaps under a future administration? Academic researchers and journalists, who might also risk being seen as contributing "specialized knowledge" in conversations with terrorist groups, signed onto an amicus brief filed by the Brennan Center for Justice. One anthropologist, for example, studies the effectiveness of peacekeeping missions and, as part of this research, speaks with insurgent groups and presents their views (among others) in the resulting studies.[26]

These scholars' work, like Jessica Stern's, will become impossible if all potential members of designated terrorist groups must be treated as radio-active, at the risk of federal prosecution. Dozens of victims or family members of victims of McCarthy-era blacklists, like the Hollywood Ten, also filed an amicus brief to tell the Court that in the current blacklist attempt to force all Americans to shun certain ideas and all people related to those ideas, they see a shameful part of our history repeating itself.[27]

Even before the Supreme Court's decision in *Humanitarian Law Project*, the U.N. Special Rapporteur on Human Rights While Countering Terrorism had criticized the breadth of American material support laws.[28] But Congress has resisted adding an intent requirement or restoring the exception for humanitarian aid to these laws. The only current exception allows provision of religious materials or medicine.[29] Doctors must now question whether they can safely provide medical care, as opposed to merely medicine, to members of groups like the LTTE,[30] or offer them advice about how to contain the spread of contagious diseases. People and organizations—including the International Red Cross—place themselves at risk of prosecution if they provide any kind of humanitarian aid (except the permitted religious materials or medicine) in conflict-torn parts of the world where designated groups may be in control of schools, orphanages, hospitals, and refugee camps. The LTTE, the insurgent Sri Lankan group HLP's co-plaintiff wanted to influence, controlled one-fifth of Sri Lanka when a devastating tsunami hit in 2004.[31] For the half million people living in those areas, the LTTE was effectively the government and so offering any meaningful humanitarian aid had to entail collaborating with this designated terrorist group.[32] As Ahilan Arulanantham, an American lawyer visiting relatives in Sri Lanka when the tsunami struck, observed: "Unlike our material support laws, the tsunami did not differentiate between areas under the LTTE's control and those controlled by the Sri Lankan government."

We have no way of knowing if counting humanitarian aid as material support has actually helped to prevent any terrorist acts, but it is clear that the threat of prosecution can do immeasurable damage to altruistic Americans—and to millions of other needy people around the world. And if American humanitarians have to steer clear of all areas of the world where designated groups operate, including the Middle East or Pakistan, the results may actually be counterproductive to our ultimate desire to disempower and discredit terrorist groups, which will be left to take credit for providing disaster relief or other forms of aid.

The Obama Administration would doubtless protest that it has no intention of prosecuting the Red Cross or Jimmy Carter. If people do trust this Administration, they may indeed be less likely to be deterred from humanitarian work by what may seem like a mere hypothetical threat of prosecution. But Congress has provided a very generous statute of limitations for prosecuting material support offenses. Instead of the usual five years, prosecutors are given eight years to start a material support prosecution and are relieved of all time limits if the offense involves a foreseeable risk of death or serious bodily injury to another person.[33] Unless Congress amends the dragnet material support law to exclude humanitarians like Ralph Fertig and supporters of democracy like Roya Rahmani, these statutes will continue to be easy trigger weapons ready to be used at will by future administrations—even against people who make decisions to act today.

3.

Charity at Home

*America's relationship with the Muslim community, the Muslim
world, cannot, and will not, just be based upon opposition to
terrorism.*—President Barack Obama, remarks to the Turkish Parliament
(2009)[1]

*[Terrorism financing investigations of Muslim charities] can
undermine support in the very communities where the government
needs it most.*—9/11 Commission Staff Report (2004)[2]

*I don't have any religious rights anymore; I ask, am I living in
America?*—Sharif B., a Muslim resident of Richardson, Texas (2008)[3]

THE REACH OF the Patriot Act–enhanced material support laws can be breathtaking, especially when combined with other aggressive post-9/11 strategies. One Bush Administration Department of Justice lawyer, for example, announced to a court that a "little old lady in Switzerland" who contributed to a charity because she intended to support an Afghani orphanage could be held in Guantánamo as an "enemy combatant"—indefinitely and without due process—if her money was passed along to Al Qaeda.[4] But President Bush decided to open an additional front in the war on terrorism financing by enlisting the International Emergency Economic Powers Act (IEEPA), a law that had been designed to clarify and limit the power of presidents to impose blockades or economic sanctions on hostile foreign nations—like Iran, Myanmar, or Libya—in emergency situations.[5] Using this statute against private American organizations or individuals was a stretch, but Bush had a surprising precedent: in 1996, Bill Clinton had branded a U.S. citizen named Muhammad Salah a "specially designated terrorist" without any hearing, notice, or trial because he was believed to be a supporter of Hamas. This declaration made it a crime for anyone in the United States to give Salah a job or sell him a sandwich—a kind of economic quarantine.[6]

Bush's Executive Order 13224, signed on September 23, 2001, extended this kind of economic quarantine to a long list of private United States–based charities and individuals. Declaring terrorism to be a national emergency, the Order announced an immediate freeze of all of the United States–based assets of twenty-seven groups Bush unilaterally designated as terrorist organizations, and authorized the Treasury Department Office of Foreign Assets Control (OFAC) to add to this new blacklist.[7] Designation meant that no one was allowed to engage in any financial transaction whatsoever with anyone on the list without applying for and receiving a special license from OFAC authorizing the transaction.

This may have seemed like a good idea in the fall of 2001. Still reeling from the events of 9/11, the Administration was frantically trying to determine whether any other threats were looming. Finding ways to prevent Al Qaeda from raising money to fund future attacks was made a priority and there had not been much time to investigate what networks for terrorist financing might exist. Alarmed officials expressed concern that there was a pipeline of money flowing from Brooklyn mosques to Al Qaeda. The government could use the broad material support laws or other criminal laws to prosecute individuals or organizations who were financing terrorists and could also use forfeiture laws, invigorated by the Patriot Act, to strip a person or individual of assets.[8] But the "blockade" approach offered one great advantage: avoidance of due process protections. In a criminal prosecution, the government would have to introduce admissible evidence amounting to proof beyond a reasonable doubt that the person or organization charged actually provided material support to terrorists, and the defendant would be afforded the full panoply of constitutional criminal procedure rights, including the right to confront witnesses and the right to a jury trial. Forfeiture proceedings do not entail as many rights, but do afford some opportunity to be heard. To the Bush Administration, due process was an unwelcome and dispensable hurdle in combating terrorism. Al Qaeda, as a foreign organization, had no constitutional rights and was regarded as our enemy in a war. Therefore, the Administration reasoned, anyone who supported Al Qaeda should also be treated as an enemy combatant and, American or not, should not enjoy any more constitutional rights than Al Qaeda itself. The administration's preference was to err on the side of overinclusion.

The problem with this reasoning is that it is circular. Without some sort of fair process, it is impossible to know whether someone actually is an Al Qaeda supporter. The Supreme Court rejected the core of this kind of flawed reasoning in *Hamdi v. Rumsfeld*,[9] holding that American citizens have a right to a hearing to determine whether they truly are an "enemy combatant" rather than being unilaterally stripped of rights by a presidential designation on the basis of shadowy and secret evidence.[10] Due process means that American citizens may not be detained on a 1 percent chance that they might be terrorists. It should also mean that the government cannot seize an American person's or organization's property on a 1 percent chance that their property might be used to support terrorists somewhere down the chain.

The designation of "Specially Designated Global Terrorists" (SDGTs) was as peremptory as the designation of Hamdi as an enemy combatant. The statute did not give the designee the right to notice of the government's suspicions or any opportunity to be heard before the designation took effect. There were no criteria provided for OFAC to apply in deciding whom to designate, no process for contesting a designation after the fact, for judicial approval, or for any form of oversight. This lack of procedural safeguards is not surprising, as the IEEPA, like the material witness law, was being enlisted in the War on Terror even though it had been designed for other purposes. Why would Congress have provided Libya, a foreign nation not covered by the United States Constitution, the right to a fair hearing before imposition of an economic blockade—a foreign policy decision? Most of the designated SDGTs were foreigners, but a number were Americans. And Americans must be treated differently from the government of Libya because we do have constitutional rights, including the right to due process before the government takes our property. The blockade approach, created as a shortcut alternative to criminal prosecution or forfeiture laws, violates basic constitutional principles and essentially amounts to punishment without due process of law.[11]

The Campaign Against Charities

The same sense of urgency that led the administration to rely on this emergency designation process also compromised implementation of this program. The campaign unleashed by this executive fiat led to a witch hunt in the world of Muslim charities. The war on terrorist financing became a war on American Muslims, who at times seemed to be presumed guilty of connections with terrorism. It probably seemed logical to investigators to start looking for those who financed Muslim terrorists by looking hard at any Muslim charity. There is no way for us to know whether targets were selected for investigation on the basis of unreliable tips, or to what extent these decisions were influenced by anti-Muslim bias. Designations of American-based charities and individuals were made behind closed doors on the basis of secret evidence. But even people of good faith anxious to find evidence of wrongdoing can come to see what they expected to see, as the overzealous prosecution of Sami al-Hussayen demonstrates. As the past decade has shown again and again, secrecy, lack of due process, and lack of accountability are a deadly combination, breeding inaccuracy as well as abuse.

Here, those who suffered were law-abiding American Muslims and the entire nonprofit sector. Within a few short months of the declaration of emergency, the three largest Muslim charities in America—the Holy Land Foundation, the Global Relief Foundation, and the Benevolence International Foundation—were blacklisted and had their assets seized in dramatic public raids during the Muslim holy month of Ramadan. These organizations were soon joined by others. Seven of the nine United States–based charities blocked under this program were Muslim; the other two were Tamil organizations providing aid relief in Sri Lanka. In the years since 2001, the government has kept some $20 million of seized assets under this Executive Order,[12] holding the assets of some organizations for over seven years despite serious questions about whether the designated charities actually were connected with terrorism financing in any way, and indeed about whether the feared Brooklyn mosque to Al Qaeda pipeline actually existed. Nothing in the applicable statutes or Executive Orders prevents these assets from being held indefinitely—that is, until the president decides that the "emergency" of terrorism has ended.

Some of the designated charities were driven out of business entirely; others were made pariahs, like Muhammad Salah. Well-intentioned donors, who had no way of knowing that their favorite charity would later be deemed to be connected with terrorism financing, found that their contributions sat sequestered for year after year, never getting to any nursery school or back to them.[13] Donors were likely to switch charities once the government blacklist besmirched an organization's reputation, so the targeted charities that remained in business struggled to raise funds for their legitimate charitable purposes and for their own self-defense. More disturbingly, American Muslims were given cause to fear contributing to any Muslim charity, even those not designated, through a persistent pattern of suspicion and harassment. Enforcement efforts infringed First Amendment religious rights as well as due process because, as noted earlier, giving generously to charity is a religious requirement for Muslims—one of the "Five Pillars of Islam." Now innocent contributions to domestic charities, not just "foreign terrorist organizations," might subject people to civil or criminal penalties, to frightening visits from the FBI, or to deportation of anyone who was not a United States citizen. Congress has not explored whether the emergency leading to these abuses continues or whether the power President Bush claimed under the IEEPA goes too far. President Obama's Administration has continued to defend actions taken under this program. And the courts have been slow to notice that this treatment of American religious rights and property ignores the Due Process Clause, the Equal Protection Clause, the Fourth Amendment's prohibition of unreasonable seizures, the First Amendment right of association, and the First Amendment right of Muslims to exercise their religion.

Congress's Patriot Act contribution to this campaign was to allow even organizations not included on the "Specially Designated Global Terrorists" blacklist to have their assets frozen without warning,[14] as a Toledo, Ohio–based charity named KindHearts for Charitable Humanitarian Development was to learn.

Having watched organizations focusing on aid in Palestine and other troubled parts of the world being shut down by the American government, the founders of KindHearts were determined to find a way to offer help to suffering people whose needs were not being met, without running afoul of American law. So in 2002, they declared their mission to provide humanitarian aid to refugees and victims of war and natural disaster around the world, especially in Lebanon and Palestine. They provided food, clean water, clothing, and medical treatment to refugees of war and natural disasters in Lebanon, Gaza, Pakistan, and in the United States following Hurricane Katrina. They sponsored health clinics and bought food and toys for needy children. They did everything recommended by the Treasury Department to avoid even the appearance of supporting terrorists. They rejected proposals for aid from groups they regarded as having political agendas. When they discovered that one of their employees was suspected of having ties to Hamas, they asked him to resign in order to show the government how determined they were to steer clear of any designated groups.[15]

But in February 2006, OFAC notified KindHearts that its assets were being frozen because the charity was under investigation. Why was this charity targeted? A Treasury Department spokesperson announced, "Kind-Hearts is the progeny of Holy Land Foundation and Global Relief Foundation, which attempted to mask their support for terrorism behind the façade of charitable giving."[16] This may have been a case of guilt by past association or assumption. Some of those involved with KindHearts had indeed been involved with organizations which the government had shut down in December 2001 for their suspected connections with Hamas (the Holy Land Foundation and Global Relief Foundation). But the Kind-Hearts founders themselves were not identified as terrorism supporters. Their experience with the blacklisted organizations was exactly what led them to recognize an unmet need and to commit themselves to complying with American law. Did the government have evidence that someone in the new organization was actually supporting Hamas or terrorists generally? Was the problem that they were suspected of running afoul of the material support law because their well-intentioned contributions of humanitarian aid to refugees in areas where Hamas was active might theoretically have freed up resources for Hamas to engage in terrorism? Was there any way KindHearts could have structured its aid to avoid that problem? We have no way of knowing and neither did KindHearts. OFAC's evidence, which could include hearsay and classified information, was not revealed at the time the organization's assets were frozen and was only partly shared in the years to follow. OFAC never offered KindHearts advice about how to avoid breaking the law, or gave them notice that they might be doing something of concern. OFAC might have issued an order to KindHearts to cease and desist from certain activities that might have left the charity able to pursue its central mission in a manner OFAC would find unob-jectionable. Instead, OFAC just put KindHearts out of business without providing evidence to back up its suspicions. Just trust us.

Without being allowed to spend its money, the charity could not do anything to help refugees or even to help itself. The charity was not per-mitted to use its own funds to hire a lawyer—paying a lawyer is, after all, a financial transaction. Lawyers are required to apply to the Treasury Department for a special license before being allowed to represent any designated organization or organization whose assets have been seized.[17] KindHearts' lawyer was granted a license, but he was told that under Trea-sury Department policy applicable at that time, he could not be paid out of the group's assets because of the blocking order. The organization had no prospect of raising additional funds (which, because of the blocking order, could only be done outside the United States), so that lawyer resigned—and was replaced by volunteer lawyers, including Lynne Bernabei, David Cole, and the ACLU, all of whom also had to apply for special licenses. In addition to being willing to work without payment, lawyers representing targeted organizations also have to be willing to explain to OFAC what their representation of the organization will entail, compromising the confidentiality of the lawyer-client relationship.

The government seized all of the organization's records and then restricted its access to those records. OFAC's review took fifteen months, but KindHearts was given a deadline of only thirty days to respond, despite being unable to review its own records or pay for legal or other professional help to document its side of the story. Former employees worried that if they helped KindHearts prepare a defense, they might be leaving themselves vulnerable under the material support law for contributing to an organization that was suspected of contributing to terrorist organizations. KindHearts was becoming radioactive.

Two and a half years after the initial blocking order, the investigation was still pending and the confiscated assets were still in the government's hands. Not only does the law neglect to provide any fair administrative process, it also fails to provide any deadlines or time limits for government action. KindHearts still had not been charged with any crime or even designated as a terrorist group, but it was being put out of business. So KindHearts went to court. The organization's complaint tells a byzantine tale of blocked documents, denied security clearances, and unresponsive bureaucracy. Early stages of the litigation were dominated by skirmishing over the availability of documents. The Obama Administration came into power, but the government's arguments did not change and neither, evidently, did the status of KindHearts. In 2009, Ohio federal judge James Carr (a Clinton appointee who is now Chief Judge of his court) wrote a sixty-five-page opinion explaining why he thought this Patriot Act provision's total disregard for fair process was unconstitutional. This confiscation of assets without any showing of wrongdoing was an unreasonable "seizure" in violation of the Fourth Amendment, he wrote, and KindHearts had been denied due process because the organization had not been given a fair opportunity to understand or respond to the government's concerns.[18] In May 2010, over four years after the initial seizure, Judge Carr ordered OFAC to tell KindHearts the basis for the original blocking order and to explain why they believed that the charity was connected with terrorist financing so that he could determine whether or not there was actually probable cause for the seizure and retention of the group's resources. He also asked OFAC, now under new management, to reconsider allowing KindHeart's lawyers to be paid out of the organization's own funds.[19]

Although it may have seemed like a good idea in the fall of 2001 to err on the side of overinclusion, a special 9/11 Commission staff report on terrorism financing later found the evidentiary basis for the early designations of charities as terrorist supporters to be weak. Asserted "links" between the designated groups and terrorists—in the form of common contacts, and so forth—were "sufficient to whet the appetite for action" but did not demonstrate that the designated groups were actually funding terrorism.[20] There certainly was not strong enough evidence of wrongdoing to justify abruptly putting these charities out of business. One former Treasury official who had been part of the December 2001 designation rush told the Commission staff, "[W]e were so forward leaning we almost fell on our face."[21] Other critics have agreed that this emergency program led to dubious designations, despite the fact that the government enjoyed an unprecedented level of access to financial information from around the world as American and international bankers and companies shared their massive databases with government officials.[22]

Because the process is secret and there is so little review by Congress or the courts, our chief source of information about the reliability of these designations comes, oddly enough, from other countries which, on being asked to join the United States in blocking particular organizations, evaluated our government's evidence and publicly announced themselves unsatisfied. On three separate occasions, the U.K. Charity Commission, for example, reviewed OFAC's assertion that a U.K.-based charity called Interpal was supporting Hamas, and concluded that "[t]he American authorities were unable to provide evidence to support their allegations."[23] This was not the only occasion on which much of the purported evidence against a group consisted of inconclusive newspaper articles which sometimes did not even name the group in question.[24] Mistranslation was also a serious problem. The evidence in a criminal trial against the Holy Land Foundation for providing material support to terrorists, for example, included a four-page FBI document which an independent translating service found to contain sixty-seven translation errors. One translation from Arabic to Hebrew to English rendered the statement "we have no connection to Hamas" as "charitable funds were channeled to Hamas."[25] Officials in other countries reached the same disparaging conclusions. As a Canadian Justice Ministry official said of one case, "We looked at the evidence and then it became clear that there was no evidence."[26]

The Holy Land Foundation (HLF) is the only one of the blocked organizations the government has had any success in prosecuting, and even that case has remained controversial. President Bush announced in a December 2001 press conference that "Hamas has obtained much of the money that pays for murder abroad right here in the U.S., money originally raised by the Holy Land Foundation."[27] But the criminal trial against HLF and some of its leaders was not based on the theory that HLF had given money to Hamas, a foreign terrorist organization, for material support purposes. Instead, the government's theory was that HLF had given money to non-designated charity committees—committees which also received aid from the International Red Cross and the United Nations—and that Foundation officials "should have known" that these committees had connections with Hamas, which might thereby receive indirect benefits from HLF's aid.[28] The 2007 criminal trial of HLF and five of its leaders, which lasted over three months, did not result in convictions on any of 197 counts. One juror at the 2007 trial referred to the prosecution evidence as "strung together with macaroni noodles."[29] Another described the case as "based on assumptions that were based on suspicions."[30] Because the jury did not agree on acquittals on all of the counts, a mistrial was declared and the government got to try again.

Having practiced, the government did better at a 2008 retrial, winning convictions of the charity and five leaders on a number of charges including charges under the material support law—which, as the last chapter showed, is a pushover.[31] The defendants appealed what they claimed had been an unfair trial. Procedural wrangling—over fundamental issues like whether an appeal should be allowed and whether HLF could be represented by counsel—persisted for additional years, almost a decade after the initial designation. But the government did not win any convictions against Benevolence International Foundation (BIF) or the Global Relief Foundation,[32] the other two of the three largest American Muslim charities, and the other designated organizations were not charged with any crimes.[33] The campaign against BIF was an enormous waste of resources on all sides. A court dismissed the 2003 criminal prosecution of BIF after finding that the government simply had not connected the dots. The organization brought a civil case to challenge its designation, but ran out of money and had to drop the litigation.

The dubious American designations had ripple effects throughout the world. The Treasury Department shut down the United States offices of a group called Al-Barakaat ("the Blessing"), with Secretary Paul O'Neill calling the group "quartermasters of terror." But no actual connection between the group and terrorism was ever established, and the government eventually returned this group's money and closed its investigation without bringing any charges.[34] Meanwhile, this unsupportable designation evidently led to shutting down a branch of Al-Barakaat in Somalia. This organization had been running what was essentially the central bank of Somalia and its closure disrupted United Nations relief operations, the country's only water purification plant and an anti-cholera program, and led to the loss of 700 jobs.[35] The 9/11 Commission staff could find no corresponding benefit to offset these costs of shutting down this group's activities, as the United States had "no direct evidence at all of any real link between al-Barakaat and terrorism of any type."[36]

With the perspective of hindsight, the 9/11 Commission staff report expressed skepticism about the whole secret and peremptory designation process. The use of emergency economic sanctions against domestic groups "raises significant civil liberty concerns because it allows the government to shut down an organization on the basis of classified information, subject only to deferential after-the-fact review," the report concluded.[37] Ironically, because the president's emergency blockade program was not anticipated by Congress, American organizations actually have fewer procedural rights than their foreign counterparts who confront a "foreign terrorist organization" designation.[38] American charities and their leaders are supposed to enjoy constitutional rights. But when domestic organizations have asked courts to review the constitutionality of their designations under the president's Executive Order, the courts have almost uniformly rejected their constitutional challenges, citing the need to be deferential to OFAC on matters of national security.[39] One court explained that because the premise of the president's program was that a national emergency exists, designees are not entitled to any due process.[40] This level of deference might be appropriate for a presidential decision to place an embargo on goods from Libya, but is simply inconsistent with the constitutional rights of Americans.

Despite its mistakes and the rough nature of its procedures, has this program succeeded in disrupting the financing of terror? Experts have their doubts. The central goal of the program—to disrupt a United States to Al Qaeda financial pipeline—may have been based on a misdiagnosis of the very nature of terrorism financing. Eric Lichtblau, who researched the asset-blocking program in connection with news articles and his book *Bush's Law*, describes the emergency need to shut down the pipeline of funds to terrorists as "built, in large part, on a myth of the administration's own making."[41] He quotes a law enforcement official as telling him that, despite the administration's confident declarations, the feared pipeline "never really existed."[42] The staff of the 9/11 Commission, which conducted its own investigation of terrorism-financing networks, agreed: "The United States is not, and has not been, a substantial source of Al Qaeda funding."[43] Furthermore, the Commission staff noted, "The premise behind the government's efforts here—that terrorist operations need a financial support network—may itself be outdated. The effort to find, track, and stop money presumes that it is being sent from a central source or group of identifiable sources."[44] The Congressional Research Service reported to Congress the 9/11 Commission's recommendation that the U.S. government "shift the focus of its efforts to counter terrorist financing from a strategy based on seizing alleged terrorist assets to a strategy based on exploiting intelligence gathered from financial investigations."[45] Congress has not responded. The administration could point to the convictions it won against Holy Land Foundation as showing that money for terrorists was being raised within the United States. But those convictions were obtained under standard criminal laws, not under the emergency authority now in its tenth year.

Collateral Damage to Freedom of Religion and Association

The search for American mosques and charities feeding money to Al Qaeda has had a devastating impact on American Muslims, creating a climate of fear, self-censorship, and distrust of government. In a 2009 report called *Blocking Faith, Freezing Charity*, based on interviews with 115 Muslims around the country, ACLU researcher Jennifer Turner documented the sources and consequences of that fear. Many Muslims reported that FBI agents interrogated them about their donations to Muslim charities, whether those charities were blacklisted or not.[46] A Muslim woman in Detroit reported:

> Our whole community was approached by the FBI about our donations. They've intimidated our whole community . . . They've been asking about every single Muslim charity. Everyone is aware of this. People aren't giving as much as they should be giving, because of this.[47]

A Dearborn lawyer said:

> The FBI goes to donors' work and ask "why do you give money to this charity, what do you know about this charity, how much do

you give". . . the government makes the donor feel like he has done something wrong.[48]

Some reported having been visited by the FBI two years in a row and asked about the same kinds of donations:

> It was very obvious to me the second time [the FBI] came [to my clients] it was to say, "If you keep giving, we'll keep coming back at you". . . [T]his was an investigation to make sure people are intimidated and scared, to cut off funding to Muslim children abroad.[49]

Others have been troubled by FBI agents recruiting informants to report charitable donations and speeches made in their mosques[50] or sending undercover agents to infiltrate mosques. One New York Police Department informant, for example, attended some 575 prayer services in mosques, sometimes at the rate of four or five a day, to record who was attending and the "tone" of religious services.[51] Federal and local guidelines that used to restrict sending undercover agents into political or religious settings were relaxed after 9/11, allowing more agents to infiltrate mosques or meetings just to fish for information, without any reason to believe the mosque or group is doing anything illegal.[52] Some Muslims fear subpoenas, surveillance, or deportation if they get too close to an organization that turns out to be under investigation. And, of course, the frightening breadth of the material support laws has convinced some to stop donating to any Muslim charity at all, even though they believe that is what their faith demands of them. As Kamal J., a Muslim resident of Bedford, Texas, told an interviewer, "Because everything is under scrutiny, I am not able to fulfill my religious obligation to give—because I am just afraid."[53] Many fear that they can be prosecuted for making a contribution to a legal charity which is later designated, a retroactive guilt theory they say Treasury Department agents do not disavow.[54] Some have stopped attending mosques for fear of attracting attention; some have resorted to making contributions only in cash, so that they cannot be traced.[55] This climate of fear was exacerbated by the government's habit of announcing decisions to block a charity in the most dramatic way possible—through public raids, sometimes insensitively timed during the holy month of Ramadan. One Muslim leader remarked, "There is a better way than having the counterterrorism Task Force raid the charity with guns drawn and with the media 'happening' to show up."[56]

This overblown campaign is not only harmful to Muslims and to the charities themselves. As the 9/11 Commission staff commented, the widespread perception that this enforcement program is unfair and biased can "undermine support in the very communities where the government needs it most."[57] Muslims interviewed agreed that the government's campaign against Muslim charities and donors is the single greatest cause of their communities' alienation and mistrust of law enforcement.[58] The leader of a mosque in Detroit said:

> We want to help in building the U.S.A., and we want to work with the Department of Homeland Security as trusted partners, but we feel they treat us as guilty until proven innocent. They want us as spies, not as partners. Bridges are not being built, no—they are being torn down.[59]

There are other reasons to be concerned that this mode of operations may be counterproductive.[60] International cooperation with our antiterrorism efforts is undermined when officials in other countries distrust American assurances that they have followed the money. The "Muslim street" has reason to believe that the United States, despite the reassuring words of Barack Obama, does equate Muslims with terrorists. Islamic banking and finance expert Ibrahim Warde notes: "Here in the U.S. you occasionally hear stories but by and large people aren't aware of this, whereas in Muslim countries everyone is aware of these stories and actions against Muslim charities."[61] Residents of other countries may also be disturbed by the fact that in addition to violating our own Constitution, limiting the religious freedom of American Muslims violates international human rights law, including the International Covenant on Civil and Political Rights[62] and the Universal Declaration of Human Rights.[63]

Cables released by WikiLeaks show that other governments continue to have mixed responses to our antiterrorism financing efforts abroad, which in many respects resemble the domestic program described in this chapter. As summarized in a *New York Times* account,[64] the cables show little evidence of significant financial support for terrorism in the United States, and greatest support in the Gulf states. Although the overall tone of the cables was described as pessimistic on this score, Treasury officials claim to have put Al Qaeda under significant financial pressure by pursuing sources and methods of terrorist financing in the Gulf region in particular. President Obama has maintained a conciliatory tone in public toward Arab nations, but uses "many of the same covert diplomatic, intelligence and law enforcement tools as his predecessor."[65] Some other nations, like Kuwait, have found the evidence Americans present about particular charities "thin" and the responses the Americans propose—like shutting down a charity—"draconian." In February 2010, the European Parliament suspended a program under which Americans monitored international banking transactions (through a Belgian banking consortium called Swift), relenting only when the United States agreed to allow greater European oversight. Opposition to American investigative techniques in Germany, where memories of the Stasi are still vivid, was especially strong.

Is the domestic side of this program worth it, given what we now know about the realities of terrorism financing? Bush's economic sanction program was added to the already overbroad material support and forfeiture laws to provide redundant methods of attacking a domestic problem that may never have amounted to much. The benefits of this program are unclear; the costs are enormous—including incursions on many rights, a tremendous waste of resources on all sides, and alienation of people who could be our allies. There are dozens of ways in which this program could be tweaked to provide greater due process and greater accuracy, or conducted with more sensitivity to constitutional rights—like providing for hearings and limiting the ability of agents to intimidate law-abiding Muslims. A coalition of nonprofit groups lobbied for change in 2006,[66] but succeeded in winning only minor modifications of the OFAC program.[67] After years of observing congressional inertia in this area, a 2008 OMB Watch/Grantmakers without Borders report declared that the government's focus on charities in its campaign against terrorist financing is simply unjustifiable.[68] The report detailed the impact of the "short-term" response to terrorism in measures like the Patriot Act and the "long-term" consequences for the nonprofit sector, and called on charities to mobilize to seek change. In his 2009 Cairo speech, Barack Obama expressed his intention of working with Muslims to alleviate the hurdles to charitable donations.[69] In August 2010, Muslim groups wrote to Obama to express their concern about how little progress had been made on this front.[70] In December 2010, the members of the coalition gave up in frustration.

Is this entire program doing more harm than good? There are alternative legal tools available to prosecute charities or freeze their assets if the government actually has reliable proof of some sort of malfeasance. George W. Bush declared a state of "emergency" to allow the same results without any of the due process. Are we really willing to let that emergency mind-set continue into a second decade and beyond? While Barack Obama would need Congress to fix the material support statutes, he could root out the cause of much of this campaign of fear and disinformation with a stroke of the pen—by revisiting Executive Order 13224.

4.
Traveling with Terror

We can't just throw a bunch of names on these lists and call it security . . . If we can't get an 8-year-old off the list, the whole list becomes suspect.—Rep. William J. Pascrell, Jr. (2010)[1]

If they have that kind of difficulty with a member of Congress [not being allowed to fly because his name is on a No Fly list], how in the world are average Americans, who are getting caught up in this thing, how are they going to be treated fairly and not have their rights abused?—Sen. Edward J. Kennedy (2004)[2]

No American should be forced to undergo a virtual strip search or subjected to such excessive groping of the body . . . when there is no suspicion of wrongdoing . . . To do so goes against every good and decent principle this country was founded upon.—John Whitehead, Rutherford Institute (2010)[3]

LIKE SENATOR EDWARD Kennedy, most Americans have had their closest encounters with antiterrorism measures and watchlists at the airport. As Senator Kennedy told an astonished Senate Judiciary Committee in August 2004, he was at Reagan Airport planning to take the US Air shuttle from Washington to Boston when an agent told him, "We can't give [the ticket] to you, you can't buy a ticket." When Kennedy asked why not, the agent replied, "We can't tell you."[4] Kennedy reported having had the same experience on other occasions when he tried to board a plane to return to his job in Washington, D.C. Apparently "T. Kennedy," a name that must be shared by thousands of Americans, was an alias that appeared on one of the watchlists airport screeners were required to consult.

If your name appears on the No Fly list, a blacklist, you will be denied a boarding pass and referred to law enforcement. If your name is on only the companion "Automatic Selectee" list, you will not necessarily be prevented from flying, but you will be subjected to extra screening, ranging from an extra search to full-blown interrogation. At one point, the TSA received some thirty reports per day from the airlines of potential matches with the watchlists, most or all of which were false positives—identifications of people who were not actually suspected of being terrorists at all.[5]

How can you tell if you're on a watchlist? You can't. But one of the first signs is being told you have to see an agent to check in for your flight. According to the Department of Homeland Security, 99 percent of the people who complain of problems at the airport "are not on the terrorist watchlist, but are misidentified as people who are."[6] Small comfort to those who have to cancel or delay their travel plans because they have common names. The Transportation Security Administration (TSA) lists on its website as a "myth" that children are on the watchlist.[7] But someone who shared a name with eight-year-old New Jersey Cub Scout Michael ("Mikey") Hicks evidently was on the Selectee list. And so Mikey's family learned to arrive early at the airport before every trip so that Mikey could be questioned, patted down, and even frisked before boarding. Anyone whose name appeared to be on the list was treated as suspicious. The Hicks family had a lot of experience with this ordeal. Special attention to Mikey began when he was two years old and persisted even on one occasion when Mikey's mother (a photojournalist who had been cleared to fly with Vice President Al Gore) enlisted her Congressman to have a TSA agent run interference for her family at the airport. Both Mrs. Hicks and Congressman Pascrell expressed their bafflement at the fact that for seven years, it had not been possible to get Mikey, who was born less than a month before 9/11, cleared of suspicion so he could be spared this ordeal.

Before 9/11, there was a No Fly list, but it had only sixteen names on it. In December 2008, the master list from which the No Fly and Selectee lists are drawn contained 1,183,447 names.[8] The size of the airport lists has fluctuated over the decade. The No Fly list apparently had about 20,000 names around the time Senator Kennedy was stopped.[9] When Congress finally took an interest in the plight of innocent travelers, after the 2004 Judiciary Committee hearing at which Senator Kennedy stole the show, that list was reduced to about 3,400. But after the Christmas 2009 incident involving Nigerian air passenger Omar Abdulmutallab, who was discovered in a plane heading for Detroit with explosives in his underwear, the number went back up, almost doubling within a few months with the prospect of additional increases.[10]

These watchlists—now proliferating beyond the airport, affecting Amtrak and cruise ship passengers too[11]—present a dramatic example of just

how challenging it can be to strike a balance between the desire for dragnets to catch the guilty and recognition of the harm they cause the innocent. The larger the number of names on the list, the more likely the list is
to include actual terrorists—and also to include innocent Americans who
will have their travel plans and their constitutional rights disrupted. Timothy Healy, Director of the Terrorist Screening Center, which administers
the master list, assured Congress that in deciding how to strike that balance, "privacy is protected and civil liberties are safeguarded throughout
the entire watchlisting and screening process."[12] Healy also told Congress
that there would inevitably be mistakes in deciding what names to place
on the lists: "[T]hese people are identified by fragments of information.
They're identified by a source saying 'this guy's involved in it.' So it's not a
black and white system."[13] Just trusting the FBI to strike its own balance
in secret, with no due process for those swept up in the enterprise and with
little real accountability or oversight, sets the stage for both constitutional
violations and ineffectual security measures. But government agencies prefer to make their own decisions in secret so they won't be second-guessed
by anyone. It is typical of post-9/11 thinking for officials to want space to
err on the side of overinclusion, and it is simply human nature for people
to believe that they can be trusted not to make mistakes.

But from the beginning, the watchlists were riddled with errors. Documents released in response to an ACLU Freedom of Information Act lawsuit in 2003 showed that watchlists were being generated long before any
coordinated policy or criteria for selecting names had been developed.[14]
A March 2008 Inspector General report found those same problems had
persisted—the "nomination" process still lacked adequate coordination
and criteria—and expressed concern about the accuracy of the lists.[15] A
follow-up May 2009 report by the same Inspector General, studying the
nominations themselves, showed that accuracy was indeed a very serious
problem: procedures for reviewing nominations of people who were not
already subjects of FBI investigations were "weak or nonexistent"; in 78
percent of cases, nominations to the list were not timely and sometimes
were based on outdated or simply incorrect information; the list was over-
inclusive but also underinclusive, as people who should have been placed
on the list (like the underwear bomber) were not. At the same time, the FBI
failed to remove names of cleared people in a timely manner in 72 percent of
cases, despite the fact that the 2004 Congress had instructed the agencies involved to create a system to enable innocent people to get off the list and the
agencies had publicly announced that their lists had been scrubbed clean.[16]

Under the dragnet principle, the agencies involved with aviation security have been far more concerned with adding names of the potentially guilty, especially at times of heightened public concern, than with finding ways to remove the names of the innocent. It took a special act of Congress in July of 2008 to finally remove the name of Nelson Mandela, who spent many years on the watchlist because of his connection with the African National Congress, which prevailed in an election making him President of South Africa in 1994.[17]

This disturbing level of inaccuracy does nothing to enhance our safety but it does compromise a number of constitutional rights, including the right to due process. American travelers are denied the right to fly within the United States without being given any real opportunity to correct mistakes. If you find that a name resembling yours is on a watchlist, how do you prove that you are not a terrorist if you are over eight years old and not a U.S. senator? And if it is indeed your name that was put on the watchlist, how can you clear yourself if you're not told what caused your name to appear on the list and therefore have no chance to rebut false rumors or to point out grudges, biases, or unpopular positions that might have led to your being targeted? As Americans, we are accustomed to the idea that we are innocent until proven guilty. But post-9/11 dragnets tend to focus on prevention rather than punishment. One consequence of this shift to a prevention paradigm, as experience with the material support laws has shown,[18] is that due process has gotten lost. Prediction is an unreliable basis for punishment or other government-imposed hardships.[19] And the individual is left to persuade the government that he is not *that* T. Kennedy if he wants to board a plane.

More than the right to travel can be at stake. At least one law-abiding American had to find a way to convince a faceless bureaucracy to remove him from a watchlist in order to keep his job. Erich Scherfen is an American citizen and Persian Gulf War veteran. He was a frontline infantryman and paratrooper and, after his honorable discharge from active duty, he served as a helicopter pilot for the National Guard. (He flew a Cobra attack helicopter and had a secret security clearance.) Beginning in 2006, he found himself being detained and harassed at airports. Airport gate agents had suggested to him that he was on a watchlist; those hints were confirmed in April 2008 when his employers at Colgan Airlines (a regional airline) told him that they had tried and failed to get his name removed from the watchlist, that he was being suspended without pay, and that he would be fired if he could not get his name removed promptly.[20]

Erich tried filing a complaint with the Department of Homeland Security (DHS), as part of the DHS TRIP program—the acronym stands for Traveler Redress Inquiry Program—designed to give innocent travelers a way to get off the watchlist. For four agonizing months he got no response. Desperate to keep his job, he consulted the ACLU and filed a lawsuit to try to get a court to help him. The agencies involved would not say whether or not Erich was actually on a list, even though his employer had already shared that information. The government repeatedly tried to get the case dismissed, but the court declined and scheduled a hearing. Shortly before the date of the hearing, Erich was surprised to learn that Colgan Airlines sent a letter to the Department of Homeland Security to confirm that Erich was being restored to his job. Even though the government had evidently relented, Erich continued to litigate because he believed he had been placed on the watchlist because of his religion. Erich is a Muslim. Having been exposed to Islam as part of his sensitivity training while serving in the Gulf, he studied comparative religion after he returned home and decided to convert—as had other Gulf War veterans. Shortly after that, he married Rubina Tareen, a Pakistani-born U.S. citizen, who is also a Muslim and who experienced airport problems even before Erich did. But not every Muslim-American ends up on the watchlist. Court records showed that in 2006, a co-worker had reported to the state police that Erich Scherfen was remodeling his car to carry bombs—a wild and false inference apparently based on the co-worker having seen Erich remove a broken seat from the car.[21]

In February 2010, the district court, having reviewed secret evidence submitted by the government and never shown to Erich's lawyer, dismissed the case. The judge reasoned that Erich had his job back and so either he had not been on the list or was no longer on the list and so, in either event, he no longer had any standing to complain about how the list worked because he was no longer being injured.[22] And so the court did not reach the issue of whether Erich's rights had been violated—or the issue of whether it is constitutional to allow careless procedures and religious bias to put other people in the same situation.

One concern about secret designations, as Erich's experience shows, is that they can be arbitrary or discriminatory. Secrecy can hide a multitude of abuses. Federal government policies aspirationally prohibit racial, religious, or ethnic profiling, but Erich Scherfen's case shows that it need not be a government agent's bias that causes Muslims to find themselves branded. Erich's co-worker may have made mental leaps in interpreting a perfectly innocent act because he knew Erich was a Muslim and in his own mind he equated Muslims and terrorists. The flawed watchlist nomination process, as the Inspector General found, can nurture and conceal all kinds of bias and sloppy fact-finding.

Another source of concern about watchlists is that behind closed doors suspicion can be based on First Amendment protected speech or associations, as well as religion. Jan Adams and Rebecca Gordon were early casualties of the No Fly list, stopped at the San Francisco airport on their way to Chicago in 2002 and told by agents that they were on "an FBI no-fly list."[23] They suspected that they were being targeted because of their anti-war activism—they were co-publishers of a newspaper called *War Times*, which was critical of the Bush Administration's domestic war on terrorism. The newspaper's slogan was "The first casualty of war is truth." So they became plaintiffs in the Freedom of Information Act lawsuit mentioned above, hoping to learn why their names had been placed on the list. They never got an explanation, but the hundreds of pages of documents they received did not assuage their concerns. They were among the first to discover that the process for selecting names was dysfunctional. In addition, the FBI declined to say whether or not activities like attending antiwar protests could lead to inclusion on the list. And neither the FBI nor the TSA could say how many people had been stopped as a result of the lists, as the agencies did not think there was any need to keep track.

Fourth Amendment rights may be infringed if people are detained at airports without sufficient cause, as prolonged detention can amount to an unreasonable seizure. Having one's name on a watchlist on the basis of insufficiently verified "fragments of information" is certainly not the equivalent of probable cause for arrest. People who want to get on an airplane, or keep their jobs, are under pressure to agree to an interrogation or polygraph test, compromising the Fifth Amendment's privilege against self-incrimination. And it is certainly a denial of equal protection to single out people for special treatment because they are Muslims. But because the whole process is secret, we have no way of knowing how often improper or arguably unconstitutional designations occur. It is also typical of the War on Terror decade that Congress has provided little oversight and the courts have played almost no role in deciding whether any of this violates the Constitution. When experiences like Erich Scherfen's come to light, most judges agree with the judge in Erich's case that a person who doesn't know for sure whether or not his name is on the list does not have standing to raise constitutional claims. Might the government try to avoid all constitutional litigation, therefore, simply by stonewalling and refusing to confirm whether a person actually has been watchlisted,[24] or by quietly removing that one squeaky wheel from the list?

Would-be litigants also encounter other difficulties, including government lawyers hiding behind secrecy and refusing to share relevant evidence with their lawyers, or even with the court, in order to keep the agencies' actions from being reviewed or questioned, as Rahinah Ibrahim, a Malaysian doctoral candidate in architecture at Stanford University, discovered. When Rahinah arrived at the San Francisco airport with her fourteen-year-old daughter to fly home to Malaysia for vacation, she was handcuffed, searched, and driven to a police holding cell. An FBI agent eventually told the local police they could release her, as her name was being moved from the No Fly to the Selectee list and so she would be allowed to fly home after all, whenever she could book another flight. She was able to fly home to Malaysia the next day, but when it came time for her to return to school, she found that her visa had been revoked. When she complained to the government, she received a form response, telling her that her case had been reviewed and any required corrections had been made. Still not knowing why she had been targeted, in January 2006 she decided to bring a lawsuit against the federal and local officials involved. Years of technical legal wrangling over matters like jurisdiction and pleading standards followed. The government agencies involved vigorously resisted revealing to Rahinah's lawyer or even to the judge what evidence had led to Rahinah being treated as a terrorism suspect. This government intransigence continued after Barack Obama became president and installed a new chain of command of lawyers in the Department of Justice.

The judge assigned to Rahinah's case, William Alsup, was someone who took civil rights very seriously. A Clinton nominee, he had served as a law clerk for Supreme Court Justice William O. Douglas and had done civil rights work in the south. Judge Alsup eventually became exasperated with the government's insistence on keeping all information about Rahinah's treatment secret. At a hearing in December 2009, he told the government lawyers that it was evident to him that a "monumental mistake" had been made and that their arguments for refusing to show the court five-year-old information on the ground that national security could be compromised were "baloney."[25] Alsup ordered the government to turn over the documents showing why Rahinah had been targeted. He entitled his order, more circumspectly although still a shade sarcastically, "Order for Production of Items Despite the Assertion of Various Privileges."[26] But there are limits to what an individual district court judge can do. The same judge had already dismissed some of the claims Rahinah had raised because they did not clear procedural hurdles set by the Supreme Court.[27] The district court still has not decided, as I write, whether any of Rahinah's rights were violated. Surviving dismissal for so many years, though, is enough to distinguish Rahinah's case from most others—and to distinguish William Alsup from most other judges.

Watching the Watchlists

Back in 2004, the ACLU filed a lawsuit on behalf of frustrated passengers who had no way to prevent recurring airport problems even once they had been cleared for a particular flight. The plaintiffs included John Shaw, a retired Presbyterian minister from Washington State; Michelle Green, a U.S. Air Force Master Sergeant stationed in Alaska; and Alexandra Hay, a Middlebury, Vermont college, student; all of whom were hassled at airports because they had name twins.[28] The lawsuit asked the agencies to develop some real program for enabling innocent people to find a way out. That December, after the lawsuit was filed, after the Senate Judiciary Committee hearings starring Senator Kennedy, after expressions of public concern, and after a 9/11 Commission recommendation,[29] Congress finally took action, directing the TSA to maintain its lists in a manner that "will not produce a large number of false positives" and to create an appeal system for persons wrongly placed on the lists—exactly what the lawsuit had asked.[30] In light of this promising legislation, the lawsuit was discontinued. But for years, the systems created in response to Congress's command remained ineffective. A December 2009 Congressional Research Service report described misidentification as a recurring issue that should be of concern to Congress.[31]

The Department of Homeland Security developed DHS TRIP, which invites someone who has experienced problems at the airport to file a form online and get a "Redress Control Number," as Erich Scherfen did. Travelers still are not told whether or not they actually are or were on the list, why they were placed on the list if they were on it, or whether they have been removed from the list as a result of their complaint. They are given no opportunity to confront or challenge unfounded accusations like the one made by Erich Scherfen's co-worker. Any review, like the original designation, will take place behind closed agency doors. The response letter they get following the review will be comically cryptic.

The letter Erich Scherfen received after his four-month wait, for example, said:

> In response to your inquiry concerning travel delays at the airline ticket counter or airport security checkpoint, we conducted a review of any applicable records in consultation with other Federal agencies, as appropriate. Where it was determined that a correction to records was warranted, these records were modified to address any delay or denial of boarding that you may have experienced as a result of the Transportation Security Administration's watch list screening process.[32]

As of June 2010, 81,793 travelers had asked the Department of Homeland Security to remove their names from the watchlist or clarify their status.[33] Many of their cases are still pending as I write; those whose cases were resolved may have no way to know whether their complaints resulted in any concrete action or whether they will have a problem the next time they go to the airport.[34] But the TSA says things have improved since the beginning of the decade. In 2007, the TSA conducted a "scrub" of its list and expressed confidence that mistakes were no longer a concern.[35] Some positive procedural changes were made during the second half of the decade, like adopting criteria (including a "reasonable suspicion" standard) for putting names on the list.[36] A 2008 article in the *Washington Times* reporting on some of these developments optimistically began, "Sen. Ted Kennedy can relax. Terrorists, not so much."[37] The recently initiated Secure Flight program aims to reduce the number of false positives at the airport.[38] The Transportation Security Administration, taking over the job of screening from the airlines, undertook to refine the list by including data on gender and date of birth, and by requiring a complete name before putting someone on the No Fly list (although someone known by a partial name or epithet—like "Ahmed the Tall"—might still be on the Selectee list). A traveler might now find it easier to show airlines that he is not *that* T. Kennedy or *that* Michael Hicks. Of course, this convenience comes at the expense of personal privacy, as airlines now ask passengers for a range of personal information, and pass on to the TSA the passenger's passport number and itinerary in addition to personal identifiers.[39]

But despite periodic flurries of procedural tweaks and positive public relations spin, the flaws in the watchlist designation process itself remain. Those whose names actually were placed on the list, for unknown reasons, continue to have problems, and their experiences do not have the cuteness quotient of little Mikey's story.

Ayman Latif, a disabled Marine Corps veteran who was born and raised in Miami, was living in Egypt with his wife and baby. His veterans' disability benefits were reduced because he was not permitted to fly back to the United States for a required in-person reassessment meeting with the Veterans Administration (VA). Ayman and his wife had decided to take the baby to Miami for a visit with the family. But at the Cairo airport they were shocked to be told that they would not be allowed on the plane. Ayman did not know why his name might have ended up on a watchlist or how to get it removed. He tried filing a form with DHS TRIP in April 2010 and was given a Redress Control Number. Three months later, not having gotten any response, he filed another form and got another Redress Control Number. Not knowing whether the redress process was accomplishing anything, he enlisted the help of the U.S. Embassy and, as a result, FBI agents met with him in Cairo and questioned him for four hours. He was told that these agents were recommending that he be granted a waiver to fly, but that did not materialize. Someone back in Washington whom he had not met evidently would not approve. While he was stranded in Egypt, Ayman missed his appointment with the VA and was unable to reschedule the appointment because he was still not allowed to fly to the United States. As a result, his benefits were reduced and Ayman had to move his family to lower-cost housing. Ayman hoped that his lawsuit might finally cause someone to review his case and realize that it had all been a mistake. That plan succeeded, at least in part. After the complaint was filed, he was permitted to fly home to the United States on a one-time "waiver."

Steve Washburn, another veteran and American citizen, took a job with a technology company in Riyadh. But he and his wife did not take to life in Saudi Arabia and so they decided to move back home to the United States. They sold their house, closed their bank account, and planned to go to Las Cruces, New Mexico, where Steve's parents lived. They got as far as Dublin, where they were visiting Steve's pregnant step-daughter, and were then told they would not be allowed to fly to the United States. Sympathetic FBI agents suggested that Steve fly to Mexico and then cross the border on foot at Ciudad Juarez, since he was only prohibited from flying to the United States, not from entering the country. Accepting this suggestion, he bought a plane ticket from London to Mexico City. His wife, a citizen of Spain, was told that she would not be permitted to accompany her husband even though she was not on any watchlist. Steve got on the flight to Mexico but, after three and a half hours in the air the plane was sent back to London. Steve was detained and interrogated for nine hours. His life savings were confiscated. His Irish visa, which he had extended twice, was expiring and he had every reason to be concerned that the Irish authorities would lose patience with their involuntary guest. Although Steve is a lifelong U.S. citizen, he had become a man without a country. He called the FBI in New Mexico to ask for help and, as a result, FBI agents met with him in Dublin. After three interrogation sessions and a voluntary polygraph test, which he passed, the agents told him they would recommend a waiver so that he could fly home. (One might wonder whether one side benefit of the watchlists, or one purpose, is to provide a strong incentive for people who might otherwise have been unwilling to submit to interrogation to answer questions about who and what they know, or to agree to serve as informants.) Steve tried again, flying to Mexico City, but when he arrived there he was handcuffed to a chair for hours, interrogated for at least an hour, and detained overnight. "Growing up in America," he says, "we're taught the great American system in that you're innocent until proven guilty."[40]

Ayman, Steve, and fifteen other United States citizens or legal residents who are not allowed to fly to, from, or within the United States for reasons they do not understand became plaintiffs in a 2010 ACLU lawsuit about the No Fly list,[41] one of the watchlists which still leave innocent Americans stranded, with no effective means of convincing the bureaucracy of their innocence—nine years, several statutes, and multiple lawsuits after 9/11.

Why have we made so little progress on the due process front over the course of a decade? Why don't we insist that Congress and the courts show more vigilance in protecting the right to travel and the right to be treated fairly by the government? Perhaps our tolerance for false positives has grown post-9/11 because we hope to tip the balance in the direction of safety.[42] But not all experts think No Fly lists as they are currently constructed are a sufficiently effective means of preventing terrorist incidents to justify their burden on constitutional rights. Security expert Bruce Schneier, who has been a persistent gadfly to the security agencies, has found it easy to imagine ways to get around the No Fly list—at least before the Secure Flight program—for anyone willing to use false identification or stolen credit cards.[43] Mario Labbé, a Canadian record company executive who lives in Quebec, found a way to thwart the watchlist system even without resorting to fraud. He had discovered that his name had been put on the watchlist after he had been a victim of identity theft, but the Department of Homeland Security told him there was no way to remove it. So he adopted the simple expedient of changing his first name, which worked to stymie the system.[44] Schneier's conclusion is that much of the money we spend on airport security is "a show designed to make people feel better" and that we would be better off spending our resources on trying to catch terrorists before they head for the airport. One author estimated the cost of the watchlist program since 9/11 as being as much as $1 billion, and also questioned whether the program is worth its costs or if it is just a form of what Schneier terms "security theater."[45] The 9/11 Commission regarded the watchlists as useful,[46] although noting that they could be more carefully administered, but also concluded that we may be fighting the last war by focusing too narrowly on the identity of air passengers rather than on paying greater attention to cargo and to the security of our ports.[47] In February 2009 the U.S. House of Representatives passed the Fair, Accurate, Secure, and Timely [FAST] Redress Act, to create a better process for individuals placed on government watch lists to challenge their classification.[48] But the bill never passed the Senate. We still have a lot of work to do on this front, but it is noteworthy that in this area, it was possible to get Congress to pay attention to the impact of counterterrorism measures on the innocent and to effect some useful changes in the redress system. It is also notable that it took so many years to accomplish so little.

Security Theater?

Conferring discretion on thousands of airport screeners and state and local police to decide who looks suspicious is another kind of recipe for violations of the Fourth Amendment (which prohibits unreasonable searches and seizures) and the Equal Protection Clause. In the post-9/11 world, it doesn't take a watchlist to interfere with one's travel plans. Almost anyone can be singled out for special screening and questioning—and not just for forgetting to discard liquids or neglecting to take off your shoes. Some joke sardonically that Muslims are singled out for the offense of "FWM"—Flying While Muslim—but non-Muslims also find themselves detained for a wide variety of reasons. Here are two examples.

Nick George, a student at Pomona College, was studying Arabic. He brought along his Arabic-English flash cards to study on the long plane ride from Philadelphia back to school. TSA agents were suspicious of the Arabic language, so Nick ended up being handcuffed, interrogated, and jailed for five hours—all for Flying with a Foreign Language ("FFL"?). He missed his flight and became so outraged that he is suing the TSA for violating his First Amendment right to study the language of his choice, and his Fourth Amendment right to be free from unreasonable seizures.[49]

Steven Bierfeldt, Director of Development for the Campaign for Liberty, a political organization that grew out of Congressman Ron Paul's presidential campaign, was detained in a small room at Lambert-St. Louis International Airport and interrogated because the metal box he put on the belt of the security checkpoint X-ray machine contained cash, which he carried in connection with his fundraising work. His lawsuit against the Department of Homeland Security for illegally detaining him for the offense of Flying with Cash ("FWC"?) was bolstered by an audio recording he had made of his interrogation.[50] His case was eventually settled when the TSA agreed to instruct its agents that their job was to search for possible terrorists and not to explore whatever conceivable offense someone might be committing by carrying a large amount of cash.[51]

The widespread introduction of what the TSA calls "advance imaging" technology in the late fall of 2010 caused many Americans to become indignant and even outraged, as the level of intrusion on personal privacy during routine airport security screening went far beyond fear of having a hole in one's sock. The TSA had installed about 500 whole-body imaging scanners by December 2010, with another 500 planned for installation in 2011, at airports around the country. These machines use backscatter (low-level X-ray) or millimeter wave technology in order to detect non-metallic objects that might pose security threats, like powders and gels. The technology produces detailed, three-dimensional images of the naked body of the person scanned. Those who favored the use of this technology told pollsters that they put a higher priority on combating terrorism than on protecting privacy.[52] Others were highly concerned about the degree of invasion of privacy—the scans could reveal intimate and potentially embarrassing details like whether the person screened had a colostomy bag or wore an adult diaper. Although the TSA said the amount of radiation involved in backscatter technology was negligible, some questioned whether there had been sufficient study of possible health risks. And others pointed to the unequal impact of such technology on religious objectors and on the disabled—one flight attendant who was a breast cancer survivor was ordered to expose and remove her prosthetic breast after a

Charlotte, North Carolina, airport machine showed that her breast was abnormal.[53] Humorist Dave Barry was pulled aside for a special pat down because his image showed a "blurry groin."[54] To appease those concerned about the machines, the TSA announced that anyone who was asked to walk through the machines could opt out, but at the price of submitting to a thorough pat down. Some were even less sanguine about this prospect. One bladder cancer survivor from Michigan was covered in urine when agents accidentally tore open his colostomy bag during a pat down.[55]

Questions were also raised about the effectiveness of this technology. The General Accounting Office, Congress's own auditing agency, repeatedly expressed doubts about whether the machines are really able to do the intended job. That office specifically told Congress that it was unclear whether the bodyscanners would have been able to detect the explosives in Omar Abdulmutallab's underwear—the very incident that led to this security upgrade.[56] Nongovernmental scientists who studied the technology concluded that the scanners were poor at identifying powder or plastic explosives, or items placed in body cavities.[57] And this technology comes with a hefty price tag—about $150,000 per machine. Security expert Bruce Schneier, for one, thinks the machines are a waste of money that could be better spent on more essential programs, like securing ports. Would the opinion of those who value security over privacy be affected if they heard more from experts who doubted whether these machines actually provide much additional security? Or are those supporters just trusting the government to decide that what they are doing is essential and involves no more invasion of privacy than necessary?[58]

Negative reactions to this technology have spanned the political spectrum, with critics of the TSA screening program including, on the conservative end, Sarah Palin, former Republican Arkansas Governor Mike Huckabee, and Texas Governor Rick Perry[59] and, on the other side of the aisle, consumer advocate Ralph Nader,[60] and Democrat Representatives Sheila Jackson Lee (TX) and Bennie G. Thompson (MS).[61] Although many individuals have expressed shock at the TSA's program, many others have expressed shock that anyone would be unwilling to submit to having a single federal employee look at their image in a private setting. But although the TSA said that the scanned images would not be preserved, additional controversy was generated when it was discovered that the machines the agency ordered had the capacity to retain images, while other machines they might have purchased did not,[62] and that federal agents actually admitted to having retained thousands of images from bodyscanners in use at courthouses.[63] The overall reaction of the general public has been difficult to gauge accurately. Poll numbers have been all over the map. A November 2010 *Washington Post*/ABC News poll concluded that about two-thirds of respondents supported the scanners while only about half supported the pat downs.[64] A Zogby International poll conducted just about the same time, on the other hand, showed that over 60 percent of likely voters opposed these measures and that 48 percent said they would avoid air travel and opt for another mode of transportation where feasible.[65] Older polls, conducted while the technology was not yet in widespread use in the United States, tended to reflect a higher rate of approval.[66] Some individuals demonstrated at airports to express their dissatisfaction, but a National Opt Out Day planned for the day before Thanksgiving in 2010 fizzled, as most people chose to proceed to their holiday destinations rather than protest. Representative Ron Paul introduced legislation he titled the American Traveler Dignity Act to reverse the TSA's decisions.[67]

Of course, the Constitution is countermajoritarian, so whether or not intrusive screening procedures are constitutional does not depend on where majority sentiment lies. Lawsuits challenging the "virtual strip search" and "excessive groping" were filed by the Rutherford Institute on behalf of three individuals, including Chris Daniels, a frequent business traveler who was subjected to a highly intrusive search after initial screening revealed an abnormality in his genital area, the result of a childhood injury. When he decided to leave the airport and skip his planned trip rather than submit to groping he found humiliating, he was told that he was not free to leave and was required to submit to the enhanced pat down.[68] The Electronic Privacy Information Center (EPIC) brought its own lawsuit against what it described as the "unlawful, invasive, and ineffective" "digital strip search."[69]

Are Americans overly willing to tolerate highly invasive security measures even if they are not proven to be effective? The 9/11 Commission commented that "Americans' love affair with [technology] leads them to also regard it as the solution" even if it is expensive and often fails.[70] Bruce Schneier says that we are hardwired to react to specific stories, and so we focus on the details of the last incident and waste money adopting measures geared to that particular story, measures which future terrorists will find easy to evade by simply changing the details of their plan. The more successful security measures, he says, tend to be invisible—like keeping cockpits locked and arming pilots, and like encouraging passengers to fight back.[71] The real security failure on Christmas Day, 2009, he says, was in our reaction. Others agree that we need to stop assuaging our fear by reacting to the last threat and pay more attention to what actually works. "We've had nine years of just grafting security measures one on another," says Bruce Hoffman, a terrorism expert at Georgetown University. "Maybe it's time to step back, take a hard look and look for a new approach."[72]

The Rights of Others

Intrusive as they are, the bodyscanners do treat everyone equally. Many Americans complained about the bodyscanner searches because they expected that they would be affected. Perhaps one reason Americans have not complained more loudly about the flawed watchlist system and other security screening measures is that we privately believe that any serious costs of this approach will be paid by someone else. Even with 20,000 names on the watchlist, the odds are that any individual American will not be seriously inconvenienced or stranded in a foreign country. Until the bodyscanners were introduced, for most of us airport security meant taking off our shoes and buying toiletries in small bottles. For Muslim-Americans, however, the stakes can mount far higher. Is it any coincidence that Erich Scherfen, Ayman Latif, Steve Washburn, and Rahinah Ibrahim, all of whom suffered extreme versions of airport problems, are all Muslims? Do Americans truly believe that Muslim-Americans are so inherently suspect that any rumor about their activities—like removing a seat from a car—should put them on the No Fly list? That stereotyping is the very kind of discrimination our country has had to work to overcome with wave after wave of hyphenated Americans.

Before 9/11, Americans had begun to reach consensus that racial profiling of African-Americans is both unconstitutional and ineffective law enforcement.[73] Sardonic references to the "crime" of DWB—Driving While Black—permeated American culture. FWM—Flying While Muslim—is another version of noxious and misguided profiling. But after 9/11, even some respected scholars argued that profiling Arabs and Muslims is different.[74] After all, hadn't the 9/11 hijackers all been Arab and Muslim?

The math just doesn't work that way. There are millions of Muslims in the United States, the overwhelmingly vast majority of whom have absolutely nothing to do with terrorism. Just as racial profiling proved to be bad law enforcement, singling out Muslims for special treatment at the airport, or in other venues, is a costly and ineffective way to identify terrorists.[75]

At the very least, because we have no empirical or theoretical basis for expecting profiling of Muslim passengers to make us safer, we should not be willing to tolerate the costs in terms of people's rights[76] and of our own descent into bias. Profiling can also prove counterproductive. Alienating Muslims who fly through American airports is not a good way to enlist the support of Muslim-American communities or to win over Muslims throughout the world. And profiling can quickly lead to "substitution." Once it is obvious that Arab and Muslim men are being stopped, would-be terrorists will quickly adapt and recruit people who do not fit that profile.

When I have spoken about this issue to various audiences, people often bristle at the suggestion that they may be more willing to give up other people's rights. But, sadly, this phenomenon is all too real,[77] which is why we need the politically insulated courts as well as our elected leaders to play a role in watching the watchlists. We have been tolerating watch-list and security programs that compromise both due process and equal protection rights. And if most Americans are willing to tolerate a flawed program, no branch of government is likely to respond.

Issues about profiling and security are not limited to the airport. Between 2005, when New York City began its subway checkpoint program, and early 2009, Jangir Sultan, a thirty-two-year-old native New Yorker of Kashmiri descent who works as a hospital manager, was stopped by the New York Police Department and had his bag searched twenty-one times. At that point, his frustration and outrage at being repeatedly singled out boiled over and he decided to sue. A mathematical expert calculated that the odds of his being stopped that often had the searches actually been as random as they are advertised were 1 in 165 million. New York City offered to settle the case for $10,000, but Jangir said he would forego the money if the city would agree to monitor the program to prevent others from being profiled on the basis of their race or ethnicity. The city declined his offer.[78]

The New York City subway search program that humiliated and outraged Jangir Sultan is a good example of the trade-offs we make without really being able to know what we are getting and we are giving up. Under this program, the New York Police Department (NYPD) visits various subway stations from time to time, sets up tables, and asks some of the people coming into the station to open their backpacks or large bags for screening. The NYPD is supposed to use a preordained system to select the subjects of these searches in order to avoid racial profiling—like stopping and searching every tenth person, for example. People who do not want to open their bags for inspection are not compelled to submit to the search. If they decline to be searched they will not be allowed to enter the subway, but they may leave without consequence—and, if they wish to do so, reenter the subway at a different time or at a different subway stop.

The Second Circuit Court of Appeals, which sits in New York, decided that, on balance, this program is "reasonable" within the meaning of the Fourth Amendment (which allows only "reasonable" searches and seizures) because the need to catch terrorists is so great and the cost to individual privacy of opening and rifling through a backpack is relatively minimal.[79] But another factor in the Fourth Amendment balancing test says that a program like this is only reasonable if it is a "reasonably effective" way to catch terrorists. The evidence offered to the court on this issue was testimony from a witness the city described as an expert, who testified that terrorists would indeed be deterred by this surveillance program because terrorists desire certainty, and even the possibility of having to leave a particular subway station at a particular time injects a note of disruptive uncertainty into their plans. The court then simply deferred to this expert's claim to know how terrorists' minds operate, remarking that judges are not competent to evaluate such matters. The court did not itself determine that the program was likely to be effective, but only that a purported police expert—whom the judges just decided to trust—thought it might be. Other experts might well disagree. The 9/11 Commission and a panel of the National Academy of Sciences tell us that we do not have a large enough base of experience with terrorism to be able to predict how terrorists will act.[80] Thus, we find ourselves either guessing or reenacting the last battle—having everyone take off their shoes because Richard Reid once hid a bomb in his shoe, for example. As Bruce Schneier says, "We defend against what the terrorists did last week."[81]

Did the NYPD genuinely believe that this professed expert knew how terrorists think and what would disrupt a terrorist's plans? Or did the NYPD simply want to do something to make New Yorkers feel safe in the subway (especially in light of recent subway and train bombing incidents in London and Madrid) and therefore set out to create the most credible program they could manage under the circumstances? The New York City subway search program does not seem like a very promising means of preventing terrorism. Only a tiny percentage of the five million people who ride the subway each day could conceivably be screened. Because searches are sporadic and because people can walk away, it does not seem highly likely that the program will actually catch any terrorists or foil their plans—although as with any dragnet, this is always a possibility. It is impossible to say that this program will prevent terrorism; it is also impossible to say that it will not. We cannot measure events that do not take place, so on the benefit side of the balance, we have a question mark. On the cost side of the balance, there is minor inconvenience to many subway riders, with the prospect of far greater insult to people like Jangir Sultan. Also on the cost side of the balance, however, is another hole in the Fourth Amendment and another occasion on which a court simply deferred to the self-proclaimed experts—a potentially dangerous practice, as shown by the infamous *Korematsu* case, where the Supreme Court deferred to government experts who claimed that it was necessary to national security to exclude Japanese-Americans from their West Coast homes during World War II.[82]

Many New Yorkers say that they do understand rationally that it is unlikely that a terrorist would be singled out for a search, and that any unlucky would-be terrorist could simply turn around and take an explosive-laden backpack to the next subway station. But, they say, the subway search program makes them feel safer. Uniformed officers with a foldout table and printed signs are a symbol of security. Is the goal being served by this program actually to prevent terrorism or to prevent terror? The phrase "War on Terror" may be a very precise description of some of our post-9/11 strategies, which hold pacifiers to be a good substitute where we don't have actual cures.

Another security program instituted in the New York City subways is the "See Something, Say Something" program. Posters urge subway riders to call the telephone number 1-888-NYC-SAFE if they observe something they find suspicious. After the program had been running for about a year, new posters crowed that the program was a success because 1,944 calls had been made to that telephone number during the previous year. The poster provided no information about whether or not any of the calls were fruitful in apprehending or deterring any terrorist plot. William Neuman, an enterprising *New York Times* reporter, decided to find out more. He learned that the hotline had actually received 13,473 calls during 2007, of which 644 (only 45 of which bore any relationship to the transit system) were deemed worthy of investigation. No one could tell him where the poster's number of 1,944 calls had come from. Most calls had nothing to do with the program, or reported a variety of personal belongings left behind on the subway, none of which was dangerous. Eleven calls reported suspicious "counting" by Muslim men, who turned out to be counting rosary-like prayer beads. No terrorists had been arrested as a result of the program, the cost of which was put at $3 million.[83] It is notable that evaluation of this program was left to the *New York Times* rather than New York's elected representatives or courts.

Like the subway search program, this program might conceivably prevent a terrorist attack, although we have no way to evaluate the likelihood of that type of success. Even if this innocuous program does not compromise anyone's rights, is it worth the $3 million? By the laws of inertia, these and other security programs are likely to continue into a second decade even though we have no way of knowing whether they are worthwhile. Once we become accustomed to a new baseline, like bag searches or bodyscanners at the airport, those practices, like the idea of watchlists, are likely to proliferate. Familiarity breeds acceptance. And so bag searches spread to the subways and bodyscanners are proliferating at the entrances of courthouses around the country.

The Fourth Amendment teaches us that law enforcement officials—whether the FBI, the TSA, or the NYPD—should not be trusted to police themselves. This is not because they are not good people, but because we give them a one-dimensional job to do—to prevent other people from harming us. We expect them to do that job zealously, and we tend to blame them if they do not keep us completely safe, even though that is not a very reasonable expectation. Under these conditions, it is not surprising if people entrusted with the weighty responsibility of protecting us against terrorists sometimes become overzealous or allow themselves to be carried away by wishful thinking. As Supreme Court Justice Louis Brandeis explained, that is why the courts have to be available to enforce the Fourth Amendment's guarantee against unreasonable searches and seizures: "The greatest dangers to liberty lurk in insidious encroachment by men of zeal, well meaning but without understanding."[84] There is indeed a balance that needs to be drawn at the airport or in the subway, but if we leave it to the FBI or the NYPD to strike that balance, constitutional values will regularly end up on the losing side. Yes, Congress and the courts should be more active in oversight. But they are unlikely to step up to that role if we don't even want to know whether or not we are being given placebos.

5.

Banks and Databanks

We regret to inform you that we have decided that it is not in our best interest to continue your banking relationship with us.—Letter from Fleet Bank to U.S. citizen Hossam Algabri (2002)

[A]nyone can recognize elements of terror planning.—Air Force "Eagle Eyes" promotion (2010)

What happened in Vegas stayed in federal data banks.—Barton Gellman, *Washington Post* (2005)

WATCHLISTS AND SECURITY screening don't only apply to travelers. Every time you go to a bank, buy a house, apply for a credit card, purchase life insurance, use a travel agent, or rent a car, the Patriot Act affects you. As a customer you may be lucky enough to be unaware of its impact. Or you might be unlucky, like Hossam Algabri, whose bank account was abruptly terminated because his bank created its own blacklist—perhaps in the hope of avoiding sanctions for not working hard enough to ferret out terrorism financing. And every time you apply for a job or rent an apartment, your prospective employer or landlord risks violating the prohibition of doing business with a blocked person if they don't know whether or not you are on the "emergency" government blacklist that caused the Muslim charities problems. A more ubiquitous companion of the No Fly list is what might be called the No Buy list.[1]

Post–Patriot Act businesses, especially financial institutions, have been swept up in the War on Terror, as the line between the private sector and government has been erased[2] by a pervasive combination of different types of government rules and activities:

1. Financial institutions, very broadly defined, are conscripted as antiterrorism agents, shouldering many duties like Suspicious Activity

Reporting and facing heavy penalties if they fail to perform their assigned duties.

2. Financial institutions are required to check extensive government watchlists before engaging in transactions; all businesses and individuals have to be wary of subjecting themselves to civil or criminal penalties for doing business with the wrong people, even if those people, like Hossam Algabri, are not on any government list. If it sounds farfetched to suggest that a Starbucks barista who is not a terrorist might have reason to be concerned, chapter 11 tells the story of what happened to a Florida waiter who was unlucky enough to serve dinner to some of the 9/11 terrorists.

3. Government agents cannibalize information people have shared with businesses by (a) imposing special obligations on financial institutions to collect and turn over a range of information about their customers, (b) using Patriot Act powers to demand records of any business—including schools, hospitals, and libraries—through watered-down court orders or, in some cases, through National Security Letters which don't require court approval at all, (c) asking businesses to turn over information or records voluntarily, which many do even where doing so violates privacy laws, and (d) buying masses of information from data aggregators, who are in the business of collecting, cross-indexing, and selling vast quantities of information about every aspect of people's lives, from religious practices to vacation plans to the medications they take.

Like the campaign against charities, this web of compulsion and obligation was initially intended to disrupt terrorism financing, hence the special focus on financial institutions and the surprising involvement of the Treasury Department's Office of Foreign Assets Control (OFAC) in all-American transactions. Another goal was to enlist the financial sector in informing on people who act suspiciously. And a third goal was to combine the forces of private record-keeping and government coercion to feed ever-expanding government databanks in order to enable data mining—searching for information about particular individuals (subject-based data mining) or using mathematical models to search oceans of data for terrorist patterns (pattern-based data mining).

Whether privacy is an anachronistic notion in the age of Google and Facebook is a hotly debated topic.[3] But whatever the pros and cons of

Amazon.com's ability to mine data about you in order to sell you a book, government collection and use of large quantities of data is qualitatively different and far more consequential. People sometimes ask why anyone should care what the government knows about them if they are not doing anything wrong. After exploring the post–Patriot Act state of what has aptly been dubbed "dataveillance,"[4] I will address that question. There are many reasons to care, as individuals and as members of society, about the government keeping digital dossiers[5] on us. It is no exaggeration to say that not only individual privacy is at stake, but also the quality of our democracy. And there is every reason to believe that we can control this genie, even if we cannot put it back into the bottle, if we decide that the new private-public spying partnership and the dataveillance approach to terrorism are costing us more than they are worth.

Financial Institutions as TIPSters

Post-9/11, the term "financial institution" has been expansively defined to apply not only to banks, but also to car rental agencies, storage warehouses, real estate brokers, private equity fund managers, broker/dealers, casinos, life insurers, jewelers, travel agencies, pawnbrokers, landlords, and "persons involved in real estate closings or settlements,"[6] whether they know it or not. People in these businesses have to master all the intricacies of highly complex and demanding laws or risk very stiff penalties. The duties imposed—"Know Your Customer" (i.e., gather and maintain information that the government can later plunder),[7] "Suspicious Activity Reporting,"[8] maintaining an anti–money laundering program,[9] conducting records searches on request,[10] and watchlist-checking—are so challenging that the Patriot Act has spawned a new business: creating and marketing Patriot Act compliance software. One merchant advertises:

- Simultaneously cross check your customer list against multiple watch lists
- Scan customer name, address, date of birth and social security number (SSN) to rule out a match with sanctioned entities or individuals
- Create "good" and "blocked" customer lists for future searches[11]

Meeting these obligations costs a lot more than the price of software. One research firm estimated that securities firms alone would have to spend $700 million on compliance in the first few years of this new regime.[12] Penalties for willful violations—either for not checking lists where required or for failing to discharge other obligations the law imposes—can go up to 10–30 years imprisonment and a $1 million fine per violation. Western Union, for example, was fined $8 million in 2002 for failing to report "suspicious transactions."[13] The company that owns Western Union, First Data Corporation, now has over 150 employees working on compliance, in addition to the hundreds of thousands of employees who regularly screen wire transfers as part of their job.[14] The costs of compliance and of penalties may be passed on to customers, of course. And there are other kinds of costs to asking companies to wear a terrorism-prevention hat in addition to their business hat: innocent Americans find themselves denied financial services because software has decided, on the basis of unknown or unreliable criteria, that they might be a threat to national security. French Clements, a young man living in San Jose, California, for example, tried to start a retirement fund by opening an online brokerage account with Harris Direct. But the system denied his request, citing the Patriot Act—probably because he was a college student who moved frequently and so the address on his application did not match the address in his credit report, a factor the software considered suspicious.[15]

Unexplained decisions may be based on religious or ethnic profiling, perhaps built into software's algorithms,[16] or perhaps as a result of human perceptions that it is risky to do business with Muslims. Hossam Algabri, a thirty-two-year-old Boston computer consultant, had banked with Fleet Bank for ten uneventful years when the bank, giving him no reason, abruptly decided to close his account, sending him the startling letter quoted above.[17] He believes that the explanation lies in his religion and background. A Muslim, Hossam immigrated to the United States from Egypt at the age of twelve. A similar upsetting encounter with a business happened to Faizah Zuberi, a Pakistani-American doctor who lives in New Jersey. She reports that American Express suddenly and inexplicably demanded that she furnish an extraordinary amount of documentation—her tax returns, employment statements, financial statements, and so forth—and then nevertheless canceled her credit card for no apparent reason.[18]

Facing complex law and an intimidating penalty structure, companies have little incentive to tell their customers about their suspicions or to give them a chance to clear up mistakes or misunderstandings. Hossam Algabri has no way to know if his bank reported some suspicion about him to the government, whether the government initiated his problem by warning the bank about him, or whether the bank simply decided to "play it safe" by cutting its ties with a foreign-born Muslim.

In many respects, the Know Your Customer/Suspicious Activity Reporting enterprise resembles another early post-9/11 idea about how to combat terrorism. In his January 2002 State of the Union address, George W. Bush proposed creating an army of truck drivers, utilities workers, and cable guys to look for and report on suspicious activities as part of a program called TIPS (Terrorism Information and Prevention System).[19] The pilot project would have enlisted a million amateur intelligence agents in ten cities. Even though images of 9/11 were still vivid, the public was horrified and Congress refused to provide funding.

There were many good reasons for rejecting TIPS. This network of informants bears a strong resemblance to the system run by the despised East German Stasi, the state security service whose operations were memorialized in the popular 2006 film *The Lives of Others*. Between 1950 and 1989, the Stasi employed over 90,000 full-time workers and over 173,000 informants to monitor their neighbors' behavior and identify possible enemies of the state.[20] A large-scale program like TIPS would have sowed a deep sense of distrust and unease among Americans worrying not only about whether their neighbors were terrorists, but also whether they were informants. American tradition, embodied in the Constitution's First Amendment freedom of speech and association and the Fourth Amendment's prohibition of unreasonable searches and seizures, promises us a "right to be let alone."[21] We expect to be able to go about our business, develop relationships, and form and express ideas without the government tracking our actions and transactions. In addition, the TIPS program inevitably would have produced countless false positives, deluging intelligence agencies with a great deal of useless information and encouraging them to waste their time pursuing worthless leads (like the account of Erich Scherfen removing a seat from his car). As the saying goes, you don't find a needle in a haystack by adding more hay.

Inviting amateurs to spot terrorists also invites racial, ethnic, and religious profiling, as the *New York Times* story on the See Something, Say Something program, described in the last chapter, showed. Asked to report suspicious activity in the subways, callers overwhelmingly reported innocuous activity and praying Muslims. Programs that were heirs to TIPS, like the Air Force's "Eagle Eyes," have encouraged these polarizing tendencies, disconcertingly promising that "anyone can recognize elements of terror planning" and urging the public to "watch for people who don't seem to belong."[22] This is the type of advice that evidently led an overly suspicious co-worker to plant suspicions about pilot Erich Scherfen that almost caused him to be fired from his job. It is always possible that an amateur sleuth might find and recognize a dangerous needle in the haystack, but the public found this possibility too slight to justify TIPS, a program that would have moved our society a giant step in the direction of totalitarianism.

But TIPS did not die. "Financial institutions," broadly defined, have taken the place of Bush's cable guys, spying on their customers on behalf of the government.

Watchlists and the Private Sector

OFAC maintains a hefty "Specially Designated Nationals" watchlist of suspected terrorists and terrorist entities—an altogether different list from the ones used at the airport. This mother list includes the smaller number of OFAC's "Specially Designated Global Terrorists" who are not allowed to buy or sell any form of property or interest in property (due to the "emergency" 2001 Executive Order that plagued the Muslim charities), plus legions of others. The current Specially Designated Nationals watchlist goes on for 500 dense, three-column, single-spaced pages,[23] is amended frequently, and contains many common names that are the equivalent of Smith or Jones (Mohammed, Ali, Taylor, Rodriguez), as well as many lengthy recitations of aliases or "doing business as" alternative names. Financial institutions are required to check these lists before engaging in business with anyone or risk civil or criminal fines.[24] If you get a "hit" on checking the list, that is, the name of your customer matches all or part of a name on the list, you then have to work your way through page after stupefying page of complex instructions on the OFAC website, telling you how to conduct further analysis and which bureaucracy to call.[25] Meanwhile, your customer's transaction—whether it's a mortgage, a job application, or the sale of a car—will be on hold while OFAC investigates. You might well decide that it is easier to just refuse that mortgage or hire someone else rather than go through the process of finding out whether your customer only happens to share a name with someone on the list.

Tom and Nanci Kubbany found out about this list when they were trying to buy their first house, in Arcata, California. They were so confident of their solid financial status that they were stunned when their mortgage application was denied. They eventually were able to figure out that this was because a credit report that made its way into their file flagged the fact that "Hassan," Tom's highly common middle name, matched part of a name on a government watchlist—where the name had been placed because it was an alias of Saddam Hussein's son.[26] (As Nanci and Tom now know, requesting an annual credit report is one way to uncover potential problems like this.[27])

The OFAC watchlists suffer from all the same defects as the No Fly and it companion lists. They are compiled with information conglomerated by multiple agencies, in secret, without due process, and therefore are highly susceptible to mistakes. And there is no procedure at all for getting one's name off this watchlist—not even the behind-the-curtains remedy of the DHS TRIP program. Unlike the government, private companies are not subject to freedom of information laws, and so someone who is rejected by a financial institution has no recourse.[28] Faizah Zuberi, the New Jersey doctor, has no effective way to fight the American Express company's decision to cancel her credit card or even to find out why they took that action. Because the OFAC list is published, it is at least possible to know if you or someone with a name similar to yours is actually on that blacklist, so at least it is possible for some consumers to anticipate problems.

Although businesses other than financial institutions are not obligated to check watchlists, some do so voluntarily for self-protection. Everyone is subject to penalties for engaging in any form of transaction with a "blocked" entity, or for providing "material support" to any terrorist, even someone not on any watchlist. This includes families buying or selling a house, shoeshine stands, and hot dog vendors. Title companies have added watchlist-checking to their real estate closing checklists.[29] Many businesses, including foundations and charities, also try to protect themselves from unwanted government attention by adding antiterrorism compliance clauses to, as one lawyer advised real estate professionals, "every document you enter into—leases, amendments, purchase and sale agreements, consents to subleases, brokerage agreements, loan documents, construction contracts, vendor contracts—everything."[30] These clauses typically ask the signers to warrant that they are not on the OFAC list, will not violate antiterrorism laws, will not do business with any entity violating antiterrorism laws, will provide certification or other evidence of compliance, and will absorb costs generated if they do violate antiterrorism laws. Given that the material support laws are so broad and therefore so easy to violate, as previous chapters have shown, these clauses won't necessarily insulate even the most cautious business from civil or criminal penalties. But Treasury officials responsible for enforcing all these vague and threatening laws say there is no need for concern: "[W]hen we issue enforcement actions—especially major enforcement actions—they are rare and only applied when appropriate."[31] Just trust us.

Once financial institutions became accustomed to checking watchlists as a matter of routine, the idea of mandatory list-checking was available to be extended to others, like charitable organizations. The Combined Federal Campaign (CFC) is a program that channels millions of dollars in charitable donations from federal employees and military personnel. The CFC provides a convenient form where people on the federal payroll can check off organizations to which they would like to contribute from a list of thousands of participating nonprofits. In deciding what groups to put on this list, the Treasury Department sets ground rules and sends eligible nonprofits a questionnaire to fill out. As of October 2003, the questionnaire required each nonprofit to certify that it "does not knowingly employ individuals or contribute funds to organizations found on" watchlists. When asked by a reporter whether this certification would require the organizations to check the watchlists, the director of the program replied that it would.[32] To many organizations, being required to check lists compiled without due process was intolerable. The lists were unreliable; the names on the lists were being obtained in mysterious and possibly unconstitutional fashion; and the requirement had troubling historical echoes: obligatory list-checking was evocative of McCarthyism. After considerable debate and turmoil, the ACLU withdrew from the program, forfeiting as much as half a million dollars in federal employee contributions.[33] A coalition of other nonprofit groups, ranging from the Sierra Club to People for the Ethical Treatment of Animals to Unitarians, also found this demand that they serve as TIPSters disturbing and joined the ACLU in a lawsuit to challenge the legality and constitutionality of the watchlist-checking requirement. The case was settled when the Treasury Department relented and said that it would not require eligible nonprofits to check the watchlists after all.[34]

But as chapter 3 described, charities, like all other businesses, are still vulnerable to sanctions if they employ or do business with someone who is deemed to be a terrorist, whether they check watchlists or not. Non-Muslim American charities have little cause to fear being abruptly shut down, so far. But they are subject to material support prosecutions if they are found to be supporting terrorists or working with designated organizations, as the Humanitarian Law Project recognized. OFAC created voluntary guidelines for charities to consult in order to protect themselves against unintended diversion of their grants to terrorist groups.[35] These guidelines are generally regarded by the charities themselves as ineffectual. A charity can follow all the guidelines—as KindHearts tried to do—and nevertheless find itself in the sights of government enforcers. A report by OMBWatch and Grantmakers without Borders describes OFAC's Voluntary Guidelines and "Risk Matrix system" as "the worst of both worlds" because the guidelines demand burdensome investigation but don't actually provide protection against legal sanctions.[36] Charities generally have their own due diligence practices, which seem to be effective. A study of charities that did check watchlists to ensure that they were not giving grants to or doing business with terrorists showed that no charity had gotten a true hit—that is, the charities were not funding or employing anyone who actually was on a watchlist in any event.[37] Do non-Muslim charities need to worry about undue government attention? The uncertainty created by the material support and blockade laws shifts a great deal of power to the government by providing a justification for investigating, prosecuting, or just pressuring an organization whose work it might disfavor, perhaps for political reasons.

Does It Work?

Is it worth the cost in time, effort, and corrosion of business relationships to require companies to search for needles in their customer haystacks in all the ways described? Blue Cross Blue Shield of Michigan, for example, conducted a costly and time-consuming search of six million customers' health insurance records, looking for possible terrorists. The search yielded 6,000 false positives—customers whose records were then investigated more fully by the company's employees before they were determined not to pose any problem—but no terrorists.[38] When MSNBC reporter Brian Braiker asked a Treasury Department spokesperson whether list-checking is effective, the spokesperson confidently responded, "The list has worked" but, the reporter noted, declined to give any specific examples, citing privacy and legal concerns.[39] Braiker tried the system himself, entering the name "Osama bin Laden," but did not get a hit because the watchlist spelled the name he had in mind "Usama bin Laden." Better comparison shopping might have gotten him less literal software which would have declared a match. But the watchlists, based on known names and aliases, don't protect against someone using a new alias or front. If Osama bin Laden had wanted to engage in any sort of financial transaction in the

United States, in all likelihood he would not have done so under his own name, whether spelled with an O or a U.

This program of business watchlist-checking and information gathering has become unmoored from its origin as a way to address terrorism financing and money laundering. The 9/11 Commission staff thought the Patriot Act's plan to disrupt terrorist financing by adapting a criminal money-laundering model was always destined to fail because it was based on a false equation between the nature of criminal money laundering and terrorism financing.[40] Bankers can recognize money laundering activity, designed to conceal the illegal source of funds, because it is common enough that patterns can be recognized. If a customer inexplicably deposits an unusually large amount of money in an account and then moves that money through layers of shell companies and offshore accounts, bankers will recognize and report these suspicious activities. But how can a bank recognize money deposited by terrorists or intended for terrorists? Efforts to develop a profile of terrorist financiers for financial institutions to apply are unlikely to succeed, according to the Commission staff, because we do not have an adequate basis for prediction. One attempt to compose a terrorist profile carefully studied the 9/11 hijackers and, as a result, identified factors like listing one's occupation as a student and spending money on flight training schools as indicators of terrorist activity.[41] These very specific factors might indeed detect terrorists who want to reenact the 9/11 hijackings in every detail, but are not likely to identify would-be terrorists with a different plan. Nothing the 9/11 hijackers did, noted the Commission staff, would have triggered any of the post–Patriot Act reporting requirements.[42] Their activities did not raise money-laundering alerts by moving large amounts of money through American financial institutions. So the chief functions of the financial institution network actually seem to be first, getting businesses to play an active TIPSter role in trying to spot terrorists (with questionable results), and second, using businesses as pass-throughs to feed the government's bulging databanks.

Collecting the Dots

The data collection and data mining approach to fighting terrorism is also reminiscent of an early post-9/11 idea that Congress rejected because it smacked of totalitarianism. In February 2002, the *New York Times* revealed to the public that a branch of the Defense Department headed by John Poindexter—a former National Security Advisor to Ronald Reagan previously

best known for his involvement in the Iran-Contra scandal and his statement that it was his duty to withhold information from Congress[43]—was
working on a secret program known as "Total Information Awareness."[44]
This program, under the motto "Knowledge Is Power," aimed to design a
gargantuan database that would collect information from both government and corporate databases on all of Americans' "transactions" and then
create algorithms and systems to mine that data to try to discover terrorist patterns. The covered "transactions" would have included "Financial,
Education, Travel, Medical, Veterinary, Country Entry, Place/Event Entry,
Transportation, Housing, Critical Resources, Government, [and] Communications" information.[45] As one of the program's designers explained, the
program's task was "much harder than simply finding needles in a haystack. . . . [O]ur task is akin to finding dangerous groups of needles hidden
in stacks of needle pieces." Therefore, he concluded, "In principle at least,
we must track all the needle pieces all of the time and consider all possible
combinations."[46] *New York Times* columnist William Safire was among the
many critics, from all points along the political spectrum, who were aghast:
"[The TIA] has been given a $200 million budget to create computer dos-
siers on 300 million Americans."[47] As public outrage about this Orwellian
vision continued to simmer, Congress delayed and ultimately decided to
defund the program.[48] This was something of a pyrrhic victory for privacy.
The TIA program was not actually abolished, but driven underground.[49]

The idea behind Total Information Awareness—to collect as many
dots of information as possible in the hope that some of those dots might
somehow be connected at some point—continued to be a centerpiece of
the Bush/Cheney approach to counterterrorism.[50] The Patriot Act gave
the government many new tools to conduct surveillance and to gather
information about Americans from third parties—including the special
obligations imposed on "financial institutions." And the Bush Administration went beyond the Patriot Act in dealing itself additional means
of gathering information—like the infamous National Security Agency
(NSA) spying program (to be discussed in chapter 10). But the easiest way
for the government to acquire data from businesses is simply to ask. Private companies can often be prevailed upon to share information without
any legal compulsion—or can be pressured into doing so by threats or
promises regarding government contracts, or exhortations to be patriotic.
As part of a Cold War operation known by the code name "Shamrock,"
Western Union voluntarily turned over the contents of private telegrams
to the government.[51] During the past decade major airlines from American

to United admitted to sharing voluntarily millions of passenger records with the FBI.[52] Antiterrorism financing programs relied heavily on the voluntary cooperation of a powerful Belgian banking consortium called Swift, as mentioned in chapter 3, to supply data about international financial transactions.[53] Most major telecommunications companies cooperated with Bush's extralegal NSA surveillance program. And more recently, Sprint Nextel was revealed to have given the government access to information about the whereabouts of its cell phone customers on over eight million occasions.[54]

Alternatively, the government can buy information from fourth parties. Businesses called data aggregators collect and market masses of information about identifiable individuals from every source imaginable—eviction notices, E-ZPass records, sex toy purchases, unlisted telephone numbers, religious affiliations, Prozac orders, child custody orders, book purchases[55]—and cross-index data to generate specialized lists like "Affluent Hispanics," "Big Spending Vitamin Shoppers,"[56] or the "Gay America Megafile." As early as 2001, the Justice Department was entering into multimillion-dollar contracts for bulk information.[57] The government is not just a customer of these private multibillion-dollar businesses, but a partner. A ChoicePoint executive told a reporter, "We do act as an intelligence agency, gathering data, applying analytics."[58] The revolving door of company executives and government officials attests to that collaboration. Some officials who have left government employment have later gone to work for these companies.[59] One has to wonder to what extent the government's antiterrorism plans have been influenced by companies lobbying to profit by selling materiel for the War on Terror.

This symbiotic relationship serves many functions for the government. By outsourcing data collection, the agencies can avoid the Constitution's and Congress's limits on their own direct acquisition of data—like the need to get a court order or to comply with privacy laws regarding government collection of information. In the United States, unlike almost any other industrialized nation,[60] federal privacy laws restricting government collection of data do not generally apply to private data collection. (As this book goes to press, the Department of Commerce, members of Congress, and many others have been advocating the passage of new privacy protection laws to promote international commerce as well as civil liberties.) The Patriot Act carved out generous exceptions to preexisting privacy laws that prohibited businesses from disclosing information in certain areas regarded as especially sensitive—like educational, library, health, and electronic services records—without a court order. Constitutional rights like the First and Fourth Amendments only apply to governmental actors. Unlike government surveillance, private data collection is not generally subject to oversight by Congress, Inspectors General, or courts. And by enlisting businesses, government agencies can pass on the costs of data collection to the private sector—ultimately to us as consumers. Thus there is no real disincentive to the government collecting and hoarding vast quantities of private data. Agencies can just keep amassing searchable dots, hoping that someday some of them will connect.

Does "dataveillance" work? The 9/11 Commission believed that lack of intelligence was not one of the problems leading to 9/11; other objective expert observers, like federal government agency Inspectors General, have not been able to find much evidence that the data mining approach is productive.[61] The National Research Council of the National Academy of Sciences launched an extensive study following the public debates over the Total Information Awareness program and, in a 2008 report, concluded that there was simply no scientific consensus that contemporary data mining techniques were ready for use in terrorism investigations.[62] Data mining is successfully used by the private sector—to detect consumer fraud or to select consumer goods to recommend to particular targets. But the Council noted that to be successful in searching for patterns, you have to know what pattern you are looking for, and we know very little about how to recognize potential terrorists because our information about patterns of terrorism is so sparse[63]—as shown by the unsuccessful attempt to create a terrorist profile described above. And beyond the problem of sparse data, it is far from clear that there are underlying terrorist patterns to be discovered, no matter how much data we amass. Acts of terrorism may just be more distinct and distinctive than acts of money laundering. A 2010 *Washington Post* study of intelligence efforts found that federal intelligence officers are in effect drowning in data and frequently don't even look at much of the information flooding into their offices and computers.[64] And imperfect understanding of what is being looked for inevitably generates an extraordinary number of false positives—attention drawn to innocent people.[65]

Why Should I Care?—Privacy and Democracy

If the benefits of dataveillance are unclear, what then are the corresponding costs? What are the consequences of omnivorous government databanks accumulating every bit of information that can be bought, compelled, collected, or googled? In his groundbreaking 1967 book on privacy, Alan Westin posed the question, "Why should I care what the government knows about me if I'm not doing anything wrong?" He then answered the question: "The answer, of course, lies in the impact of surveillance on human behavior."[66] Students of privacy since then have identified many different ways in which behavior is affected by pervasive government data collection and data mining.

Intrusion. Business records about you, including bank records of the checks you write or online payments you make and your medical or school records, provide a detailed and profoundly revealing picture of your whole life to any reviewer. Have you written a check to an HIV-testing clinic? Made a contribution to a splinter political group? Planned a trip to Yemen? Entered an institution for alcohol rehabilitation? Failed physics? The broader the dissemination of information about your life, the more you are exposed to others' suspicion or scorn. Is it more or less upsetting that you won't know how many people on the government payroll may be reviewing and reacting to details about your life? Will your behavior be affected if you don't want to expose yourself by leaving tracks—perhaps paying for the HIV test in cash or deciding to go to the Grand Canyon instead of Yemen?

Confidentiality. If you share information about your physical or mental condition with a doctor at a hospital, or information about your finances with a bank in order to apply for a mortgage, you agree to share with a limited audience for a limited purpose. Your sense of trust in that relationship may be shaken by knowing that the doctor or bank may be passing that information on to government databanks, voluntarily or not. Without any real guarantee of confidentiality, you may not be willing to share information the doctor or mortgage broker needs in order to help you.

Control. If you cannot choose the extent to which your information will be shared, you lose control of who will have access and whether you will be judged out of context.[67] Scott McNealy, CEO of Sun Microsystems, famously said, "You already have zero privacy—get over it." But young Facebook users who do not mind exposing their views or their bodies on the Internet nevertheless care deeply about whether or not they themselves are in control of what information they decide to post.[68]

Identity Formation. Michel Foucault found a powerful image of the modern world in Jeremy Bentham's "Panopticon," a circular prison where the inmates are within view of their guards at all times. This constant exposure, he said, causes those on view to internalize the gaze.[69] People who think they are always on view are likely to change their behavior, as Westin observed, to avoid acting in ways that might attract negative attention from the guards. This kind of behavioral self-censorship can over time transform a person's identity.

Fear of Government Action. There is a substantial difference between the potential consequences of sharing any kind of information with a business, a school, or a medical provider as opposed to the government. If your information is regarded negatively, a bank might refuse to give you a mortgage; the government, on the other hand, might decide to prosecute you on terrorism or tax evasion charges, or lock you up as a material witness. The Fifth Amendment privilege against self-incrimination gives us an enforceable right to have the government leave us alone. If the government asks you to supply information about your activities, you have a constitutional right to remain silent. You have no comparable right to refuse to tell the bank that you once defaulted on a mortgage.[70] The bank is allowed to punish you for refusing to divulge such information by refusing to do business with you. The Constitution guarantees individuals a private enclave as against the government, not against private individuals or businesses.

The more information your bank and other businesses and institutions share with the government, voluntarily or not, the more "points of contact" the government then has with you, and "the stronger the grip of the government on the governed."[71] One reason Sami al-Hussayen was prosecuted was that federal agents were free to study his bank records and discover that he had made contributions to Muslim charities. As Sami's prosecution also shows, adverse government action can be based on mistaken assumptions, so individuals do have reason to be concerned even if they are supremely innocent of any wrongdoing. But the reality is that many, probably most of us, have done something illegal or embarrassing at some point. By putting everyone under a microscope, the huge databanks give the government the power to have something on almost anyone, a power that can be used to go after political enemies or whatever religious or ethnic group is currently considered suspicious.

Blurring the boundary between what businesses can do and what government can do transforms the relationship of the individual and the government, reducing individual autonomy and increasing governmental power. Ultimately, blurring the boundary between the individual and the government is one of the hallmarks of a totalitarian state.[72]

Privacy and Democracy. We all lose when any American loses privacy[73] because the private enclave is the birthplace and incubator of democracy.[74] Privacy, the subject of the Fourth Amendment's guarantee against unreasonable searches and seizures, is essential to the exercise of First Amendment freedoms of religion, speech, and association.[75] Our concept of the role of the individual in society could not exist without adequate protection of privacy.[76] Hannah Arendt, while advocating for involvement in public life, recognized a "danger to human existence from the elimination of the private realm." There are, she said, "a great many things which cannot withstand the implacable bright light of the constant presence of others on the public scene," and so a "life spent entirely in public, in the presence of others, becomes . . . shallow."[77] The democratic structures reinforced by private thought and action then protect all of our rights, not only our right to privacy. Legal scholar Daniel Solove maintains that the better metaphor for the range of concerns raised by government dataveillance is not Orwell's Big Brother, but Kafka's *The Trial*.[78] In Kafka's haunting story, Josef K. is arrested and ultimately executed by an inaccessible and faceless bureaucracy that employs arbitrary and incomprehensible procedures and never tells him for what crime he is being prosecuted. The hallmark of Josef K.'s experience is his powerlessness against an omnipotent state. The motto of the Total Information Awareness program was, quite aptly, "Knowledge Is Power." Innocent Americans caught in the web of watchlists and Suspicious Activities Reports experience not only a lack of privacy but a lack of power to understand or to fight back against an all-knowing, all-powerful, and incomprehensible state.

Americans still value their privacy, even after 9/11.[79] The National Academies of Science Council concluded that challenges to our national security do not warrant fundamental changes in the level of privacy to which innocent Americans are entitled.[80] Some blame technology for destroying privacy, but law professor James Rule assures us that our technology is not our destiny.[81] It is incoherent laws[82] and odd interpretations of the Constitution, as chapter 7 will explain, that have left us exposed. Congress can strengthen privacy laws by imposing meaningful limits on acquisition, retention, and dissemination of sensitive information. Even if it is politically impossible—or even unwise—to curtail the government's acquisition of information, at least privacy laws can limit how widely that information can be shared, and how long it can be retained in databanks. In response to widespread concerns about privacy, George W. Bush created a President's Privacy and Civil Liberties Oversight Board.[83] But as I write, this Board is not engaging in any oversight because President

Obama, more than two years into his term of office, has yet to appoint any members to it.

If we want to preserve our privacy and arrest the slide to a more totalitarian state, we need to exercise the powers we do have as citizens and as consumers. Hossam Algabri decided to go public with his complaint against Fleet Bank because he thinks that consumers, whether Muslims or not, have been far too passive in accepting arbitrary treatment. As shown by the history of the airport watchlists, if people don't complain loudly and persistently, their interests are unlikely to get much attention from government officials—who are more focused on the terrorists the dragnet might catch than on the innocent people whose lives are disrupted—or from businesses worried about staying in the government's good graces. Legal scholar Jack Balkin summarizes:

> The question is not whether we will have a surveillance state in the years to come, but what sort of surveillance state we will have. Will we have a government without sufficient controls over public and private surveillance, or will we have a government that protects individual dignity and conforms both public and private surveillance to the rule of law?[84]

It is worth the effort to wrestle with imposing adequate controls to rein in this genie. As lawyer Ben Wizner recently commented to me, "The reason we don't regard privacy as fundamental is that we have it"—or maybe we just think we do.

II.

SURVEILLANCE AND SECRECY

6.

Gutting the Fourth Amendment

We think that the Fourth Amendment should be no more relevant than it would be in cases of invasion or insurrection.[1]—John Yoo, Office of Legal Counsel memo (2001)

When legislation is written that waters down the standard of the Fourth Amendment, it is not the guilty who suffer, but the innocent.—Brandon Mayfield (2007)

How do you file a brief in a secret court?—Ann Beeson, ACLU lawyer (2003)

BRANDON MAYFIELD, the Oregon lawyer who was the innocent victim of a stupendous FBI mistake, came to understand the significance of what might look like the Patriot Act's tiniest change to previous law: replacing the word "the" in a statute about foreign intelligence surveillance with the words "a significant." This deceptively trivial rewording was part of a sea change that has increasingly allowed American citizens to be treated the same way we treated the Soviet Union during the Cold War. Brandon's story is a disturbing example of how our right to be free from unreasonable searches and seizures is being chipped away, chunk by chunk, and how the courts have failed to intervene.

Brandon thinks that FBI agents were inclined to believe that he was involved in the March 2004 bombing of several commuter trains in Madrid, Spain, because he is a Muslim. He converted to Islam shortly after meeting his Egyptian immigrant wife, Mona. Brandon is an American citizen, born in Oregon and reared in Kansas, and a former Army officer with an honorable discharge. At the age of thirty-eight, he had never been convicted of any crime and had not traveled outside the United States since 1994 when he completed his military duty in Germany. He did not even have a current passport.

Then the FBI entered his life. Employing unprofessional procedures, FBI experts mistakenly declared that his fingerprint matched a partial fingerprint discovered on a blue plastic bag containing detonators that was found near one of the Madrid commuter train stations. The fingerprints evidently did have some remarkably common features. In fact, one court-appointed expert subsequently thought the identification was correct. But after the initial identification, the FBI did not seriously test whether the fingerprints really were a match. Examiners who were supposed to function independently were told that their colleagues had identified the fingerprint as Brandon's, a violation of sound forensic practice. One retired FBI employee who served as an independent examiner had been reprimanded on at least three previous occasions for mistaken identifications of fingerprints.[2] A lengthy 2006 Inspector General report provides a detailed study of how the mistake occurred, blaming circular reasoning and simple carelessness for a conclusion that, by professional standards, should not have been reached.[3]

After deciding that Brandon's fingerprint matched the print on the plastic bag, the FBI began to follow Brandon and his family as they went to work (Mona worked as a legal assistant in Brandon's office), to school, and to their mosque. Attorney General John Ashcroft personally signed an application to the Foreign Intelligence Surveillance Court for permission to eavesdrop in private areas of the Mayfield family home. The FBI used the Foreign Intelligence Surveillance Act (FISA) to set up extensive wiretapping in Brandon's home and office because at least some of the agents involved doubted that they could meet the more rigorous standards required to wiretap Americans suspected of crimes. In the course of their surveillance, the FBI intercepted a large number of conversations in Brandon's home and office and covertly searched his home and office computers. They seized a massive amount of material, including his client files and his children's homework. (They labeled his son's Spanish homework "Spanish documents.") They did not notify him that they were searching his home (notice is the usual practice in executing a regular search warrant), but they were careless enough to leave traces of their activities—bolting doors that the family had left unbolted, leaving open blinds that had been closed—so that Brandon, Mona, and their three children had every reason to think they had been burglarized. Despite intense surveillance efforts, the agents found nothing to bolster their suspicions for a simple reason—Brandon Mayfield had no connection whatever with the bombing or the plastic bag.

The FBI also reported the identification of Mayfield to the Spanish police. But Spanish experts who examined the two fingerprints advised the American agents that their identification of the fingerprint on the bag as Brandon Mayfield's was wrong. On April 21, FBI agents met with Spanish investigators in Madrid in order to explain and defend their conclusion. At this meeting, the Spaniards complimented their American counterparts on a detailed presentation and said they would reexamine the fingerprints to check their own conclusions.

On May 4, reporters began to inquire about the existence of an American suspect in the Madrid bombings and the FBI, concerned about potential media leaks, decided that it would be a good idea to arrest Brandon Mayfield promptly. But the agents recognized that they did not have probable cause to believe he had committed a crime—just questions about how his fingerprint (as they thought) had gotten on that bag. And so they decided to arrest him as a "material witness," the same jury-rigged technique used against Abdullah al-Kidd (who was detained on the pretext that he was needed to testify at the trial of Sami al-Hussayen). On May 6, agents submitted affidavits in support of their request for a material witness arrest warrant and for additional search warrants. In these affidavits, they continued to affirm that the FBI considered the fingerprint a "100% positive identification." The material witness affidavit mentioned that the Spanish police had made "preliminary" findings which were "not consistent" with the FBI's findings (although not that the Spaniards had flat out disagreed with their identification). But, the affidavit averred, the Spanish police "felt satisfied" with the FBI's conclusion after the April meeting. The intimation was that the Spaniards had come to recognize that their preliminary investigation was not as thorough as the FBI's and had bowed to the Americans' superior skills. The Inspector General later noted the FBI agents' "overconfidence" in their own identification—they never asked the Spanish police to explain the basis for their negative conclusion, and they never seriously reexamined their own conclusion.[4] The Inspector General's report also repudiated excuses FBI agents offered after the fact for their incorrect fingerprint identification (like lack of access to the plastic bag itself).

The material witness affidavit also acknowledged that Brandon did not have a current passport issued in his name but declared there was a "likelihood" that he had false or fictitious travel documents. These affidavits also made much of Brandon's religion, offering his attendance at a mosque and the fact that he advertised his legal practice in a publication nicknamed the "Muslim Yellow Pages" as evidence connecting him to the bombing as a material witness. Brandon's lawyers later pointed out that among other businesses advertising in the "Muslim Yellow Pages" were Avis, Best Western, and United Airlines. The Inspector General later characterized a number of assertions in this affidavit as misleading. Contrary to the affidavit's statement that the Spaniards had come to be satisfied with the FBI's identification of Brandon Mayfield, the Spaniards had not expressed any such agreement. In fact, on reexamination of the fingerprints, they adhered to their conclusion that the FBI was wrong.[5] And there was no basis whatever for the affidavit's statement that it was "likely" that Brandon had gotten a fake passport,[6] except for the same kind of backward reasoning that had led to the misidentification of his fingerprint in the first place—if Brandon was involved with the Madrid bombing, he must have been there and if he had no genuine passport he therefore must have had a fake one. But the judge reading these affidavits had no reason to doubt the fingerprint identification or to question whether the FBI actually had evidence of a fake passport. And so, on the basis of these dubious affidavits, a material witness arrest warrant was issued.

The arrest was suitably dramatic. The FBI announced to the media that they had made a 100 percent match of Brandon's fingerprint with the Madrid fingerprint. Mona was not told where her husband was being held, but she was cruelly told that he was a prime suspect in a crime punishable by death—despite the fact that he was ostensibly only being held as a material witness. Brandon spent two horrible weeks in the Multnomah Detention Center until, on May 19, the Spanish police announced to the FBI and the media that they had definitively matched the fingerprint in question with an Algerian suspect—who had absolutely no connection with Brandon Mayfield. At the request of the Portland prosecutor, Brandon was released from prison the next day, but he was held in home detention for three more days as the FBI agents continued to resist the conclusion that they had targeted the wrong man.

After his ordeal finally ended, Brandon and his family were so outraged about their persecution that they decided to sue. Government lawyers must have thought that any jury would be shocked by the FBI's campaign against Brandon Mayfield because they settled his claim for unjustified arrest and imprisonment for $2 million. The settlement[7] included not only money damages, but a formal apology:

> The United States of America apologizes to Mr. Brandon Mayfield and his family for the suffering caused by the FBI's misidentification

of Mr. Mayfield's fingerprint and the resulting investigation of Mr. Mayfield, including his arrest as a material witness in connection with the 2004 Madrid train bombings and the execution of search warrants and other court orders in the Mayfield family home and in Mr. Mayfield's law office.[8]

As part of the settlement, the Mayfields preserved the right to continue their constitutional challenge to the Patriot Act provision that authorized part of their unjustifiable harassment—the expansion of the authority of the Foreign Intelligence Surveillance Court over an American citizen in Oregon—as the government was not willing to apologize for that. The government argued that the Patriot Act amendment in question did not violate the Fourth Amendment, even if it did encourage eavesdropping on and searching the home of an American family without the usual Fourth Amendment–required probable cause. The Mayfields won a fleeting victory from a federal judge who understood and valued the Fourth Amendment's safeguards against government overreaching. Oregon District Court Judge Ann Aiken held that the Patriot Act expansion of FISA permitted an illegal end run around the Fourth Amendment which, she said, "has served this Nation well for 220 years, through many other perils."[9] But Obama Administration lawyers succeeded in getting Judge Aiken's decision reversed on appeal for a very peculiar and disconcerting reason. Before getting to this surprise litigation twist, I need to explain why it was that Brandon Mayfield, an American citizen in the State of Oregon, was subject to the Foreign Intelligence Surveillance Court in the first place and why the Fourth Amendment, a critical part of our constitutional heritage, is not protecting Brandon and others like him from this kind of ordeal.

The Fourth Amendment and Terrorism

The authors of the Fourth Amendment understood deeply why unlimited government power to spy on people is intolerable. Excessive governmental power to search or to seize "persons, houses, papers, and effects" (in the words of the Fourth Amendment) was a primary cause of the American Revolution.[10] The framers took search and seizure authority very personally, perhaps because many of them had seditious literature in their basements and tea or rum on which they had not paid detested duties in their pantries, but also because they recognized the inherent connection between privacy and democracy. Like the Fifth Amendment privilege against self-incrimination, the Fourth Amendment guarantees people space to form their thoughts and live their lives without government intrusion. Within private enclaves, especially in our homes, there is a wealth of information about us that the government cannot either buy or google—evidence of our habits and opinions, what we read and write, and what we say to our family and friends when we think no one is listening.

The framers were especially outraged by the general warrants the King's agents employed to search at will,[11] recognizing that unlimited power to search invites arbitrary or discriminatory use—to discomfit political rivals, for example, or to trawl for potential critics or revolutionaries. So in the Fourth Amendment, they provided a constitutional guarantee of the "right of the people to be secure against unreasonable searches and seizures." This right has been interpreted as having two components: first, government officials are not to search or seize anyone or anything unless they have good reason to believe that the target is involved with a crime. The default standard for defining what counts as a good enough reason to search or arrest is probable cause. This requirement of individualized suspicion prevents general searches or fishing expeditions just to see if someone has done something wrong—a power associated with totalitarian states. Second, before searching, government officials prototypically have to convince an objective magistrate that they indeed have probable cause and are not being overzealous, engaging in wishful thinking, or acting in an arbitrary or discriminatory manner. This is nothing more than the classic detached second opinion we all want before we do something important, like agree to let a doctor operate on us.[12] By requiring agents who want to search or seize someone to explain their reasons to someone detached from the investigation, the judicial check limits the government's ability to trample on our privacy, target political opponents, or focus on people of a particular race or religion. The Supreme Court has created countless exceptions to this basic protocol, but both elements remain essential to our idea of who we are as a nation: we have a right to be let alone if we have not done anything to justify suspicion, and we have the right to have a neutral court act as a check on possible executive branch overreaching. As Supreme Court Justice and Nuremberg war crimes prosecutor Robert Jackson warned, "Uncontrolled search and seizure is one of the first and most effective weapons in the arsenal of every arbitrary government."[13]

In creating the new post-9/11 search and seizure authority, Congress exploited and stretched preexisting Fourth Amendment exceptions and loopholes to allow the government to conduct more searches with less individualized suspicion and less judicial review. Some of those exceptions the Supreme Court had already endorsed; others had been created by statutes that everyone assumed the Court would approve if the occasion arose. One of the preexisting statutory modifications of the Fourth Amendment prototype was the Foreign Intelligence Surveillance Act of 1978. That statute, with its subsequent amendments both before and after 9/11, progressively lowered the baseline for eavesdropping and searching, even for an American citizen in Oregon. This chapter and the next four chapters in this section will explore the consequences of lowering the Fourth Amendment baseline of probable cause and independent court review, showing how the Patriot Act–enhanced powers in each chapter veer further and further away from the Fourth Amendment paradigm. Would the framers have agreed to set aside the Fourth Amendment to allow an all-out search for possible terrorists? In answering that question, we need to bear in mind that our founding fathers were themselves regarded by the British as dangerous revolutionaries and that they lived in a world where British sleeper cells posed a very real threat to the young American republic.

"Foreign" Intelligence Surveillance, Americans, and the Patriot Act

Ironically, the Foreign Intelligence Surveillance Act of 1978 (FISA)[14] began as part of a design to protect Americans against unwarranted government eavesdropping. In 1975–1976, the bipartisan Church Committee, headed by Senator Frank Church of Idaho, held hearings in response to widespread concern that warrantless surveillance was out of control—spurred in part by revelations that President Richard Nixon had been using what he claimed were inherent presidential powers to spy on Americans he or FBI Director J. Edgar Hoover believed to pose a threat to national security. The Church Committee conducted the first extensive congressional review of American intelligence activities and discovered much to be concerned about, including, in one notorious example, the FBI's aggressive surveillance of Dr. Martin Luther King.[15] One result of these hearings was the enactment of FISA. This compromise Cold War-era statute preserved Fourth Amendment protections for "United States persons" but lowered the barriers to investigating foreign powers, prototypically the Soviet Union. Investigators who wanted to search or eavesdrop on foreign powers and their agents—by placing a bug in the Soviet

Embassy, for example—still needed to go to a court: the newly created Foreign Intelligence Surveillance Court. But they were not required to show that they had probable cause to believe that the "foreign power" in question was involved in a crime. Instead, they only had to show that they had probable cause to believe that their target was a foreign power or agent, and that their purpose was to obtain foreign intelligence information rather than evidence of a crime. In addition to changing the standards required to obtain a search warrant, FISA also designed a special court to conduct judicial review of the government's applications. Both the nature of the FISA court and the method of selecting the judges to serve on it represent a substantial departure from the federal court norm. The members of the FISA court are handpicked by the Chief Justice of the Supreme Court without any second opinion or review of whether the appointments are balanced.[16] All other courts presumptively operate in public, publishing opinions explaining their decisions and inviting the public to attend proceedings, except to the extent that the government can meet a heavy burden of showing that secrecy is necessary for some particular part of an occasional opinion or proceeding. The FISA court rarely publishes opinions[17] and always meets in secret. Thus the power to select the judges who will serve on this court is enormously consequential, as current Chief Justice John G. Roberts, Jr., acknowledged at his confirmation hearing.[18]

Since 1978, the year in which FISA became law, the Chief Justices have been Warren E. Burger, William H. Rehnquist, and Roberts, all Republican appointees tending to favor government positions. University of Pennsylvania law professor Theodore Ruger conducted an empirical study of William Rehnquist's twenty-five FISA court designations and concluded that the profile of the judges Rehnquist selected was not remarkably different from the profile of a randomly selected group of federal judges. Rehnquist tended to select conservative Republican appointees, but also included some Democratic appointees. Nevertheless, Ruger concluded, "[T]he actual FISA judges' Fourth Amendment behavior was more consistently pro-government than the individual random judges."[19] Reports to Congress show that between 1979 and 2009, the FISA court has approved 28,807 out of approximately 28,816 applications.[20] Around the time of the Mayfield searches, the FISA court had granted 16,970 out of 16,974 applications.

If Brandon Mayfield had actually been involved with the Madrid train bombing, he would fit the statute's definition of "agent of a foreign power" even though he is an American citizen. The definition includes anyone who "knowingly engages in sabotage or international terrorism"—terrorists as well as spies, Americans as well as foreigners.[21] What is different about being treated as the agent of a foreign power instead of an ordinary American? The FISA probable cause requirement is different, because there is no need to establish probable cause to believe that the target has committed a crime. The agents were divided on the issue of whether or not this difference would have mattered in Brandon's case. Some believed that a regular court would have found probable cause to issue the requested warrants in light of the FBI's assertion that the fingerprint match was 100 percent certain—even though the agents turned out to be wrong. But another difference is that operating under FISA means that the judicial second opinion in Brandon Mayfield's case was that of the highly predictable FISA court instead of a randomly selected judge.

An additional difference between operating under FISA as opposed to the usual rules covering investigations of Americans concerns whether and when the government has to give notice of the searches or wiretaps. Notice is regarded as essential under the Fourth Amendment. Officials executing a search warrant are supposed to knock and announce their arrival, except under extraordinary circumstances.[22] Due process requires agents who seize someone's property to provide notice that the property has been taken so the owner can pursue available remedies for its return.[23] The statute authorizing wiretaps to investigate crimes requires that notice be given to the person wiretapped within ninety days of the end of the surveillance.[24] Under the usual rules covering Americans, Brandon Mayfield would have had a right to be notified that he had been searched—after the fact, if not at the time of the search itself.

The specter of secret searches of Americans had led to considerable outrage over another Patriot Act loophole-expansion: the so-called sneak and peek provision,[25] which allows the government to execute a search warrant covertly and to delay telling the target about the search—although only with the court's permission and presumptively for not longer than thirty to ninety days.[26] (In a telling example of mission creep, the sneak and peek provision, touted as an antiterrorism measure, has been used overwhelmingly in drug cases rather than terrorism investigations.[27]) Had a non-FISA search warrant been issued, a regular court would have considered when the Mayfields should have been given notice that they were being searched, but FISA strips an American who is deemed to be a "foreign agent"—that is, a terrorist—of this right. And so the targets of a FISA search will never have an opportunity to question the constitutionality of the search—unless they are criminally prosecuted or find themselves in the highly unusual position of the Mayfields.

This complete lack of notice made sense when the target was the Soviet Embassy. But because the FISA statute is so dense and mind-bogglingly intricate, many critics of the sneak and peek provision did not notice that FISA subjected some selected Americans to an even greater unfairness: covert searches with notice denied instead of just deferred, with no court approval required for concealment. Some commentators had assumed that the controversial "sneak and peek" provision was used in the Mayfield case, but the Inspector General reassuringly noted that it was not—but that was only because FISA allowed the agents to dispense with notice without even asking a court's permission and so there was no need for the agents to invoke the "sneak and peek" authority. And of course the fact that the FISA court operates in secret, not even publishing redacted opinions, means that the public generally has no idea what the court is doing and so cannot provide any check on this world of secret spying.

Pre–Patriot Act, the chief legal limitation on use of the relaxed standards of FISA instead of a search warrant or regular court order was that obtaining foreign intelligence had to be "the" purpose of the investigation. This seemingly technical limitation is important because it is the reason courts could regard FISA as constitutional even though it bends Fourth Amendment standards. The Supreme Court had developed an exception to usual Fourth Amendment rules if the government can show a "special need" for information other than criminal investigation, and that serving this special need is "the primary purpose" of the investigation.[28] The original FISA statute compliantly declared that its alternate surveillance procedure was available only if "the" purpose of the surveillance was to obtain foreign intelligence information—for example, to find out what the Soviet Union was up to. But the Patriot Act defied the Supreme Court's "primary purpose" precondition by allowing the use of FISA's diluted form of judicial review any time gathering foreign intelligence is "a significant" purpose of an investigation—obviously covering many more instances than bugging the Russian Embassy. Judge Aiken, in the *Mayfield* case, aptly described this expansion as allowing the executive branch "to bypass the Fourth Amendment in gathering evidence for a criminal prosecution."[29] Although the FISA court is allowed to review whether or not a target is an "agent of a foreign power," the statute requires the court to defer to the government's assertion that finding foreign intelligence and not evidence of a crime is their purpose, and that they have reason to believe they will find foreign intelligence by eavesdropping or searching in the place they select.[30] And so the second opinion requirement is doubly diluted. These departures from the Fourth Amendment norm explain why Judge Aiken believed the Patriot Act "the/a significant" amendment was unconstitutional. Eliminating the primary purpose requirement potentially subjects many more Americans to the FISA court and to Brandon Mayfield's disturbing surveillance experience.

Mayfield v. United States Part II

Judge Aiken's ruling invalidating this expansion of FISA was vacated, however, because the Court of Appeals concluded that the Mayfield family did not have standing to raise any constitutional claim about the search and seizure of their own property. How could that be? The Court of Appeals agreed with Judge Aiken that the family had indeed been injured and continued to suffer invasions of their privacy because of the FBI's far-reaching surveillance. As part of the settlement agreement, the government had promised to return things the agents had taken from Mayfield's home and office—like Mayfield's physical files or records—but they had not promised to return or destroy "derivative evidence" they still had. According to the District Court, this "derivative" category included a great deal:

> photocopies or photographs of documents from confidential client files in Mayfield's law office, summaries and excerpts from the computer hard drives from the Mayfield law office and plaintiffs' personal computers at home, analysis of plaintiffs' personal bank records and bank records from Mayfield's law office, analysis of client lists, websites visited, family financial activity, summaries of confidential conversations between husband and wife, parents and children, and other private activities of a family's life within their home.[31]

This material, according to the government's lawyers, had already been distributed among various government agencies and would remain rooted in their files and databanks. The relevant statutes do not prevent the government from retaining and disseminating this trove of information about an innocent man and his family.[32] In the post–Patriot Act world, information is added to the government's hoard but not subtracted. Everyone agreed that the Mayfields were suffering ongoing injury because of the government's retention of all of this private information. But the appellate court reluctantly found that the family nevertheless could not challenge the constitutionality of the procedures the government had used to gather all this evidence because the government would not agree, if the Mayfields won their case, to actually return or destroy all this "derivative" evidence. Because the court's ruling in favor of the Mayfields would not make any tangible difference under the circumstances, the case was dismissed.

There was a technical legal reason behind this ruling. In the settlement agreement, the Mayfields had agreed to drop their request for an injunction (the kind of order a court uses to compel the government to take action) and to pursue only a claim for a declaratory judgment (a judicial declaration of illegality). Judge Aiken did not think this concession mattered, remarking: "[I]t is reasonable to assume that the Executive branch of the government will act lawfully and make all reasonable efforts to destroy the derivative materials when a final declaration of the unconstitutionality of the challenged provisions is issued."[33] But the government won its appeal by assuring the Court of Appeals that—unreasonable or not—it had no intention of correcting the mistake.[34] The Obama Justice Department refused to voluntarily destroy or return the illegally obtained derivative evidence that the courts agreed could continue to harm the Mayfields, and the court was not in a position to force them to do so, and so the appellate court reversed Judge Aiken's now toothless ruling and the case ended there. The Mayfields tried to get the Supreme Court's attention, but the high Court declined to become involved. This was the second decision finding the Patriot Act "the/a significant" expansion of FISA to be unconstitutional that was then erased on appeal.

The Secret Court and the One-Sided Litigation

The Foreign Intelligence Surveillance Court itself had also found this Patriot Act expansion of FISA to violate the Fourth Amendment not long after the statute was enacted. The FISA court, as the figures above show, had never been much of a stumbling block for federal agents wanting to wield FISA powers. In March 2002, Attorney General Ashcroft asked the FISA court to adopt new procedures for implementing the Patriot Act expansion by extending the use of FISA to law enforcement instead of just intelligence officials. If gathering foreign intelligence no longer had to be "the" purpose of FISA searches, he reasoned, criminal investigators could also now use FISA as long as they could assert that gathering intelligence was "a significant" goal of their investigation. In May 2002, the FISA court wrote an opinion rejecting the proposed procedures, finding that the Patriot Act amendment was unconstitutional. As a result, that court denied an unprecedented seventy-five surveillance applications.[35] Although the FISA court usually operates in secret, the court decided to publish its important opinion in this case after Senator Patrick Leahy inquired about how the Patriot Act provision in question was being implemented.

Congress had created a special review court to hear appeals from the FISA court—the Foreign Intelligence Surveillance Court of Review—but that court had never convened because the government, the only party allowed to argue in the FISA court, had essentially never lost a case. If you win, you have nothing to appeal; if you aren't a party, you aren't allowed to appeal, even if you are somehow able to find out that you have lost. Since the appellate process was just as one-sided as the FISA court itself, only the government was invited to appear in front of this court. But since it was now public knowledge that the review court would be convening to consider this case, the ACLU and the National Association of Criminal Defense Lawyers asked permission to file an amicus ("friend of the court") brief to defend the FISA court's conclusion and argue that the Patriot Act provision in question was unconstitutional. That position otherwise would not be defended in the one-sided appeal. ACLU lawyer Ann Beeson bemusedly described the bizarre challenges of trying to figure out how to file a brief with a court that had no physical location, had never met, and had no procedures.[36] After some successful detective work, the court's "friends" were told that they would be permitted to file a brief—which the court might or might not read—with the clerk of the court, who worked for the Department of Justice. The review court met, as secretly as might be expected, in a secure room inside the Justice Department building. Members of Congress who wanted to attend were turned away.

Although Theodore Ruger's study found that Chief Justice Rehnquist had tried for some bipartisanship in his appointments to the FISA court, Rehnquist's selections for the Court of Review were all Nixon or Reagan appointees.[37] The review court judges did read the amicus brief, complimenting its authors for their excellent presentation, but ruled that the Patriot Act amendment was constitutional—reversing the FISA court in the first appeal ever of one of its decisions and thus keeping the statistics overwhelmingly pro-government. Addressing the Fourth Amendment issue, the review court said that whether or not the statute was consistent with the Supreme Court's "primary purpose" test was a question with "no definitive jurisprudential answer."[38] But, the court went on, even if the requirements of the Patriot Act provision do not meet the minimum Fourth Amendment warrant standards, they "certainly come close."[39] And so, because national security matters were involved, the FISA expansion was declared to be reasonable and the Fourth Amendment was brushed aside. The litigation ended there. How could the Supreme Court review this ruling when there was only one party in the case—the government—and that party had won and so had no reason to appeal? Ann Beeson and her colleagues filed a motion with the Supreme Court asking to be allowed to intervene in the case for the purpose of petitioning for Supreme Court review. The Court refused the invitation.[40]

Judge Aiken, in the *Mayfield* case, is the only judge who subsequently agreed with the FISA court and disagreed with the review court's ruling. The only other courts to have considered whether the Patriot Act went too far in expanding FISA have been courts in criminal cases where defendants were challenging the constitutionality of government surveillance in order to have incriminating evidence against them excluded from their trials. If the government prosecutes someone and wants to use evidence derived from FISA searches at the trial, the government is then and only then required to tell the "aggrieved person" about the origins of the evidence so that person can challenge its admissibility.[41] However, if the "aggrieved person" (the criminal defendant) does challenge the admissibility of the results of the surveillance, the Attorney General may require the court to review the challenge in secret, so the defendant and defense counsel never get to see the surveillance applications or any of the other materials involved. The statute does allow the court to disclose materials to the defense attorney and to hold an adversary hearing if that is regarded as necessary to reach an accurate result but, evidently, courts never find such hearings to be necessary.[42] Procedure matters.

In a criminal case, the result of a court finding the Patriot Act FISA amendment unconstitutional would be to exclude actual evidence of a criminal defendant's guilt. And in a criminal case, defense attorneys are unable to see or respond to the relevant materials. Is it a coincidence that judges considering the Fourth Amendment issue in this context have all upheld the Patriot Act FISA amendment?[43] The *Mayfield* court, in the context of considering the case of a demonstrably innocent man, in a public civil proceeding, was far more skeptical about the sufficiency of the FISA safeguards. While the results are lopsided, it should also be noted that the number of constitutional challenges to this Patriot Act amendment heard by courts is quite small. The fact that targets of FISA searches, unlike targets of regular search warrants or eavesdropping orders, are never given notice that they have been subject to a search unless they are prosecuted means that the government can control when and if challenges will occur. By deciding not to prosecute someone, or not to use a particular piece of evidence, or by offering a defendant an attractive plea bargain, the government can prevent courts from considering motions to suppress FISA-derived evidence. But there seems to be little need for the government to avoid the courts, which have almost unanimously accepted the lowering of the FISA bar. Judge Aiken and, notably, the FISA court itself were unusual in their dedication to Fourth Amendment principles. And the combination of all the procedures surrounding the FISA court and review of its rulings truly stacks the deck.

A Job for Congress and the Courts

The section of the Patriot Act that broadened the reach of FISA by eliminating the "primary purpose" requirement was highly controversial and so it was scheduled to expire in 2005. Realizing that it was passing the Patriot Act hastily, barely over five weeks after 9/11 with virtually no debate or reflection, Congress provided that sixteen of its more controversial provisions would "sunset" after four years unless they were intentionally renewed. There was no controversy and no real discussion when Congress decided to make this particular expansion of FISA permanent in 2005–2006, or during the 2009 reauthorization hearing process. Congress evidently does not hear much on this subject from disgruntled constituents. Who other than Brandon Mayfield and a few people convicted of crimes would know if they have been subject to "foreign intelligence" searches? The whole point of secret surveillance is that the targets do not know they are under surveillance. Judging from Brandon Mayfield's case, there is no way to escape the reach of the FISA power, since avoiding all international travel and contacts is not enough to prevent being designated an "agent of a foreign power." But how many people are willing to absorb the complexities of this body of law to understand how the Fourth Amendment is being diluted here and why that matters?

Very few judges today are willing to push back against the government's ever increasing power to search and eavesdrop with less and less supervision. Since 9/11, the U.S. Supreme Court has decided about thirty-one cases raising Fourth Amendment claims. The Court has ruled against the Fourth Amendment in twenty-six of those cases.[44] At the oral argument of the first search and seizure case the Court heard post-9/11, Justice Sandra

Day O'Connor remarked that "[w]e live in perhaps a more dangerous age today than we did when this event took place."[45] Judge Aiken was right to worry that expanding this dragnet threatens our Fourth Amendment rights by allowing too much discretionary executive authority: "In place of the Fourth Amendment, the people are expected to defer to the Executive Branch and its representation that it will authorize such surveillance only when appropriate."[46] There was a brief period during the 1960s when the Supreme Court seemed on the verge of holding all electronic eavesdropping unconstitutional because it is such a powerful tool and so difficult to contain.[47] Justice William Brennan, one of the stalwarts of the Warren Court, said: "Electronic surveillance . . . makes the police omniscient; and police omniscience is one of the most effective tools of tyranny."[48]

The Patriot Act's expansion of FISA is not consistent with previous Supreme Court interpretations of the Fourth Amendment but, if the Court ever consents to hear a case on the subject, it is quite likely to shrink the Fourth Amendment one more size in order to validate this expanded authority. Congress is unlikely to roll back FISA to its pre-9/11 size. But even if the expanded power to acquire dossiers on Americans is with us to stay, Congress or the courts could at least fashion meaningful limits on the ability of the government to retain and distribute information so that other families won't have the experience of the Mayfields.[49] Do we need another Church Committee to make that happen? It might seem unlikely that we could muster such a constructive process in our highly partisan age, but it should not be impossible. One concern people across the political spectrum, liberals and libertarians alike, share with the framers of the Fourth Amendment is suspicion of allowing the government too much arbitrary power over our lives and our property. What is at issue here is not whether or not the government will be allowed to search for terrorists, but what procedures the government must follow in order to do so. As the authors of the Fourth Amendment clearly saw, procedure matters.

7.

The Patriot Act and Library/Business Records

If the lady from Toledo can be required to disclose what she read yesterday and what she will read tomorrow, fear will take the place of freedom in the libraries, bookstores, and homes of the land.—Justice William O. Douglas (1953)[1]

Revised Patriot Act Will Make It Illegal to Read Patriot Act.—The Onion (2003)

American Librarians

It was probably predictable that librarians would be among the first to recognize how great a threat the post-9/11 surveillance regime poses to our First Amendment traditions as well as to our privacy. Among the framers of the Constitution were dedicated librarians. In 1731, Benjamin Franklin convinced his friends to pool their book collections to start the Library Company of Philadelphia, said to be the country's first subscription library.[2] Franklin was so widely admired that a town in Massachusetts decided to name itself in his honor and asked him to bless their choice by donating a church bell. Instead, he sent a crate of books, declaring that "sense" is preferable to "sound." The town of Franklin claims to have instituted the first American public library when it voted in 1790 to make the books its namesake had provided available to all residents for free.[3] Thomas Jefferson, a famously prodigious reader, maintained the largest private collection of books in the country. After the British burned the Library of Congress during the War of 1812, the library was restocked with books from Jefferson's collection.[4]

The twenty-first-century librarians of the American Library Association (ALA), custodians of this intellectual tradition, passed a resolution in January 2003 condemning the Patriot Act's threat to ideas, the fuel of democracy.[5] The ALA, which has over 60,000 members, is the oldest library association in the world. Its policy is to oppose "any use of governmental prerogatives that lead to the intimidation of individuals or groups and discourages them from exercising the right of free expression guaranteed by the First Amendment."[6] To the librarians, libraries are a bulwark of democracy and so spying on people in the library, where ideas are formed and expressed, seems as wrong as spying on them in the voting booth.

The librarians' concern focused mainly on Patriot Act Section 215, which went far beyond the special treatment of financial institutions by allowing agents to get a court order requiring *any* custodian of records to turn over *any and all* of their customers' records—business, educational, medical, Internet, and, yes, library records. This court order is even easier to get than the orders in Brandon Mayfield's case. Instead of following the Fourth Amendment's usual rule of asking a court to provide a second opinion about whether seizing the records in question is justified, the Patriot Act instructs the court—the secret Foreign Intelligence Surveillance Court again—that it "must" sign an order requiring the custodian to turn over business records (perhaps with a modification or two) as long as the government's application recites that the information sought is "relevant" to a terrorism investigation. Unlike the FISA order in Brandon Mayfield's case, these orders are not based on any kind of probable cause or any particular reason to believe that the target is a terrorist. And the agents applying for the order, not judges, make the decision about what is relevant. The provision does contain one caveat: an instruction that people should not be targeted "solely" on the basis of their First Amendment activities.[7] But this instruction is easy enough to evade. Under the terms of the statute, one's religious practices, antiwar activism, or taste in books may become the basis for government investigation as long as the government can also claim some additional reason for wanting to look at someone's records. And even this feeble limitation is virtually impossible to enforce because both the decision to target someone and the court order happen in secret.

These Just Trust Us orders worried the librarians because they empower government agents to command a world of private information—including the books library patrons check out and e-mails they send or websites they visit on library computers—without any meaningful judicial oversight. No one contended that library records should be sacrosanct—just that in order to protect both First Amendment intellectual and associational rights and Fourth Amendment–oriented privacy concerns, this kind of highly personal information should remain private unless a neutral court agrees with the FBI that a search is justified. Under cover of these pushover orders, the FBI can trawl through the records of innocent people if they think that by doing so they might find something they would consider "relevant" to a terrorism investigation. "Relevance," a very open-ended standard, may be viewed by some agents as including the names of people who have checked out biographies of Osama bin Laden or researched how dams are built. Will people think twice about trying to understand Osama bin Laden if they fear that checking out his biography might bring the FBI to their doorstep? Will they hesitate to visit websites of radical political parties, or support groups for HIV-positive patients, if information about what they are reading and thinking is only one easy step away from a government database? These concerns are not just hypothetical. In New Mexico, for example, a former public defender was arrested by federal agents and interrogated for five hours after using a computer at a Santa Fe academic library, apparently as a result of posting a chat room statement opining that President Bush was out of control.[8] The story of the schoolboy who was visited by the FBI after checking out a book on dams for a school project may or may not be apocryphal, but stories like this spread and contribute to an atmosphere of apprehension that is likely to induce self-censorship. This chilling effect can influence people's decisions and their sense of freedom regardless of whether these court orders are actually being used, and will be magnified to the extent that people believe the orders can and will be used.

Attorney General Ashcroft responded by accusing the librarians of "baseless hysteria."[9] Citing national security considerations, however, he refused to share any information at all about how the suspect provision was actually being implemented. But librarians are not as quiet as their stereotype. Librarians around the country kept asking questions and raising the alarm about this threat to our constitutional values.[10] Their campaign generated enough public concern that Ashcroft decided to "declassify" information about Section 215's use and announce that there was no reason for concern because, as of September 2003, that provision had not been used at all.[11] At the time, most librarians did not suspect that this reassurance was quite misleading because the FBI actually was knocking on library doors and demanding information about library patrons—under a different Patriot Act provision. That story will be told in the next chapter.

Post-9/11 was not the first time the FBI attempted to enlist librarians in national security efforts, and not the first time this kind of attempt sparked public outrage. During the 1970s and '80s, the FBI instituted a secret "Library Awareness" program as part of its Cold War counterintelligence efforts. Librarians, especially at academic libraries, were asked to look out for library users who might be diplomats from hostile powers recruiting spies or gathering information that might be harmful to our national security—the "agents of foreign powers" cited in the Foreign Intelligence Surveillance Act. Some librarians reported having been asked to track the books checked out by foreigners from Communist countries. A *New York Times* story exposed this program in 1987[12] and documented the outraged reactions of librarians at having been asked to take part. The Executive Director of the New York Library Association at the time, Nancy Lian, said:

> I find it amazing that a librarian could be supposed to recognize someone who is a national of a hostile power. . . . Does anyone with an accent come under suspicion? These things are so far removed from the professional duties of a librarian that I find it almost inconceivable that this whole thing is happening.

In response to this episode, forty-eight states passed library confidentiality laws, providing greater privacy protection for library records than for most other business records.[13] Although the content of these laws varies, they generally prohibit librarians from turning over patron information except as necessary to comply with a court order.[14] These laws can be trumped by the Patriot Act, however, even if the court order it countenances is a sham or indeed if the requirement of a court order is entirely eliminated. The federal government, under the United States Constitution's Supremacy Clause,[15] is empowered to ignore state laws that get in the way of its investigations.[16]

During the initial Patriot Act debates, Senator Russell Feingold (the only Senator to vote against the Patriot Act) proposed an amendment providing that the Act would not preempt existing federal and state privacy laws. He did not succeed in his effort to maintain preexisting privacy standards that protected library and other sensitive business records from fishing expeditions—by requiring a meaningful court order.[17] In the years since Feingold's lonely effort to preserve privacy, Congress has not been wholly unreceptive to the librarians' crusade. On several occasions Congress came close to enacting special legislation to protect libraries and bookstores by requiring a court order involving an actual decision by a court before seizure of their records. Representative Bernie Sanders's "Freedom to Read Protection Act"[18] failed in 2003 when it was wrestled to a 210 to 210 tie because the Republican House leadership left the vote open twice as long as scheduled while they rounded up opposing votes. In June 2005, Sanders tried again and his bill passed the House by a vote of 238–187 but was not adopted by the Senate.[19] During the 2005 Patriot Act reauthorization hearings, Section 215 was one of the sections scheduled to sunset, so Congress had to decide whether to renew this provision. The Senate voted to modify Section 215 by raising the standard for obtaining a court order and requiring some showing of an actual connection with terrorism that a court could review. But the House Rules Committee did not allow floor votes on these proposed amendments or on a reprise of Sanders's bill for special treatment of libraries. And so the court order required by Section 215 remained not much more than a fig leaf for another four years.

Judicial Fumbling

Although Section 215 came to be known as the "library provision" because of the publicity surrounding the librarians' campaign, the concerns raised by this power to raid business records at will are not limited to libraries and bookstores. Many other businesses and organizations also maintain sensitive records that should not be exposed to fishing expeditions without the protection of a suspicion standard and a court's second opinion. That is why, pre-9/11, federal privacy laws provided special protection for the confidentiality of educational records,[20] for medical records,[21] and for privacy on the Internet.[22] Those were the laws Feingold's amendment would have preserved.

After 9/11, freedom of religion was also on the endangered list. By 2003, the leaders of the Muslim Community Association of Ann Arbor, Michigan (MCA), an organization that ran community mosques and Islamic schools, had become very worried that FBI agents would arrive in their offices with a court order to search their records, despite Section 215's nod to the First Amendment. They knew about the Muslim charities that had been abruptly put out of business on the basis of spurious fact-finding. They knew that FBI or local agents were infiltrating worship services and other meetings following the relaxation of guidelines governing undercover activities in political or religious settings. They had heard the librarians discuss the breadth of the Section 215 orders. And a number of their members had already been visited by the FBI for reasons they did not understand. Homam Albaroudi, for example, reported that the FBI had come to question him on two occasions, just to find out, they said, whether he knew about any conspiracies against the United States. This Syrian-born engineer, who had become a naturalized United States citizen in 1998, was offended by their attentions and their evidently low opinion of his patriotism, and replied that if he had known of any conspiracies he would have reported them. He was afraid that the FBI had not liked his attitude and might be investigating him, including possibly searching through records about his activities at MCA.[23]

The MCA leaders were also aware that Section 215 contained an automatic and absolute gag provision that prohibited recipients of a court order issued under that section from ever telling anyone they had received such a demand.[24] They were concerned that if they were indeed asked to turn over their records under Section 215, the gag provision would then prevent them from speaking out, even if they thought the demand was improperly based on religious profiling. The absolute language of the gag order at the time evidently even prohibited consulting a lawyer or going to court to challenge the constitutionality of the demand for production of records. And so rather than placing themselves in an untenable situation where they would have to risk violating the law in order to challenge it, they decided to preemptively ask the court to find that Section 215 violates the First, Fourth, and Fifth Amendments by exposing records like theirs to easy capture.

They were joined by a number of other nonprofit organizations, some of which, like the American-Arab Anti-Discrimination Committee and the Council on American-Islamic Relations, specifically served Arab and Muslim populations, working with those communities on economic, cultural, or civil liberties issues. Other organizations joining the challenge to this provision did not particularly identify themselves with Arab or Muslim causes. Mary Lieberman, a social worker, was Executive Director of Bridge Refugee Services, a Knoxville, Tennessee–based ecumenical organization affiliated with Church World Services (a ministry of thirty-six Protestant, Orthodox, and Anglican denominations in the United States), and Episcopal Migration Ministries, which provided aid to refugees from anywhere.

Bridge had an Iraqi refugee client, Muwafa Albaraqi, who, in 1991, had participated in an unsuccessful uprising against the government of Saddam Hussein, with the encouragement of the United States. When this effort failed and he had to flee Iraq, Bridge helped him to settle in Tennessee, find a job as a checkout clerk in a grocery store, enroll in a part-time electrical engineering program at the University of Tennessee, and apply for citizenship. Muwafa was alarmed and upset when FBI agents came to his workplace in January 2003 to question him, telling him the interview was not optional and insultingly asking him if he would engage in terrorism if an Iraqi agent cut off his brother's finger and sent it to him in the mail. He saw no reason why the FBI should suspect him of anything. When he told his contacts at Bridge about this experience, they thought it not unlikely that the FBI might decide to cast its net wider if they wanted to know more about Muwafa, for whatever reason. The records that Bridge kept about people the organization helped, including notes on personal interviews, seemed a likely focus of interest. The FBI had already asked Bridge for records about some of its other clients, which Bridge had refused to turn over voluntarily as its records often covered a range of sensitive personal issues, sometimes including notes on family problems, substance abuse issues, or health issues a client had shared with an interviewer in connection with a request for help.[25] So Mary Lieberman and Bridge decided to join the lawsuit.

Arguing that they were likely to be targeted because of the ethnicity, religion, or political associations of some or all of their members, the organizations told the court about numerous instances of FBI contacts with their members or clients, including Homam Albaroudi's and Muwafa Albaraqi's experiences. They also explained that the prospect of the government demanding their records was currently having a serious impact on their own and their members' exercise of their First Amendment rights of speech and association. Mosque attendance had declined dramatically; members now insisted on giving donations to these nonprofit organizations anonymously. At least one person had insisted that the Muslim Community Association permanently expunge all records mentioning his name, for fear that the FBI might obtain the records and then subject him to scrutiny. "John Doe," a formerly active member of the Muslim Community Association who wanted to remain anonymous in his affidavit because he was afraid of piquing the government's interest, reported that he had stopped speaking out on issues that concerned him, had pulled back from his connection with the MCA, and had changed his customs of donating to charity. He took to heart the experience of the Muslim charities and was chilled in his speech, his associations, and his religious observances by the very existence of Section 215, for fear that government agents might find some reason in the MCA records to arrive at his door.[26]

The threat to the confidentiality of their business records also made it difficult for organizations like Bridge or MCA to do their work. Some of the groups, like some librarians, had begun to omit sensitive information from their own records for fear of compromising their members', clients', or patrons' privacy. And many began to think twice about keeping some kinds of records at all. People like Muwafa Albaraqi were not likely to share personal information with them if their organization's computers and file cabinets were a way station to FBI databases. Fear of the consequences of candor might lead to self-censorship which, in turn, might prevent people in need from seeking or receiving meaningful help.

The government moved to dismiss the case on the ground that the organizations did not have standing—that is, could not prove that they had actually been injured—because they could not prove that they had in fact been targeted to receive Section 215 orders or that they were likely to be. In support of this argument, the government filed secret evidence about the use of Section 215, for the judge's eyes only. The judge found herself in a difficult situation. She was obviously reluctant to dismiss the case for lack of standing on the basis of material the plaintiffs' lawyers could not see and therefore could not answer, but she seemed equally reluctant to second-guess the government's assertion that it could compromise national security to reveal how often Section 215 was or was not being used.

The government's secrecy argument was based on the "mosaic theory." This theory, which proliferated following 9/11, maintains that any tiny piece of information made available to the American people would also be available to potential enemies and might endanger our national security because it might then be combined with other tiny pieces of information to form a revealing picture of our antiterrorism strategy[27]—a contention courts were finding difficult to assess. On the one hand, it is certainly true as a matter of observation that one apparently insignificant bit of information might turn out, in combination with other information, to be revealing. But on the other hand, this type of reasoning has no logical limit. Because there is no way for anyone to disprove the possible significance of any piece of information, taking this observation as a defense to any disclosure of any information gives the executive branch a blank check to withhold all information.[28] And so the judge avoided deciding the government's motion to dismiss for month after month and then year after year.

In October 2002, the ACLU had tried filing a Freedom of Information Act (FOIA) lawsuit in the District of Columbia to find out about the use of Section 215, but the judge in that case accepted the government's mosaic theory argument—after reviewing secret submissions by the government—and denied the request.[29] Following September 2003, when Attorney General Ashcroft declassified information about Section 215's use in answer to the librarians, the ACLU tried again, requesting information about the total number of times FBI field offices had compiled Section 215 applications and sent them to FBI headquarters for further required approvals.

The District of Columbia district judge in the case seemed sympathetic to this request, noting the widespread public interest in the use of this power (mentioning the librarians, of course), but again deferred to the government's national security claim because the D.C. Circuit Court of Appeals had affirmatively endorsed the mosaic theory.[30] Secrecy was foiling the MCA's lawsuit challenging Section 215 and also preventing the American people from having enough information to weigh in about that provision's renewal at the Patriot Act reauthorization hearings.

The *MCA* case was still pending in April 2005, when sections of the Patriot Act including 215 were up for renewal. At a Senate reauthorization hearing, Attorney General Alberto Gonzales testified that, according to the most recent figures, Section 215 had been used only thirty-five times and never in a library or bookstore.[31] The government lawyers in the *MCA* case then followed up by filing more secret evidence on the issue of whether the case should be dismissed, perhaps outlining the prospects for future use of Section 215. Once again the plaintiffs' lawyers were not allowed to read the government's submissions. Unable to resolve the dilemma secrecy had created, the judge continued to let the case languish undecided.

Finally, the judge found a way out. At the 2005 reauthorization hearings, several issues concerning Section 215 were debated. Although Congress did not revise the statute to require meaningful court participation as a precondition to seizure of library or other business records, Congress did amend Section 215's nondisclosure provision. In response to litigation that will be described in chapter 9, Congress amended the provision by including an exception to the gag order in order to allow recipients of records demands under Section 215 to consult a lawyer and to enlist a court if they had concerns about the legality or constitutionality of a demand. In 2006, after this revision, the judge finally issued an opinion in the *MCA* case. She denied the government's motion to dismiss, ruling that the plaintiff organizations did have standing, even if they could not show that they actually had been or would be asked for their records, because they reasonably feared that they would be targeted and also because Section 215 had a chilling effect on their own speech and associations. And so, three years after the complaint had been filed, she invited the plaintiffs to decide whether or not they still wanted to continue their challenge to the Patriot Act section in light of the recent revisions, which at least ameliorated the plaintiffs' concern that it would never be possible to challenge a demand for records without risking criminal prosecution.[32] The plaintiffs decided to drop the lawsuit and to use the opportunity afforded by the revised gag order to challenge Section 215 orders if and when they were served. And thus the only court in a position to consider the constitutionality of this provision hung back and waited for Congress to act—for the unbelievable period of three years—instead of deciding whether this Patriot Act provision is unconstitutional. It has been impossible so far to get any court to make that decision.

Despite this protracted and frustrating litigation experience, Mary Lieberman, who now teaches social work at the University of Texas, describes her participation in this lawsuit on behalf of her clients at Bridge Refugee Services as "the privilege of a lifetime."

Third-Party Records and the Fourth Amendment

Although the 2005 Patriot Act amendments did address the problem of Section 215's gag order (albeit not fully, as later chapters will describe), they did not, as noted above, do anything to resolve the underlying constitutional problem—that government agents can search and seize private records without having to convince a court that they have probable cause or at least some real basis for suspicion. The Fourth Amendment issues at stake have not been addressed by the courts for two reasons. First is the ironclad theory of standing that the government raised in *MCA*. The federal courts only consider constitutional claims of people who can show that they personally have been injured by the practice they are challenging. The *MCA* court was persuaded that the members of the plaintiff organizations had standing because their own First Amendment rights were being affected even if the FBI never actually asked to look at their records. Fear that the FBI would do so was itself causing concrete harm to First Amendment values because people had become afraid to share information. But the people who have standing to raise Fourth Amendment claims, the subjects of the records at stake, cannot complain about invasion of their privacy if they do not know that their records are being seized. The whole point of the gag order is to ensure that targets will not learn that the FBI is seeking information about them. And so secrecy itself can prevent Fourth Amendment challenges from being brought.

The second problem is that, standing issues aside, courts are unlikely to find that targets have any Fourth Amendment rights in these circumstances.[33] This is because the Supreme Court has interpreted the Fourth Amendment as irrelevant in situations where a person has exposed information to a third party—like a bank or a telephone company. According to the Court's rather breathtaking reasoning, we give up any "legitimate expectation of privacy" in information we voluntarily turn over to third parties, whether that information is our bank balance or the telephone numbers we call. Because our bankers and telephone companies have access to that information, in the Court's view it all therefore becomes subject to government seizure without any of the procedural protections the Fourth Amendment would otherwise impose. In other words, the Fourth Amendment, in the Court's interpretation, does not cover records in the hands of a third party.

Two cases in the 1970s established this courthouse door–closing idea. In *United States v. Miller*,[34] Treasury agents bearing a defective subpoena had asked the presidents of two banks to produce "all records of accounts, i.e., savings, checking, loan or otherwise, in the name of Mr. Mitch Miller." The bank presidents cooperated. Miller then complained that the government had violated his Fourth Amendment rights by first requiring his bankers to keep such records and then demanding the production of those records without a valid court order. The Court disagreed that the government's doubly coercive actions mattered. By using a bank, the Court said, Miller had exposed his private information to his bankers and therefore assumed the risk that those bankers would share his information with the government. The Court considered it irrelevant that the bankers did not turn over the information voluntarily, or that using a bank may not really be optional in the modern world. The second case, *Smith v. Maryland*,[35] applied the same exaggerated "assumption of risk" idea to allow government agents to obtain telephone records showing the telephone numbers Smith had called and from which he had received calls—on the theory that Smith had "voluntarily" shared that information with his telephone company and therefore could no longer expect that those numbers would remain private from anyone. To obtain the contents of telephone calls, the government would need a court order; to obtain telephone logs, the government was excused from paying attention to Fourth Amendment niceties.

Although the Supreme Court declared in these cases that "society" was not prepared to recognize any legitimate expectation of privacy in such instances, American society seemed to disagree. Congress reacted to *Miller* by enacting the Right to Financial Privacy Act of 1978[36] in order to protect customers of financial institutions from "unwarranted intrusion into their records while at the same time permitting legitimate law enforcement activity."[37] The Act prevented fishing expeditions in financial records by requiring the kinds of protection the Fourth Amendment would have, had it been deemed applicable, like notice and judicial involvement. This was the law until the Patriot Act crafted exceptions so that financial institutions could collaborate in filling government databanks. And the decision in *Smith* led Congress to enact the Electronic Communications Privacy Act, requiring agents to obtain a court order before seeking an individual's telephone log from a telephone company.[38] This statutory privacy protection too was later diluted by the Patriot Act, as chapter 9 will recount, leaving telecommunications information again exposed to government collection without any court order at all.

Scholars have been critical of the *Miller/Smith* assumption of risk theory.[39] And there are cogent arguments that highly intrusive post-9/11 surveillance mechanisms are indeed unconstitutional despite *Miller* and *Smith*, especially where the highly revealing records of Internet service providers are involved.[40] The third-party doctrine made more sense in the pre-Internet world where the locus of most private activity was in the home. The Supreme Court has been very protective of the privacy of activities in the home, even if those activities are illegal—like growing marijuana,[41] or watching obscene videos.[42] But especially since the advent of "cloud computing," there is little distinction between what an individual does at home and the information that individual shares with an Internet service provider. While the framers of the Constitution stored their constitutionally protected "papers and effects" at home, Miller and Smith did not possess their own records; they had to share certain types of information in order to use a bank or a telephone. Many Internet users, because of cloud computing, share an infinitely broader variety of information with their Internet service providers. Current technology allows Internet users to store their personal calendars, contacts lists, documents, and photographs on third-party servers, which provide convenient access to one's information from any computer, instead of just on their home computers.[43] The Internet is also redefining what it means to have a conversation, to buy music, or to obtain a book to read. The potentially limitless theory of *Miller* and the increasingly unsatisfying content/non-content distinction the Court drew in *Smith* expose the type of information that Benjamin Franklin would have been able to keep private in his home, unless the government was able to obtain a search warrant. The Patriot Act allows searches and seizures of personal information that the framers might well have equated with the despised general warrant.

But the Supreme Court has not yet declared any limit to the *Miller/ Smith* third-party doctrine, and so those decisions are the chief reason why debates over protection of personal information in the hands of a third party have taken place in Congress rather than in the courts.[44] The *Miller* and *Smith* cases, abdicating the Court's responsibility for protecting Fourth Amendment values, are also one reason why American data privacy laws are so much less protective than those of comparable nations. Once the courts have declared that a practice is not unconstitutional, in our court-centered culture we are likely to assume that the practice is consistent with our values and need not be reexamined. As a result, Congress has also become less inclined to vindicate privacy values. The bottom line, at least so far, is that Congress gets to decide where the floor of protection for records kept by businesses, libraries, schools, hospitals, community organizations, and Internet providers should be set and, in the Patriot Act, Congress decided to lower the floor. The Supreme Court had already left the building.

Reconsidering the "Library Provision"

Enough members of the 2001 Congress had been dubious about whether or not conferring such a broad surveillance power was a good idea that in enacting the Patriot Act, they imposed an expiration date on Section 215. But four years after the Patriot Act, Congress voted to extend this power for another four years before it had any significant information on how the power had been used—beyond Attorney General Gonzales's testimony about the infrequency of its use. During the 2005 reauthorization deliberations, however, Congress finally showed some interest in exercising oversight and asked the Inspector General of the Justice Department, Glenn Fine, to investigate how this power had been used. Inspector General Fine's first report on the use of Section 215 was released in March 2007, five and a half years after the provision's adoption. The report concluded that Section 215 had not been misused because, as Gonzales had said, it simply had not been used much at all. Because of procedural complexities in getting the process started, the FBI had not begun using this new power until May 2004. The Inspector General also found that Ashcroft and Gonzales had spoken truthfully in saying that Section 215 had never been used in a library. It seems the outspoken librarians had an impact even in the secret recesses of the FBI offices. According to the report, on several occasions agents had proposed obtaining a Section 215 court order to review

library records, but their proposals did not survive the FBI's internal review process. One supervisor explicitly declined a proposal to apply for a
library-related order because of the controversy the librarians had ignited.
And so, the report said, the FBI got the information it sought "through
other investigative means."[45] But Section 215 is now loaded and ready for
action, and only the Inspector General has any means of learning whether
the FBI's self-restraint with respect to libraries will continue.

In light of the fact that the FBI has never used the Section 215 authority
in libraries, so far as we know, and that this power does not actually seem
to be necessary, creating an exemption for libraries and bookstores seems
like an easy way for Congress to make a statement about our commitment
to free speech and thought. Library records could still be obtained if agents
could show a court that they have a good reason to want to see them,
just as Fourth Amendment norms should require. But special treatment of
libraries and bookstores should not deflect pressure for more meaningful
protections of other types of private information too. The records of social
work agencies like Bridge, schools, medical providers, and many others
also implicate important privacy issues. Congress would do better to re-
instate meaningful privacy protections for all of the information we share
with businesses and librarians by adopting a real standard of individualized suspicion and giving the reviewing court something to review.

While business leaders had generally been supportive of the Patriot
Act, some became concerned about the problems the new massive security apparatus was creating for themselves and their customers.[46] The
mayor of Las Vegas, for example, complained about the FBI gathering
information from local businesses concerning close to a million people
who had visited Las Vegas during a particular time period, characterizing this prodigious collection of business records as "Kafkaesque":
"The central component to our economy is privacy protection. People
are here to have a good time and don't want to worry about the government knowing their business."[47] In addition to sensitive customer information, businesses may be required to expose their confidential data
and trade secrets. Multinational companies have particular reason to
worry because, like Pavlov's dogs, they are subject to conflicting sets of
demands: under United States law they may be required to share confidential customer data with the government; under the more protective
data privacy laws of other countries, like the European Union and Canada, they may be prohibited from divulging that same information.[48]
And they risk prosecution on charges unrelated to terrorism once the

government is examining their records. Might the government find what it would regard as evidence of tax evasion or price-fixing? And so at the 2005 reauthorization hearings, some business leaders lobbied for greater protection of their customers' privacy.[49]

Perhaps it was to appease this powerful lobby as well as the feisty librarians that the Senate had wanted in 2005 to adopt a new, more rigorous standard for court orders under Section 215. But because the House of Representatives did not concur, in the end, only minor changes were made to the substance of this provision. Nevertheless, Congress showed that it was still concerned about the scope and impact of this authority. Although fourteen of the sixteen originally sunsetting Patriot Act provisions were renewed and made permanent during the 2005 reauthorization hearings, the "library provision" was not made permanent. A new sunset was imposed on Section 215, requiring Congress to revisit these issues in 2009.

When the second round of Patriot Act sunset hearings came around in 2009–2010, the Obama Administration and a Democratic Congress seemed interested in modifying this authority. Both the House and Senate Judiciary Committees approved bills to raise the standard for Section 215 orders. Although the administration supported continuing the "library provision,"[50] in 2009–2010 Obama seemed willing to negotiate about procedural modifications. The proposed amendments never came to a vote on the floor, however. Instead, Congress, with the administration's support, punted. Congress simply reauthorized the provisions until February and then May 2011.[51] On May 26, 2011, the very day the extended provisions were to expire at midnight, Congress again extended Section 215, without modification, by a Senate vote of 72-23. (The rush was so great that President Obama, who was in Europe, signed the bill remotely by autopen.) Senator Rand Paul (R-KY) had forced a floor vote on whether to provide greater protection for records involving gun sales and banking.

Senator Ron Wyden (D-OR), who had sponsored a different unsuccessful amendment to Section 215, dropped a bombshell: "When the American people find out how their government has secretly interpreted the Patriot Act, they will be stunned and they will be angry."[52] A Justice Department spokesperson declined to explain Wyden's cryptic reference, insisting that there was no problem because congressional oversight committees and the FISA court were aware of the controversial interpretation in question. Ask the librarians whether that's good enough.

Graduate student Sami al-Hussayen, shown here with his sons, was prosecuted for posting links on a website.

College football player Lavoni T. Kidd, who converted to Islam while at the University of Idaho and changed his name to Abdullah al-Kidd, found himself arrested and detained as a "material witness" even though he was never called to testify at any proceeding.

Roya Rahmani (a pseudonym) was jailed and tortured in Iran for supporting a pro-democracy group. She was granted political asylum in the United States and then prosecuted here for supporting the same pro-democracy group.

Erich Scherfen, a Gulf War veteran, was told by his boss that he would lose his job as a commercial pilot if he could not get his name removed from a No Fly list.

Homeland
Security

Traveler Inquiry Form

I. Your Travel Experience

Thank you for contacting the Department of Homeland Security Traveler Redress Inquiry Program (DHS TRIP).
Please check ALL scenarios that describe your travel experience:

- ☐ I am always subjected to additional screening when going through an airport security checkpoint
- ☐ I was denied boarding
- ☐ I am unable to print a boarding pass at the airport kiosk or at home
- ☐ I am directed to the ticket counter every time I fly
- ☐ The airline ticket agent stated that I am on a Federal Government Watch List
- ☐ I was detained during my travel experience
- ☐ A ticket agent took my identification and called someone before handing me a boarding pass
- ☐ I missed my flight while attempting to obtain a boarding pass
- ☐ I am repeatedly referred for secondary screening when clearing U.S. Customs and Border Protection
- ☐ I was denied entry into the United States
- ☐ I am a foreign student or exchange visitor who is unable to travel due to my status
- ☐ I was told my fingerprints were incorrect or of poor quality
- ☐ I feel I have been discriminated against by a government agent based on race, disability, religion, gender, or ethnicity
- ☐ I believe my privacy has been violated because a government agent has exposed or inappropriately shared my personal information
- ☐ I was given an information sheet by a CBP Officer
- ☐ Other travel related issue

II. Personal Information

Full Name:

First   Middle   Last

Date of Birth: Place of Birth:
mm/dd/yyyy   City or Town/Province/Country

Sex: ☐ Male ☐ Female   Height: Weight: Hair Color: Eye Color:

III. Contact Information

Mailing Address:

Street or PO Box   Apt. No.

City or Town   State or Province   Zip or Postal Code   Country

Physical Address (if different):

Street   Apt. No.

City or Town   State or Province   Zip or Postal Code   Country

Home Telephone: Work Telephone:

E-mail Address:

1 of 4

Department of Homeland Security Traveler Redress Inquiry Program (DHS TRIP) form.

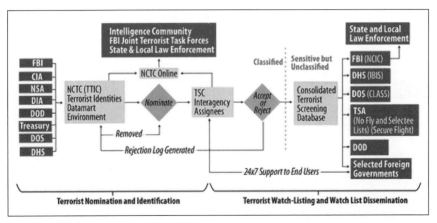

A chart showing the watchlists used by various agencies.

Packing Arabic-English flashcards to study on a flight back to Pomona College turned into a detention and interrogation nightmare for student Nick George.

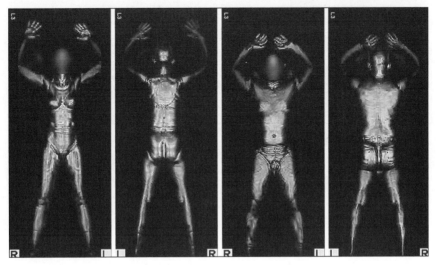

A representation of the kind of image captured by bodyscanner machines in use at airports across the country.

FinCEN Form 109
March 31, 2007
Previous editions will not be accepted after September 30, 2007
(Formerly Form TD F 90-22.56)

Suspicious Activity Report by Money Services Business

▶ **Please type or print. Always complete entire report. Items marked with an asterisk * are considered critical. (See instructions.)**

OMB No. 1506-0015

1 ☐ Check this box only if amending or correcting a prior report (see item 1 instructions)   1a ☐ Check this box if this is a recurring report

Part I   Subject Information   2 ☐ Multiple subjects (see item instructions)

3 Subject type (check only one box)   a ☐ Purchaser/sender   b ☐ Payee/receiver   c ☐ Both a & b   z ☐ Other

*4 Individual's last name or entity's full name	*5 First name	6 Middle initial

*7 Address

*8 City	*9 State	*10 ZIP Code	*11 Country Code (If not US)

*12 Government issued identification (if available)

a ☐ Driver's license/state I.D.   b ☐ Passport   c ☐ Alien registration   z ☐ Other _____

e Number | | | | | | | | | | | | | | | | | | | | | | f Issuing state/country _____

| *13 SSN/ITIN (individual) or EIN (entity) | *14 Date of birth ___/___/___ MM DD YYYY | 15 Telephone number (| | |) | | | - | | | | |

Part II   Suspicious Activity Information

*16 Date or date range of suspicious activity	*17 Total amount involved in suspicious activity a ☐ Amount unknown
From ___/___/___ To ___/___/___	$			,			,			,			.00
MM DD YYYY MM DD YYYY	

*18 Category of suspicious activity (check all that apply)

a ☐ Money laundering   b ☐ Structuring   c ☐ Terrorist financing   z ☐ Other (specify) _____

*19 Financial services involved in the suspicious activity and character of the suspicious activity, including unusual use (check all that apply).

a ☐ Money order   b ☐ Traveler's check   c ☐ Money transfer

z ☐ Other _____   e ☐ Currency exchange

Check all of the following that apply

(1) ☐ Alters transaction to avoid completing funds transfer record or money order or traveler's check record ($3,000 or more)

(5) ☐ Individual(s) using multiple or false identification documents

(2) ☐ Alters transaction to avoid filing CTR form (more than $10,000)

(6) ☐ Two or more individuals using the similar/same identification

(7) ☐ Two or more individuals working together

(3) ☐ Comes in frequently and purchases less than $3,000

(8) ☐ Same individual(s) using multiple locations over a short time period

(4) ☐ Changes spelling or arrangement of name

(9) ☐ Offers a bribe in the form of a tip/gratuity

(10) ☐ Exchanges small bills for large bills or vice versa

If mailing, send each completed SAR report to:
Enterprise Computing Center - Detroit
Attn: SAR-MSB
P.O. Box 33117
Detroit, MI 48232-0980

A free secure e-filing system is available to file this report. Go to http://bsaefiling.fincen.treas.gov for more information and to register.

Catalog No. 49340J   (Rev. 3/07)

Suspicious Activity Reporting form, page 1.

OFFICE OF FOREIGN ASSETS CONTROL

SPECIALLY DESIGNATED NATIONALS AND BLOCKED PERSONS

January 21, 2011

2ND ACADEMY OF NATURAL SCIENCES (a.k.a. ACADEMY OF NATURAL SCIENCES; a.k.a. CHAYON KWAHAK-WON; a.k.a. CHE 2 CHAYON KWAHAK-WON; a.k.a. KUKPANG KWAHAK-WON; a.k.a. NATIONAL DEFENSE ACADEMY; a.k.a. SANSRI; a.k.a. SECOND ACADEMY OF NATURAL SCIENCES; a.k.a. SECOND ACADEMY OF NATURAL SCIENCES RESEARCH INSTITUTE), Pyongyang, Korea, North [NPWMD]

3MG (a.k.a. MIZAN MACHINE MANUFACTURING GROUP), P.O. Box 16595-365, Tehran, Iran [NPWMD]

7 KARNES, Avenida Ciudad de Cali No. 15A-91, Local A06-07, Bogota, Colombia; Matricula Mercantil No 1978075 (Colombia) [SDNTK]

7TH OF TIR (a.k.a. 7TH OF TIR COMPLEX; a.k.a. 7TH OF TIR INDUSTRIAL COMPLEX; a.k.a. 7TH OF TIR INDUSTRIES; a.k.a. 7TH OF TIR INDUSTRIES OF ISFAHAN/ESFAHAN; a.k.a. MOJTAMAE SANATE HAFTOME TIR; a.k.a. SANAYE HAFTOME TIR; a.k.a. SEVENTH OF TIR), P.O. Box 81465-478, Isfahan, Iran; Mobarakeh Road Km 45, Isfahan, Iran [NPWMD]

7TH OF TIR COMPLEX (a.k.a. 7TH OF TIR; a.k.a. 7TH OF TIR INDUSTRIAL COMPLEX; a.k.a. 7TH OF TIR INDUSTRIES; a.k.a. 7TH OF TIR INDUSTRIES OF ISFAHAN/ESFAHAN; a.k.a. MOJTAMAE SANATE HAFTOME TIR; a.k.a. SANAYE HAFTOME TIR; a.k.a. SEVENTH OF TIR), P.O. Box 81465-478, Isfahan, Iran; Mobarakeh Road Km 45, Isfahan, Iran [NPWMD]

7TH OF TIR INDUSTRIAL COMPLEX (a.k.a. 7TH OF TIR; a.k.a. 7TH OF TIR COMPLEX; a.k.a. 7TH OF TIR INDUSTRIES; a.k.a. 7TH OF TIR INDUSTRIES OF ISFAHAN/ESFAHAN; a.k.a. MOJTAMAE SANATE HAFTOME TIR; a.k.a. SANAYE HAFTOME TIR; a.k.a. SEVENTH OF TIR), P.O. Box 81465-478, Isfahan, Iran; Mobarakeh Road Km 45, Isfahan, Iran [NPWMD]

7TH OF TIR INDUSTRIES (a.k.a. 7TH OF TIR; a.k.a. 7TH OF TIR COMPLEX; a.k.a. 7TH OF TIR INDUSTRIAL COMPLEX; a.k.a. 7TH OF TIR INDUSTRIES OF ISFAHAN/ESFAHAN; a.k.a. MOJTAMAE SANATE HAFTOME TIR; a.k.a. SANAYE HAFTOME TIR; a.k.a. SEVENTH OF TIR), P.O. Box 81465-478, Isfahan, Iran; Mobarakeh Road Km 45, Isfahan, Iran [NPWMD]

7TH OF TIR INDUSTRIES OF ISFAHAN/ESFAHAN (a.k.a. 7TH OF TIR; a.k.a. 7TH OF TIR COMPLEX; a.k.a. 7TH OF TIR INDUSTRIAL COMPLEX; a.k.a. 7TH OF TIR INDUSTRIES; a.k.a. MOJTAMAE SANATE HAFTOME TIR; a.k.a. SANAYE HAFTOME TIR; a.k.a. SEVENTH OF TIR), P.O. Box 81465-478, Isfahan, Iran; Mobarakeh Road Km 45, Isfahan, Iran [NPWMD]

8TH IMAM INDUSTRIES GROUP (a.k.a. CRUISE MISSILE INDUSTRY GROUP; a.k.a. CRUISE SYSTEMS INDUSTRY GROUP; a.k.a. NAVAL DEFENCE MISSILE INDUSTRY GROUP; a.k.a. SAMEN AL-A'EMMEH INDUSTRIES GROUP), Tehran, Iran [NPWMD]

17 NOVEMBER (a.k.a. EPANASTATIKI ORGANOSI 17 NOEMVRI; a.k.a. REVOLUTIONARY ORGANIZATION 17 NOVEMBER) [FTO] [SDGT]

32 COUNTY SOVEREIGNTY COMMITTEE (a.k.a. 32 COUNTY SOVEREIGNTY

MOVEMENT; a.k.a. IRISH REPUBLICAN PRISONERS WELFARE ASSOCIATION; a.k.a. REAL IRA; a.k.a. REAL IRISH REPUBLICAN ARMY; a.k.a. REAL OGLAIGH NA HEIREANN; a.k.a. RIRA) [FTO] [SDGT]

32 COUNTY SOVEREIGNTY MOVEMENT (a.k.a. 32 COUNTY SOVEREIGNTY COMMITTEE; a.k.a. IRISH REPUBLICAN PRISONERS WELFARE ASSOCIATION; a.k.a. REAL IRA; a.k.a. REAL IRISH REPUBLICAN ARMY; a.k.a. REAL OGLAIGH NA HEIREANN; a.k.a. RIRA) [FTO] [SDGT]

101 DAYS CAMPAIGN (a.k.a. CHARITY COALITION; a.k.a. COALITION OF GOOD; a.k.a. ETELAF AL-KHAIR; a.k.a. ETILAFU EL-KHAIR; a.k.a. I'TILAF AL-KHAIR; a.k.a. I'TILAF AL-KHAYR; a.k.a. UNION OF GOOD), P.O. Box 136301, Jeddah 21313, Saudi Arabia [SDGT]

2000 DOSE E.U. (a.k.a. DOMA E M), Calle 31 No. 1-34, Cali, Colombia; NIT # 805015749-3 (Colombia) [SDNT]

2000-DODGE S.L., Calle Gran Via 80, Madrid, Madrid, Spain; C.I.F. B83149955 (Spain)

2904977 CANADA, INC. (a.k.a. CARIBE SOL; a.k.a. HAVANTUR CANADA INC.), 818 rue Sherbrooke East, Montreal, Quebec H2L 1K3, Canada [CUBA]

A A TRADING FZCO, P.O. Box 37089, Dubai, United Arab Emirates [SDNTK]

A K DIFUSION S.A. PUBLICIDAD Y MERCADEO, Calle 28N No. 6BN-54, Cali, Colombia; NIT # 900015699-8 (Colombia) [SDNT]

A K EDUCAL S.A. EDUCACION CON CALIDAD, Calle 28N No. 6BN-54, Cali, Colombia; NIT # 900015704-7 (Colombia) [SDNT]

A RAHMAN, Mohamad Iqbal (a.k.a. ABDURRAHMAN, Abu Jibril; a.k.a. ABDURRAHMAN, Mohamad Iqbal; a.k.a. MUQTI, Fihiruddin; a.k.a. MUQTI, Fikiruddin; a.k.a. RAHMAN, Mohamad Iqbal; a.k.a. "ABU JIBRIL"); DOB 17 Aug 1958; POB Tirpas-Selong Village, East Lombok, Indonesia; nationality Indonesia (individual) [SDGT]

A Y A LA CASCAJERA S.A. (a.k.a. COMERCIALIZADORA INTERNACIONAL ASFALTOS Y AGREGADOS LAS CASCAJERA S.A.), Calle 100 No. 8A-49, Trr. B, Oficina 505, Bogota, Colombia; NIT # 900155202-1 (Colombia) [SDNT]

A.I.C. COMPREHENSIVE RESEARCH INSTITUTE (a.k.a. A.I.C. SOGO KENKYUSHO; a.k.a. ALEPH; a.k.a. AUM SHINRIKYO; a.k.a. AUM SUPREME TRUTH) [FTO] [SDGT]

A.I.C. SOGO KENKYUSHO (a.k.a. A.I.C. COMPREHENSIVE RESEARCH INSTITUTE; a.k.a. ALEPH; a.k.a. AUM SHINRIKYO; a.k.a. AUM SUPREME TRUTH) [FTO] [SDGT]

A.T.E. INTERNATIONAL LTD. (a.k.a. RWR INTERNATIONAL COMMODITIES), 3 Mandeville Place, London, United Kingdom [IRAQ2]

A.W.A. ENGINEERING LIMITED, 3 Mandeville Place, London, United Kingdom [IRAQ2]

ABADIA BASTIDAS, Carmen Alicia (a.k.a. ABADIA DE RAMIREZ, Carmen Alicia), c/o DISDROGAS LTDA., Yumbo, Valle, Colombia; c/o RAMIREZ ABADIA Y CIA. S.C.S., Cali, Colombia; Calle 9 No. 39-65, Cali, Colombia; DOB 15 Jul 1934; POB Palmira, Valle,

Colombia; Cedula No. 29021074 (Colombia) (individual) [SDNT]

ABADIA DE RAMIREZ, Carmen Alicia (a.k.a. ABADIA BASTIDAS, Carmen Alicia), c/o DISDROGAS LTDA., Yumbo, Valle, Colombia; c/o RAMIREZ ABADIA Y CIA. S.C.S., Cali, Colombia; Calle 9 No. 39-65, Cali, Colombia; DOB 15 Jul 1934; POB Palmira, Valle, Colombia; Cedula No. 29021074 (Colombia) (individual) [SDNT]

ABAROA DIAZ, Victor Manuel, c/o TIENDA MARINA ABAROA, La Paz, Baja California Sur, Mexico; C. Antonio Navarro S/N, Col. Centro, La Paz, Baja California Sur 23000, Mexico; DOB 30 May 1955; POB La Paz, Baja California Sur, Mexico; citizen Mexico; nationality Mexico; C.U.R.P. AADV550530HBSBZC00 (Mexico); R.F.C. AADV550530UQ0 (Mexico) (individual) [SDNTK]

ABAROA FOX MARINE (a.k.a. MATERIALES Y REFACCIONES ABAROA; a.k.a. TIENDA MARINA ABAROA), Abasolo S/N, Col. El Manglito, La Paz, Baja California Sur 23060, Mexico; Leona Vicario 1000 E/Alvaro Obregon, Benito Juarez, Cabo San Lucas, Baja California Sur 23469, Mexico; R.F.C. AADV550530UQO (Mexico) [SDNTK]

ABAROA PRECIADO, Aristoteles (a.k.a. ABAROA PRECIADO, Aristoteles Alejandro), La Paz, Baja California Sur, Mexico; DOB 29 Sep 1981; POB La Paz, Baja California Sur, Mexico; citizen Mexico; nationality Mexico; C.U.R.P. AAPA810929HBSBRR19 (Mexico) (individual) [SDNTK]

ABAROA PRECIADO, Aristoteles Alejandro (a.k.a. ABAROA PRECIADO, Aristoteles), La Paz, Baja California Sur, Mexico; DOB 29 Sep 1981; POB La Paz, Baja California Sur, Mexico; citizen Mexico; nationality Mexico; C.U.R.P. AAPA810929HBSBRR19 (Mexico) (individual) [SDNTK]

ABAROA PRECIADO, Rosa Yolanda Nabila, Ave. Mariano Abasolo S/N Barr, La Paz, Baja California Sur 23060, Mexico; DOB 19 May 1985; POB Baja California Sur, Mexico; citizen Mexico; nationality Mexico; C.U.R.P. AAPR850519MBSBRS00 (Mexico); Passport 05070005312 (Mexico) (individual) [SDNTK]

ABAROA PRECIADO, Victor Hussein, C. Antonio Navarro S/N, La Paz, Baja California Sur 23000, Mexico; DOB 23 Jun 1978; POB La Paz, Baja California Sur, Mexico; citizen Mexico; nationality Mexico; C.U.R.P. AAPV780623HBSBRC09 (Mexico) (individual) [SDNTK]

ABASTECEDORA NAVAL Y INDUSTRIAL, S.A. (a.k.a. ANAINSA), Panama [CUBA]

ABAUNZA MARTINEZ, Javier; DOB 1 Jan 1965; POB Guernica, Vizcaya Province, Spain; D.N.I. 78.865.882 (Spain); Member ETA (individual) [SDGT]

ABBAKAR MUHAMAD, Abdul Aziz; DOB 1961; POB Sudan; Passport 562605 (Sudan) issued 28 Oct 1998; IARA Peshwar, Pakistan Director (individual) [SDGT]

ABBAS, Abdul Hussein, Italy (individual) [IRAQ2]

ABBAS, Abu (a.k.a. ZAYDAN, Muhammad); DOB 10 Dec 1948; Director of PALESTINE LIBERATION FRONT - ABU ABBAS FACTION (individual) [SDT]

ABBAS, Kassim, Lerchesbergring 23A, D-60598, Frankfurt, Germany; DOB 7 Aug 1956; POB Baghdad, Iraq (individual) [IRAQ2]

The first of 500 pages of the Office of Foreign Assets Control Specially Designated Nationals Watchlist.

American citizen Brandon Mayfield and his family were searched under the Foreign Intelligence Surveillance Act after the FBI mistakenly matched his fingerprint with one found in Spain.

George Christian was prohibited from telling Congress about his own experience with an FBI demand for information about library patrons.

George Christian, with his Executive Committee colleagues at Library Connection of Connecticut, Barbara Bailey, Peter Chase, and Janet Nocek, at a press conference held after nine months of litigation and after the Patriot Act provision they wanted to testify about had been reenacted.

Internet service provider Nick Merrill spent over six years gagged from telling anyone that he was the John Doe challenging the constitutionality of this National Security Letter demanding information about one of his clients.

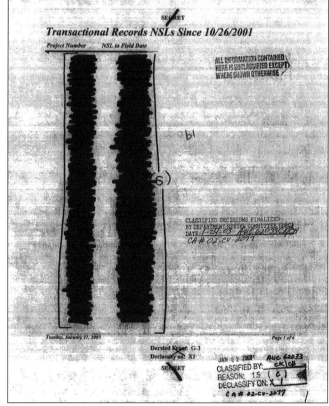

Page 1 of a document released in response to an ACLU Freedom of Information Act request for information about the frequency of use of National Security Letters.

8.
Gagging the Librarians

The Patriot Act affects real lives and even an ordinary American like me can end up being targeted by the FBI.—Barbara Bailey, President, Library Connection Inc.; Director, Welles-Turner Memorial Library, Glastonbury, Connecticut (2006)

The Patriot Act inverts the constitutional requirement that people's lives be private and the work of government officials be public; it instead crafts a set of conditions in which our inner lives become transparent and the workings of the government become opaque. Either one of these outcomes would imperil democracy; together they not only injure the country but also cut off the avenues of repair.—Elaine Scarry (2004)[1]

The Library Connection

George Christian isn't sure if it's accurate to call him a librarian. As Executive Director of Library Connection of Connecticut, he works with computer systems in the libraries that belong to his consortium. It is certainly accurate to call him a true patriot. When he had an unexpected brush with the War on Terror, he put his personal comfort and convenience aside and stood up for principle—the principles of First Amendment freedom of speech and of democracy itself.

It all started on July 13, 2005, when George was handed a National Security Letter, on FBI letterhead:

Under the authority of Executive Order 12333, dated December 4, 1981, and pursuant to Title 18, United States Code (U.S.C.), Section 2709 (as amended October 26, 2001), you are hereby directed to provide to the Federal Bureau of Investigation (FBI) any or all subscriber information, billing information and access logs of any person or entity related to the following: IP address 216.47.180.118, Date: 2/16/2005; Time: 16:00 to 16:45 PM EST. . . .

You are further advised that Title 18, U.S.C., Section 2709(c) prohibits any officer, employee or agent of yours from disclosing to any person that the FBI has sought or obtained access to information or records under this provision.

George hadn't known about the National Security Letter provision in Section 505 of the Patriot Act. Along with his librarian colleagues, he had been concerned about the "library provision" (Section 215, described in the last chapter, which watered down the standard for court-ordered seizure of library records). Librarians were worried about the consequences of allowing FBI agents to check out whether library users were checking out a biography of Osama bin Laden. They were also worried about how to handle their new role as assistant government agents. George had discussed with leaders of other library consortiums in Connecticut whether they should hire a lawyer to help them develop a privacy policy and procedures to cope with Patriot Act enforcement. But when Attorney General Ashcroft announced in September 2003 that Section 215 had never been used in a library or bookstore, George and his colleagues accepted the assurance and decided not to spend money on a lawyer. "We trusted them but apparently we shouldn't have," he says.[2]

A number of librarians were mystified by Ashcroft's and then Gonzales's statements that the controversial court order provision had never been used in libraries because FBI agents had come to them and demanded information about their patrons.[3] It turned out that the FBI was indeed asking librarians for records, but using National Security Letters (NSLs) instead of the Section 215 court orders, so Ashcroft and Gonzales were technically correct. The NSL—a kind of do-it-yourself order the FBI and some other agencies can use to gather certain kinds of information—had started out as a narrow exception to consumer privacy laws but had expanded to cover not only financial records and credit reports, but also Internet subscriber information including electronic records. This authorization applies to libraries that offer computers for public use. The range of information available under a National Security Letter is not nearly as broad as what can be obtained under Section 215. Under an NSL, the FBI is not entitled to get the content of records showing what books a patron is reading. But agents do not have to go to a court at all in order to issue an NSL and so if they are only looking for particular kinds of information about customers and patrons, like names, addresses, and billing records, this form of self-help is very convenient. At the time George received his

NSL, the FBI interpreted the statute in question as also covering information about what websites patrons visit, what e-mail addresses they use, and other information about the patrons themselves. (As chapter 9 will discuss, a 2008 Office of Legal Counsel memo later rejected that interpretation.[4]) If Section 215 removed the alarm from the front door, the National Security Letter provision blasted a large hole in the back door.

It turned out that the apparently simple demand for information in the NSL George received would have involved turning over a massive amount of information about Connecticut library patrons. Library Connection is a consortium of twenty-six libraries in the Hartford, Connecticut, area, which was organized to provide a common computer system to control catalog information, patron records, and circulation information for its member libraries. Modern libraries rely on a lot more technology than just paper card catalogs and books. The IP address given in the NSL was a router at one of the libraries, and there was no way to trace the path from a particular router to a specific computer. And so complying with the NSL would involve telling the FBI who was using every computer in the library in question on that day. And because there was no way to determine who had used computers in that library on a particular day five months earlier, "subscriber information of any entity related" to that IP address would have to be construed as a request for information on all the patrons of that library—a very broad dragnet indeed. Approximately 288,000 people held library cards with the Connecticut libraries involved in the consortium; many people without library cards also use the libraries.[5]

George's indignant reaction was that he wanted to testify before Congress to "raise a big patriotic American flag of caution about how our civil liberties are being sorely tested by law enforcement abuses of national security letters." Congress, as he knew, was currently debating whether or not to extend Patriot Act provisions including Section 215, but was being lulled by the misleading reassurance of Attorney General Gonzales that any concern about undue intrusion on libraries was baseless because that specific power was not being used.[6] But the absolute gag order under this provision, like the gag order attached to Section 215, commanded him not to tell anyone at all (except perhaps his own "officer, employee or agent") that he had received an NSL. The gag order was so stark that it did not, on its face, allow him to consult an attorney or go to court to challenge either the constitutionality of the gag order, or the production demand that turned out to be extremely burdensome and perhaps impossible. But George decided that he would not let the threat of the gag order stop him from consulting a lawyer. In addition to his concern about the gag order, George also thought hard about whether the information sought might be urgently needed in connection with the FBI's hot pursuit of a dangerous suspect. In considering what to do, he thought it was significant that the NSL he received was dated several months before it was served on him, that it referred to computer use five months earlier, and that several days before serving the NSL, an FBI agent had called to inquire about the correct name of the person who should receive the demand. These circumstances, in combination, made him think that the information sought was not so urgently needed that he could not at least consult a lawyer to help him figure out how to respond. His conclusion that this was not an urgent request was borne out when, months later, the government withdrew the request for information.

The lawyer George consulted had never heard of National Security Letters either. But the lawyer's assistant did some research, which turned up the story of an Internet service provider known as "John Doe" who, on receiving a National Security Letter consulted the ACLU, went to court, and won his constitutional challenge to the statute's absolute gag order provisions. Before the 2005 Patriot Act reauthorization hearings, a New York federal court in John Doe's case had ruled that despite the statute's absolute terms, the Constitution requires giving NSL recipients a chance to consult a lawyer and to ask a court to relax the demands made of them. The same judge had also ruled that permanent, absolute gag orders violate the First Amendment unless they are actually justified by the circumstances of the individual case.[7]

George's attorney told him that the only way to challenge his National Security Letter or his gag order was to follow in John Doe's footsteps and bring a lawsuit against the Attorney General in federal court. Reluctant to make such a weighty and potentially costly decision by himself, George decided to consult the three other members of the Executive Committee of Library Connection, his organization's officers: Barbara Bailey (President; Director, Welles-Turner Memorial Library, Glastonbury), Peter Chase (Vice President; Director, Plainville Public Library), and Janet Nocek (Secretary; Library Director, Portland Library). All four officers fully appreciated the importance of antiterrorism investigations—Janet Nocek had a friend who had died on one of the planes that crashed into the World Trade Center—but they agreed that they were defending democracy by insisting that the checks and balances established in the Constitution be observed. So the four decided to engage the ACLU to bring a lawsuit on

Library Connection's behalf to seek relief from the gag order. (The ACLU became a co-plaintiff because its own lawyers and agents were also gagged from discussing the litigation.) The first stage of the litigation aimed to achieve modest goals: first, to allow the Executive Committee's actions to be presented to the full Library Connection Board, and second, to allow the four to identify themselves and testify before Congress so that the fact that a demand like this had indeed been made in a library could become part of the national debate surrounding renewal of the Patriot Act. "Everyone has the responsibility," says George, "to make sure the government plays by the rules." George and his colleagues did not seek permission to disclose the letter's actual contents. In deference to the government's national security concerns, the Library Connection Executive Committee members were willing to keep quiet about the particular information that had been sought. They just wanted to speak about their own experience and to impress upon Congress their view that the FBI should not be allowed to demand information like this without judicial review.

But George and his colleagues were to discover that the gag order's impact went beyond prohibiting them from testifying before Congress. George prepared an affidavit to submit to the Connecticut federal court in the case of *John Doe v. Gonzales*, explaining what had happened. He was then surprised to learn that he and his three colleagues could not attend the court hearing in their own case because of the risk that they might be identified as the plaintiffs. He had become a genuine "John Doe," along with his colleagues. So at the attorneys' request, the court arranged for them to watch the hearing on closed-circuit TV in a locked room in the Hartford Federal Court building, sixty miles from the courthouse in Bridgeport where the case was being argued.[8] The documents in the case were initially filed under seal and could not be viewed on the court's website. On the morning of the hearing, the court permitted a redacted version of the complaint and motion papers to be posted.

The government's insistence on maximum secrecy was based on the "mosaic" theory, as described in the last chapter.[9] Since there is no way to know when a seemingly innocuous piece of information (like a challenge to the scope of statutory gag orders?) might be useful to America's enemies, the government insisted on keeping as much information as possible under wraps. This is another example of dragnet thinking: if there is a 1 percent chance that revealing information might conceivably do harm to national security in some remote manner, that information should remain secret even though enforcing secrecy necessarily defeats the exercise of constitutional rights. There were several constitutional rights at odds with the government's desire to muzzle George and his colleagues. In addition to having a right to freedom of speech under the First Amendment, the librarians also had a right under the First Amendment to petition the government for redress of grievances.[10] The public also has an independent First Amendment right of access to judicial proceedings.[11] And as the judge who was assigned the case concluded, there was no basis for believing that enemies of the United States would gain any advantage by learning the identity of this "John Doe."

Federal judge Janet Hall, who was assigned to hear the case, had worked for the Department of Justice and the U.S. Attorney's Office in Virginia, and was in private law practice when President Bill Clinton nominated her to the bench in 1997. Hall asked the government what reasons it had for keeping the four John Does from describing their NSL experience to Congress or their colleagues. The government initially told Judge Hall that the relevant information was classified and could not even be revealed to her, but Hall pointed out that in her previous work, she had already been granted the highest level of security clearance. As in the *MCA* case, the government insisted on providing its response to Judge Hall ex parte, in secret. The plaintiffs' lawyers, as in the *MCA* case, were not allowed to see the government's evidence and therefore were hard-pressed to reply. Nevertheless, after reviewing the secret evidence, Judge Hall found that the First Amendment gave the librarians a right to speak and that the government had not shown a sufficiently compelling reason to keep the librarians totally gagged. On September 9, she ordered that the government modify the gag order to permit the Library Connection Four to identify themselves and therefore to offer personal testimony to Congress: "Doe's speech would be made more powerful by its ability to put a 'face' on the service of the NSL . . . Doe's statements as a known recipient of a[n] NSL would have a different impact on the public debate than the same statements by a speaker who is not identified as a recipient."[12]

But the government was still determined to prevent the librarians from talking to Congress. At the government's request, Judge Hall stayed her order until September 20, meaning that it would not take effect until after the government had a chance to appeal her decision. The government did appeal and on September 20, the Court of Appeals granted the government a continuing stay. This meant that the librarians would not be able to testify until after the appeal itself was over—if they won. The Patriot Act hearings were expected to conclude by the end of the year, as the provisions at issue were slated to expire at the end of December, and so the librarians and their lawyers were caught in a real-life version of *Beat the Clock*.

Throughout the months since July, the rigors of secrecy had been taking their toll. George and his colleagues were very troubled by the fact that they could not even tell the members of their Board of Directors that they were engaging in this now highly public litigation. That felt to them like an involuntary violation of their fiduciary duty. They could not advise other libraries to prepare for possible receipt of a National Security Letter by establishing policies or procedures to follow. Peter Chase, who was Chairman of the Intellectual Freedom Committee for the Connecticut Library Association and served as a public spokesperson on the subject of the Patriot Act, began to refuse invitations to speak on the topic of surveillance in libraries. The League of Women Voters in Hartford invited Peter and United States Attorney Kevin O'Connor to debate each other on the question of applying the Patriot Act to libraries, reprising a debate the two men had held in March. Peter felt he had to decline the invitation because he now knew too much about the subject and feared that he might slip and divulge something about his personal experience; O'Connor, who was representing the government in the Library Connection case, accepted. Peter says he found it "galling" that O'Connor was traveling around the state "telling people that their library records were safe, while at the same time he was enforcing a gag order preventing me from telling people that their library records were not safe."

Barbara Bailey says, "It was difficult to sit among colleagues and listen to them discuss 'John Doe.' I had to work hard to keep my mouth shut or I would risk jail time." The gag order prevented the four from accepting recognition for their courageous stance, including the 2005 Robert Downs Intellectual Freedom Award presented to "John Doe" by the University of Illinois Graduate School of Library and Information Science. When colleagues talked about the litigation, the four had to keep poker faces; when colleagues were asked to rise and applaud "John Doe" for standing up for principle, they had to stand and applaud themselves appreciatively, for fear of discovery if they acted any differently from people who did not know who John Doe was. More difficult than professional forbearance was maintaining silence with their friends and families. Although no one was supposed to know their identities, reporters speculated and called Library Connection members to request interviews. Peter Chase's son asked at one point, "Dad, is the FBI after you?" To his horror, Peter realized that he was not allowed to reassure his son by answering that question honestly. George Christian's sixteen-year-old son, aware of law enforcement contacts with his father, was afraid that his father would be arrested. To comply with the gag order, George had to be evasive with both his son and his wife, an impossible situation for a man who prides himself on being open and honest. No wonder no NSL recipient beyond one other John Doe had ever challenged the government or the gag order.

On September 21, the day after the Court of Appeals had extended the gag order, a *New York Times* article outed George and his colleagues. Alison Leigh Cowan reported that a "close reading" of the court record revealed that the "John Doe" in the Connecticut case was Library Connection of Connecticut. The story bore the ironic title, "Librarians Must Stay Silent in Patriot Act Suit, Court Says."[13] Cowan had solved the mystery of John Doe's identity because the court's own website inadvertently referred to the case in one spot as *"Library Connection Inc. v. Attorney General"* instead of *"John Doe v. Attorney General."* In addition, some FBI or Justice Department lawyer who had redacted some previously sealed documents before they were posted had failed to omit some telltale facts, including a description of one of the plaintiffs as Chairman of the Intellectual Freedom Committee for the Connecticut Library Association. No one but Peter Chase fit that description.

In light of the *New York Times* report, the ACLU asked to have the stay lifted, given that the entire point of the stay was to prevent anyone from finding out John Doe's identity. That identity had now been disclosed and the clock on the congressional hearings was running. But the government replaced the sloppily redacted documents on the court's website with more carefully redacted versions and argued vigorously against vacating the stay, maintaining that the stay had not become moot: "mere publication of an article that purports to identify the NSL recipient does not let the cat out of the bag."[14] Government lawyers told the court that people in Connecticut do not read the *New York Times* and that studies show that 58 percent of people do not believe what they read in newspapers anyway. The government required all court documents filed in connection with this motion to be filed under seal, at least initially, and also asked to have the argument held in a closed session,[15] all to avoid any public discussion of the formerly secret identity of "John Doe." Bizarrely enough, among the documents that had to be filed under seal was the already published *New York Times* story correctly identifying the Library Connection as John Doe, which had been attached to court papers as an exhibit. Phrases like "the cat is out of the bag" or "the genie is out of the bottle" were censored, as were direct quotations from Supreme Court cases on the right to disclose information that has already been revealed to the public.

One appellate judge, musing on these events in a later opinion, quoted Benjamin Franklin's *Poor Richard's Almanack*: "Three may keep a secret if two of them are dead."[16]

The Court of Appeals refused to vacate the stay. On October 3, the lawyers asked Circuit Justice Ruth Bader Ginsburg to lift the stay, noting that the Patriot Act debates were expected to conclude in the very near future. Although commenting on the irony that the gag was continuing after the cat was in fact out of the bag, Justice Ginsburg declined to vacate the stay, finding that the circumstances were not extraordinary enough to warrant interfering with a pending appellate process that she hoped would be concluded with dispatch. So the Library Connection Four remained mute.[17]

The Court of Appeals heard argument on the government's appeal on November 2, 2005,[18] as the Patriot Act debates continued. On November 6, *Washington Post* reporter Barton Gellman told the story the librarians couldn't tell, beginning his front-page exposé on the proliferation of use of NSLs:

> The FBI came calling in Windsor, Conn., this summer with a document marked for delivery by hand. On Matianuk Avenue, across from the tennis courts, two special agents found their man. They gave George Christian the letter, which warned him to tell no one, ever, what it said.[19]

Gellman reported that George Christian was far from alone: over 30,000 NSLs were being served each year.[20] Congress had not been engaging in much oversight of NSLs at the time and so might not have known what the public was now learning. Thanks to the chain of events set in motion by Gellman's article and the John Doe litigation, we now have official figures. In the year 2000, the FBI had issued 8,500 NSL requests. (Each NSL can contain multiple requests.) After the Patriot Act's expansion, the numbers jumped to 39,346 requests in 2003; 56,507 in 2004; 47,221 in 2005; and 49,425 in 2006.[21] George Christian's experience had been repeated hundreds of thousands of times but, so far as we can tell, he was only the second person to question why he was so utterly gagged.

On March 9, 2006, after protracted debate, a filibuster, and a lot of un-gainly procedural maneuvering, Congress voted to renew the Patriot Act, including Section 215 and the National Security Letter provision, without having had the benefit of testimony from anyone at Library Connection. The following week, the Court of Appeals asked the parties to file additional papers to explain how the extension of the Patriot Act provision in question, with some modest amendments, affected the litigation. One of the modifications provided a procedure for having an NSL gag order lifted, as will be more fully described in the next chapter. The government lawyers announced that because the new statute allowed for the possibility of a gag order not being absolute and permanent, they would no longer contest the Library Connection members revealing their identity. The government had another belated surprise in store for Library Connection: a resounding "never mind." In April, the government not only dropped its legal battle to preserve the gag order, but also withdrew its original demand for Connecticut library records. George Christian was off the hook. He did not have to figure out how to comply with the NSL's difficult—and evidently noncritical—demands. And so the librarians were finally free to speak— six weeks *after* the prolonged and contentious Patriot Act debates had ended. It still took a number of weeks for the necessary court procedures to be completed so the plaintiffs could hold their first press conference.

At that press conference, on May 30, the librarians spoke up at last. Janet Nocek pointed out that "[t]he government's gag order also kept us from having a free discourse with our elected officials when they needed it most. No one got to hear the real story." And George Christian said, "The fact that I can speak now is a little like being permitted to call the Fire Department only after a building has burned to the ground."[22]

On August 2, Justice Ginsburg granted a motion to unseal the Supreme Court's records in the case, and similar motions unsealed records in the Court of Appeals and District Court. All the documents I describe, once treated as explosive, can now be read on the courts' or the ACLU's web-sites. And starting in June 2006, the Library Connection Four freely accepted awards and speaking engagements, recognizing that they are just about the only people in the country allowed to talk about what it is like to be conscripted by the government to turn over information about one's customers or patrons, and then gagged. Janet Nocek told an audience of New Jersey librarians that most of the feedback she has received since her identity was revealed has been quite positive—librarians and others thank her for her willingness to uphold American values of free speech and thought, even at risk of federal prosecution. The only negative commentary she received was one e-mail accusing her of being a "trader" to the United States.[23] Probably not a message from another librarian.

Other Librarian Tales

How many other librarians have shared George Christian's experience? We don't know. The American Library Association, frustrated at the lack of information about the impact of surveillance measures on libraries, administered its own survey in June 2005. One hundred thirty-seven librarians responded that federal, state, or local law enforcement agents had asked them for information about their patrons between October 2001 and June 2005.[24] In light of gag orders, respondents could not be asked for details. And it is possible that, because of gag orders, not all respondents who had received requests for information were willing to say so in response to the questionnaire. Have NSLs been served on librarians under the Obama Administration? We don't know. But we do know that the law still empowers the FBI to use this method of compelling information in libraries and elsewhere and that Barack Obama's Justice Department has been arguing for an extension of the NSL's reach (to be discussed in the next chapter).[25]

A few other librarians have been able to tell their stories publicly. Joan Airoldi, director of the library district in Whatcom, Washington, tells of an FBI agent who stopped by the Deming branch of the Whatcom County Library System (in northeastern Washington) to ask for a list of everyone who had borrowed a particular biography of Osama bin Laden. Like George Christian, the Whatcom librarians consulted their attorney. They concluded that the request was probably a fishing expedition and certainly a problem under the First Amendment. It turned out that a library patron had sent the volume in question to the FBI after noticing words handwritten in the margin describing hostility toward America as "a religious duty." The words were a quotation from a statement bin Laden had made in a news interview. The librarians decided not to turn over the patron records without a subpoena (which is issued by a court, grand jury, or prosecutor, rather than an investigating agency like the FBI).

The FBI returned to the Deming library with a subpoena. (In this case, of course, a National Security Letter would not have been adequate because the FBI was seeking information beyond the bounds of what the NSL statute authorizes—the actual content of library records.) The librarians decided to continue resisting, by asking the court to quash the subpoena on constitutional grounds if necessary. "Who would check out a biography of bin Laden knowing that this might attract the attention of the FBI?" asked Joan Airoldi. Two weeks later, the FBI withdrew the request. Airoldi recognized that she was fortunate that the FBI had gotten a subpoena rather than proceeding under any of the Patriot Act authorities that have gag orders attached, including Section 215 (under which the FBI would be able to seek the identity of someone who borrowed a specific book). "With a Patriot Act order in hand," she said in an op-ed in *USA Today*, "I would have been forbidden to disclose even the fact that I had received it and would not have been able to tell this story."[26]

There are a few other librarian anecdotes publicly available. Former ALA President Carol Brey-Casiano recently told how she came close to being fired in the fall of 2001 for not turning over sign-up sheets for the computer in her El Paso, Texas, library, either in response to someone who showed up at her library identifying himself as a Texas Ranger (accompanied by an unidentified person citing the Patriot Act), or in response to a later court order. She was not able to comply with these requests because her library routinely shredded the computer sign-up sheets every night. But the Texas Ranger filed a complaint about her, perhaps feeling that she had not been sufficiently cooperative or regretful. This led to an extensive investigation during which 140 members of her staff were interrogated. The mayor of El Paso agreed to allow her to remain in her job pending the investigation only if she promised not to tell anyone what was happening—an informal gag order.[27]

Only one other librarian has contested a National Security Letter, so far as we know. Brewster Kahle, founder of the Internet Archive, a digital library used by researchers, historians, scholars, and government agencies, received a demand for personal information about one of the archive's users, including name, address, and "electronic communication transactional records." The demand included a gag order. He turned to the Electronic Frontier Foundation, which, together with the ACLU, brought a lawsuit challenging the constitutionality of the NSL. He believed that the NSL in his case was actually improper under the terms of the statute itself.[28] As had happened to George Christian, Brewster Kahle could not tell his own Board of Directors about the NSL, the legal issues it presented, or his decision to litigate. And his lawyers could not talk about this instance of NSL usage directed at a library even though one of those lawyers, Jameel Jaffer, was testifying on behalf of the ACLU at a congressional hearing on the FBI's use and misuse of NSLs. The case was settled, with results similar to the ultimate resolution of the Library Connection case. The FBI agreed to lift the gag order in part, to allow Brewster Kahle and his attorneys to talk about their experiences with this NSL. As had happened in the case of the Library Connection officers, the only other librarians to challenge an NSL, the government also withdrew the NSL request for information about a library patron. For its part, the Internet Archive agreed not to disclose the contents of the demand, the same distinction the Library Connection Four had been willing to observe. If the demands that were litigated were representative of the kind of information the government used NSLs to get librarians to provide, it may not be essential to use NSLs in libraries after all.

It seems unlikely that these two examples—Library Connection and the Internet Archive—are the only instances in which NSLs have been served on a library given that there have been hundreds of thousands of NSL requests. But we don't know. In 2003 the House Judiciary Committee asked Assistant Attorney General Viet Dinh how many times a Section 215 court order had been issued to libraries and was told that the answer was classified.[29] In 2007, the Senate Judiciary Committee asked the FBI how many NSLs had been served on libraries in 2007 and was told that figure was unknown but determinable.[30] The answer may have been transmitted to Congress, but it was not made public.[31] Appearing on a panel at a bar association event in New York, Viet Dinh was later asked what he had learned from his experiences with the Patriot Act. His response? "Don't ever cross librarians!"

The expanded NSL provision, Section 505 of the Patriot Act, had not been scheduled to sunset in 2005 but, following the *John Doe* litigation brought by the Library Connection Four and the Internet service provider described in the next chapter, Congress nevertheless made some changes to this provision. Two of those changes—concerning the rights of NSL recipients and the gag order—will be discussed more fully in the next chapter. Another was a theatrical gesture in the direction of exempting libraries from National Security Letters—a sop for the librarians.[32] Language in the revised law says that a library functioning in a "traditional role" is not subject to an NSL—unless it is providing "electronic communication services."[33] The exception swallows the exemption because any library providing Internet service—basically every library in the country—is still subject to NSLs. (If the intimation of the amendment seems to be that "traditional" library transactions, like borrowing a book, are now protected, it is worth noting again that the NSLs never applied to the contents of "traditional" records, like the identity of people who borrowed books, in any event.) FBI Director Robert Mueller, in a letter responding to a Senate Judiciary Committee inquiry, opined that the new librarian-appeasing language "did not actually change the law."[34] During the second round of reauthorization hearings, beginning in 2009, Section 215 and its application to libraries was once again a subject of debate, as the previous chapter described, but that provision was extended without any modifications. Limiting the scope of National Security Letters, like the scope of Section 215, continues to be the subject of a number of proposed bills as this book goes to press.

Even if Congress favored any of the proposed revisions, the modification to the Patriot Act authority granted would be small and would have been slow in coming. This seems surprising in light of the widespread support the librarians generated. The public reacted viscerally to the specter of the FBI in the library, more so than to any of the other Patriot Act revisions of the law.[35] Both Section 215 and the NSL threaten First and Fourth Amendment values of librarians and their patrons by exposing so much private information to the government with so little oversight. This is a significant threat. But fewer people have been aware of the absolute, permanent gag order the Library Connection Four challenged, a limitation on speech that compromises democracy itself. As Elaine Scarry so elegantly put it, the combination of government-imposed secrecy and individual loss of privacy not only inverts the preconditions for democracy, but also cuts off the "avenues of repair."[36] How can the American people make sound decisions about the acceptability of something like the "library provision" if everyone who knows how that provision has actually been used is silenced?

The best place to end this story is with Janet Nocek's invitation: "Let the American people decide whether a shroud of secrecy has descended upon all of us that might affect not just a few librarians, but any ordinary 'John Doe.'"

9.

John Doe and the National Security Letter

No more National Security Letters to spy on citizens who are not suspected of a crime.—Candidate Barack Obama (2007)

My name is not John Doe and this is not my real voice.—Unidentified actor reading a statement written by "John Doe" (2007)

THE LIBRARY CONNECTION Four lived under government-imposed silence for about the length of a pregnancy. The John Doe who preceded and inspired them, the president of a small Internet access and consulting business in New York, was gagged for over six years. When he received a National Security Letter in February 2004 demanding that he provide information about one of his clients, "Doe" says he immediately noticed two things: that there was no judge's signature and that he was commanded not to tell anyone, ever, about his grave concern that this demand was unconstitutional. With no precedent to reassure him, he nevertheless dared to consult lawyers at the ACLU and go to court even though he was always aware that challenging the government might not be easy. "Doe" says that when he met with his lawyers for the first time, he asked them, "How do I know if I file this lawsuit they won't put me in a sack and drag me away?" When the lawyers told him that they could not predict what would happen, he replied that he was nevertheless willing to go ahead.

The lawsuit he filed in April 2004 to challenge his National Security Letter was originally entitled *John Doe v. Ashcroft*. As the years passed, it was renamed *Doe v. Gonzales*, then *Doe v. Mukasey*, and then *Doe v. Holder*, as each successive Attorney General took office. In an anonymous 2007 op-ed in the *Washington Post*, "Doe" described living under this prolonged regimen of silence as "stressful and surreal":

When I meet with my attorneys I cannot tell my girlfriend where I am going or where I have been. I hide any papers related to the case where she will not look. When clients and friends ask me whether

I am the one challenging the constitutionality of the NSL statute, I have no choice but to look them in the eye and lie.[1]

Amy Goodman of *Democracy Now* co-wrote a book in which she mentioned John Doe's story—but without knowing at the time that the John Doe she was describing happened to be someone she knew.[2] Although Obama Administration lawyers initially argued that John Doe had to keep concealing his identity for national security reasons, they ultimately agreed to a compromise settlement in the summer of 2010. After more than six years of forced guile and deceit, "John Doe" could finally reveal his secret identity: Nicholas Merrill, whose Internet company, Calyx Internet Access Corporation, served clients ranging from IKEA to Snapple to *Democracy Now*. Why did Nick Merrill risk litigating despite the gag order and then keep litigating for over six stressful years? In his own words:

> [I]t's a total cliché, but, you know, all that's necessary for evil to triumph is for good men to do nothing. I felt this was something I had to do. And as an internet provider or a systems administrator or a telephone technician, you have a lot of information that paints a really vivid picture about people's personal, private lives and communications.[3]

In addition to challenging the gag order, Nick Merrill challenged the National Security Letters themselves, arguing that the Patriot Act provision expanding their use violated the First and Fourth Amendments. It was important to him that his lawyers urge not only widely known First Amendment free speech rights, but also less appreciated Fourth Amendment privacy rights. Nick had taken Constitutional Law at Hampshire College and had considered at one point becoming a lawyer because the rights he learned about, including the Fourth Amendment, seemed to him to be critically important. As it turned out, he found a way to defend those rights without going to law school. Since his lawsuit began, the National Security Letter has become a key battleground where dragnet surveillance methods contend with fundamental constitutional values of privacy and free speech, where our desire to trust the executive branch is challenged by the fact that we know abuses are engendered by secrecy, and where secrecy's threat to democracy is most apparent.

One reason NSLs loom large is that, unlike the infrequently used Patriot Act section that had become known as the "library provision" before George Christian discovered that nickname was misplaced, National Security Letters have been used for hundreds of thousands of "requests."

Another is that, as the last chapter suggested, National Security Letters take one more giant step away from Fourth Amendment norms beyond even the hollow "library provision" court orders: the letters need not be preceded by any individualized suspicion and they do not involve any court at all. The FBI decides when to use them and then requires the people who experience this technique firsthand to remain silent, on pain of federal prosecution. Because NSLs are used against electronic service providers, including both librarians and Internet service providers, First Amendment values are very much at stake. If the FBI can indeed use a self-service NSL to gather information about what websites Internet users visit or what e-mail addresses appear in their correspondence, the government has much of the Big Brother power the librarians feared, but with no judicial check at all.

The Library Connection plaintiffs challenged the NSLs themselves as well as the gag orders, but they only actually litigated the constitutionality of the gag orders. Like the Library Connection Four, Nick wanted to testify before Congress but was not allowed to do so. He would have told Congress that he believed that gag orders do damage beyond preventing Americans from speaking to their own legislators and courts—they actually enable abuses of power by giving government agencies too much space to hide. At the time Nick started his lawsuit, the public, like George Christian's first lawyer, knew very little about National Security Letters. Barton Gellman's informative 2005 *Washington Post* article had not yet been published; no other court had been asked to consider the constitutionality of this authority; and Congress was not doing much in the way of oversight. The ACLU had succeeded in getting some documents pertaining to the use of NSLs released in Freedom of Information Act litigation: six almost entirely blacked-out pages, which suggested that NSLs were being used, but not to what extent.[4] As more was revealed over time, Nick's fears proved to be quite justified. The chain of events set in motion by his lawsuit led Congress to a long overdue decision to exercise greater oversight over the use of National Security Letters, leading in turn to shocking revelations about how the FBI behaved when it was not being checked by Congress, the courts, or the people themselves. In May 2007, the Inspector General of the Justice Department reported that by that date, the FBI had racked up about 3,000 violations of its own NSL rules and procedures, and had provided false information to Congress in the few areas where it did report.[5] That secrecy could cover up abuse of power was no longer just a hypothetical fear. Had Nick and the Library Connection officers been permitted to share their experiences and their concerns with Congress and the public earlier, might some of that abuse have been averted?

Although the law did change in some respects as a result of Nick's litigation, the central problem remains: NSLs still allow the FBI to collect a great deal of information about innocent people and to avoid the courts. And Barack Obama has embraced this power. Obama changed his position on National Security Letters with his change of position from candidate to president, even asking Congress to expand the scope of information NSLs can command.[6]

Why National Security Letters?

When the first procedure resembling a National Security Letter was created, it was, ironically enough, as part of the 1978 Right to Financial Privacy Act[7] (Congress's response to the *Miller* case's declaration that financial records were not protected by the Fourth Amendment at all). The statute provided procedural protection for financial records but created a narrow exception allowing specific executive agencies to invite "financial institutions" to share limited kinds of credit information about suspected terrorists or spies.[8] These invitations were designed to be a less coercive alternative to court orders. The point of the exception was just to assure custodians that if they provided their customers' records in response to a national security investigation, they would not be liable for violating federal privacy law.[9] This was another legislative baby step.

The authors of this exception probably would not recognize the vast, coercive power the NSL has become today. The statute under which most NSLs are issued currently, the Electronic Communications Privacy Act (ECPA), was also written to protect privacy—the privacy of electronic communications after the *Smith* case (which permitted government to demand telephone company records at will) left information like telephone logs outside the Fourth Amendment's umbrella. The ECPA also allowed a narrow exception to its privacy protections, authorizing the use of NSLs to require electronic communication service providers to turn over subscriber information, billing records, and "electronic communication transactional records,"[10] a term the statute does not define. This is the section covering libraries that offer their patrons computers and, of course, Internet service providers.[11] NSLs can obviously scoop up an enormous quantity of information in either area—financial records or electronic communications records. As Barton Gellman's 2005 *Washington Post* exposé, "The FBI's Secret Scrutiny: In Hunt for Terrorists, Bureau Examines Records of Ordinary

Americans," reported and the mayor of Las Vegas deplored, the FBI used NSLs to gather information from car rental companies, casinos, and other "financial institutions," concerning the activities of nearly a million people who had visited Las Vegas during a certain time period. Internet service providers like AOL, as Nick says, have access to vast quantities of information about their subscribers—and what if the term "electronic service provider" is deemed to cover Internet hosts like Google, social network providers like Facebook, and perhaps even cafés and businesses that, like Starbucks or Delta Airlines, offer WiFi access to their customers?[12]

That's why it matters that Congress kept lowering the standard for using an NSL. Like the FISA provisions that applied to Brandon Mayfield (the mismatched fingerprint case), the original NSL provisions in the Financial Privacy and Electronic Communications Acts distinguished between ordinary Americans on the one hand, and "foreign" spies or terrorists on the other. To use an NSL, agents had to have "specific and articulable facts" that their target was a foreign power or a foreign power's agent, the kind of individualized suspicion requirement that applied in the *Mayfield* case. All other Americans were exempt from this convenient form of surveillance.[13] In 1993, Congress relaxed the standard for getting an NSL[14] and then, in October 2001, the Patriot Act went a giant step further and removed the suspicion requirement altogether. The combination of these amendments allowed agencies to gather data about Americans they don't actually find suspicious at all if they think information about those people might lead to information about terrorists or spies. FBI agents now only have to certify that the information they seek is "relevant" to a counterterrorism or counterintelligence investigation.[15] They certify this to themselves. FBI agents do not have to persuade a court that information they want is relevant to a terrorism investigation, but only their colleagues, and those colleagues may view "relevance" as a very easy standard to satisfy. One model FBI request to be submitted for a supervisor's signature consisted of one sentence: "This subscriber information is being requested to determine the individuals or entities that the subject has been in contact with during the past six months."[16]

Lowering the threshold encouraged the proliferation of NSLs; as previously noted, the numbers climbed into the hundreds of thousands.[17] Other factors also contributed to the phenomenal growth in the use of NSLs post-9/11. The Patriot Act made this power more widely available by allowing the fifty-six FBI field offices to issue their own NSLs instead of only high officials in the central FBI office, as the law had previously required. Attorney General guidelines were changed in January 2003 to allow NSLs to be used in preliminary investigations instead of only in full investigations.[18] And exacerbating the Big Brother aspect of all this data collection, Attorney General Ashcroft rewrote the applicable Department of Justice guidelines to allow greater retention and sharing of the data collected—regardless of whether anything suspicious was actually found.[19] Databases could be stuffed with information about innocent people as long as someone once thought that collecting information about those people might lead to evidence about someone else. As the Mayfield family discovered, once information was collected, it was in the data banks to stay. And since no court—not even the FISA court—is involved when NSLs are used, there is not even an opportunity for judicial review of the scope of the information gathered, retained, or disseminated.

The scope of the information NSLs can amass has also exploded since 1986 because of the growth of the Internet and the increasingly central role "electronic services" like computers play in people's lives. Although it has not always been clear whether or not agents can obtain website use and e-mail address information using NSLs, Internet service providers can certainly be required to furnish the FBI with a subscriber's name, address, telephone number, account name, e-mail headers, credit card and billing information, and transaction/activity logs. The FBI used its authority, at least until quite recently, to gather data not only about people actually suspected of some sort of terrorist activity, but also about any target's "community of interest"—the entire network of people who had contact with the target.[20]

This astonishingly vast power was virtually untethered. The courts could not serve as a check since there is no provision for judicial involvement. Unlike Section 215, the Patriot Act provision expanding NSL authority did not sunset. The only legislative oversight required was the submission of a semi-annual classified report to congressional intelligence and judiciary committees.[21] But even those reports were secret and NSL recipients themselves were gagged. The public and the rest of Congress were left in the dark and the FBI evidently was left to police itself—until Nick Merrill came along.

John Doe and Victor Marrero

Are National Security Letters unconstitutional? The litigation Nick Merrill and the ACLU brought established that the Patriot Act provision involved violated Nick's First Amendment rights by indiscriminately gagging him, and the First Amendment rights of his Internet clients—to preserve their anonymity in using the Internet—by subjecting them to government scrutiny without a court order. This happened because Nick's case was randomly assigned to a federal judge who was willing to take on hard constitutional questions and evaluate vociferous government demands for secrecy. Most other judges had blinked when confronted with Patriot Act challenges. (When Nick was finally allowed to reveal his identity, he commented wistfully that he wished he could someday meet Judge Marrero, who had presided over his case for years. Like the Library Connection Four, Nick had been instructed by his lawyers not to attend any judicial proceeding where he might be identified.)

Victor Marrero was born in Santurce, Puerto Rico, and was serving as the United States Permanent Representative to the Organization of American States when President Bill Clinton selected him, in 1999, to fill the seat in the Southern District of New York vacated by Sonia Sotomayor, who had just been elevated to the Court of Appeals. His experience with *John Doe v. Ashcroft* began with having to mediate disputes about how deeply secret this litigation would be. Under the mosaic theory (that any bit of information might become dangerous when combined with other bits), the government did not want a single piece of information about the case to be made public. Judge Marrero concluded that it would not compromise national security for the public to know that this cryptically named lawsuit existed. Allowing the lawsuit to be conducted in secret would have conflicted with the Constitution's view of the importance of the right of public access to judicial proceedings. But when the ACLU then posted a cautious press release on its website, the government demanded removal of innocuous material like the court's briefing schedule and a description of National Security Letters that scrupulously tracked the language of the statute. Judge Marrero had to issue another ruling declaring which details could be posted.[22] Battles over redaction continued throughout the case, with the government insisting that the ACLU withdraw a sentence that described its anonymous client's business as "provid[ing] clients with the ability to access the Internet" and a direct quote in a brief from a Supreme Court case.[23] One of the lawyers on the case, Ann Beeson, remarked on the irony that the government was using the Patriot Act to silence people who questioned the Patriot Act, even in court.

Loosening the Gag

Judge Marrero agreed with Nick and the ACLU that the statute's automatic, absolute, and permanent gag order violated the First Amendment. While noting that judges are not national security experts and so "the Government should be accorded a due measure of deference when it asserts that secrecy is necessary for national security purposes in a *particular situation* involving *particular persons* at a *particular time*," Marrero reasoned,

> [h]ere, however, the Government cites no authority supporting the open-ended proposition that it may universally apply these general principles to impose perpetual secrecy upon an entire category of future cases whose details are unknown and whose particular twists and turns may not justify, for all time and all places, demanding unremitting concealment and imposing a disproportionate burden on free speech.[24]

Contending with the government's asserted need for utter secrecy were First Amendment values: "[D]emocracy abhors undue secrecy, in recognition that public knowledge secures freedom."[25] Marrero also recognized that too much secrecy could create other kinds of problems:

> [A] categorical and uncritical extension of non-disclosure may become the cover for spurious ends that government may then deem too inconvenient, inexpedient, merely embarrassing, or even illicit to ever expose to the light of day. At that point, secrecy's protective shield may serve not as much to secure a safe country as simply to save face.[26]

It was virtually unprecedented for such a gag order to apply in circumstances where no court had authorized the method of investigation in question, and Marrero thought that the self-service nature of NSLs would increase the likelihood of secrecy concealing abuses of power.[27] Using National Security Letters, the FBI gets to decide what records to seek, make its demands without getting any second opinion, and then require everyone who knows what they are doing never to tell anyone. This, to Marrero, looked like a dangerous combination. When the Justice Department's Inspector General later studied how National Security Letters were actually being used behind closed doors at the FBI, Marrero's analysis proved prescient.

The government appealed his decision. While the appeal was pending, Congress held the 2005–2006 debates on whether to reauthorize the expiring Patriot Act provisions. Although the National Security Letter authority was not one of the provisions slated to sunset, Victor Marrero's decision in the *John Doe* case (even though it was pending appeal) was a subject of significant discussion on the floor of Congress[28] and led to several amendments of that authority. Heeding the opinion's reasoning on the First Amendment issue, Congress revised the nondisclosure provision covering NSLs (as well as in Section 215) to make gag orders discretionary instead of automatic. To justify a gag order under the revisions, a special agent would have to certify that disclosure of the request might result in danger to national security, interference with an FBI investigation, or danger to any person—in that particular case, as Victor Marrero had said the First Amendment required. Congress also added a provision allowing a recipient to go to court to challenge the scope or duration of a gag order—but then eviscerated the court's authority to decide such challenges by requiring the court to defer to an FBI certification that the gag order is still necessary.[29] And having finally seen an example of resistance, Congress also added an explicit penalty for violation of the gag order—five years' imprisonment and a fine.[30]

The new gag provision, however, was only a very minimal improvement, replacing some major constitutional flaws with different but equally significant constitutional flaws, and so Nick and the ACLU continued to litigate. In this second round, both the District Court and Court of Appeals agreed that the new protocol was still unconstitutional because it imposed too great a burden on the recipient and still gave too much unilateral authority to the government.[31] By this time, the Inspector General's damning report had been published, so the fact that executive branch officials still got to make final decisions about who was allowed to speak and who wasn't, without any judicial review, now seemed more than theoretically problematic. What was to prevent the FBI from using its discretion in an arbitrary or discriminatory fashion?[32] The answer, to Marrero, was that this was the job of the courts. "[W]hen the judiciary lowers its guard on the Constitution, it opens the door to far-reaching invasions of liberty."[33] His skepticism about the FBI's capacity for limiting itself proved justified here too. Nothing in the statute prevented the FBI from exercising its discretion so that very little changed, despite the amendment. The Inspector General reported that after the 2005 revisions, despite internal guidance telling agents not to use gag orders reflexively, the FBI continued to impose gag orders in connection with 97 percent of all National Security Letters.[34]

The Obama Administration had continued to fight to uphold the statutory gag order but did not ask the Supreme Court to review the ruling on the gag orders. The FBI agreed to comply with the court's interpretation of the First Amendment as a matter of internal policy.[35] But the new decision still did not allow Nick Merrill to identify himself.

Fourth Amendment Rights for NSL Recipients

Nick contended that the NSL process also violated the Fourth Amendment rights of his clients. The *Smith* and *Miller* cases (described in chapter 7), however, had theorized that by sharing information with one's bank or telephone company, one has forfeited any reasonable expectation of privacy and therefore has no Fourth Amendment rights if the government then demands that information. Judge Marrero accepted the conclusion of other courts that this assumption of risk theory would also apply to information shared with an Internet service provider like Nick's company, Calyx, and so his clients were deemed to have no Fourth Amendment right protecting the privacy of their information.[36] But Judge Marrero thought that Nick himself had a Fourth Amendment right to ask a court to review whether the NSL served on him was unreasonable or oppressive to him[37]— a right George Christian also might have exercised after he realized that the demand made of him could entail turning over names of thousands of Connecticut library patrons. The government was attempting to seize information from records in his possession, and the statutes governing the NSL did not provide the customary safety valve for the recipient of a demand for information—the right to ask a court to quash or modify that demand. Without any prospect of judicial review, the government might demand an oppressive amount of material, or might target someone as an NSL recipient for arbitrary or discriminatory reasons. Due to Judge Marrero's decision on this issue, future John Does no longer have to worry about whether it is permissible for them to consult a lawyer or a court. Congress was impressed by the judge's conclusions on this front too, and during the 2005 reauthorization hearings amended the statute by explicitly providing a right for recipients to seek judicial review of an NSL if they want to claim that a demand for information violates their own rights.[38]

Nick and the ACLU had won this second victory in both the courts and Congress because, unlike the judge in the *Muslim Community Association* case described in chapter 7 (challenging the constitutionality of Section 215 orders to turn over records), Judge Marrero did not hang back and wait to see whether Congress might do something to fix the statute's constitutional defects on its own. He played the role federal judges are supposed to play in our national dialogue about what constitutional rights mean, and Congress responded, as did the Department of Justice. Six months after the Second Circuit dismissed the government's appeal on the judicial review issue as moot in light of Congress's action,[39] the government dropped its original demand for information about John Doe's client.[40] Thus, in all three of the cases where NSL recipients contested the demands made of them—Library Connection, the Internet Archive, and Nick Merrill's pioneering John Doe case—the government decided not to pursue its NSLs when challenged. What might this suggest about the utility of NSLs? Has the government backed down in the face of every challenge so far because the FBI actually has adequate alternatives to this shortcut process, or is it perhaps because there have been so few challenges that the few demands meeting opposition are easy enough to write off?

First Amendment Rights for Internet Users

Under the terms of the 2010 settlement, the gag order still prevents Nick from saying anything about the client who was the subject of the NSL—a prohibition he entirely respects. But Judge Marrero also recognized that clients' and all Internet service clients' First Amendment rights, finding that Internet users have a right to anonymity grounded in the First Amendment guarantees of freedom of speech and association. He then ruled that this right is compromised by the overly easy availability of NSLs.

> [T]he FBI theoretically could issue to a political campaign's computer systems operator a § 2709 NSL compelling production of the names of all persons who have email addresses through the campaign's computer systems. The FBI theoretically could also issue an NSL under § 2709 to discern the identity of someone whose anonymous online web log, or "blog," is critical of the Government. . . . These prospects only highlight the potential danger of the FBI's self-certification process and the absence of judicial oversight.[41]

At the time this case was brought, the FBI seemed to assume that NSLs could be used to obtain information about the websites an ISP's customer had visited and the addresses for all e-mails sent and received. As noted above, a 2008 Office of Legal Counsel memo subsequently disavowed that interpretation.[42] Because the Obama Administration has asked for the scope of NSLs to be expanded (or restored, according to proponents), it is worth considering just what's at stake if the reach of NSLs is again extended to website and e-mail logs. As Judge Marrero observed:

> NSLs can potentially reveal far more than constitutionally-protected associational activity or anonymous speech. By revealing the websites one visits, the Government can learn, among many other potential examples, what books the subscriber enjoys reading or where a subscriber shops. As one commentator has observed, the records compiled by ISPs can "enable the government to assemble a profile of an individual's finances, health, psychology, beliefs, politics, interests, and lifestyle."[43]

Another commentator noted that the amount of information at issue could expand exponentially depending on the definition of who is an "electronic communications service provider" and therefore eligible to be served with an NSL instead of a court order:

> Consider that the definition of "electronic communications service providers" doesn't just include ISPs and phone companies like Verizon or Comcast. It covers a huge range of online services, from search engines and Webmail hosts like Google, to social-networking and dating sites like Facebook and Match.com to news and activism sites like RedState and Daily Kos to online vendors like Amazon and Ebay, and possibly even cafes like Starbucks that provide WiFi access to customers.[44]

Another vast dragnet. If Judge Marrero is right that the *Smith/Miller* assumption of risk cases leave Internet users without any Fourth Amendment rights, and if the Supreme Court neither overrules nor distinguishes the *Smith/Miller* cases in this context, Congress will be deciding whether or not to extend or reform NSLs without any possibility of a judicial second opinion.

The Inspector General Exposés, 2007–2010

The 2005 Patriot Act reauthorization hearings took place before there was any real data about the use or abuse of NSLs for Congress to consider, and without testimony from any of the five John Does who wanted to participate in the legislative process. Attorney General Gonzales testified that he was not aware of any abuses of the Patriot Act authorities.[45] He was about to learn a great deal from the Inspector General of his department.

One of the most important decisions Congress made in connection with the 2005–2006 Patriot Act reauthorization was to ask Department of Justice Inspector General Glenn Fine to review the FBI's use of its NSL authority and to prepare a public report. Fine's first report, published in March 2007 and weighing in at 199 pages (including a 50-page executive summary), was a shocker. Congress had quite modestly asked to monitor the numbers of NSLs used and the number of United States persons (FISA's term for American citizens and residents) involved.[46] But it turned out that the FBI had been providing inaccurate reports on the number of NSLs it used for the simple reason that no one was keeping track. Fine estimated that 22 percent more NSL requests had been issued than the totals the FBI had supplied.[47] This report published, for the first time, the number of NSL requests (a higher number than the NSLs because many letters include more than one request for information) as amounting to hundreds of thousands from 2001–2007—even more than the 30,000 per year Barton Gellman had reported (to indignant denials).[48] The FBI reports to Congress had also seriously understated the number of "United States persons" whose information was sought through NSLs, even though such requests had grown to more than 50 percent of the total. Furthermore, the report concluded that, despite Gonzales's reassuring assertion that he was not aware of any abuses, over 60 percent of the files reviewed showed violations of one or more FBI internal control policies and 22 percent revealed violations the FBI had failed to report to its own executive branch watchdogs. The report also found that even if information obtained under NSLs cleared a target of suspicion, it remained in the databases available for later data mining, regardless of whether it involved an innocent person or a "United States person."[49] What the report did not find, according to ACLU policy counsel Michael German, formerly with the FBI, was much concrete evidence that the hundreds of thousands of NSL requests had resulted in catching any terrorists.[50] The Inspector General had difficulty finding any evidence to suggest that the use of NSLs was productive[51] because the FBI did not keep records that would allow that kind of assessment.

Two weeks later, answering questions about this stinging report before a bipartisanly irate House Judiciary Committee, Fine estimated that there had been about 3,000 violations and abuses by the FBI in its first four years of experience with the Patriot Act–improved NSL.[52] The FBI's General

Counsel, in her own testimony, described this as "an F report card."[53] Evidently, allowing the FBI to police itself behind closed doors was just as bad an idea as the framers of the Fourth Amendment, Nick Merrill, and Victor Marrero had thought.

Alarming revelations about how the FBI had been misusing its NSL powers did not end there. It turned out that some agents had taken to using Post-it notes as a substitute for NSLs. One reason more recipients do not challenge NSLs is that a large percentage of the requests go to major telecommunications providers, which do not need to be forced to cooperate. Fine found that FBI agents in field offices, especially in the New York office, had developed a cozy relationship with some of these repeat players. Expecting that compliance with their demands would be routine, some agents began to take shortcuts, requesting subscriber information by e-mail, and even by Post-it note. This level of informality meant that these requests were not reviewed or documented even within the FBI. Fine's January 2010 report revealed that the FBI had circumvented even the minimal administrative procedures required to use an NSL in some 2,000 requests for information.

One technique agents used to avoid the internal NSL process and get information immediately was to issue "exigent letters," a streamlined procedure designed to dispense with the administrative NSL process in case of emergency. Fine discovered that FBI agents frequently issued exigent letters when there was clearly no emergency, promised recipients that subpoenas would follow when no subpoenas had been requested, and issued blanket NSLs to cover up for the fact that they had already received the requested information through unauthorized use of exigent letters.[54] Among those whose telephone numbers were obtained through exigent letters were reporters for the *New York Times* and *Washington Post*,[55] highlighting the potential of NSLs to be used to silence critics, whether those critics are reporters or John Does.[56] It seems that after reviewing a draft of the Inspector General's highly negative 2010 report on the FBI's misuse of exigent letters, the FBI asked the Department of Justice's elite Office of Legal Counsel for an opinion on the legality of its actions. Evidently, the OLC's opinion, issued about two weeks before the IG's report was published, retroactively declared that the use of exigent letters had been proper.[57] But the OLC opinion itself is secret, so it is impossible to evaluate.

What can we learn from this saga? First, real congressional and judicial oversight of searches and seizures truly is essential. Just trusting the FBI, or the other agencies that wield NSL power—or borrow it, like the

Department of Defense[58]—invites abuse. In this instance, the abuse was carefully documented by the Inspector General, suggesting that there is indeed reason to be concerned about what has been happening in other areas where painstaking public reports do not exist. Second, instead of accepting Obama's invitation to expand the NSL, Congress would do better to adopt one of the reform proposals to reintroduce some sort of individualized suspicion threshold.[59] Third, the draconian gag rule hid abuses and prevented public debate and reform. Nick Merrill thinks that without the shield of the gag orders it is doubtful that the FBI would have been able to abuse its NSL power. With the gag order, abuses are far less likely to come to light. Secrecy breeds overconfidence and abuse. Finally, we need the courts to be open to claims that even measures touted as increasing national security may be unconstitutional. Nick Merrill was enough of a patriot to stand up to Congress and the FBI, but he needed the third branch of government, the judiciary, to make his voice heard.

Now that his ordeal by silence is over, Nick Merrill is continuing his campaign against gag orders and NSLs. He is in the process of forming a new not-for-profit organization, to be called Calyx like his former company, which will be committed to protecting the privacy of telephone and Internet customers. "All of this," he says, "has totally distracted me from making money." He thanked one of his lawyers by giving him a sweatshirt bearing a picture of one of his own heroes, Fred Korematsu—the Japanese-American who challenged the constitutionality of his exclusion from his California home during World War II. He has celebrated his freedom by granting some interviews.[60] Of course, it has never been possible to squelch Nick altogether. During the years that he was prohibited from identifying himself, he scrupulously complied with the gag order but also wrote his anonymous op-ed. He even found a way to accept an award recognizing his extraordinary commitment to civil liberties at a public dinner in 2007. At the point when his award was to be presented, the lights in the room dimmed and a video showed a blue-dotted face as an actor's voice began to read a statement Nick had written: "My name is not John Doe and this is not my real voice."

10.

The President's Surveillance Program

These are tens of millions of Americans who are not suspected of anything . . . Where does it stop?—Senator Patrick Leahy (2006)[1]

This debate is going to cost American lives.—Mike McConnell to Congress (2008)

I hope we'll not hear any more irresponsible rhetoric about congressional inquiries risking American lives.—Senator Patrick Leahy to Mike McConnell (2008)

Abuse of power comes as no surprise.—Jenny Holzer (circa 1989)

TRAWLING THROUGH MILLIONS of telephone and e-mail conversations for evidence of terrorism may be the biggest dragnet of them all. Beginning in early 2002, President Bush authorized the NSA to capture international telephone conversations and e-mails without consulting any court and without following the procedures Congress had prescribed in the 1978 Foreign Intelligence Surveillance Act (FISA). The program Bush began on his own account is still with us, in expanded form, through at least 2012, now courtesy of Congress. And most courts refused to review serious claims that the program tramples on a range of constitutional rights even if individual people can't tell exactly when the government is listening. Defense attorneys find that their clients and potential witnesses are afraid to speak with them for fear of being overheard and ending up on a watchlist, implicating the Sixth Amendment right to counsel; authors and scholars find their sources in other countries drying up, affecting their First Amendment rights; human rights investigators at organizations like Amnesty International have good reason to fear that their international calls will be intercepted en masse, compromising their Fourth Amendment right to be free from unreasonable searches and seizures. All Americans who place or receive an international call or send an international e-mail, especially to a country like Afghanistan, have no way to know whether they have an unexpected eavesdropper.

When George W. Bush authorized the National Security Agency (NSA) to start its new massive spy program, his lawyers were aware of arguments that the program was illegal[2] and possibly unconstitutional as well. FISA, as described earlier, had been Congress's response to an earlier president's claim that he did not need a warrant to spy on Americans for national security purposes. Its procedures, specifically intended to prevent presidential power grabs, required FISA court approval before eavesdropping on suspected terrorists or spies, even during time of war. In an epitome of overreaching, Bush took the precaution of not letting Congress or the FISA court know what he was doing so that his program would not be challenged or stopped.

It was not until four years later, when the *New York Times* published James Risen and Eric Lichtblau's article, "Bush Lets U.S. Spy on Callers Without Courts,"[3] that Americans learned about the highly secret "Terrorist Surveillance Program (TSP)," one aspect of Bush's personal multipronged surveillance scheme. The *Times* had delayed publication of this story for a year at the urging of the administration, which desperately wanted to preserve its secret. The story reported that Bush had authorized the NSA to eavesdrop on multitudes of people, including Americans within the United States, capturing their telephone and e-mail conversations without any court order at all as long as one party to the conversation was outside the country and was believed to have some sort of connection with terrorists. Even today, we do not know the details of how this still-classified TSP program, or its successor under the 2008 FISA Amendments Act (FAA), works. Intercepting these calls and e-mails apparently involves gaining access, with the help of telecommunications providers, to signals that are routed through United States communications systems, even when people outside the country are talking to others outside the country.[4] The revelation that such a paradigm-shifting policy had been created and carried out wholly within an executive branch bubble created quite a stir at the time. Members of Congress and the general public were outraged by Bush's aggressive hijacking of democracy. Judge James Robertson, a member of the FISA court that would have reviewed the applications the law required, resigned from the court.

But the leaks had not yet ended. A second round of stories disclosed another facet of the president's surveillance program: the accumulation of the largest collection of information ever assembled, intended to create a database of every telephone call made within the nation's borders. In May 2006, Leslie Cauley reported in *USA Today* that the NSA had been secretly collecting information about tens of millions of telephone calls, reaching "into homes and businesses across the nation by amassing information about the calls of ordinary Americans—most of whom aren't suspected of any crime."[5] This collection did not involve the contents of the conversations but did record data about who was calling whom that could easily be cross-referenced with other information to find out a tremendous amount about the callers. Although the workings of this program too are still cloaked in mystery, Mark Klein, a former technician for AT&T, explained that his company had enabled the collection of call-detail information by splicing fiber optic cables and running a duplicate set of information to a secret room in San Francisco: Room 641A at 611 Folsom Street.[6] Total Information Awareness, the megaspying program proposed by Admiral Poindexter that Congress had repudiated in 2003, had been resurrected in a new form.

On learning about this additional program, Republican Sue Kelly, chair of a House banking subcommittee, asked in exasperation, "What else is it that we don't know?" White House spokesperson Dana Perino assured the press that even though government activities had been concealed from everyone including Congress, all of the intelligence activities involved were "lawful, necessary and required for the pursuit of al-Qaeda and affiliated terrorists."[7]

Five years later, the Terrorist Surveillance Program continues in a legalized and expanded form despite the fact that neither Congress nor any court has actually taken a hard look at whether the program is constitutional, whether it is worth its costs, or whether it needs procedural modifications. Congress placed its imprimatur on this radical spying program in 2008, expanding it beyond Bush's concept, and also granted the telecommunications companies retroactive immunity for their illegal cooperation.[8] Then-Senator Barack Obama voted in favor of both measures. Obama Administration lawyers have been employing the same extreme procedural arguments Bush-era lawyers crafted to persuade the courts not to do their job of deciding whether the eavesdropping program violates the Constitution—arguments based on the state secrets privilege, standing, and governmental immunity. In fact, the Obama lawyers have taken those arguments to new heights—or, more accurately, to new depths. In one case, Obama Department of Justice lawyers argued that the government is immune from lawsuits on this subject unless the government decides to reveal on whom it is spying and actively cooperates in the litigation (the state secrets privilege).[9] In the same case, the Obama lawyers also came up with an audacious standing argument, convincing the court that no one should be allowed to challenge a spy program if so many people have been spied on that grievances have become "generalized."[10] In another case, the government lawyers argued that the plaintiffs could not show they had standing to bring a lawsuit because the government had forced them to pretend that a document once in their possession, which proved that their conversations were being intercepted, did not exist.[11] Even when a later challenge was brought to the statute Congress had passed to authorize questionable surveillance, the Obama lawyers argued that no one could have standing unless they knew for a fact that they had been spied on—thus insulating the statute itself from constitutional review.[12] Acceding to Congress and the administration, until very recently the courts have fouled away all of the serious challenges to the legality of the NSA's and the telecoms' actions, with one very odd exception I will describe and one case whose outcome is still in doubt as I write.

It is well worth spending some time on the story of how the Bush Administration's excessive penchant for secrecy and self-regard, some of which the Obama Administration has inherited, had a devastating impact on the ability of each of the three branches of government to do its job. The Constitution took a hit as internal checks in the Department of Justice failed, Congress was manipulated, and the courts were confounded.

In the Halls of the Department of Justice

One article of faith of the Just Trust Us philosophy woven into the Patriot Act was trust that requiring high-level executive branch officials to approve surveillance requests could substitute for checks and balances by Congress, the courts, and the American people. What went on behind the tightly closed doors of the Justice Department demonstrates dramatically, once again, that the framers knew what they were doing in requiring involvement of all three branches of the federal government as well as the American people in important policy decisions. Even the best and most independent legal minds at the Department of Justice got caught up in the fight to neutralize the fundamental checks and balances built into the Constitution, in a bizarre series of events that ranged from the hospital bed of John Ashcroft to the isolated office of John Yoo.[13]

The Office of Legal Counsel (OLC), an elite division within the Department of Justice, by tradition is expected to provide a special check on unconstitutional executive branch action through objective legal analysis. The OLC was asked in the fall of 2001 to write a memo analyzing the legality and constitutionality of the president's surveillance program. Many have commented on the extraordinary degree of influence the White House exercised over the Department of Justice, including the OLC, during the Bush years.[14] Alberto Gonzales, first as White House counsel and then as Attorney General, seemed determined to afford President Bush all the powers he wanted in meeting the threat of terrorism. In addition, the White House was so intent on maintaining the secrecy of this program that it exerted extraordinarily tight control over information about these covert operations, even within the Justice Department itself. Very few people were "read in"—that is, allowed to know about the program and how it worked. One lawyer in OLC, John Yoo, was chosen to be read in and prepared a memo confidently dismissing concerns that the surveillance program violated either existing statutes or the Fourth Amendment. In his view, Article II of the Constitution gives the president capacious inherent authority to respond to emergencies like 9/11 regardless of Congress or everyday constitutional rights, and so the Fourth Amendment simply had to step out of the way. This was the same type of argument Richard Nixon had made before the passage of FISA. Yoo's memo was not subject to the usual peer review because his boss, Jay Bybee, was not "read in." Even Ashcroft's requests to have his own chief of staff and Deputy Attorney General read in were not granted. Jack Goldsmith, who later replaced Bybee as head of the OLC, said, "in practice Yoo worked for Gonzales."[15] Relying on Yoo's memo, Ashcroft approved and Bush reauthorized the new surveillance program about every forty-five days, sometimes with modifications, for over two years.

During those years, Bush did not tell Congress what he was doing—out of a desire for secrecy and also, according to insiders, because he feared Congress might not approve his plan.[16] Instead, he briefed only a congressional "Gang of Eight": the House and Senate majority and minority leaders, and the heads and ranking members of the House and Senate Intelligence Committees. This end run around Congress was an unorthodox and inadequate means of seeking constitutionally required congressional agreement for a major change in the law. The participants could not even agree on what had happened, as the secret briefings of the "Gang of Eight" took place off the record and without reliable staffers to take thorough notes. Alberto Gonzales reported that the group had reached consensus approving the president's action; Representative Nancy Pelosi and Senators Jay Rockefeller and Tom Daschle denied that there had been any such agreement.[17] Senator Rockefeller wrote to Vice President Cheney expressing his skeptical views about the legality and constitutionality of the program but, when he found his concerns deflected, kept the White House's secret.

When Yoo and Bybee left the office, their successors, Patrick Philbin and Jack Goldsmith, were then "read in" and allowed to read Yoo's memo. They concluded, two years after the fact, that the memo was deficient. The Inspectors General of the five agencies involved with the program later agreed when they were eventually allowed to read the memo, finding that Yoo's analysis of the FISA statute was incomplete, his supersized view of the inherent power of the president inconsistent with Supreme Court case law, and his consideration of the scope of the program inadequate. Goldsmith and Philbin shared their concerns with James Comey, the new Deputy Attorney General. (The Yoo memo is still classified, although parts of it were quoted in the Inspectors General report. This is one of the documents sought in a pending Freedom of Information Act claim.[18])

Comey was troubled by the dubious legality of the program and its procedures.[19] The extreme secrecy surrounding the program also generated a number of worrisome legal and ethical issues. What could the FBI tell its field offices when sharing information obtained as a result of the secret surveillance? Would an agent applying for a search warrant on the basis of evidence gathered under this program have to lie to the court about its source? If someone were prosecuted for a crime discovered as a result of this program, would that person's attorney be told about the actual, legally precarious source of the evidence, as the law required? How would judges react if they found out that judicial authority required by FISA was being ignored? Illegality breeds cover-up illegality.

A spellbound Senate Judiciary Committee later listened to James Comey testify about the dramatic developments that followed.[20] Comey had unexpectedly become Acting Attorney General[21] on March 4, 2004, when John Ashcroft was rushed to the hospital with severe gallstone pancreatitis. Comey therefore was the one whom Gonzales, along with David Addington, Vice President Cheney's lawyer, asked to reauthorize the program as it was about to expire (again) in March 2004. But with doubts cast on the soundness of the Yoo memo, Comey made up his mind to decline to do so. After a series of frantic meetings and consultations, Gonzales and White House Chief of Staff Andrew Card decided (apparently at the request of the president himself) to call Ashcroft at the hospital to ask him to sign off on reauthorization of the program instead. Janet Ashcroft answered the telephone, however, and refused to allow them to speak to her husband, who was in intensive care recovering from surgery. Gonzales and Card decided that the only way to get past Mrs. Ashcroft was to go to the hospital in person. But Ashcroft's chief of staff tipped off Comey, who raced to head them off at the pass, enlisting a posse of Robert Mueller (Director of the FBI), Jack Goldsmith, and Patrick Philbin to meet him at the hospital. That evening, Gonzales and Card stood across from Mrs. Ashcroft at the head of her husband's hospital bed, with Comey, Goldsmith, and Philbin behind them. Ashcroft told Gonzales that he was not feeling very well but nevertheless explained his legal concerns about the program. He concluded: "But that doesn't matter, because I'm not the Attorney General. There's the Attorney General [pointing to Comey]." Gonzales and Card walked out. The next morning the program was reauthorized for two more months over the signature of White House counsel Alberto Gonzales.

If these events are dramatic enough to command a popcorn-eating audience's attention, the embarrassing incident at the hospital, combined with the unprofessionalism of the Yoo memo and the corrosive effect of excessive secrecy even within the department, were earthshaking to insiders. Many resignation letters were drafted that week. Comey, Goldsmith, and Ashcroft (according to his chief of staff) all considered resigning. Mueller threatened to resign if the president commanded the FBI to continue with the program. But the unsatisfying denouement of this part of the story is that Philbin and Goldsmith then drafted a new memo opining that the surveillance program was both legal and constitutional after all, although on a different theory—that the Authorization for Use of Military Force Congress had enacted in September 2001 allowed the president to make decisions about how to conduct the war Congress had authorized, including how to use the tactic of eavesdropping. Therefore, in their analysis, there was still no need to consult Congress because this authorization had supplanted FISA. (This OLC memo also remains classified and is another subject of the pending Freedom of Information Act litigation.) This argument is farfetched, as the Congressional Research Service, among many others, concluded.[22] In authorizing the use of force against Al Qaeda, Congress had not repealed or amended FISA, which by its own terms applies even during a declared war.[23] But, evidently satisfied, Ashcroft continued to sign off on extensions. The program continued—still without Congress knowing or approving or the FISA court playing the role Congress had given it, until the *New York Times* story broke a year and a half later—for a total of about four years.

We have now come to the Deep Throat part of the story. After years of watching the president run an illegal and unchecked surveillance program, close to a dozen insiders decided to become whistleblowers and agreed to talk to Risen and Lichtblau. Jack Goldsmith, who was in the eye of the storm, believes that these insiders were reacting to what they perceived as a crisis of legitimacy—a lack of checks to ensure that the government did not act illegally or unconstitutionally.[24] "The Bush administration's failure to engage Congress," he wrote, "eliminated the short-term discomforts of public debate, but at the expense of many medium-term mistakes."[25] It is probably not coincidental that while these insiders were reflecting on the events of and before March 2004 and pondering the future of the surveillance program after May 2004, when it again expired, April saw the publication of the shocking photographs from Abu Ghraib. Jane Mayer, in her book *The Dark Side*, draws a connection between the shameful conduct documented in those photos and the politicization of the Justice Department and OLC under the influence of Dick Cheney and David Addington, as well as the questionable craftsmanship of memos by John Yoo.[26] Abu Ghraib served as an excruciating reminder of what can happen when people who expect to operate in secret believe they are justified in bending the rule of law.

In January 2006, after the *New York Times* story was published, the president publicly acknowledged the existence of the NSA program. A year later, after the midterm elections, the president finally "withdrew the program," having found a way to get the Foreign Surveillance Intelligence Court to review applications and give permission for surveillance en masse. Goldsmith believes that had the president taken that approach in the first place, this whole sorry episode could have been avoided.[27] But later that spring, the Foreign Intelligence Surveillance Court evidently wanted to revise the procedures covering this surveillance, perhaps giving the court a greater role in decision-making—all conversations on this subject were secret—so Bush decided to try his luck with Congress.

The Rubber Stamp Congress

It turned out that Bush need not have worried about congressional cooperation. Even though the midterm elections had left the Democratic Party in control, Congress not only approved the eavesdropping program twice, first in the temporary Protect America Act in 2007, passed after four days of discussion with no hearings, and then in the FISA Amendments Act of 2008 (FAA), but also actually overshot the president's program. Bush had only claimed the right to eavesdrop on people who were connected with Al Qaeda, however loosely. The FAA does not require any type of individualized suspicion—not even a finding that the target is connected with terrorism. In addition, the statute does not require any individualized court orders authorizing surveillance; does not require identifying people or places to be searched; and does not impose any meaningful limits on the acquisition, retention, analysis, or dissemination of "foreign intelligence" information obtained. The only prerequisites for an eavesdropping order are (1) that acquiring "foreign intelligence" is a "significant purpose" of the eavesdropping, and (2) that one party to the conversation or e-mail is believed to be overseas and not an American. This amounts to letting the FISA court approve blanket, en masse eavesdropping as long as an application states that people abroad are being monitored for the purpose of gathering foreign intelligence—an order, for example, allowing monitoring of all calls between the United States and Afghanistan. Because there is always someone at the other end of telephone calls or e-mails, Americans will inevitably be involved. And because it can be impossible to determine where an e-mail originates, some of the communications intercepted will be purely domestic. The statute resolves all doubts in favor of allowing the government to eavesdrop more with fewer checks.

Senator Patrick Leahy, Chair of the Senate Judiciary Committee, remarked that the media had been doing Congress's job. "Shame on us for being so far behind and being so willing to rubber stamp anything this administration does. We ought to fold our tents."[28] It may not be strictly accurate to describe Congress's actions here as a rubber stamp, as Congress did give the FISA court some role (albeit a toothless one) and adopted a program that was more extreme than the president's. But Leahy was appropriately critical of Congress's decision-making process. In 2008, Congress did not know enough to make an independent judgment about whether these changes to FISA were either wise or necessary. Bush Administration officials were making extravagant claims about the program's necessity that were never documented and indeed seem impossible to substantiate. Vice President Cheney declared to CNN News, for example, that eavesdropping without warrants had saved thousands of lives.[29] The information Congress had before it to evaluate claims like this was insubstantial, unreliable, and one-sided. Just as the secrecy surrounding the program had roiled the Justice Department, it also impaired Congress's ability to make a considered judgment about the costs and benefits of this eavesdropping program. Having tight control of information about the program, administration spokespersons could pick and choose examples of alleged success to showcase in their testimony. They did not need to fear contradiction by the members of Congress, who had few independent sources of information about the program. In fact, no one outside the administration had access to the whole picture and few knew anything at all about the impact of this program because, of course, the people spied on generally did not know they were targets.

Was there another side to the story that Congress wasn't hearing? Leahy was also right that reporters were doing a better job than Congress at uncovering what the administration was trying to bury. Lawrence Wright, Pulitzer Prize–winning author of *The Looming Tower*,[30] a book exploring the connections between terrorism and 9/11, wrote a *New Yorker* article about Mike McConnell, Director of National Intelligence, which was published in January 2008, during the period when Congress was considering whether to make permanent the temporary surveillance authority it had approved in the 2007 Protect America Act. The article contended that McConnell was telling Congress things that were demonstrably untrue. One of the episodes McConnell liked to cite as proof that the president's courtless surveillance was necessary involved the capture of three American soldiers in Iraq. Analysts at the NSA in Fort Meade, Maryland, wanted to examine communications traffic in Iraq to try to locate the missing soldiers but, because those communications might pass electronically through U.S. circuits, McConnell would explain, this surveillance would require a court order under the pre-2008 Foreign Intelligence Surveillance Act—a perverse requirement when speed was of the essence in trying to find the soldiers.[31] But why, Wright asked him, was there any problem with speed, given that the FISA statute in force at the time actually allowed a three-day grace period after monitoring begins to seek a court order? The preexisting statute simply did not prevent immediate surveillance. When Wright did not buy McConnell's vague alternative explanation—that applications would nevertheless have to go through an administrative process—McConnell exploded: "This debate is going to cost American lives."[32]

As Wright reported, McConnell was forced to modify his congressional testimony after the fact in a number of respects. He testified that it took about twelve hours to get the Attorney General to issue an emergency wiretap order. But after the Chair of the House Intelligence Committee, Silvestre Reyes, requested a timeline of the kidnapping, his office retracted that statement.[33] It was not the FISA law that was at fault for delay, it seemed, but interagency wrangling. McConnell also retracted a statement to another committee[34]—that Patriot Act FISA–bypassing legislation had contributed to the capture of terrorists in Germany.[35] And in response to McConnell's unequivocal statement, "[t]here's no spying on Americans," Wright pointed out that he personally knew otherwise. Wright had discovered that a transcript of a telephone call he had made from his home in Austin, Texas, to a source in Egypt was in an intelligence file because the FBI came to his home to question him about the contents of that conversation—and at least one other conversation he had with an English solicitor. Wright had also learned, to his horror, that the FBI was under the mistaken impression that his daughter had made the calls, and so she was listed on an FBI chart as an Al Qaeda connection—probably her debut in a terrorist-related database and her opportunity to be treated, like Brandon Mayfield, as the "agent of a foreign power."

Congress commissioned the Inspectors General of the NSA and the four other agencies involved, including the Department of Justice, to evaluate the TSP program—in a report to be published *after* they had already decided to amend FISA. The joint Inspector General report came up with little or no concrete evidence of any successful terrorism prevention or prosecution that could be attributed to this spying program. Executive branch officials the Inspectors General interviewed "had difficulty citing instances" of success but nevertheless declared the program useful. The leads generated by this type of surveillance, the report found, had no demonstrable connection to terrorist activity, with the possible exception of several cases that "may have" directly contributed to counterterrorism successes, but which were discussed only in the classified version of the report.[36] There is indeed reason to be skeptical about how useful this unprecedented spying program actually is. The program aims at collecting vast quantities of data without targeting data that really may be useful. Like the 9/11 Commission, James Bamford, Pulitzer Prize–winning historian of the NSA, has consistently argued that the NSA needs to pay more attention to processing information rather than to the quantity of information it collects.[37] Again, the executive branch insiders clung to their dragnet because it might at some point catch something useful—if that bit of information was noticed—even though the program operates at the expense of a variety of constitutional rights.

On the other side of the scale, the hearings could not include more than abstract testimony about the costs of the surveillance program because most victims of international eavesdropping do not, unlike Wright, know with certainty that the government has been intercepting their conversations. On one side, officials like Mike McConnell avowed that they were saving American lives and that evidence supporting that claim had to remain secret; on the other, there were no human faces associated with the costs of the program.

Although the program Congress adopted in the FAA is vastly intrusive and unproven, the only real controversy on the floor of Congress in 2008 was over an amendment granting retroactive immunity to the telecommunications providers that had collaborated in providing access to the requested information, in violation of the law in force at the time. The three biggest telecommunications companies, AT&T, Verizon, and BellSouth, had cooperated and provided an inside track to their customers' conversations without insisting on court orders. But another telecom, Qwest, had been squeamish about the legality of the program, fearing substantial fines for violating federal privacy law that was still very much on the books. On being asked to collaborate, Qwest suggested that the NSA comply with the law by obtaining an order from the Foreign Intelligence Surveillance Court. Officials responded that they didn't want to do that because the FISA court might not approve. The NSA tried appeals to patriotism and threats to withhold future lucrative government contracts, but CEO Joseph Nacchio remained obdurate and refused to provide the records of Qwest's fifteen million customers in this legally questionable situation. Nacchio later said that the government actually did withdraw hundreds of millions of dollars of contracts in retaliation.[38] Libertarians were as concerned as civil libertarians about the government's strong-arm tactics. Supporters of Representative Ron Paul organized a bipartisan political action committee, Accountability Now, to fund advertisements against members of Congress who supported retroactive immunity, whatever their party.[39]

The sunset hearings in 2012 will give Congress another opportunity to examine this program more fully. Meanwhile, what has been at least as concerning as Congress's action has been the refusal of the courts to consider cases alleging that the president's unauthorized surveillance program was illegal or unconstitutional. One recent ray of hope is a decision by the United States Court of Appeals for the Second Circuit, in New York, allowing the continuation of a lawsuit challenging the constitutionality of the successor to that program, the FAA.

Closing the Courthouse Doors

ACLU v. NSA—In 2006, after the NSA eavesdropping and data mining programs were exposed by reporters, ACLU lawyers Ann Beeson, Jameel Jaffer, and Melissa Goodman brought a lawsuit claiming that these programs were illegal and unconstitutional. Goodman, the newest member of the team, was involved in the lawsuit "from the minute we read about this program in the *New York Times*." She and her colleagues thought that the "illegal" part would be easy enough to establish, as the FISA statute expressly prohibited this type of spying without a court order. The clients they were representing had compelling explanations of why the program violated a range of constitutional rights, even if they could not say for sure that their own conversations had been intercepted.

Nancy Hollander, a criminal defense attorney, found that people overseas whom she needed to consult or interview in connection with representation of her clients were afraid to talk openly with her. Legal experts said that she would be violating her ethical responsibilities by holding conversations with her clients that were likely to be intercepted. Larry Diamond, a scholar of democracy development, believed that the global surveillance program would inhibit people who live in repressive countries from making phone calls or sending e-mails to the United States to "report developments and deliver opinions and analyses critical of their own governments, or of the United States government, or even perhaps of powerful American or international business interests." Scholar Barnett Rubin, Director of the Afghanistan Regional Project at NYU's Center on International Cooperation, who researches and writes about conflict prevention in Afghanistan and the surrounding region, found that his collaborators, moderate Muslims and Islamic scholars, had become afraid to talk with him for fear that their conversations would end up in a federal databank and cause the U.S. government to harass them or put them on watchlists. Members of the environmental organization Greenpeace, previously targeted for surveillance by the NSA, feared that their social activism and opposition to Bush Administration environmental policies might make them a target once again, as secrecy and lack of oversight readily conceal use of discretionary surveillance powers to serve political agendas. Other plaintiffs included writer Christopher Hitchens ("I believe the President when he says that this will be a very long war, and insofar as a mere civilian may say so, I consider myself enlisted in it. But this consideration in itself makes it imperative that we not take panic or emergency measures in the short term, and then permit them to become institutionalised"), historian James Bamford ("What greatly concerns me as someone who has written more about NSA than any other writer is that in the past, when NSA was allowed to operate in absolute secrecy, without oversight, it became a rogue agency"), and the ACLU itself.

The Bush Administration fought back, first arguing that the courts should not review the legality of the programs because of the "state secrets privilege." Even to defend the NSA surveillance programs in court, the government argued, would necessarily compromise the government's national security secrets. The Detroit-based district judge assigned to hear this lawsuit, Anna Diggs Taylor (a 1979 Carter appointee who was the first African-American woman on her court, and who had served as Chief Judge) bisected the case. She honored the government's desire to keep the curtain closed on its data mining program and dismissed claims about that program on the basis of the state secrets privilege. But she thought that the facts already publicly revealed about the eavesdropping program were telling enough to allow a court to make a decision—and her decision was that the program was both illegal and unconstitutional.[40]

When this ruling was appealed, however, the Sixth Circuit Court of Appeals, which covers Michigan even though it is based in Cincinnati, was unsympathetic to the plaintiffs' concerns about the impact of this program on their work, our rights, and our democracy.[41] The appeals court decided that Nancy Hollander and the other plaintiffs did not have standing to raise any constitutional or statutory claims because they could not, predictably, establish that they personally had been under surveillance—the same problem the Muslim Community Association encountered in trying to challenge the Patriot Act. Paradoxically, the very secrecy of the program was deemed to prevent a challenge to the program. The Supreme Court declined to hear the case.[42] Would anyone ever be able to establish standing and get a judicial ruling on the constitutional issues involved?

Post-FAA Litigation

Amnesty v. McConnell—Within an hour of President Bush signing the FAA, litigators Jaffer and Goodman were back in court, in New York this time, with a new roster of authors, scholars, and human rights and labor organizations as clients. These included Amnesty International, whose American branch frequently calls and e-mails Amnesty's London-based researchers to discuss human rights investigations and abuses related to terrorism and counterterrorism, and to events in Afghanistan and Iraq—certainly information that could be classified as "foreign intelligence" information. Under the FAA, the government could intercept all of Amnesty's calls between the United States and London, en masse, compromising Amnesty's confidential sources and strategy discussions. Another plaintiff, Scott McKay, was one of the Idaho lawyers who had represented Sami al-Hussayen in his material support prosecution. He feared that his continuing conversations with his client, now living in Saudi Arabia, were being monitored. The lawsuit argued that the FAA program violated the First and Fourth Amendments—the same type of constitutional claims Judge Taylor had accepted.

This case was pending in the district court when Barack Obama was sworn in. The Obama lawyers did not change course, however, and continued to argue that the plaintiffs should not be allowed to raise their claims. The district court ruled in favor of the government, finding that the plaintiffs lacked standing, even though the number of people threatened with eavesdropping is far greater than under the original Bush program and even though this decision immunizes the statute itself.[43] But in March 2011, the Second Circuit Court of Appeals disagreed with this dismissive decision, finding that the lawyers, journalists, and labor, legal, media, and human rights organizations bringing the lawsuit had shown that they had a reasonable fear of future injury and that they were incurring costs in trying to protect the confidentiality of sensitive international communications[44]—like the cost of traveling overseas to hold meetings in person. This decision, if it stands, only means that the lawsuit can continue, not that the court has found the law unconstitutional. As this book goes to press, the Obama Administration had just asked the Second Circuit to rehear this decision.

Jewel v. NSA—The Electronic Frontier Foundation (EFF) had taken a different tack in its approach to the president's Terrorist Surveillance Program, representing outraged customers who wanted to sue their telecommunications providers for jeopardizing their privacy by collaborating with an illegal program. Over forty cases brought against the telecoms from 2006 on by people ranging from AT&T clients like Tash Hepting to author Studs Terkel (who had been blacklisted during the McCarthy era) were eventually consolidated before one judge: Vaughn Walker in San Francisco. Walker had been nominated to the federal bench by Ronald Reagan but was not confirmed because senators including Ted Kennedy thought he was too conservative. He had belonged to a private club that excluded blacks and women and, while in private practice, had represented the Olympics Committee in its attempt to keep the "Gay Olympics" from using that name.[45] He was subsequently renominated by George H. W. Bush and confirmed in 1989.

When Congress granted retroactive immunity to the telecoms in 2008, the EFF had to narrow its sights and focus on claims against the NSA itself. One of the arguments made in favor of the 2008 immunity provision in Congress had been that people who wanted to challenge the eavesdropping program should have to sue the government, which had persuaded the telecoms to violate the law in the name of national security, rather than the companies, which had merely complied with what authoritative government officials had told them was a legal and patriotic program.[46]

After Obama took office, the EFF agreed to give the government an extension of time to file papers in their lawsuit against the NSA, hoping that the Obama lawyers would not be so relentlessly opposed to allowing the court to decide, once and for all, whether the NSA program had been illegal or unconstitutional. But the tenor of the government's arguments did not change. Judge Walker found that although the plaintiffs would have had standing to sue the telecoms (based on their private contractual relationships), they did not have standing to sue the government because their grievances were "generalized."[47] In other words, so many people were affected by the surveillance programs that no one would be allowed to challenge them. So where there was standing (against the telecoms), there was no possibility of raising a claim because Congress had shut the courthouse door; where there was a possibility of a claim (against the government agency), the courts found that there was no standing unless someone could prove that they had actually been spied on. The Obama lawyers also argued that the government was immune from this lawsuit and every other lawsuit on the subject unless the government were to voluntarily disclose that the plaintiffs in the case had been spied on, and actively participate in the litigation.[48] In other words, no one could sue the administration for acting unconstitutionally unless the administration decided that it wanted to be sued. The EFF vented its frustration with the new administration on its website: "In Warrantless Wiretapping Case, Obama DOJ's New Arguments Are Worse Than Bush's."[49]

Al-Haramain But Benjamin Franklin's maxim that three people are unable to keep a secret struck again—putting Judge Walker in a position to rule on the legality and constitutionality of the pre-2008 eavesdropping program. The case involved the Al-Haramain Islamic Foundation, an Oregon charity affiliated with a Saudi organization of the same name, which was one of the Muslim-affiliated charities to have its assets frozen in February 2004 while OFAC was investigating whether or not the organization had ties to Al Qaeda. Lynne Bernabei, a lawyer for the organization, found herself in the highly unusual position of knowing definitively that OFAC had reviewed intercepted conversations between Al-Haramain's Saudi-based director, Soliman al-Buthi, and its American attorneys, Wendell Belew and Asim Ghafoor.[50] But she and her colleagues were in the even stranger position of not being allowed to offer this proof to satisfy the court that they had indeed been spied on.

Here's how they came to know about the top secret document. The lawyers for Al-Haramain had requested that OFAC provide them with documentation to explain why they were suspected of having terrorist connections. Someone at OFAC gathering documents to send in response to this request mistakenly included a classified log of captured attorney-client conversations. The FBI advised Lynne Bernabei that this document, now in her possession, was still classified, and she agreed to return all of the lawyers' copies of the document, as requested. It was impossible to put the entire cat back into the bag, however, because the document in question had already been distributed to the organization's Board of Directors and read by a *Washington Post* reporter. Bernabei and her colleagues were threatened with prosecution if they revealed what was in the logbook to anyone else.[51]

The Bush Administration lawyers argued that this case should be dismissed both because of the state secrets privilege and because the plaintiffs had no standing. One of the things retroactively considered to be top secret was Al-Haramain's surrendered documentation that the NSA had eavesdropped on them. This now-quarantined evidence distinguished Al-Haramain from the plaintiffs in the earlier case against the NSA, who had seen their victory evaporate because they did not have concrete proof that anyone had spied on them. The vexing question of whether the organization should have to or could establish that it had standing without relying on the out of bounds document was not the only stumper Judge Walker faced in wrestling with this case over the course of the next four years.

This litigation too spilled over into Obama's term. Obama's lawyers continued to argue that the court should pretend that the "secret" document did not exist, and so the plaintiffs could not rely on it. They argued that nothing short of "the government's frank admission of the unlawful electronic surveillance and active cooperation in the litigation against it under FISA would suffice" for standing.[52] In other words, if you don't have evidence that you've been spied on, you can't bring a constitutional challenge because you can't show you have standing; if you do have evidence, the evidence is secret and can't be used. Either way, the door remains shut. As an alternative, the Obama lawyers also argued that the case had to be dismissed because of the state secrets privilege. Because the Bush Administration had been criticized in many quarters for its overreliance on the state secrets privilege, Attorney General Holder, as mentioned earlier, announced that he was instituting a new, leaner state secrets privilege. He promised that he could be trusted to withhold information from the courts only when he thought it was really necessary to do so.[53] Of course, if evidence is hidden even from the court, the court cannot review whether a claim of privilege is actually justified, or perhaps a cover-up for misconduct. The Obama lawyers perceived this problem and dealt with it by promising the court that they had not committed any misconduct and therefore could be trusted.

Vaughn Walker thought the state secrets claim in this context was the height of arrogance. "Under defendants' theory, executive branch officials may treat FISA as optional and freely employ the [state secrets privilege] to evade FISA, a statute enacted specifically to rein in and create a judicial check for executive-branch abuses of surveillance authority."[54] In an order issued in January 2010, he walked a tightrope between national security considerations and fairness to the plaintiffs by asking the Obama lawyers (1) to produce the quarantined document for private review by the court (after which the court would decide whether or not the plaintiffs had established that they had been under surveillance and therefore had standing), (2) to begin the process of procuring security clearances for some of the plaintiffs' lawyers so that they could respond to the government's arguments about the document, and (3) to reconsider whether any pertinent documents could be declassified. Over the next several months, the defendants refused to cooperate, according to Judge Walker. The government lawyers said that they did not have authority to allow the document to be shared with the plaintiffs' lawyers if the agencies involved, their clients, objected. Although two of the plaintiffs' attorneys were found suitable for security clearances, the Director of the NSA "refused to cooperate with the court's orders, asserting that plaintiffs' attorneys did not 'need to know' the information that the court had determined plaintiffs' attorneys would need in order to participate in the litigation."[55] The government lawyers refused to work with the plaintiffs' lawyers and the court to draft a protective order that might have solved the confidentiality problem. At one point, the lawyers threatened that if the judge insisted on sharing the secret document with Al-Haramain's lawyers, they would "withdraw" the document from the file, raising a specter of agents forcibly raiding the file cabinet in the judge's chambers. The report on whether or not this document could be declassified evidently mentioned at one point that there was an "error" in the document. Skeptics wondered if the Obama lawyers were acting out of an exaggerated sense of principle in trying to preserve secrecy, or if revealing the document would indeed expose some sort of malfeasance.[56] Trying to litigate constitutional claims against the Obama executive agencies was turning out to be just as much of an ordeal as it had been under Bush. The plaintiffs' lawyers were able to come up with a number of public statements by government officials suggesting that their conversations had indeed been intercepted under the NSA program they challenged, and the judge mercifully agreed that these statements added up to standing—even without the quarantined document. The government lawyers, however, resolutely refused to defend the legality of the NSA's actions on the theory that the court should not be considering those arguments at all, and so the court declared the plaintiffs to have won by default. The government continued to argue against the organization getting any form of relief. Meanwhile, the Oregon branch of Al-Haramain had gone out of business.[57] Even if Judge Walker's ruling on the merits of the case survives appeal, his decision may not have much impact. The decision does not concern the current law, but only the legality of the NSA program before it was approved by Congress. And this case was brought by a group whose circumstances could not conceivably be duplicated. So Judge Walker's decision about the legality of the NSA program, with Judge Taylor's similar ruling, may be of only historical interest, while the constitutionality of the current FAA-approved program remains untested.

While the Justice Department worked to immunize all versions of the surveillance program from litigation in 2009, Attorney General Holder reported to congressional intelligence and judiciary committees, as he was required to do by the FAA, that there had been a problem with overcollection of data, but that the administration was fixing it. It is not clear from the public record just what mistakes had been made. The New York Times story reporting this admission also reported that during the previous administration, the eavesdropping program had been used to spy on a member of Congress—highlighting the danger of minimizing judicial review.[58] As Frederic A. O. Schwarz, Jr., who was counsel to the Church

Committee, ruefully observes, we keep forgetting the hard-won lessons of the Church Committee report about the costs of unilateral executive branch surveillance powers.[59]

The Secret Court Strikes Again

Meanwhile, the secret FISA Court of Review had gotten in on the action. After Congress passed the Protect America Act in 2007, temporarily extending the president's surveillance program, an unidentified company brought a Fourth Amendment challenge in the FISA court to an order they received under that Act, arguing that it should not have to comply because the statute violated the Fourth Amendment. Like Nick Merrill, who received a National Security Letter ordering him to turn over client information in his possession, the company had Fourth Amendment rights of its own. Because the company clearly did have standing,[60] the FISA court ruled against its constitutional claim on the merits. The company appealed and the FISA Court of Review made one of its rare appearances to affirm the decision. As previously noted in chapter 6, although Chief Justice Rehnquist's appointees to the FISA court had been somewhat balanced politically, his choices for Court of Review were all Republican appointees.[61] A similar pattern held true for Chief Justice Roberts, who chose seven Republican appointees and one Democratic appointee for the FISA court, but only Republican appointees for the Court of Review.

The corporate John Doe in this case argued that affording so much unreviewable discretion to the executive branch invites abuse. But the new judges on the review court were as dismissive of Fourth Amendment concerns as their predecessors had been in the challenge to the law that affected Brandon Mayfield: "[T]his is little more than a lament about the risk that government officials will not operate in good faith"[62]—dismissing, in other words, the raison d'être of the Fourth Amendment. Unless the company could show actual abuses of power instead of just the potential for abuse, the court said, the statute was entirely reasonable as applied in this case. The Attorney General would play the role a court would have played in preventing abuses, the court said, and after all, the government promised that the manner in which its agents were implementing the statute avoided potential constitutional difficulties. Just trust us. On the same day that Jaffer and Goodman filed their challenge to the FAA, they also filed a motion in the FISA court asking to be notified of any FAA-related challenges, for leave to participate in any decision about the FAA as amicus curiae, and for publication of any relevant opinions.[63] The FISA court ordered the government to respond to the request, but then denied the motion.

The 2007 Protect America Act had already expired by the time of this court's ruling, and so this decision too lacks real-world impact. But the opinion does reveal the inclinations of the members of the FISA review court. Although the 2008 FAA that replaced that 2007 Act is even more expansive, there does not seem to be any reason to expect that this custom-made review court would regard the FAA any differently. Once again, it turns out that structure and process matter. In a regular federal court, judges are randomly assigned to hear cases, which means that a litigant may encounter a Victor Marrero or Ann Aiken who will take constitutional claims very seriously and not just trust the government. Regular federal courts operate publicly, inviting the public to attend arguments, and publish their opinions, only closing arguments or redacting their opinions in strictly limited measure in rare cases; the FISA courts operate in deep secrecy and only occasionally decide to publish opinions. Accountability and transparency matter. And unlike regular federal courts, which have to mediate between two parties with opposing views and their contending lawyers, the FISA court and Court of Review never see the individual people, like Brandon Mayfield, Studs Terkel, or Nancy Hollander, whose rights are actually affected by their rulings. Under the circumstances, getting the FISA Court of Review to approve whatever spying the government wants to do seems about as difficult as getting a notary public to put a stamp on a lease or a will.

"What Else Is It That We Don't Know?"

The FISA Amendments Act sunsets in 2012 and bills have already been introduced to modify it, like a 2009 bill introduced by Representatives Conyers, Nadler, and Scott to reverse the retroactive immunity provision, to impose additional limits to prevent listening in on Americans, and to control retention of the information collected. If this program does continue, Congress or the courts at least should insist on meaningful procedures to control retention and dissemination of information swept up.[64] Innocent people whose conversations are tapped should not find, as Brandon Mayfield did, that records of their private lives have burrowed into federal databanks.

Although the FAA required periodic reports to Congress, those reports aren't public. In June 2010, Melissa Goodman and her colleagues filed a lawsuit to enforce a Freedom of Information Act request for records related to government agencies' implementation of the invasive FAA surveillance power, seeking information about how the FAA spying power is being interpreted and used, how many Americans are affected, and what safeguards are in place to prevent abuse of Americans' privacy rights.[65] In response to this lawsuit (which is still ongoing), the government released over 900 pages of records in November 2010. The documents confirm that there have been abuses of the FAA power but, given the heavy redaction, it is impossible to determine what those abuses were or how systemic they might have been. The documents also confirm that the effective decisions about whom the government monitors under this program are made by the executive branch and not by the courts. All discussion and information about whether this surveillance program has been effective are entirely redacted.[66]

If anyone is going to fix FAA, it has to be Congress. The courts in this area have, for the most part, been hog-tied by secrecy and exclusionary procedures. But will Congress be interested if its constituents don't know that there are reasons to be concerned? Can the public take part in the coming debate without more information than we have now? And the most critical question remains the one asked by Representative Sue Kelly: "What else is it that we don't know?"

III.

AMERICAN DEMOCRACY

11.

Losing Our Checks and Balances: The President, the Congress, and the Courts

We do not believe it is possible to defeat all terrorist attacks against Americans, every time and everywhere. A president should tell the American people: No president can promise that a catastrophic attack like that of 9/11 will not happen again.—9/11 Commission (2004)[1]

[M]y single most important responsibility as President is to keep the American people safe. It's the first thing that I think about when I wake up in the morning. It's the last thing that I think about when I go to sleep at night.—President Barack Obama (2009)[2]

A S THE PREVIOUS chapters have shown, the post-9/11 Just Trust Us frame generates systemic pressure on all three branches of the federal government—the president, the Congress, and the courts—to move in lockstep. Again and again, the executive branch overreacted or was tempted by secrecy to exceed its powers; again and again, Congress failed to rein in abuses or to fulfill its responsibility to monitor executive agency actions; again and again, the courts discarded serious constitutional challenges to the president's and Congress's actions for trumped-up procedural reasons. Throughout the first post-9/11 decade, there was too much apparent unanimity among the three branches and too little determination to respect our rights and our traditions. This superficial unanimity, combined with pervasive secrecy, has papered over serious constitutional and policy questions—questions about who we want to be as a nation going forward. The stories of the past ten chapters show some of the price we and our fellow Americans have paid due to this failure of the Constitution's checks and balances. One necessary step to restoring and preserving our rights and our democracy is to reflect on what we can expect from each of the three branches of government while terrorism challenges us, and compare our expectations to what we have gotten so far.

The View from the Oval Office—From Bush to Obama and Beyond

By now it should be clear that the excesses of the War on Terror decade did not end when its architects-in-chief left the White House. The administration of the second post-9/11 president, Barack Obama, endorsed dragnet material support laws, despite their threat to First Amendment values; adopted the entire Bush arsenal of court-free spying techniques, despite their threat to privacy and First Amendment values; urged Congress to expand (or, in their word, "clarify") the scope of National Security Letters, one of the powers Obama had deplored as a candidate; urged Congress to renew all of the Patriot Act with virtually no changes at the 2009 reauthorization hearings; and responded to the first aborted airplane terrorism incident on Obama's watch by dramatically increasing the size of the notoriously problematic airport blacklists and then introducing an unprecedented level of privacy invasion in the TSA bodyscanner program. Obama's lawyers defended seizing the assets of a charity without even minimal due process. They have pulled out all the stops to keep the courts from reviewing the constitutionality of any aspect of the Bush/Obama antiterrorism campaign, cozying up to legal doctrines candidate Obama had criticized, like the state secrets privilege. Their radical procedural arguments urge the courts to turn away people who have been injured by our antiterrorism policies without ever considering whether their rights have been violated. President Obama tells us that we should turn the page and not worry about abuses committed under the Bush Administration, denigrating the importance of accountability and the claims of history. Like his predecessor, Obama has publicly touted the desirability of judicial restraint and judges who "interpret" rather than "make" law.[3]

In some respects, Obama and his cabinet have shown that they have indeed learned from mistakes of the previous decade. Promising a change of direction from the excesses of the War on Terror, Obama eloquently expressed his belief that we "cannot keep this country safe unless we enlist the power of our most fundamental values."[4] His administration seemed determined to be more respectful of rights, more tolerant of diverse viewpoints, and less inclined to demonize Muslims. The Bush Administration, for example, had garnered criticism and lawsuits for ideological exclusion, denying visas to teach or to attend conferences in the United States to dozens of Islamic scholars including Tariq Ramadan, who taught at the University of Oxford, and Adam Habib, Vice-Chancellor of Research at the University of Johannesburg. Obama's Secretary of State, Hillary Clinton, reversed those decisions, ending the McCarthyist attempt to keep ideas from crossing the border. (It should be noted that her decision followed a pro–First Amendment judicial decision concluding five years of litigation about the right of Americans to engage with Ramadan's ideas—a rare and welcome judicial intervention.[5]) In his tone-setting Cairo speech as well as in domestic speeches, Obama declared that the war on terrorism is not a war on Islam,[6] perhaps encouraging American Muslims to believe that, at least while Obama's term lasts, they could go to a mosque or contribute to a charity without fear of repercussions. Or perhaps not. Good intentions at the top of the pyramid do not automatically translate into action. George W. Bush visited mosques in the aftermath of 9/11 and exhorted Americans not to blame all Muslims for the acts of extremists. The Patriot Act itself included a "sense of Congress resolution" condemning discrimination against Muslims.[7] But these public statements of principle did not always square with discriminatory actions by government agents at the FBI, OFAC, or TSA, as the cases discussed in earlier chapters have shown. Even if Muslim-Americans wanted to trust Barack Obama personally, the agencies they had learned to distrust during the Bush Administration continued to employ many of the same people.

It is not surprising that President Obama quickly developed different views from candidate Obama about the relationship between our fundamental values and national security. The Just Trust Us frame pushes presidents to favor dragnets of all kinds. Held responsible for our safety and subject to blame for any terrorist incident, it is natural that presidents will opt for strategies that might just possibly prevent another attack rather than truly prioritizing preservation of our civil liberties. Terrorist attacks, concrete and visible, will lead to blame; avoiding violation of rights, an abstract goal, is unlikely to reap rewards. And of course all presidents will believe that they personally can be trusted to use their vast powers wisely. But the Just Trust Us frame is as harmful to those who wield the power as it is to those who suffer the consequences of its use. Presidents take on an impossible task if they believe, and encourage us to believe, that they will have failed if any terrorist plot succeeds, as the 9/11 Commission cautioned. But in December 2009 when Omar Abdulmutallab got on an airplane with explosives in his underwear, Obama took responsibility, telling the public that the system had failed and leading the public to believe that his administration could prevent any recurrences by doubling or tripling the size of the No Fly list and developing highly intrusive screening procedures. This evidently was what the public wanted to hear. Expecting that presidents can guarantee our safety may be childish, but presidents respond to our unrealistic expectations for personal as well as political reasons. Any president will also be subject to other forms of pressure, including the momentum of the masses of people on the huge federal government payroll. For Obama to have reversed course on some post-9/11 programs would in all likelihood have alienated members of the military and the intelligence community, who presumably believed that they were doing good and necessary work under his predecessor. Career lawyers at the Justice Department, like their client agencies, would certainly have resented being compelled to reverse their positions in ongoing cases. So the considerable force of inertia combined with the pressures of politics and position to push Barack Obama toward morphing into what some termed "Bush Lite."

While critics like Mary Cheney attacked Obama for not being more aggressive, many Bush supporters were either publicly or secretly relieved that Obama's domestic antiterrorism policies turned out to be almost indistinguishable from Bush's.[8] Some Obama supporters were disappointed that their candidate did not rescind or revise more of the Bush War on Terror policies. Some accused Obama of having made empty campaign promises, while others recognized that the presidency itself generates enormous pressure to follow the Bush/Cheney "1 percent" path. Jack Goldsmith, who served in the Bush Office of Legal Counsel, recounts how President Bush began each day by reviewing a "threat matrix" that listed and analyzed every threat directed at the United States during the preceding twenty-four hours, including both credible reports and false alarms—a document often extending over dozens of pages.[9]

Even before he began his term of office, Barack Obama had to contend with an alarming terrorism alert that involved him personally. Intelligence sources warned him that terrorists planned to hijack his inauguration. Obama's incoming security advisors worked closely with the outgoing Bush team to make contingency plans; Obama himself canceled what was to have been a final rehearsal of his inaugural address in order to analyze updates about the threat.[10] It turned out to be a false alarm. But how is a president to resist overreacting to this constant specter of dire possibilities unless there is enough pressure from the other direction to provide balance? Libertarians, civil libertarians, and librarians can sound alarms, but if the American people are unaware of the costs of our counterterrorism policies, if they assume that the costs must be necessary to keep us safe because the president says so, or if they believe that any costs will be paid by someone other than themselves, the president will not hear many voices asking him to reduce the size of the dragnets. And so, Goldsmith posits, "Every foreseeable post 9/11 President, Republican or Democrat, will embrace [unremitting fear of devastating attack, an obsession with preventing the attack, and a proclivity to act aggressively and preemptively to do so], just as Lincoln, Roosevelt, and other presidents did in time of war or emergency."[11]

That Obama adopted most of his predecessor's strategies for combating terrorism does not necessarily verify that those strategies are sound. Some might like to believe that once he became president, Obama gained access to secret information, unknown to us, that justifies Bush's approaches. We have no way to know what information presidents share, but we cannot blindly trust that any president is doing what is needed to keep us safe because the temptation to use dragnets comes with the position. If Goldsmith's prognosis applies even to a former Constitutional Law professor like Barack Obama, we cannot realistically expect any president to act aggressively to restore our rights.

The War on Terror decade challenged more than the Constitution's guarantees of rights. It also rocked another of the Constitution's essential safeguards of rights and democracy: the checks and balances among the three branches of the federal government. In George W. Bush's view, he was the "decider" and he was justified in preventing Congress, the courts, and the public from second-guessing his decisions. Many books have been written describing how Bush and Cheney worked aggressively to outmaneuver Congress and the courts. And Congress and the courts, for the most part, acceded, sometimes by affirmatively ratifying actions, but mostly by remaining silent. When all three branches of the government seem to agree that particular strategies are constitutionally acceptable, it is tempting to conclude that we have no problem. But what sounded like a chorus of agreement was actually just one voice overdubbed in an echo chamber. As the last chapter described, where Congress has acted, its actions, beginning with the Patriot Act, have not been preceded by meaningful independent deliberations. The courts have not added much voice because they have been silenced by dismissive procedural arguments or just declined to get involved, because they have been overly deferential, or, in the case of the FISA Court of Review, because they have been stacked. Worst of all, the wall of secrecy has prevented the American people from having enough information to talk back to our elected officials as they've bartered away our rights.

Obama's views on the proper role of Congress and the courts, like his views about rights, have been more nuanced than his predecessor's, at least in theory. In one of his first Executive Orders, Obama vowed that his administration would be more transparent, reversing the previous administration's grudging "Ashcroft rule," which discouraged agencies from disclosure. Instead, Obama told federal agencies that they should presume that information about what they were doing should be shared with the public, even if it is embarrassing.[12] Consistently with that promise, President Obama agreed to release controversial Office of Legal Counsel memos on the subject of torture, in response to a Freedom of Information Act (FOIA) lawsuit.[13] But he then decided that he did not want to comply with another FOIA decision ordering the release of photographs portraying United States–connected victims of torture in detention facilities in Afghanistan and Iraq.[14] Obama explained that even though the photographs were clearly of great public interest and related to issues about controversial interrogation methods (which he had banned), he had decided that releasing the photos could be harmful because they might provoke anti-American reactions. Because defying the order would have amounted to contempt of court, Obama enlisted Congress to change the law on which the order was based. Congress readily agreed to amend the Freedom of Information Act to prevent any court from reviewing a Secretary of Defense's decision not to release photographs to the public.[15] The basis for this exception to the rule of transparency is troubling. The more outrageous the government's conduct, the more reason to keep it concealed because it might provoke anger. Therefore, the public is guaranteed the right to hear about innocuous activities and minor mistakes but not about government conduct that is truly shocking. Congress agreed with Obama, as it had with Bush, that it is best to avoid the courts on issues like this and allow the executive branch to make a unilateral decision.

Backpedaling on the issue of transparency aligned Obama more closely with the Bush/Ashcroft philosophy of presidential prerogative. But Obama defended himself against that accusation in a 2009 speech at the National Archives, one of his few major speeches on national security issues:

> Here's the difference, though: Whenever we cannot release certain information to the public for national security reasons, I will insist that there is oversight of my actions—by Congress or by the courts.[16]

For example, although Obama's Justice Department had decided to keep relying on a version of the state secrets privilege that would shut out the courts, Obama promised that he would voluntarily report to Congress when the privilege was invoked.[17] The promise is encouraging, but it remains to be seen whether Congress or the courts will really be treated as equal partners by Obama or by any future Terror President.

The Sleeping Watchdog

The Constitution establishes Congress as the representative of the people. Whether a president insists on or resists congressional oversight, Congress is supposed to provide a check and not just a rubber stamp. It was as easy for Obama to get Congress to collaborate in shrinking FOIA as it had been for Bush to get Congress to shrink other rights. The preceding chapters have shown how, during the Bush years, Congress failed to provide a real check on the president or to exercise meaningful oversight over agencies that were spying on Americans, harassing Americans at the airport, closing down charities, and making businesses jump through elaborate hoops. As previous chapters have also shown, executive agencies left to operate independently and in secret are not likely to do a good job of honoring rights. When the Justice Department's Inspector General, Glenn Fine, was finally asked to study the airport watchlist system in 2008, he found that the list was riddled with errors and that the system did not provide innocent people with any effective way out. He also found that the agencies involved, accustomed to operating independently and focused on their mission, were dragging their heels in fulfilling mandates to develop more traveler-friendly procedures.[18] When the same Inspector General eventually studied the FBI's use of the self-help National Security Letters, his 2007, 2008, and 2010 reports found that allowing the FBI to operate independently and in secret had enabled a staggering number of abuses and misleading reports to Congress. In his September 2009 testimony before the Senate Judiciary Committee in connection with reauthorization of the Patriot Act, Fine strongly urged Congress to wake up and start holding hearings to find out how the FBI is using its antiterrorism powers, through "continual and aggressive" oversight.[19] The 9/11 Commission agreed, describing congressional oversight in the first half of the decade as "dysfunctional":

> Of all our recommendations, strengthening congressional oversight
> may be among the most difficult and important. So long as oversight

is governed by current congressional rules and resolutions, we believe the American people will not get the security they want and need.[20]

Part of the reason for Congress's failure to pay attention to the use and abuse of the post-9/11 powers it launched lies in partisan politics. Like so many other vexing issues, national security became a Republican versus Democrat issue. While the president and the majority of Congress were both Republican, there was a strong political disincentive for Congress to hunt for executive branch transgressions. When Democrats gained a majority, Congress ramped up oversight of the Republican president to some extent, leading to more Inspector General reports and more frequent hearings. Bills were introduced to reform National Security Letters,[21] although they did not command a majority. But when a Democratic president took over and adopted Bush's positions on issues like National Security Letters, Democrats in Congress who had been playing the role of critic were disarmed. There is little political advantage to reviewing antiterrorism strategies that people assume are keeping them safe, especially when a new Democratic president makes them his own. Commentator Glenn Greenwald points out that "by advocating for the continuation of so many Bush/Cheney policies, [Obama] weakened opposition to that approach." He noted that Obama was not just following public will on issues concerning national security but was actually leading public opinion to greater approval of the Bush/Cheney policies.[22] "[W]hat were once viewed as controversial right-wing, Bush/Cheney Terrorism policies have been transformed, under Obama, into bipartisan consensus." Obama was converting emergency post-9/11 policies into "the New Normal."[23]

New baselines are far less likely to be questioned once they have become familiar. The Patriot Act, as previous chapters have described, built incrementally on rights-diluting provisions in Bill Clinton's 1996 Antiterrorism and Effective Death Penalty Act, which had come to seem normal by 2001. In 2012, when the FISA Amendments Act expires, will Congress take a hard look at whether this spying program, already over a decade old, should be continued, or will we have become accustomed to our reduced privacy and let the program slide into permanency? When now-entrenched Patriot Act provisions come up for renewal, is Congress likely to do anything more than tweak a few provisions—perhaps appeasing the vocal librarians or slightly easing the burden on nonprofit organizations? Congress is not likely to take on the job of seriously reexamining the effectiveness and costs of antiterrorism strategies unless the voters want it done.

I have speculated that voters have not expressed more concern about those strategies because we have been kept unaware of the extent of their costs, and perhaps because we don't really want to know if post-9/11 strategies promising to keep us safe are actually impotent. Fear is a powerful motivator. But certainly another reason Congress is not hearing more outrage from constituents is that the brunt of the impact of our post-9/11 program has fallen on Muslims, a minority in the United States practicing a widely misunderstood religion and easily stereotyped as resembling the 9/11 hijackers. The stories in this book show quite clearly that the people who have suffered the greatest collateral damage—pretextual arrests as "material witnesses," actual rather than merely potential prosecution for posting links on a website or associating with watchlisted charities, mysteriously closed bank accounts, and *de facto* exile—are Muslims.[24] The milder impact felt by non-Muslim Americans—loss of privacy, occasional cooptation as government agents, and embarrassing experiences at the airport—may seem to many like an acceptable bargain. This view, of course, discounts the deeper and less visible damage the New Normal is doing to our constitutional principles, to our democracy, and to our way of life. Nevertheless, as polling data suggest, people find it all too easy to bargain away liberty in the hope of gaining safety if the liberty belongs to someone else.[25] Pew Center polls conducted between 2001 and 2006, for example, show that more than twice as many respondents were in favor of allowing airport personnel to do extra checks on passengers who appear to be of Middle Eastern descent than were in favor of allowing the government to monitor their own telephone conversations, e-mails, or credit card purchases. A *New York Times*/CBS poll in January 2006 showed that "respondents overwhelmingly supported [70%] email and telephone monitoring directed at 'Americans that the government is suspicious of;' they overwhelmingly opposed [68%] the same kind of surveillance if it was aimed at 'ordinary Americans.'"[26] A 2005 Gallup poll revealed that "[m]ore than half [of Americans polled] are in favor of subjecting all Arabs, including Arab Americans, to special security checks at airports" while only 48 percent favored allowing police to stop people at random on the street, and 46 percent favored requiring "Arabs" to carry a special ID.[27] A Gallup poll conducted in January 2010 showed that 71 percent of those polled felt that those who "fit the profile" of suspected terrorists should be subjected to more intensive security checks before being permitted to board airplanes.[28]

Why give up a dragnet that might possibly catch someone dangerous unless you care about the innocent people who predictably will be swept up? Beneath the attitudes these polls reveal seems to be an assumption that "Arabs" or Muslims are presumptively guilty and that they are not like the rest of us. John Hart Ely, in his classic book *Democracy and Distrust*,[29] points out that democracy is at its worst when it comes to protecting the rights of minorities—which is why politically insulated courts have an indispensable role to play in our constitutional democracy.

Secrecy and the Courts

One critically important reason the courts have not been more active in reviewing the constitutionality of the array of antiterrorism measures I have been discussing, as the previous chapters have shown, is the hydra-headed invocation of secrecy. The executive branch's addiction to secrecy has had a devastating impact on the ability of the courts to do their traditional job of guarding rights and protecting minorities against discriminatory enforcement. To be sure, there are certainly aspects of the government's antiterrorism activities that should be treated as confidential. But secrecy claims can be overblown—like the mosaic theory—and can sometimes amount to nothing more than cover-ups. Take the state secrets privilege. The Bush and then Obama lawyers have invoked this privilege, as already described, to keep cases out of court altogether, sometimes without even allowing the court to review whether an asserted national security concern is credible. Recognizing this "privilege" as the nuclear option of litigation, a number of judges have been reluctant to accept such a diminished role, and for good reason. One of the two cases creating the state secrets privilege,[30] a 1953 case called *Reynolds v. United States*,[31] is a perfect example of why the courts need to be able to evaluate national security secrecy claims.

Robert Reynolds, who worked for an Air Force contractor, was one of nine people who died in the crash of a B-29 airplane in Waycross, Georgia, in 1948. His widow, together with the widows of two of his colleagues, brought a wrongful death action against the government. The Air Force had investigated and written a report on the accident, but the government refused to allow Mrs. Reynolds to see it, telling the court that the plane had been testing a new missile guidance system and so disclosing the report was not in the public interest. Although the lower courts were not so tractable, the Supreme Court cooperatively agreed to dismiss the case in order to preserve the government's self-declared secrets. But when the report in question eventually was publicly released in 1996, it turned out that it did not actually contain any military secrets. It did, however, provide a great deal of support for Mrs. Reynolds's claim that the government had been negligent: a record of serious pilot error, prior knowledge that the B-29 engines tended to catch fire, and a disgraceful history of maintenance and safety procedures. Under the cover of national security arguments, the government was simply trying to conceal its own negligence.[32]

As described earlier, both Bush and Obama lawyers have often argued that key documents were too secret to be shared with plaintiffs' attorneys or with a court. The result of concealing documents, with or without the court's agreement, has been to leave some plaintiffs unable to pursue their cases, and others at a disadvantage in arguing against evidence they have not seen. And of course the "John Does" challenging the constitutionality of gag orders have had to comply with the gag orders throughout their litigation, adding another element of secrecy to complicate litigation and leaving the public in the dark. But the reductio ad absurdum of the government's drive for secrecy has been insistence that certain cases not even be listed on the court's docket. Beyond being asked to pretend that an individual document does not exist (as in the *Al-Haramain* case described in chapter 10), courts and litigants have been instructed to pretend that entire cases do not exist. We do not know how many cases have been thoroughly buried in the name of national security, for obvious reasons, but another clerical Internet error exposed one early post-9/11 example.

Mohamed Kamel Bellahouel, who had been a veterinarian in Algeria, came to the United States in 1996 to study biology at Florida Atlantic University. He and his wife, an American citizen, lived in Fort Lauderdale. When Mohamed ran out of money for tuition, he took a job as a waiter at a Middle Eastern restaurant in Boca Raton where, as it happened, several Al Qaeda hijackers had eaten a few weeks before the 9/11 attacks. The FBI thought it "likely" that Mohamed had served the hijackers their food. So in October 2001, Mohamed was arrested on a charge that he had failed to comply with the conditions of his 1996 student visa. He was then turned over to the FBI as a material witness. While he was in custody, he filed a habeas corpus petition asking the court to order his release. Five months later, after testifying before a grand jury, he was released on bond. He set out to change his immigration status, as someone married to an American citizen usually is able to do as a matter of routine.

While his case was pending, Mohamed and his lawyers at the Miami Federal Public Defender's office were surprised to learn that the government was insisting that his habeas corpus petition be treated by the courts as an absolute secret. The case was not listed on the court's docket; all court opinions were filed under seal; all courtrooms were closed to the public and press during argument.[33] The court did not explain its reasons for acceding to this extraordinary level of secrecy. Although Mohamed was now free and so no longer needed the court to order his release, he insisted on filing an appeal in order to challenge the gag order burying his case. Mohamed's lawyer, Paul Rashkind, shakes his head over the fact that, of all the people involved in this case, it was the noncitizen who cared passionately enough about the First Amendment to want to pursue this issue.

Due to a clerical error that left some information available on the Internet for a short time, Dan Christensen, a reporter for the *Miami Daily Business Review*, discovered the existence of the appeal and published an article about it,[34] which was picked up by national news media. A *Christian Science Monitor* article began, "It's the case that doesn't exist."[35] Paul Rashkind could tell swarming reporters little about the case because of the gag order, which he still honors. In the Eleventh Circuit Court of Appeals, headquartered in Atlanta, Georgia, the argument about whether all this violated the public's right of access to judicial proceedings, ironically, took place in secret. The court followed up by filing a secret opinion. The court's decision was that all documents in the case should remain sealed. Rashkind asked the Supreme Court to review this decision, compliantly filing two versions of the petition under the cryptic name *M.K.B. v. Warden*: one a heavily censored public version (the first public document filed in the case) and the other a full version for the Court's eyes only. The Reporters Committee for Freedom of the Press urged the Supreme Court to take the case, arguing that this extreme level of secrecy was a drastic departure from regular court procedures and unconstitutionally prevented the press from reporting on a matter of national interest:

> [I]t is impossible to judge whether M.K.B. was legitimately detained, or whether he was the victim of racial or ethnic profiling. It is also impossible to evaluate whether the government has a valid reason for deporting a man who had lived and worked peacefully in the United States for six years prior to his detainment.[36]

The Supreme Court declined to hear the case.[37] But shortly afterward, the case was listed on the lower court's docket in a redacted form. The public was then able to see sixty-five uninformative docket entries like: "SEALED DOCUMENT, SEALED MOTION, SEALED ORDER, SEALED NOTICE OF SEALED HEARING, SEALED MINUTES OF HEARING, SEALED TRANSCRIPT OF HEARING, and SEALED NOTICE OF APPEAL." No court order had led to the sealing of the record, evidently, and no court order led to its partial unsealing.

The closure of the *M.K.B.* case, like the web of secrecy surrounding some of the cases discussed earlier (the Library Connection case in chapter 8 and the John Doe litigation in chapter 9), shows that another constitutional right endangered during the War on Terror decade was the public's First Amendment right of access to judicial proceedings. This right is not only for the benefit of the litigants. Opening judicial proceedings to scrutiny by the press and public is one of the Constitution's methods for preventing injustice and providing accountability to the "jury of the whole"— the general public.[38] Countering this tradition of open court proceedings, in the fall of 2001, the government also began using the "mosaic theory" to urge the courts to exclude the public and press from deportation hearings in an entire group of cases designated as "special interest" cases.

Rabih Haddad, a well-known imam in Detroit, was included on the list of special interest cases—apparently because of his connection with the Global Relief Foundation, one of the Muslim charities blacklisted by President Bush. He was not charged with any crime; the government opportunistically decided to deport him for overstaying his visa. Because he was a public figure, a number of people became interested in his case, including Michigan Representative John Conyers, Jr., one of the most diligent of Congress's watchdogs. (At a recent public event, Senator Richard Durbin quipped that "John Conyers is to justice as John Coltrane is to jazz.") Conyers was highly skeptical of the notion that Rabih Haddad was financing Al Qaeda and wanted to attend the hearing to see what was going on. And so he joined the *Detroit Free Press* in challenging the constitutionality of closing the deportation proceeding.

Judge Nancy Edmunds asked the government what harm might be done if members of the public attended this hearing—given that any classified documents or testimony the government offered could be kept confidential even in a public hearing. The government's lawyers responded that it might aid terrorists to know whom the government was targeting for deportation. Judge Edmunds didn't understand how that argument applied to the case of Rabih Haddad, who had already broadcast far and wide that the government was seeking to deport him—including to a Congressman and the press. Not getting any further explanation from the government lawyers about just how national security was threatened in this case, she ruled that this hearing, at least, should be open to the public.[39] The Sixth Circuit Court of Appeals, which covers Michigan, agreed. In an opinion vindicating the First Amendment right of access to the courts, Judge Damon Keith majestically declared, "Democracies die behind closed doors."[40]

Government lawyers saw a special need in terrorism-related cases to shut out the public; others, especially members of the press, saw a special need for the public to be able to observe what was happening, given the controversial nature of these proceedings and the possible implication of religious profiling. The Sixth Circuit respected the traditional presumption in favor of First Amendment rights instead of just deferring to the government's all-encompassing national security claims:

> The Government could use its "mosaic intelligence" argument as a justification to close any public hearing completely and categorically, including criminal proceedings. The Government could operate in virtual secrecy in all matters dealing, even remotely with "national security," resulting in a wholesale suspension of First Amendment rights.[41]

But other courts have been far more deferential to mosaic theory claims,[42] including the Third Circuit Court of Appeals, which covers New Jersey, in a more general challenge to secret deportation hearings[43] and the D.C. Circuit Court of Appeals in Freedom of Information Act litigation.[44]

The Eclipse of the Courts

The failure of the courts even to consider the constitutionality of so many post-9/11 programs is perhaps the most disturbing aspect of the stories I have recounted because the federal courts are supposed to be our constitutional safety net. Article III of the Constitution designed the federal judiciary to be independent of politics in order to protect us against too much democracy. Even if a majority of Americans are willing to barter the rights of Muslims—or freedom of speech, privacy, and even democracy itself—in exchange for a greater sense of safety, it is the job of life-tenured judges to keep us from selling our constitutional birthright for a mess of pottage. Typically, courts do that by demanding that the government demonstrate that rights-compromising strategies really do serve a compelling need—like promoting our safety—and that there is no equally effective way to do what is needed without sacrificing rights. This was the approach of the Sixth Circuit in the *Detroit Free Press* case. It should have been the Supreme Court's task in the *Humanitarian Law Project* case to judge independently whether the material support law dragnet actually promotes the compelling interest of keeping us safe and whether it is worth its cost in freedom of speech—not just to nod along with executive branch assurances. To be sure, this is a challenging job, since judges are also human beings who feel fear and, as many judges are the first to say, are not generally national security experts. But the job of a judge is to choose rationality over fear, and to learn enough from experts to make informed independent decisions—as judges do every day in all kinds of cases ranging from eye-crossing antitrust cases to scientifically sophisticated patent claims.

The Supreme Court rose to this challenge in the Guantánamo and enemy combatant cases—*Rasul v. Bush, Hamdi v. Rumsfeld, Hamdan v. Rumsfeld*, and *Boumediene v. Bush*. The Court listened to experts, exercised independent judgment, and preserved fundamental constitutional principles of due process and judicial review, all in the face of fervent executive branch claims that our safety depended on allowing the president to decide who is an enemy combatant without being second-guessed by the courts. But during the War on Terror decade, the Court bowed to a comparable argument in the *Humanitarian Law Project* case, one of only three cases about domestic antiterrorism strategies it has agreed to hear so far. The Court has distanced itself from other important constitutional claims, simply refusing to hear cases including:

- the Third Circuit Court of Appeals case holding that it was permissible to exclude the public and the media from a whole category of deportation cases,[45] even though that decision was in tension with the Sixth Circuit *Detroit Free Press* decision.[46] (Ordinarily, the Court prioritizes resolving conflicts between Courts of Appeals.)
- the ruling of the one-sided Foreign Intelligence Surveillance Court of Review that the expansion of FISA that later affected Brandon Mayfield was constitutional[47]
- the *M.K.B.* "supersealing" case[48]
- the D.C. Circuit's broad endorsement of the "mosaic theory"[49]
- the Second Circuit's ruling that expansive use of the material

witness statute for arresting people who might have information about terrorism investigations is permissible[50]

- the Sixth Circuit's ruling that the lawyers and journalists who wanted to challenge the illegal NSA spying program, before Congress had laundered it, lacked standing[51]
- Roya Rahmani's appeal from the Ninth Circuit decision prohibiting her from challenging the "foreign terrorist" designation of the Iranian pro-democracy group she supported[52]
- Brandon Mayfield's appeal from the Ninth Circuit decision dismissing his challenge to the FISA provisions under which he was searched as an "agent of a foreign power"[53]
- the Fourth Circuit's dismissal of a case brought by "extraordinary rendition" victim Khaled el-Masri as precluded by the state secrets privilege,[54] despite the fact that the details of what happened to him—he was kidnapped with the collusion of American agents from a Macedonian bus and taken to a cell in Afghanistan where he was locked up, interrogated, and tortured for five months because his name was similar to that of a suspected terrorist[55]—had been published in media around the world and all Khaled really wanted was an apology[56]
- the Second Circuit's dismissal of another extraordinary rendition case brought by Canadian Maher Arar, on different procedural grounds.[57] The Canadian government had investigated Arar's complaint that American agents had kidnapped him at JFK airport and sent him to Syria where he was abused and tortured, concluding that his claims were all true and that suspicion of him had been unfounded. The Canadian government issued a formal apology to Arar for its role in his mistreatment and offered him damages in the amount of $10.5 million.[58] He got no hearing and no apology in the United States of America—just procedural excuses for slamming the courthouse door in his face. Obama Administration lawyers urged the Supreme Court not to review the decision; neither the executive branch nor Congress has shown any interest in finding out whether Maher Arar or Khaled el-Masri is owed an apology.

In our judiciocentric society, when the courts, especially the Supreme Court, remain silent on the constitutionality of government actions, that silence begins to sound like acquiescence. It is also notable that the three cases concerning the domestic impact of antiterrorism strategies that the Supreme Court did agree to hear—*Holder v. Humanitarian Law Project*, *Ashcroft v. al-Kidd*, and *Ashcroft v. Iqbal*—were all cases in which the government had lost. In all of the cases the Court refused to hear, the government's position had prevailed in the courts below.

The record in the lower courts has been only slightly less one-sided. Bush and Obama Administration lawyers, as many of the cases discussed have shown, offered the lower federal courts a smorgasbord of procedural excuses for avoiding constitutional questions about antiterrorism measures—not just the state secrets privilege—and most courts, especially the Courts of Appeals, played along. The NSA spying program, even while it was clearly illegal, evaded judicial scrutiny because of one of two hyperextended versions of the standing doctrine: either (1) that lawyers unable to talk to their clients do not suffer any recognizable injury,[59] or (2) that everyone suffers injury because of this program and so the plaintiffs are not special enough for a court to hear.[60] The *Al-Haramain* case—where the plaintiffs could not prove that they were injured because they were forced to pretend that the document proving that they had been spied on did not exist[61]—represented a new low in standing arguments. Bush and Obama lawyers have also argued that government officials should be declared immune from lawsuits about patently illegal activities—in another NSA challenge, for example.[62] Obama lawyers continued to argue that John Ashcroft should be found immune from Abdullah al-Kidd's lawsuit challenging his pretextual arrest as a "material witness."[63]

Another extraordinary rendition victim, Ethiopian citizen Binyam Mohamed, tried to get his day in court to complain of his shocking detention and torture at the behest of American agents. He had spent eighteen months locked up and, among other horrifying abuses, had his genitals repeatedly sliced with razor blades and hot, stinging liquid poured into the open wounds. The district court dismissed his case without letting him or his co-plaintiffs prove that the defendant, Jeppesen Dataplan, had collaborated with the CIA in illegally flying him to Morocco, Afghanistan, and finally Guantánamo Bay. The plaintiffs' lawyers had learned from the earlier extraordinary rendition cases that it was impossible to have the government held responsible for his treatment, so they sued the government's ally and enabler—the company described in an article by Jane Mayer as "the C.I.A.'s travel agent."[64] Jeppesen couldn't claim governmental immunity, but the government insisted that the state secrets privilege should bar all litigation about extraordinary renditions anyway and the district court agreed, dismissing this case too.

The plaintiffs appealed. After Bush Administration lawyers had filed an appellate brief maintaining that the district court was right to dismiss the case, Obama took office—about three weeks before the case was scheduled to be argued. At the argument, Court of Appeals Judge Mary Schroeder slyly asked the government attorney, "Is there anything material that has happened" recently that might have caused the Justice Department to shift its views?[65] The court and spectators were stunned when the government lawyer replied that the Justice Department was continuing to press the state secrets privilege argument. Ben Wizner, the lawyer representing Binyam Mohamed, remarked, "The only place in the world where these claims can't be discussed is in this courtroom." Judge Schroeder's panel ruled in favor of the plaintiffs, ordering that the case be allowed to continue in light of the fact that most of the information involved, although embarrassing to the United States, was indeed public. But the entire Ninth Circuit Court of Appeals reversed that decision and the Supreme Court declined to review the case.[66] The federal courts, then, had reached unanimity, refusing to hear every single victim of torture or extraordinary rendition who had sought their help.

In yet another example of procedural avoidance that has roiled the entire world of American civil litigation, the Supreme Court dismissed another complaint against John Ashcroft, brought by Muslim men arrested and detained in the fall of 2001.[67] One of those men, Javaid Iqbal, was a Pakistani citizen who had been working as a cable installer in Hicksville, Long Island, when he was arrested in New York City in November 2001 for suspected immigration fraud and locked up in the Metropolitan Detention Center for six months. While there, he was brutalized by guards, denied medical treatment, and prevented from exercising his religion. His description of this abusive treatment is entirely credible: an Inspector General report on the fall 2001 detentions had documented the practices he described.[68] But the Supreme Court came up with new rules about what kinds of facts lawyers had to put in their complaint before a lawsuit could begin and found that Iqbal's claim did not satisfy this new standard.[69]

Of course, reliance on procedural excuses to keep civil rights victims out of court is not limited to national security cases. It is a part of what Erwin Chemerinsky, in a recent book, calls "the conservative assault on the Constitution."[70] This phenomenon threatens to diminish our constitutional rights by neutralizing the courts and allowing the political branches to do whatever a majority of their constituents will approve. There is a very big difference between a democracy and a constitutional democracy. That is the difference on which the United States of America is founded. The Constitution binds us to fundamental principles and the courts are supposed to hold us to those commitments when we waver.

Is it unrealistic to expect that the courts will hold the line and protect our rights in an anxious era when the political branches claim that surrendering rights will promote our safety?[71] American history is full of examples of the Supreme Court failing to protect rights during times of war or crisis. As Norman Dorsen once said, "National security . . . has been a graveyard for civil liberties for much of our recent history."[72] Often heading the list of ignominious cases is *Korematsu v. United States*,[73] where the Court upheld the government's shameful treatment of West Coast Japanese-Americans during World War II.[74] *Korematsu* stands as a warning that judicial deference to national security claims must have its limits. The Court's approval of exclusions of over a hundred thousand innocent people from their homes was based, as was later disclosed, on highly misleading evidence submitted by the government. A federal appellate court in California, later reexamining the evidence the government had presented to the courts (primarily a report by General DeWitt) and the considerable amount of contradictory evidence it had withheld, believed that the Supreme Court might well have reached a different conclusion had it known all the facts. Perhaps some representatives of the government were so confident that this program promoted national security that they did not want to take the risk that the Supreme Court would disagree. Or perhaps they wanted to cover up how thin or how embarrassing the full record actually was. The original version of DeWitt's report, the California court noted over four decades after the fact, did not even "purport to rest on any military exigency, but instead declared that because of traits peculiar to citizens of Japanese ancestry it would be impossible to separate the loyal from the disloyal."[75] The Supreme Court's deference allowed a disgraceful course of conduct to proceed and left as its legacy an opinion that, in hindsight, is an abject embarrassment. Legal historian Geoffrey Stone notes that while our history is full of instances where courts, including the Supreme Court, have made the mistake of underprotecting rights of minorities or all Americans, there is no demonstrable instance where American courts have undermined our national security by overprotecting rights.[76]

There have been instances of judicial courage as well as cowardice, even during wartime—like Robert Jackson's eloquent paean to First Amendment values in *West Virginia v. Barnette*,[77] where the Court upheld the right of Jehovah's Witnesses to decline to salute the American flag in 1943, right in the middle of World War II. The historic Guantánamo decisions also show how the Supreme Court can lead a national conversation about controversial constitutional and policy questions and spearhead much-needed change. A handful of district judges described in the previous chapters—Ann Aiken, William Alsup, Janet Hall, Victor Marrero, Anna Diggs Taylor, Vaughn Walker—and a few appellate panels—the Sixth Circuit in the secret deportation hearing case and the Second Circuit in reviewing the exclusion of Tariq Ramadan and the dismissal of the challenge to the FISA Amendments Act of 2008—have played a critical role in the national dialogue about our own rights. Marrero's and Hall's decisions set the stage for Congress to review gag orders; the Second Circuit's pro–First Amendment decision forced Hillary Clinton's hand in granting scholars like Ramadan visas. But when the courts remain silent or offer unearned approval of actions the political branches favor, we are deprived of a critical voice speaking for our fundamental values.[78]

To restore our rights and our balances, we have to tell the president, any president, that we are not willing to sacrifice our rights for placebos. Franklin Roosevelt is said to have told an individual who was giving him advice about something what he should do, "You have to make me do it." Elected officials pay attention to what their constituents think. We have to demand that our representatives exercise independent oversight, with our participation, whether they want to or not. As other commentators have observed, Congress is actually our best hope for protecting our privacy and our other rights at this point.[79] Restoring the courts to a full partnership position will be a long-term project. But the first step is to recognize that the role that both of those branches have been neglecting is essential.

Conclusion

What is clear is that this "war on terror" will never come to a public, decisive end. It is likely, however, to shape the way we think about and experience American democracy as well as its rights and privileges for generations to come.—Anthony D. Romero (2007)[1]

As nightfall does not come all at once, neither does oppression. In both instances, there is a twilight when everything remains seemingly unchanged. And it is in such twilight that we all must be most aware of change in the air—however slight—lest we become unwitting victims of the darkness.—Justice William O. Douglas[2]

Democracy isn't what governments do, it's what people do.—Howard Zinn

PERHAPS THE MOST important reason the destructive War on Terror campaign has been allowed to continue with so few modifications is the assumption that 9/11 was such a unique event that we are justified in making exceptions to our usual principles to meet the extraordinary threat of terrorism. But the threat of terrorism is neither new nor unique. The framers of our Constitution lived in a world of British sleeper cells and reactionaries threatening to reverse the results of the American Revolution itself.[3] It is impossible to read James Madison's Federalist Papers account of his concerns for the security of New York without an uncanny sense of déjà vu:

[N]o part of the Union ought to feel more anxiety . . . than New-York. . . . The great emporium of its commerce, the great reservoir of its wealth, lies every moment at the mercy of events, and may almost be regarded as a hostage, for ignominious compliances with the dictates of a foreign enemy, or even with the rapacious demands of pirates and barbarians.[4]

The Constitution Madison and his contemporaries drafted in their turbulent era was not a document for fair weather only, to be put aside in any storm. It was a document of essential principles intended for war, peace, and twilight stages.

Threats of terrorism from domestic or foreign sources have vexed most of the world at various times, and many other countries have also been tempted to modify their laws and principles to cope with those threats. We can learn a great deal from their experiences. An Eminent Jurists Panel established by the International Commission of Jurists and chaired by Arthur Chaskalson, former president of the Constitutional Court of South Africa, spent several years conducting hearings around the world to study the clash between antiterrorism laws and previously accepted rights and principles in countries ranging from Argentina to Israel to the United States. After three years of hearings and deliberations, the panel found that the nations they studied made a serious mistake by characterizing the threat of terrorism as unique and then changing their laws or ignoring international treaties and conventions in response, rather than simply adhering to their established rule of law:

> Terrorism sows terror, and many States have fallen into a trap set by the terrorists. Ignoring lessons from the past, some States have allowed themselves to be rushed into hasty responses, introducing an array of measures which are undermining cherished values as well as the international legal framework carefully evolved over at least the last half-century.[5]

As Harold Hongju Koh, now Legal Advisor to the State Department and a Yale Law School faculty member at the time, put it in 2002:

> In the days since [September 11], I have been struck by how many Americans—and how many lawyers—seem to have concluded that, somehow, the destruction of four planes and three buildings has taken us back to a state of nature in which there are no laws or rules. In fact, over the years, we have developed an elaborate system of domestic and international laws, institutions, regimes, and decision-making procedures precisely so that they will be consulted and obeyed, not ignored, at a time like this.[6]

The Eminent Jurist Panel's chief recommendation was that we need to take stock and reexamine our reactions to threats like 9/11 in order to avoid normalizing exceptional responses.[7] This echoes the 9/11 Commission recommendation that we should reevaluate our post-9/11 policies and demand that the executive branch carry the burden of justifying the continuation of policies that are costly in terms of liberty.[8]

Ordinary Americans and the Constitution

That is where we come in. The greatest problem we face in restoring our rule of law is mustering the political will to begin that reevaluation, given that all three branches of the federal government have been bunched on one side of the scale. But the stories I have recounted in this book, although troubling in many respects, show us what needs to happen and what can happen when some of the Constitution's strategies for preservation of our values—like providing us with rights enforceable in court and with governmental checks and balances—are not heeded. During the War on Terror decade, it fell to people who were not on the government payroll to fight to preserve our rights and our democracy. The victims of mistakes, dragnets, and watchlists—like Brandon Mayfield (the American "foreign agent"), like Abdullah al-Kidd (who was arrested on the pretext that he was a "material witness"), like Erich Scherfen (who almost lost his job as a pilot), like Hossam Algabri (who was banished by his bank)—told their stories publicly; many endured years of litigation in the hope that others could be spared having the same things happen to them. Reporters with major news media, like Barton Gellman, Eric Lichtblau, and James Risen; librarians, like George Christian; and their fellow John Does including Internet service provider Nick Merrill, patriotically stood up for First Amendment freedoms of thought and speech, including our right to talk back to the government. Scholars, humanitarians, lawyers, social workers, and historians fought in the courts and in the media to defend our privacy, our freedom of speech, and our freedom of association. Muslim-Americans have contested the demonization of their religion.

This is all part of the Constitution's design too. That remarkable document provides multiple layers of protection for its fundamental structures so that even when our courts and representatives fail us, we can keep democracy alive if we have the will. The Constitution's bottom line is that the people who, in the end, have the responsibility to safeguard our constitutional heritage are the very people who truly are the government: "we, the people," in the first words of the Preamble. Our government is not just for the people but, truly, of the people and by the people. The Constitution casts us in active roles. We are the ultimate policymakers, deciding on what the laws will contain by voting and by lobbying our representatives. If we have a complaint, the First Amendment guarantees us the right to petition the government for redress of grievances. We are the ultimate adjudicators. The Constitution empowers us to serve on juries so, like John Steger of Idaho, we can use that power to thwart unjust prosecutions. We are the ultimate watchdogs. The First Amendment right of access to the courts and the Sixth Amendment right to public trials enable us to monitor what the courts are doing. The First Amendment also encompasses a guarantee of freedom of the press so that reporters can provide us with information we need to make policy decisions and to monitor the conduct of our elected officials and courts. As several of the previous chapters have shown, the press has been invaluable during the past decade in revealing attempts to subvert democracy, like President Bush's self-approved Terrorist Surveillance Program. The lawyers who brought a constitutional challenge against the NSA program were able to do so only because they read about the program in the *New York Times*. Lawyers who were seeking justice for extraordinary rendition victims learned from an article in the *New Yorker* about the role of Jeppesen Dataplan in transporting victims to sites where they were detained and tortured. Without investigative journalists, we would know far less than we do today about how our elected officials have chosen to fight terrorism.

The Constitution also guarantees us the right of association so that we don't have to do our jobs alone. Alexis de Tocqueville once famously observed that we are a nation of joiners. Civic associations have proven indispensable in enabling individuals to stand up to the government in the past decade, as they have at other points in our history. Organizations like the ACLU, the Cato Institute, the Center for Constitutional Rights, the Electronic Freedom Foundation, Human Rights First, Human Rights Watch, and the Rutherford Institute, among many others, have worked hard to educate the public, Congress, and the courts about the side of the balance elected officials tended to ignore—and were able to do so only because of the support of their members. It is because ACLU membership practically doubled during the War on Terror decade that ACLU lawyers were able to participate in most of the cases I have described, helping all the John Does to make their voices heard.

In addition to organizing in civic associations, individuals can organize through their state and local governmental units.[9] Yet another facet of the Constitution's design for protecting freedom and democracy is the structure of federalism. James Madison called the two interlocking layers of federal and state government a "double security"[10] for our freedoms. If the states deny people fundamental rights, the federal government is given power to intervene—to protect an individual's right to vote, for example. And if the federal government is stingy in protecting rights, the states can afford greater protections through their own state constitutions or laws. Oregon law, for instance, provides limitations on when state or local police can infiltrate a religious group that are more stringent than the limitations binding federal officers in the same situation.[11] This flexibility creates what one scholar called a "self-correcting constitutional compass."[12] Because of the U.S. Constitution's Supremacy Clause, the states cannot control federal agents and so a state could not, for example, declare that federal agents may not use Patriot Act powers within their state. But state and local governments can generate grassroots pressure to change federal law. In the late eighteenth century, the states of Virginia and Kentucky passed resolutions declaring their judgment that Congress's Alien and Sedition Acts violated constitutional principles[13] even if the federal government did not think so at the time. In the early twenty-first century, over 400 cities, towns, and villages as well as eight states fought back against the Patriot Act, declaring its provisions inimical to American values by signing on to variations on a Bill of Rights Defense Committee resolution.[14] These resolutions could not prevent federal officials from implementing federal law, but they could and did prohibit state employees from exacerbating the impact of Patriot Act provisions by providing voluntary assistance. The Portland, Oregon, City Council withdrew from a Joint Terrorism Task Force because it was concerned that joint federal-state operations might engender violations of the Oregon law limiting the ability of Oregon agents to infiltrate political or religious groups.[15]

Local politics can also lead individual local law enforcement officers to dissent from federal policy.[16] For example, when the FBI tried to enlist local law enforcement officials to help conduct mass interrogations of some 5,000 Arab and Muslim men in the fall of 2001, some, like the Chiefs of Police in Detroit and in Portland, Oregon, declined to participate.[17] Because of the Tenth Amendment (which reserves certain rights to the states), they could not be compelled to act as federal agents[18] and so their resistance served as another kind of check on federal overreaching. If more than a few local officials declined to help the FBI, the federal government would have to come up with the money to hire more federal agents in order to implement such an extensive interrogation program. Federalism is very much a two-way street, however, and one of the greatest sources of civil liberties violations committed during the course of terrorism investigations in recent years has been the Fusion Centers, multi-jurisdictional intelligence centers designed to combine and provide access to intelligence to and from federal, state, and local sources.[19]

Creative lawyers found other ways to use the "dual security" of state and local law to resist federal overreaching. When it was discovered that telecommunications companies had been violating federal law with impunity by providing the NSA with their customers' private phone records, the ACLU filed complaints with the Public Utilities Commissions of twenty-four states to trigger investigations into whether the companies had also violated state laws.[20] A number of the state commissions began investigations, but federal will prevailed when Congress asserted its supremacy and ordered the state commissions to leave the telecoms alone, in the same statute granting the telecoms immunity from lawsuits.[21] Congress was unwilling to share decision-making power with the states, the press, or the people. The House of Representatives even passed a resolution condemning the *New York Times* for having published the article revealing the NSA surveillance.[22] But the law Congress passed blocking the state Public Utilities Commissions and providing the telecoms with retroactive immunity expires in 2012 and can be reexamined if we want it to be. Congress cannot shut us out or shut us up permanently because we are the government.

The Constitution is resilient. It only needs us.

Restoring Balance

If we are willing to follow the lead of the John Does and take on the job of defending the Constitution, we can start by trying to learn from our history how to change. Critics of War on Terror measures frequently cite a canonical list of American violations of rights during times of war or crisis: the Alien and Sedition Acts, Lincoln's suspension of habeas corpus during the Civil War, suppression of speech during World War I, the Palmer Raids, the Japanese-American internments of World War II, the McCarthy-era Communist witch hunts, Richard Nixon's practices of spying on Americans and repressing dissent. Their point is often to compare our past mistakes with our present mistakes in order to evaluate whether we have learned as a society.[23] Evaluation is important, but so is action. Instead of looking to grade ourselves on our progress or lack of progress, or to flagellate ourselves again for the mistakes of the past, I propose that we look at these episodes to study *how* we restored our balance where we did, and what went wrong where we did not. A substantial exploration of this history is far more than I can accomplish here, but I will offer a few examples to invite further study and discussion.

John Adams and the Federalists justified the draconian Sedition Act of 1798, which criminalized speech critical of the government, on the ground that spies and foreign agents inciting insurrection were jeopardizing the nation's security.[24] That controversial law, which the Republicans had opposed, expired at the end of Adams's term and the political process offered recovery in two stages. When the Republicans won the next election, Thomas Jefferson promptly pardoned everyone who had been convicted under the Sedition Act and released those who were still serving sentences. Some forty years later, Congress repaid the fines collected under this Act and issued a committee report declaring the Sedition Act to have been unconstitutional, just as Virginia and Kentucky had thought at the time.[25] The Alien Enemies Act of the same vintage (allowing detention or deportation of citizens or subjects of a nation at war with us), on the other hand, is still with us.

Change in our antiterrorism policies, as I have shown, did not follow the election of Barack Obama. It seems unlikely that our future presidents will be more sensitive to constitutional values than former Constitutional Law professors like Obama and Bill Clinton, both of whom have fully supported rights-restrictive antiterrorism measures. And it could well be forty years before Congress is ready to apologize to Abdullah al-Kidd for his unjustified arrest, or to revise the vague and threatening material support laws.

There are more reasons for pessimism. In other times, the wars that prompted emergency action ended, so there was a trigger to prompt consideration of whether to restore abridged rights. But there will never be an armistice with terror to inspire our return to normal, especially if the War on Terror is, as it was under the Bush Administration, perceived as a war on all terrorists—Iranians who support pro-democracy groups, Kurdish nationalists, and anti-Israel Palestinians alike—rather than only on Al Qaeda. And even after a finite war, true restoration of balance can be painfully slow. After World War II, for example, Congress reacted fairly promptly to authorize compensation for property lost by Japanese-Americans driven from their homes by our internment policy.[26] But it was not until 1971 that Congress passed a statute prohibiting the future detention of Americans without congressional approval.[27] And it was not until 1988 that President Ronald Reagan signed an act proclaiming the internments an injustice, and offering an apology and reparations.[28] It took actions by all three branches of the federal government as well as a commission to effect those corrections. President Gerald Ford had issued a presidential proclamation in 1976, in connection with the bicentennial celebration of the Constitution. In 1980, Congress followed up by establishing a blue-ribbon commission, which spent several years hearing from hundreds of witnesses and reviewing hundreds of documents before concluding, in 1983, that the internment decisions were due to "race prejudice, war hysteria and a failure of political leadership" rather than military necessity.[29] And both Fred Korematsu and Gordon Hirabayashi, who had lost their cases in the wartime Supreme Court, brought new federal court cases during the 1980s in which they won reversals of their convictions (for disobeying an exclusion order and defying a curfew, respectively)—over four decades after the fact—so the courts also played a significant role in the national dialogue.[30] Of course the *Korematsu* opinion itself, although in disrepute, was not actually overruled.

On some occasions, the Supreme Court has corrected its own course. But this too can be a painfully slow process, when it happens at all. During World War I and its aftermath, the Court had not been willing to reverse convictions for antiwar or anti-American speech, but after the war the Court gradually reformed its First Amendment doctrine to provide fuller protection for unpopular speech—although it then relapsed in the 1940s and 1950s in the face of the Communist scare. It took half a century before meaningful First Amendment protection of extreme or radical speech reached its high water mark.[31]

Perhaps the most encouraging model we have is the Church Committee, the robust commission process that restored balance and the rule of law after Richard Nixon subjected Americans to excessive and unwarranted surveillance—quite speedily, by historical standards. Frederick A. O. Schwarz, Jr., who was counsel to the Church Committee, along with co-author Aziz Huq, tells the fascinating story of how several years of bipartisan effort led to a thorough study of the nation's history of surveillance.[32] As a result, Senators Frank Church and Charles Mathias reported that the United States had been deemed to be in an almost constant state of emergency since 1933 and identified about 470 examples of emergency power legislation that had remained on the books.[33] Based on its study of history and bipartisan deliberations, the Church Committee attempted to move the country out of a perpetual state of emergency into a carefully considered rule of law. Schwarz and Huq see many parallels between that committee's work and the work of the 9/11 Commission, while ruing the fact that we never did internalize the lessons of the Church Committee well enough to avoid repeating the mistakes that committee tried to put behind us.[34]

My sketchy foray into history suggests that a bipartisan commission may have the best chance of rising above the politics that hamstring all three branches of government and inspiring reflection and perhaps change. The 9/11 Commission process was exemplary and some of its recommendations have made a difference, but its report is now over five years old. Will the innocent victims of the War on Terror have to wait for forty years, like the victims of the Sedition Act and World War II internment policies, before we are able to consider whether we have made any mistakes? Will inertia lead us into a second and perhaps third decade of War on Terror, or can we rise above fear and restore our democracy by initiating a process of reevaluation, as the 9/11 Commission itself recommended? Are we too deeply partisan to be able to launch a bipartisan effort?

The challenges are substantial, but we cannot afford to be daunted. Constitutional rights like the First Amendment freedoms of speech, association, religion, and access to the courts, Fourth Amendment privacy rights, due process, and equal protection rights should not just be written off as regrettable casualties of a metaphorical War on Terror. In this book, I have offered an account of how seriously we have jeopardized our rights and our democracy by going along with post-9/11 emergency measures that are supposed to be keeping us safe. I have also offered reasons to question whether some of those policies are misguided and even counterproductive. I do not offer a particular program for how to combat terrorism. Instead, my solution is process-based, like so much of the Constitution. My chief goal is to convince Americans to play the role the Constitution relies on us to play—to inform ourselves and take part in the serious policy debates we need to have, rather than passively trusting our elected leaders to make decisions for us. I hope that focusing attention on the costs of our antiterrorism strategies will help to inspire a reexamination of the policies themselves, greater public pressure on the president and Congress to restore our rights, greater expectations of the courts, and greater determination to preserve our rights in the future.

The Constitution, as our foundational document, is a lot like a marriage contract. Sometimes we may be tempted by strong emotions, like fear, to cheat on our commitments to our fundamental principles. But if we want to keep our privacy, our freedom of speech and thought, and our right to talk back to the government, we need to recommit ourselves to resisting that temptation and doing our own part to protect and defend the Constitution. After all, any worthwhile relationship takes work.

Notes

Introduction

1. RON SUSKIND, THE ONE PERCENT DOCTRINE SINCE 9/11 52 (New York: Simon & Schuster, 2006).

2. Uniting and Strengthening America by Providing Adequate Tools Required to Intercept and Obstruct Terrorism (USA PATRIOT Act), Pub. L. No. 107–56, 115 Stat 272 (2001).

3. Senator Russ Feingold explained his reasons for voting against the Patriot Act:

> Of course, there is no doubt that if we lived in a police state, it would be easier to catch terrorists . . . But that probably would not be a country in which we would want to live. And that would not be a country for which we could, in good conscience, ask our young people to fight and die. In short, that would not be America.

147 Cong. Rec. S10990-02, S11020 (daily ed. Oct. 25, 2001) (statement by Sen. Feingold).

By contrast, Senator Tom Daschle, the Democratic majority leader largely responsible for pushing through the Patriot Act, said "we made the best judgment we could, taking into account the very delicate balance between civil liberties and law enforcement that we had to achieve in bringing a bill of this complexity to the floor . . . all of those involved did a terrific job under the most difficult of circumstances." 147 Cong. Rec. S10547-07, S10574 (daily ed. Oct. 11, 2001) (statement by Sen. Daschle).

4. NAT'L COMM'N ON TERRORIST ATTACKS UPON THE U.S., 9/11 COMMISSION REPORT 394–95 (Washington, DC: USGPO, 2004), http://www.gpoaccess.gov/911/pdf/fullreport.pdf.

5. President Barack Obama, inaugural address (Jan. 21, 2009), http://www.whitehouse.gov/the_press_office/President_Barack_Obamas_Inaugural_Address/.

6. Transcript of Oral Argument at 47, ll. 17–22, Holder v. Humanitarian Law Project, ___ U.S. ___, 130 S. Ct. 2705 (2010) (No. 08–1498) (argued Feb. 23, 2010).

7. Editorial, *Breaking a Promise on Surveillance*, N.Y. TIMES, July 29, 2010, http://www.nytimes.com/2010/07/30/opinion/30fri1.html?_r=1.

8. *See* Marc Ambinder, *Clash with Congress: Obama Threatens Veto of Intelligence Funding Bill*, THE ATLANTIC, July 8, 2009, 4:47 P.M., http://www.theatlantic.com/politics/archive/2009/07/clash-with-congress-obama-threatens-veto-of-intelligence-funding-bill/20921/.

9. Press Release, U.S. Dep't of Justice, *Attorney General Establishes New State Secrets Policies and Procedures* (Sept. 23, 2009), http://www.justice.gov/opa/pr/2009/September/09-ag-1013.html.

10. Memorandum to the Heads of Exec. Dep'ts, Agencies & Dep't Components from Eric Holder, Attorney Gen., U.S. Dep't of Justice, Policies and Procedures Governing Invocation of the State Secrets Privilege 1 (Sept. 23, 2009), http://www.justice.gov/opa/documents/state-secret-privileges.pdf.

11. PLATO, THE REPUBLIC 2.359a–2.360d (Jowett trans., New York: Vintage Classics 1991).

12. In re Nat'l Sec. Agency Telecomm. Records Litig., 700 F. Supp. 2d 1182 (N.D. Cal. Mar. 31, 2010).

13. *See* Susan N. Herman, *Patriotic Dissent*, 45 WASHBURN L.J. 21 (2005).

14. There have been sporadic complaints of groups being targeted based on their viewpoints (antiwar, pro-Arab, pro-Palestinian, or socialist) during Obama's watch, but most of the incidents cited have occurred in Fusion Centers, where state officers supplement federal agents in counterterrorism roles. *See Spying on First Amendment Activity-State-by-State*, ACLU (Sept. 29, 2010), http://www.aclu.org/spy-files/spying-first-amendment-activity-state-state; *More About Fusion Centers*, ACLU (June 25, 2010), http://www.aclu.org/spy-files/more-about-fusion-centers.

15. *See* DIR. OF THE ADMIN. OFFICE OF THE UNITED STATES COURTS, REPORT ON APPLICATIONS FOR DELAYED-NOTICE SEARCH WARRANTS AND EXTENSIONS (2009), http://big.assets.huffingtonpost.com/SneakAndPeekReport.pdf.

16. J. M. Kalil & Steve Tetreault, *PATRIOT ACT: Law's Use Causing Concerns*, LAS VEGAS REVIEW-J., Nov. 5, 2003, http://reviewjournal.printthis.clickability.com/pt/cpt?action=cpt&expire=&urlID=8164533&fb=Y&;partnerID=565.

17. GEOFFREY R. STONE, PERILOUS TIMES (New York: W.W. Norton 2004); *see also* GEOFFREY R. STONE, WAR AND LIBERTY (New York: W.W. Norton 2007).

18. Korematsu v. United States, 323 U.S. 214, 246 (1944) (Jackson, J., dissenting).

19. *Poll Finds Trust of Federal Government Runs Low*, CNN (Feb. 25, 2010, 8:38 P.M.), http://www.cnn.com/2010/POLITICS/02/23/poll.government.trust/index.html.

20. *See* chapter 11, notes 25–28 and accompanying text.

21. *See* STONE, PERILOUS TIMES, *supra* note 17, at 222–26.

22. BENJAMIN FRANKLIN, AUTOBIOGRAPHY OF BENJAMIN FRANKLIN 104 (New York: Macmillan 1914).

23. GEORGE LAKOFF, DON'T THINK OF AN ELEPHANT (White River Junction, VT: Chelsea Green 2004).

24. *Humanitarian Law Project*, 130 S. Ct. 2705 (2010).

25. ANDREW BACEVICH, THE LIMITS OF POWER (New York: Holt 2009).

26. *See* BRUCE FEIN, CONSTITUTIONAL PERIL (New York: Palgrave Macmillan 2008).

27. *See* Anthony Lewis, *Civil Liberties in a Time of Terror*, 2003 WISC. L. REV. 257.

28. E. D. Kain, *Ron Paul Introduces the American Traveler Dignity Act*, WASH. EXAMINER, Nov. 19, 2010, http://washingtonexaminer.com/blogs/opinion-zone/2010/11/ron-paul-introduces-american-traveler-dignity-act#ixzz18aOQR4sJ.

29. Amy Schatz, *Paul Camp, Liberals Unite on Spy Bill*, WALL ST. J., June 26, 2008, http://online.wsj.com/article/SB121443403835305037.html?mod=googlenews_wsj.

30. *Bierfeldt v. Napolitano*, ACLU (Nov. 10, 2009), http://www.aclu.org/national-security/bierfeldt-v-napolitano.

31. Timothy Lynch, *Breaking Our Vicious Cycle: Preserving Civil Liberties While Fighting Terrorism*, POLICY ANALYSIS, no. 443, 2002, http://www.cato.org/pubs/pas/pa443.pdf .

32. BENJAMIN H. FRIEDMAN, JIM HARPER, & CHRISTOPHER A. PREBLE, EDS., TERRORIZING OURSELVES (Washington, DC: Cato Institute 2010).

33. DAVID COLE, ENEMY ALIENS (New York: New Press 2005).

Chapter 1

1. Al-Kidd v. Ashcroft, 580 F.3d 949, 953 (9th Cir. 2009), *aff'd en banc*, 598 F.3d 1129 (9th Cir. 2010), *cert. granted*, ___ U.S. ___, 131 S. Ct. 415 (2010).

2. My account of the circumstances surrounding Sami al-Hussayen's arrest relies on interviews with lawyer David Nevin and Idaho Law Professor Liz Brandt, on court records, and on the admirable reporting of Maureen O'Hagan in *A Terrorism Case That Went Awry*, SEATTLE TIMES, Nov. 22, 2004, http://seattletimes. nwsource.com/html/localnews/2002097570_sami22m.html, and by other reporters including Bob Fick, *Idaho Graduate Student Acquitted of Using Internet to Support Terrorism*, SEATTLE TIMES, June 11, 2004, http://seattletimes.nwsource.com/html/localnews/2001952936_webstudentacquitted10.html; *Sami al-Hussayen Case*, IDAHO PUB. TELEVISION, May 27, 2004, http://idahoptv.org/dialogue/diaShowPage. cfm?versionID=118747 (discussion with four reporters covering the trial); Betsy Hiel, *Trial Ties Suspect to Calls for Jihad*, PITTSBURGH TRIBUNE-REV., May 16, 2004, http://www.pittsburghlive.com/x/pittsburghtrib/news/middleeastreports/s_194369. html; and Betsy Z. Russell in the IDAHO SPOKESMAN-REVIEW, *e.g.*, *Sami Al-Hussayen on His Way Home*, July 22, 2004, http://www.spokesman.com/stories/2004/jul/22/sami-al-hussayen-on-his-way-home/.

3. Bureau of Consular Affairs, U.S. Dep't of State, A New Form DS 157, Supplemental Nonimmigrant Visa Application (2002), http://travel.state.gov/visa/laws/telegrams/telegrams_1432.html. The requirement applies to "all male nonimmigrant visa applicants between the ages of 16 and 45."

4. *See* 18 U.S.C. §§ 1001(a)(2); 1546(a) & 3238 (2006).

5. *See* Fox Butterfield, *A Nation Challenged: The Interviews; A Police Force Rebuffs F.B.I. on Querying Mideast Men*, N.Y. TIMES, Nov. 21, 2001, http://www. nytimes.com/2001/11/21/us/nation-challenged-interviews-police-force-rebuffs-fbi-querying-mideast-men.html.

6. O'Hagan, *supra* note 2.

7. United States v. al-Hussayen, Second Superseding Indictment, No. CR 03–048 at 8–9, (D. Idaho Mar. 4, 2004), http://news.findlaw.com/hdocs/docs/terrorism/usal-hussyn304sind2.pdf.

8. Providing Material Support to Terrorists, 18 U.S.C. § 2339A.

9. Brandenburg v. Ohio, 395 U.S. 444 (1969).

10. Betsy Z. Russell, *Free Speech or Terrorism?* IDAHO SPOKESMAN-REV., May 4, 2004, http://www.spokesman.com/blogs/boise/2004/may/04/free-speech-or-terror-ism/.

11. Betsy Z. Russell, *Eye on Boise: Expert Cross-Examined*, IDAHO SPOKESMAN-REV., May 20, 2004, http://www.spokesman.com/blogs/boise/2004/may/20/expert-cross-examined/.

12. Violent Crime Control and Law Enforcement Act of 1994, Pub. L. No. 103–322, § 120005(a), 108 Stat. 1796, 2022 (1994).

13. *Id.* at § 120005(c)(2).

14. H.R. REP. NO. 104–383, at 81 (1995).

15. Patriot Act § 805(2)(B).

16. The only witness called by the defense was a former CIA official who testified that the website was analytical and did not bear the marks of terrorist-recruiting enterprises. *See* Betsy Z. Russell, *Terrorism Case Goes to Jury*, IDAHO SPOKESMAN-REV., June 2, 2004, http://spokesmanclassifieds.com/pf.asp?date=060204&ID=s1525547.

17. The sources for my account are interviews with Abdullah al-Kidd and his lawyer, Lee Gelernt, affidavits of Abdullah al-Kidd, the opinion in *al-Kidd*, 580 F.3d 949, and Adam Liptak, *For Post-9/11 Material Witness, It Is a Terror of a Different Kind*, N.Y. TIMES, Aug. 19, 2004, http://www.nytimes.com/2004/08/19/politics/19witness.html.

18. Liptak, *supra* note 17.

19. *Id.*

20. *FBI's Fiscal Year 2004 Budget: Hearing Before the Subcomm. on the Dep'ts of Commerce, Justice & State, H. Appropriations Comm.*, 108th Cong. (2003) (statement of Robert S. Mueller, III, Dir., FBI), http://www.fbi.gov/congress/congress03/mueller032703.htm.

21. Release or Detention of a Material Witness, 18 U.S.C. § 3144.

22. United States v. Awadallah, 349 F.3d 42 (2d Cir. 2003), *cert. denied*, 543 U.S. 1056 (2005). The District Court noted that Awadallah had been kept in solitary confinement for most of his stay and was continuously strip-searched and bruised. 349 F.3d at 47–48. A 2003 Inspector General Report confirmed that at least a few detainees like Awadallah were being treated abusively and that terrorism suspects were not distinguished from "uninvolved witnesses." *See* OFFICE OF THE INSPECTOR GEN., U.S DEP'T OF JUSTICE, THE SEPTEMBER 11 DETAINEES: A REVIEW OF THE TREAT-MENT OF ALIENS 20 (2003), http://www.justice.gov/oig/special/0306/full.pdf.

23. United States v. Awadallah, 202 F. Supp. 2d 55, 61–79 (S.D.N.Y. 2002), *rev'd*, 349 F.3d 42, 49–64 (2d Cir. 2003), *cert. denied*, 543 U.S. 1056 (2005).

24. *See Witness to Abuse: Human Rights Abuses Under the Material Witness Law Since September 11*, 17 HUM. RTS. WATCH, no. 2(G), 2005 at 2, http://www.aclu.org/files/FilesPDFs/materialwitnessreport.pdf; *see generally* Anjana Malhotra, *Overlooking Innocence: Refashioning the Material Witness Law to Indefinitely Detain Muslims Without Charges*, INT'L C.L. REP. 1–2 (2004), http://www.aclu.org/files/iclr/malhotra.pdf.

25. Patriot Act § 412. Detention of noncitizens who are expected to be deported may be extended up to six months.

26. Al-Kidd, 580 F.3d at 953.

27. Al-Kidd v. Ashcroft, 598 F.3d 1129 (9th Cir. 2010) (*en banc*) (8 judges dissenting), *cert. granted*, ___ U.S. ___, 131 S. Ct. 415 (2010).

28. *See* Ashcroft v. al-Kidd, No. 10–98, *cert. granted*, 131 S. Ct. 415 (2010).

29. David Cole, *Out of the Shadows: Preventive Detention, Suspected Terrorists, and War*, 97 CALIF. L. REV. 693, 705, 724 (2009).

30. DAVID COLE & JULIUS LOBEL, LESS SAFE, LESS FREE 49, 109–16 (New York: New Press 2007).

31. *See id.* at 3–15 (critiquing the prevention paradigm).

32. *See* BERNARD HARCOURT, AGAINST PREDICTION (Chicago: Univ. of Chicago Press 2007).

33. *See* Robert M. Chesney, *Beyond Conspiracy? Anticipatory Prosecution and the Challenge of Unaffiliated Terrorism*, 80 S. CAL. L. REV. 425, 425, 475–79 (2007).

34. Richard B. Zabel & James J. Benjamin, Jr., *In Pursuit of Justice: Prosecuting Terrorism Cases in the Federal Courts*, HUM. RTS. FIRST (2008), at 28, http://www.humanrightsfirst.info/pdf/080521-USLS-pursuit-justice.pdf (statistics for convictions under 18 U.S.C. §§ 2339A & B).

35. *Criminal Terrorism Enforcement in the United States During the Five Years Since the 9/11/01 Attacks*, TRANSACTIONAL RECS. ACCESS CLEARINGHOUSE [hereinafter TRAC], http://trac.syr.edu/tracreports/terrorism/169/.

36. *See* OFFICE OF THE INSPECTOR GEN., U.S. DEP'T OF JUSTICE, THE SEPTEMBER 11 DETAINEES: A REVIEW OF THE TREATMENT OF ALIENS HELD ON IMMIGRATION CHARGES IN CONNECTION WITH THE INVESTIGATION OF THE SEPTEMBER 11 ATTACKS (2003), http://www.justice.gov/oig/special/0306/full.pdf.

37. *Immigration Enforcement Under Obama Returns to Highs of Bush Era*, TRAC, http://trac.syr.edu/immigration/reports/233/.

38. *As Terrorism Prosecutions Decline, Extent of Threat Remains Unclear*, TRAC, http://trac.syr.edu/tracreports/terrorism/231/; Zabel & Benjamin, *supra* note 34, at 25.

39. *See* David Bario, *By Any Means Necessary*, AMER. LAWYER, 2008, http://www.law.com/jsp/tal/PubArticleTAL.jsp?id=1196279828736&slreturn=1&hbxlogin (focus shifting from prosecution to intelligence).

40. *Who Is a Terrorist? Government Failure to Define Terrorism Undermines Enforcement, Puts Civil Liberties at Risk*, TRAC, http://trac.syr.edu/tracreports/terrorism/215/.

41. JOHN ROTH, DOUGLAS GREENBURG, & SERENA WILLE, STAFF REPORT TO THE 9/11 COMMISSION, NATIONAL COMMISSION ON TERRORIST ATTACKS UPON THE UNITED STATES: MONOGRAPH ON TERRORIST FINANCING 50 (2004), http://govinfo.library.unt.edu/911/staff_statements 9/11_TerrFin_Monograph.pdf.

Chapter 2

1. My sources for this section include an interview with Roya Rahmani, her attorneys, and translator Ali Safavi, as well as court documents.

2. Ali Safavi, *Reality Check: Understanding the Politics Behind the MEK's Terrorist Designation*, HUFFINGTON POST, Mar. 31, 2010, http://www.huffingtonpost.com/ali-safavi/reality-check-understandi_b_520592.html.

3. *See* Designation of Foreign Terrorist Organizations, 8 U.S.C. § 1189(a)(4)(B).

4. People's Mojahedin Org. of Iran v. United States Dep't of State, 182 F.3d 17, 18–19, 25 (D.C. Cir. 1999), *cert. denied*, 529 U.S. 1104 (2000).

5. United States v. Afshari, 426 F.3d 1150 (9th Cir. 2005), *reh. & reh. en banc denied*, 446 F.3d 915 (9th Cir. 2006), *cert. denied sub nom.* Rahmani v. United States, 549 U.S. 1110 (2007).

6. *See* David Stringer, *Britain Removes Iran Opposition Group from Terror List*, SEATTLE TIMES, June 23, 2008, http://seattletimes.nwsource.com/html/nationworld/2004479589_apbritainiran.html; Philippa Runner, *EU Ministers Drop Iran Group from Terror List*, EUOBSERVER, Jan. 26, 2009, http://euobserver.com/9/27472.

7. The Liberation Tigers of Tamil Eelam, an insurgent group in Sri Lanka, was militarily defeated and is now defunct.

8. Humanitarian Law Project v. Ashcroft, 309 F. Supp. 2d 1185 (C.D. Cal. 2004).

9. Intelligence Reform and Terrorism Prevention Act of 2004, Pub. L. No. 108–458 § 6603, 118 Stat. 3762–64 (2004).

10. Providing Material Support or Resources to Designated Foreign Terrorist Organizations, 18 U.S.C. § 2339B.

11. 18 U.S.C. § 2339A(b)(3).

12. Humanitarian Law Project v. Mukasey, 552 F.3d 916 (9th Cir. 2009), *rev'd sub nom.* Holder v. Humanitarian Law Project, ___ U.S. ___, 130 S. Ct. 2705 (2010).

13. Holder v. Humanitarian Law Project, ___ U.S. ___, 130 S. Ct. 2705 (2010).

14. Transcript of Oral Argument at 47, ll. 17–22, *Humanitarian Law Project*, 130 S. Ct. 2705 (No. 08–1498) (argued Feb. 23, 2010).

15. *Humanitarian Law Project*, 130 S. Ct. at 2723–24.

16. *Id.* at 2729.

17. JESSICA STERN, TERROR IN THE NAME OF GOD (New York: HarperCollins 2003).

18. *Humanitarian Law Project*, 130 S. Ct. at 2728.

19. *See id.* at 2724 (majority); *id.* at 2735 (Breyer, J., dissenting).

20. 18 U.S.C. § 2339(i).

21. *Humanitarian Law Project*, 130 S. Ct. at 2727.

22. Transcript of Oral Argument, *Humanitarian Law Project*, *supra* n.14, at 47–48. *See also* United States v. Al-Arian, 308 F. Supp. 2d 1322, 1337 (M.D. Fla. 2004) (under the government's broad interpretation, "a cab driver could be guilty for giving a ride to an FTO member to the UN").

23. *See* Ahmed Yousef, *What Hamas Wants*, N.Y. TIMES, June 20, 2007, http://www.nytimes.com/2007/06/20/opinion/20yousef.html?_r=1.

24. Brief for ACLU et al. as Amici Curiae Supporting Respondents/Cross-Petitioners at 14, *Humanitarian Law Project*, 130 S. Ct. 2705, http://www.aclu.org/files/assets/08-1498_and_09-89_tsac_The_Carter_Center.pdf ("peace-making, conflict resolution, human rights advocacy, and the provision of aid to needy civilians sometimes requires direct engagement with groups and individuals that resort to or support violence, including some that are, have been, or might in the future be designated as FTOs").

25. *Id* at 2.

26. Brief for Academic Researchers and the Citizen Media Law Project by the Brennan Ctr. for Justice as Amici Curiae Supporting Respondents/Cross-Petitioners

at 4, 14, *Humanitarian Law Project*, 130 S. Ct. 2705 (Nos. 08–1498 & 09–89) http://brennan.3cdn.net/17d1e217d2edf1043a_d3m6yfe19.pdf.

27. Brief for Victims of the McCarthy Era as Amici Curiae Supporting Respondents/Cross-Petitioners, *Humanitarian Law Project*, 130 S. Ct. 2705, http://ccrjustice.org/files/HLP/Holder_v_HLP_McCarthy_Era_Victims_amicus_brief.pdf.

28. Martin Scheinin, A/HRC/6/17/Add.3, Nov. 22, 2007, paras. 41, 47, http://daccess-dds-ny.un.org/doc/UNDOC/GEN/G07/149/55/PDF/G0714955.pdf?OpenElement.

29. 18 U.S.C. § 2339B(g)(4), referencing definitions in § 2339A(b)(1).

30. United States v. Shah, 474 F. Supp. 2d 492, 497 n.5 (S.D.N.Y. 2007).

31. *Implementation of the USA PATRIOT ACT: Prohibition of Material Support Under Sections 805 of the USA PATRIOT ACT and 6603 of the Intelligence Reform and Terrorism Prevention Act of 2004 Before the H. Comm. on the Judiciary, Subcomm. on Crime, Terrorism and Homeland Sec.* 26 (2005) (Testimony of Ahilan T. Arulanantham, Staff Attorney, ACLU) (firsthand account).

32. *Id.* at 25–26.

33. 18 U.S.C. § 3286.

Chapter 3

1. President Barack Obama, Remarks to the Turkish Parliament (Apr. 6, 2009) (transcript available through the White House Office of the Press Sec'y, http://www.whitehouse.gov/the_press_office/Remarks-By-President-Obama-To-The-Turkish-Parliament/).

2. JOHN ROTH, DOUGLAS GREENBURG, & SERENA WILLE, NATIONAL COMMISSION ON TERRORIST ATTACKS UPON THE UNITED STATES, MONOGRAPH ON TERRORIST FINANCING: STAFF REPORT TO THE COMMISSION 50 (2004), http://govinfo.library.unt.edu/911/staff_statements/911_TerrFin_Monograph.pdf.

3. ACLU, BLOCKING FAITH, FREEZING CHARITY 14 (ACLU ed., 2009), http://www.aclu.org/human-rights/report-blocking-faith-freezing-charity.

4. *Government Argues for Holding Detainees*, MSNBC (Dec. 1, 2004, 5:44 P.M.) http://www.msnbc.msn.com/id/6631668/ns/us_news-security.

5. International Emergency Economic Powers Act, Pub. L. No. 95–223, tit. II, 91 Stat. 1626 (1977) (codified as amended at 50 U.S.C. §§ 1701–06).

6. *Aiding Terrorists: An Examination of the Material Support Statute: Hearing Before the S. Comm. on the Judiciary* (2004) (testimony of Professor David Cole, Geo. Univ. L. Ctr.); *see* Executive Order 12,947 (1995). There is considerable controversy over whether Salah, said to be a supporter of Hamas, was actually guilty of anything. *See* Michael E. Deutsch & Erica Thompson, *Secrets and Lies: The Persecution of Mohammad Salah (Part II)*, 38 J. OF PALESTINE STUD., no. 1, 2008, at 25–53, http://caliber.ucpress.net/doi/abs/10.1525/jps.2008.38.1.25.

7. *See Specially Blocked Nationals and Blocked Persons*, OFFICE OF FOREIGN ASSETS CONTROL, U.S. DEP'T OF THE TREASURY (Mar. 17, 2011), http://www.treasury.gov/ofac/downloads/t11sdn.pdf.

8. *See* Patriot Act §§ 106, 317, 319(a), 320, 323, 371–73, and 806.

9. Hamdi v. Rumsfeld, 542 U.S. 507 (2004).

10. The courts have found a high level of unreliability in the "enemy combatant" designations leading to detention at Guantánamo. *See* Susan N. Herman, *The Limits*

of Advocacy: Lawyers for Terrorists/Lawyers for Torturers, HARV. L. & POLICY REV., July 9, 2010, nn. 42–43, http://www.hlpronline.com/2010/07/herman_limits.

11. *See* Eric Sandberg-Zakian, *Counterterrorism, the Constitution, and the Civil-Criminal Divide: Evaluating the Designation of U.S. Persons Under the International Emergency Economic Powers Act*, 48 HARV. J. LEGIS. 301, 333–34 (2010).

12. OFFICE OF FOREIGN ASSETS CONTROL, U.S. DEP'T OF THE TREASURY, TERRORIST ASSETS REPORT 2010 6 (2010), http://www.treasury.gov/resource-center/sanctions/Documents/tar2010.pdf.

13. The Treasury Department has authority to return or refer seized assets, *see generally* 31 C.F.R. §§ 501.701(a)(2) & (4) & 597.201 (2010), but has denied all requests to do so. *See* OMB WATCH & GRANTMAKERS WITHOUT BORDERS, COLLATERAL DAMAGE: HOW THE WAR ON TERRORISM HURTS CHARITIES, FOUNDATIONS, AND THE PEOPLE THEY SERVE 61–66 (2008).

14. Patriot Act § 106 (codified at 50 U.S.C. § 1702).

15. My account of the facts is based on Complaint, Kindhearts for Charitable Humanitarian Development, Inc. v. Paulson, 676 F. Supp. 2d 649 (N.D. Ohio 2009) (No. 3:08CV2400), http://www.aclu.org/files/pdfs/safefree/kindhearts_complaint.pdf.

16. Press Release, Dep't of the Treasury, *Treasury Freezes Assets of Organization Tied to Hamas* (Feb. 19, 2006), http://www.ustreas.gov/press/releases/js4058.htm.

17. *See* Terrorism Sanctions Regulations, 61 Fed. Reg. 3,805-01 (Feb. 2, 1996) (codified at 31 C.F.R. § 595.204; 31 C.F.R. §§ 501.801–501.808).

18. KindHearts for Charitable Humanitarian Dev. v. Geithner, 647 F. Supp. 2d 857 (N.D. Ohio Aug. 18, 2009).

19. KindHearts for Charitable Humanitarian Dev. v. Geithner, 2010 U.S. Dist. LEXIS 45175 (N.D. Ohio May 10, 2010).

20. ROTH ET AL., *supra* note 2, at 9.

21. *Id.* at 79.

22. *Id.* at 111.

23. Sean O'Neill, *Britain Rejects Bush's Charge Against Charity*, DAILY TELEGRAPH, Sept. 25, 2003, http://www.telegraph.co.uk/news/worldnews/northamerica/usa/1442381/Britain-rejects-Bushs-charges-against-charity.html.

24. IBRAHIM WARDE, THE PRICE OF FEAR 95–102 (Berkeley: Univ. of Calif. Press 2007).

25. Greg Krikorian, *Questions Arise in Case over Islamic Charity*, L.A. TIMES, June 18, 2006, http://articles.latimes.com/2006/jun/18/nation/na-holy18.

26. John Riley, *Taking Liberties: Part 3: A Powerful Weapon: Financial Sanctions Are Popular Tool in War on Terror*, NEWSDAY, Sept. 17, 2002.

27. Press Release, White House Office of the Press Secretary, *President Announces Progress on Financial Fight Against Terror* (Dec. 4, 2001), http://georgewbush-whitehouse.archives.gov/news/releases/2001/12/20011204-8.html.

28. Greg Krikorian, *Terror Financing Case Ends in Mistrial*, L.A. TIMES, Oct. 23, 2007, http://articles.latimes.com/2007/oct/23/nation/na-holyland23.

29. David Koenig, *Mistrial Declared in Islamic Charity Case*, USA TODAY, Oct.22, 2007, http://www.usatoday.com/news/topstories/2007-10-22-2117674574_x.htm.

30. Greg Krikorian, *Weak Case Seen in Failed Trial of Charity*, L.A. TIMES, Nov. 4, 2007, http://articles.latimes.com/2007/nov/04/nation/na-holyland4.

31. Gretel C. Kovach, *Five Convicted in Terrorism Financing Trial*, N.Y. TIMES, Nov. 24, 2008, http://www.nytimes.com/2008/11/25/us/25charity.html.

32. ROTH ET AL., *supra* note 2, at 111.

33. BLOCKING FAITH, *supra* note 3, at 59.

34. ROTH ET AL., *supra* note 2, at 11 n.4.

35. WARDE, *supra* note 24, at 102.

36. ROTH ET AL., *supra* note 2, at 82–83.

37. *Id.* at 8.

38. *See* Designation of Foreign Terrorist Organizations, 8 U.S.C. § 1189(b).

39. *See* Holy Land Found. for Relief & Dev. v. Ashcroft, 219 F. Supp. 2d 57, 74 n.28 (D.D.C. 2002).

40. Islamic Am. Relief Agency v. Unidentified FBI Agents, 394 F. Supp. 2d 34, 49–50 (D.D.C. 2005), *aff'd*, 477 F.3d 728 (D.C. Cir. 2007), *cert. denied*, 552 U.S. 816 (2007).

41. ERIC LICHTBLAU, BUSH'S LAW 240 (New York: Pantheon 2008).

42. *Id.* at 241.

43. ROTH ET AL., *supra* note 2, at 4, 24.

44. *Id.* at 51.

45. MARTIN WEISS, CONG. RESEARCH SERV., RS21902, CRS REPORT FOR CONGRESS: TERRORIST FINANCING: THE 9/11 COMMISSION RECOMMENDATION CR-3 (2005).

46. BLOCKING FAITH, *supra* note 3, at 69–75.

47. *Id.* at 72.

48. *Id.* at 71.

49. *Id.*

50. *Id.* at 75–78.

51. Robin Shulman, *The Informer: Behind the Scenes, or Setting the Stage?*, WASH. POST, May 29, 2007, http://www.washingtonpost.com/wp-dyn/content/article/2007/05/28/AR2007052801401.html.

52. *See* Tom Lininger, *Sects, Lies and Videotape: The Surveillance and Infiltration of Religious Groups*, 89 IOWA L. REV. 1201 (2004); GEOFFREY R. STONE, WAR AND LIBERTY: AN AMERICAN DILEMMA: 1790 TO THE PRESENT 141 (New York: W.W. Norton 2007).

53. BLOCKING FAITH, *supra* note 3, at 99.

54. *Id.* at 93–96.

55. *Id.* at 122–24.

56. *Id.* at 67.

57. ROTH ET AL., *supra* note 2, at 50, 112.

58. BLOCKING FAITH, *supra* note 3, at 118.

59. *Id.* at 119.

60. *See* Nina J. Crimm, *The Moral Hazard of Anti-Terrorism Financing Measures: A Potential to Compromise Civil Societies and National Interests*, 43 WAKE FOREST L. REV. 577, 619–26 (2008).

61. ROTH ET AL., *supra* note 2, at 122.

62. International Covenant on Civil and Political Rights, art. 18[1]–[2] (Dec. 16, 1966), G.A. Res. 2200A [XXI], 21 UN GAOR Supp. (No. 16) at 52, UN Doc. A/6316 (1966), 999 U.N.T.S. 171, *entered into force* Mar. 23, 1976, ratified by the U.S. June 8, 1992 (protecting religious freedom and expression).

63. Universal Declaration of Human Rights, art. 18 (Dec. 10, 1948), G.A. Res. 217A[III], UN Doc. A/810 at 71 (1948).

64. Eric Lichtblau, *Cash Flow to Terrorists Evades U.S. Efforts*, N.Y. TIMES, Dec. 6, 2010.

65. *Id.*

66. "[W]e worry that sweeping statements . . . misrepresent the prevalence of terrorist abuse of the U.S. charitable organizations that are the intended audience for the revised Guidelines." Letter from Steve Gunderson, President and CEO, Council on Founds., to Office of Terrorist Financing and Fin. Crime (Feb. 1, 2006), http://www.usig.org/PDFs/Comments_to_Treasury.pdf.

67. Michael W. Ryan, *Not All Practice Makes Perfect: How the Treasury's Revised Anti-Terrorist Financing Guidelines Still Fail to Adequately Address Charitable Concerns*, 43 WAKE FOREST L. REV. 739 (2008).

68. OMB WATCH, *supra* note 9, at 32–33.

69. President Barack Obama, Remarks by the President on a New Beginning, at Cairo University, Cairo, Egypt (June 4, 2009), http://www.whitehouse.gov/the_press_office/Remarks-by-the-President-at-Cairo-University-6-04-09.

70. Letter from Am. Muslim Health Prof'ls et al., to President Barack Obama (Aug. 11, 2010), http://www.muslimadvocates.org/documents/Obama%20Charity%20Letter%20II%20FINAL.pdf; *see* Sahar Aziz, *Ease Restrictions on International Charities*, CNN (June 4, 2010, 12:08 P.M.), http://www.cnn.com/2010/OPINION/06/04/aziz.cairo.charities/index.html.

Chapter 4

1. Lizette Alvarez, *Meet Mikey, 8: U.S. Has Him on Watch List*, N.Y. TIMES, Jan. 13, 2010, http://www.nytimes.com/2010/01/14/nyregion/14watchlist.html.

2. Rick Bowmer, *Terror List Snag Nearly Grounded Ted Kennedy*, USA TODAY, Aug. 19, 2004, http://www.usatoday.com/news/washington/2004-08-19-kennedy-list_x.htm.

3. *Insisting on Right to Privacy, TRI Defends Airline Passengers, Sues DHS & TSA over Scanners, Virtual Strip Searches & Full-Body "Rub-Downs,"* THE RUTHERFORD INSTITUTE NEWS (Dec. 5, 2010), http://www.rutherford.org/articles_db/press_release.asp?article_id=870.

4. Rachel L. Swarns, *Senator? Terrorist? A Watch List Stops Kennedy at Airport*, N.Y. TIMES, Aug. 20, 2004, http://nytimes.com/2004/08/20/national/20flight.html.

5. Sara Kehaulani Goo, *Faulty "No Fly" System Detailed*, WASH. POST, Oct. 9, 2004, http://www.washingtonpost.com/wp-dyn/articles/A18735-2004Oct8.html.

6. *DHS Traveler Redress Inquiry Program*, U.S. DEP'T OF HOMELAND SEC., http://www.dhs.gov/files/programs/gc_1169676919316.shtm.

7. *See* Alvarez, *supra* note 1.

8. OFFICE OF THE INSPECTOR GEN., U.S. DEP'T OF JUSTICE, THE FEDERAL BUREAU OF INVESTIGATION'S TERRORIST WATCHLIST NOMINATION PRACTICES 1 (2009), http://www.justice.gov/oig/reports/FBI/a0925/final.pdf [hereinafter *Inspector Gen. Report, Watchlist Practices*].

9. *See* WILLIAM J. KROUSE & BART ELIAS, CONG. RESEARCH SERV., RL33645, TERRORIST WATCHLIST AND AIR PASSENGER PRESCREENING 11 (2009).

10. *After Christmas Incident, No-Fly List Nearly Doubled*, USA TODAY, Mar. 10, 2010, http://www.usatoday.com/travel/flights/2010-03-10-no-fly-list_N.htm.

11. Intelligence Reform and Terrorism Prevention Act of 2004, Pub. L. No. 108–458 § 4071(a)(1), 118 Stat. 3638, 3729 (2004).

12. *Five Years After the Intelligence Reform and Terrorism Prevention Act: Stopping Terrorist Travel, Hearing Before the S. Comm. on Homeland Sec. & Gov't'l Affairs* 111st Cong. 2 (2009) (statement of Timothy J. Healy, Dir., Terrorist Screening Ctr., FBI, U.S. Dep't of Justice).

13. Angela M. Hill & Brian Ross, *U.S. Government Sued by ACLU over No Fly List*, ABC NEWS (June 30, 2010), http://abcnews.go.com/Blotter/us-government-sued-aclu-fly-list/story?id=11054805.

14. *Unprecedented Release of Government Documents Reveal Confusion and Absence of Policy in Implementing No-Fly Lists, ACLU Says*, ACLU (Oct. 9, 2004), http://www.aclu.org/national-security/unprecedented-release-government-documents-reveal-confusion-and-absence-policy-imp.

15. *See generally* OFFICE OF THE INSPECTOR GEN., U.S. DEP'T OF JUSTICE, AUDIT OF U.S. DEPARTMENT OF JUSTICE TERRORIST WATCHLIST NOMINATION PROCESS (2008), http://www.justice.gov/oig/reports/plus/a0816/final.pdf.

16. *Inspector Gen. Report, Watchlist Practices, supra* note 8.

17. *Mandela Off U.S. Terrorism Watch List*, CNN (July 1, 2008), http://articles.cnn.com/2008-07-01/world/mandela.watch_1_president-mandela-apartheid-anc?_s=PM:WORLD.

18. *See* DAVID COLE & JULES LOBEL, LESS SAFE, LESS FREE 3–15 (New York: New Press 2007) (critiquing the prevention paradigm).

19. *See* BERNARD HARCOURT, AGAINST PREDICTION (Chicago: Univ. of Chicago Press 2007).

20. Jeanne Meserve, *Name on Government Watch List Threatens Pilot's Career*, CNN (Aug. 22, 2008, 10:07 A.M.), http://www.cnn.com/2008/US/08/22/pilot.watch.list/.

21. Mike McIntire, *Ensnared by Error on Growing U.S. Watch List*, N.Y. TIMES, Apr. 6, 2010, http://www.nytimes.com/2010/04/07/us/07watch.html?pagewanted=all.

22. Scherfen v. U.S. Dep't of Homeland Sec., No. 3:CV-08-1554, 2010 U.S. Dist. Lexis 8336 (M.D. Pa. Feb. 2, 2010).

23. *Statement by Rebecca Gordon and Jan Adams*, ACLU (Apr. 23, 2003), http://www.aclu.org/files/FilesPDFs/042203-statement-nofly.pdf.

24. *Cf.* Gilmore v. Gonzales, 435 F.3d 1125, 1132 (9th Cir. 2006), *cert. denied*, 549 U.S. 1110 (2007) (government refused to concede whether a written order or directive requiring identification existed, or if it did, who issued it or what it said).

25. McIntire, *supra* note 21.

26. Ibrahim v. U.S. Dep't of Homeland Sec., No. C 06-00545 WHA, 2009 U.S. Dist. Lexis 122598, at *3–4 (N.D. Cal. Dec. 17, 2009).

27. Ibrahim v. U.S. Dep't of Homeland Sec., No. C 06-00545 WHA, 2009 U.S. Dist. Lexis 64619 (N.D. Cal July 27, 2009).

28. Complaint at 3, Green et al. v. Transp. Sec. Admin., No. CV04-0763 (W.D. Wash. Apr. 6, 2004), http://www.aclu.org/national-security/aclu-complaint-no-fly-list-case.

29. *See* NAT'L COMM'N ON TERRORIST ATTACKS UPON THE U.S., THE 9/11 COMMISSION REPORT 385–87 (Washington, DC: USGPO, 2004), http://www.gpoaccess.gov/911/pdf/fullreport.pdf [hereafter *9/11 Commission Report*].

30. Intelligence Reform and Terrorism Prevention Act of 2004, Pub. L. No. 108–458, § 4012(a)(1)(C)(iii)(II), 118 Stat. 3638, 3715 (2004) (codified as amended at 49 U.S.C. § 44903(j)(2)(C)(iii)(II)).

31. KROUSE & ELIAS, *supra* note 9, at 19.

32. *Scherfen*, 2010 U.S. Dist. Lexis 8336, at *10.

33. *See* Alvarez, *supra* note 1.

34. Procedures could be developed to spare people futile, disruptive, and humiliating trips to the airport. One author suggests that people be allowed to visit an airport or embassy before a planned trip, and that federal agents might be willing to share with a lawyer representative who had a security clearance information that is currently being withheld, and thus enable accurate fact-finding. Justin Florence, *Making the No Fly List Fly: A Due Process Model for Terrorist Watchlists*, 115 YALE L.J. 2148 (2006); Justin Florence, *A Better No-Fly List*, WASH. POST, Jan. 4, 2010, http://www.washingtonpost.com/wp-dyn/content/article/2010/01/03/AR2010010301811.html.

35. *Inspector Gen. Report, Watchlist Practices, supra* note 8, at 82; *Myth Buster: TSA's Watch List Is More Than One Million People Strong*, TRANSP. SEC. ADMIN., http://www.tsa.gov/approach/mythbusters/tsa_watch_list.shtm.

36. U.S. GOV'T ACCOUNTABILITY OFFICE, REPORT TO CONGRESSIONAL REQUESTERS: TERRORIST WATCH LIST SCREENING: OPPORTUNITIES EXIST TO ENHANCE MANAGEMENT OVERSIGHT, REDUCE VULNERABILITIES IN AGENCY SCREENING PROCESSES, AND EXPAND THE USE OF THE LIST 19 (2007), http://www.gao.gov/new.items/d08110.pdf.

37. *Airport Watch List Now Reviewed Often*, WASH. TIMES, Apr. 11, 2008, http://www.washingtontimes.com/news/2008/apr/11/airport-watch-list-now-reviewed-often/.

38. *Secure Flight Program*, TRANSP. SEC. ADMIN., http://www.tsa.gov/what_we_do/layers/secureflight.

39. *See* 73 Fed. Reg. 64,023–64,024 (Oct. 28, 2008) (codified at 49 C.F.R. subpts. 1540, 1544, & 1560) for a list of the information that might be included.

40. Hill & Ross, *supra* note 13.

41. *See* Complaint, Latif et al. v. U.S. Dep't of Justice., No. 3:10CV00750 (D. Or. June 30, 2010), http://www.aclu.org/national-security/latif-et-al-v-holder-et-al-complaint.

42. *See* Daniel J. Steinbock, *Data Matching, Data Mining, and Due Process*, 40 GA. L. REV. 1, 17–18 (2005).

43. Jeffrey Goldberg, *The Things He Carried*, THE ATLANTIC (November 2008), http://www.theatlantic.com/doc/200811/airport-security/2.

44. *Quebec Man Changes Name to Dodge Relentless Airport Screening*, CBC NEWS (Sept. 11, 2008, 10:48 P.M.), http://www.cbc.ca/canada/montreal/story/2008/09/11/nofly-name.html.

45. Marcus Holmes, *Just How Much Does That Cost, Anyway? An Analysis of the Financial Costs and Benefits of the "No-Fly" List*, 5 HOMELAND SEC. AFF. J., no. 1, 2009, http://www.hsaj.org/?article=5.1.6.

46. *9/11 Commission Report, supra* note 29, at 385.

47. *Id.* at 390–91.

48. H.R. 559, 111st Cong. (1st Sess. 2009).

49. Complaint for Damages, George v. TSA, No. 2:10-CV-00586 (E.D. Pa. Feb. 10, 2010), http://www.aclu.org/national-security/george-v-tsa-complaint-damages.

50. *ACLU Client Steve Bierfeldt's Detention and Interrogation by the TSA* (audio recording), http://www.aclu.org/national-security/audio-recording-aclu-client-steve-bierfeldts-detention-and-interrogation-tsa.

51. *TSA Fixes Search Policy After ACLU Sues*, ACLU (Nov. 10, 2009), http://www.aclu.org/national-security/tsa-fixes-search-policy-after-aclu-sues.

52. Jon Cohen & Ashley Halsey III, *Poll: Nearly Two-Thirds of Americans Support Full-Body Scanners at Airports*, WASH. POST, Nov. 23, 2010, http://www.washingtonpost.com/wp-dyn/content/article/2010/11/22/AR2010112205514.html.

53. *TSA Makes Cancer Victim Remove Prosthetic Breast*, CBS NEWS (Nov. 19, 2010), http://www.cbsnews.com/stories/2010/11/19/national/main7070415.shtml.

54. *Humorist Dave Barry and His TSA Pat-Down*, NPR (Nov. 15, 2010), http://www.npr.org/2010/11/15/131338172/humorist-dave-barry-and-the-tsa.

55. David Porter, *For Disabled, Airport Security Hassles Are Old Hat*, ABC NEWS (Nov. 24, 2010), http://abcnews.go.com/Business/wireStory?id=12231458&tqkw=&;tqshow=.

56. Terry Jeffrey, *GAO: "Unclear" If Airport Body Scanners Will Detect Underwear Bombs*, TOWNHALL (Dec. 19, 2010), http://townhall.com/columnists/TerryJeffrey/2010/12/09/gao_unclear_if_airport_body_scanners_will_detect_underwear_bombs/page/full/.

57. *See* Leon Kaufman & Joseph W. Carlson, *An Evaluation of Airport X-Ray Backscatter Units Based on Image Characteristics*, 4(1) J. OF TRANSP. SEC. 73 (2011).

58. Julie Pace, *Obama Says Understands Ire over Airport Screenings*, SEATTLE TIMES, Nov. 20, 2010, 9:47 P.M., http://seattletimes.nwsource.com/html/nationworld/2013484360_presidentairport21.html.

59. Editorial, *Politicizing Airport Security*, N.Y. TIMES, Nov. 23, 2010, http://www.nytimes.com/2010/11/24/opinion/24wed2.html?_r=1.

60. Ralph Nader, *TSA Is Delivering Naked Insecurity*, USA TODAY, Nov. 17, 2010, http://www.usatoday.com/news/opinion/forum/2010-11-18-column18_ST1_N.htm.

61. Dave Michaels, *Lawmakers Asking TSA to Reconsider Pat-Down Procedures*, DALLASNEWS.COM (Nov. 19, 2010, 5:37 P.M.), http://aviationblog.dallasnews.com/archives/2010/11/lawmakers-asking-tsa-to-recons.html.

62. *See* Jeffrey Rosen, *The TSA Is Invasive, Annoying—and Unconstitutional*, WASH. POST, Nov. 28, 2010, http://www.washingtonpost.com/wpdyn/content/article/2010/11/26/AR2010112604290.html.

63. Mary Forgione, *New Uproar over Security Scanners After Agency Acknowledges Storing Images*, L.A. TIMES, Aug. 9, 2010, http://travel.latimes.com/daily-deal-blog/index.php/new-uproar-over-secu-7335/.

64. Cohen & Halsey, *supra* note 52.

65. *61% Oppose Full Body Scans and TSA Pat Downs; 48% Will Seek Alternative to Flying*, ZOGBY.COM (Nov. 23, 2010), http://www.zogby.com/templates/printnews.cfm?id=1925.

66. *See* Jeffrey M. Jones, *In U.S., Air Travelers Take Body Scans in Stride* (Jan. 10, 2010), http://www.gallup.com/poll/125018/Air-Travelers-Body-Scans-Stride.aspx (poll conducted Jan. 5–6, 2010 found 78 percent approval rating).

67. E. D. Kain, *Ron Paul Introduces the American Traveler Dignity Act*, WASH. EXAMINER, Nov. 19, 2010, http://washingtonexaminer.com/blogs/opinion-zone/2010/11/ron-paul-introduces-american-traveler-dignity-act#ixzz18aOQR4sJ.

68. *Insisting on Right to Privacy, TRI Defends Airline Passengers, Sues DHS & TSA over Scanners, Virtual Strip Searches & Full-Body "Rub-Downs,"* RUTHERFORD INSTITUTE NEWS (Dec. 5, 2010), http://www.rutherford.org/articles_db/press_release.asp?article_id=870.

69. *EPIC v. DHS (Suspension of Body Scanner Program),* ELECTRONIC PRIVACY INFORMATION CENTER, http//epic.org/privacy/body_scanners/epic_v_dhs_suspension_of_body.html.

70. *9/11 Commission Report, supra* note 29, at 88.

71. Bruce Schneier, *Our Reaction Is the Real Security Failure,* AOL NEWS (Jan. 7, 2010), http://www.schneier.com/essay-303.html.

72. Scott Shane, *Administration to Seek Balance in Airport Screening,* N.Y. TIMES, Nov. 21, 2010, http://www.nytimes.com/2010/11/22/us/22tsa.html.

73. *See Racial Profiling Seen as Widespread, Particularly Among Young Black Men,* GALLUP NEWS SERV. (Dec. 9, 1999), http://www.gallup.com/poll/3421/racial-profiling-seen-widespread-particularly-among-young-black-men.aspx (81 percent of those polled disapproved of racial profiling).

74. *See, e.g.,* Paul Sperry, *When the Profile Fits the Crime,* N.Y. TIMES, July 28, 2005, http://www.nytimes.com/2005/07/28/opinion/28sperry.html); Samuel R. Gross & Debra Livingston, *Racial Profiling Under Attack,* 102 COLUM. L. REV. 1413, 1437 (2002); William J. Stuntz, *Local Policing After the Terror,* 111 YALE L.J. 2137, 2161, 2179 (2002).

75. Sharon Davies, *Profiling Terror,* 1 OHIO ST. J. CRIM. L. 45, 76–81 (2003); Christopher Edley, Jr., *The New American Dilemma: Racial Profiling Post-9/11, in* THE WAR ON OUR FREEDOMS 180–86 (Richard C. Leone & Greg Anrig, Jr. eds., New York: Public Affairs 2003).

76. Bernard Harcourt, *Muslim Profiles Post-9/11: Is Racial Profiling an Effective Counterterrorist Measure and Does It Violate the Right to Be Free from Discrimination?,* 2 JOHN M. OLIN L. & ECON. WORKING PAPERS, no. 288, 2006, http://www.law.uchicago.edu/files/files/286.pdf.

77. *See, e.g.,* W. Kip Viscusi & Richard J. Zeckhauser, *Sacrificing Civil Liberties to Reduce Terrorism Risks,* 26 J. RISK & UNCERTAINTY 99 (2003) (finding that law students polled were more willing to approve of intrusive airport screening measures if they did not belong to a group that historically experienced being singled out). *See* chapter 11, notes 25–28 and accompanying text.

78. *See* Complaint, Sultan v. Kelly et al., No. 09 CV 00698(RJD)(RER), 2009 WL 464013 (E.D.N.Y. Feb. 19, 2009), http://www.nyclu.org/case/sultan-v-kelly-et-al-challenging-nypds-subway-bag-search-program.

79. MacWade v. Kelly, 460 F.3d 260 (2d Cir. 2006).

80. NATIONAL RESEARCH COUNCIL OF THE NATIONAL ACADEMY OF SCIENCES, PROTECTING INDIVIDUAL PRIVACY IN THE STRUGGLE AGAINST TERRORISM 58–59 (Washington, DC: National Academies Press 2008), http://books.nap.edu/openbook.php?record_id=12452&page=7.

81. Goldberg, *supra* note 43.

82. *See* Daniel Solove, *Data Mining and the Security-Liberty Debate,* 75 U. CHI. L. REV. 343, 347–48 (2008) (criticizing the *MacWade* court's version of balancing interests).

83. William Neuman, *In Response to M.T.A.'s "Say Something" Ads, a Glimpse of Modern Fears,* N.Y. TIMES, Jan. 7, 2008, http://www.nytimes.com/2008/01/07/nyregion/07see.html?_r=1&oref=slogin>;.

84. Olmstead v. United States, 277 U.S. 438, 479 (1928) (Brandeis, J., dissenting).

Chapter 5

1. SHIRIN SINNAR, THE OFAC LIST: HOW A TREASURY DEPARTMENT TERRORIST WATCHLIST ENSNARES EVERYDAY CONSUMERS (San Francisco: Lawyers' Comm. for Civ. Rights of the San Francisco Area 2007), http://www.lccr.com/03%202007%20 OFAC%20Report.pdf.

2. Jack M. Balkin, *The Constitution in the National Security State*, 93 MINN. L. REV. 1, 7 (2008).

3. *See* JEFFREY ROSEN, THE NAKED CROWD (New York: Random House 2005); JAMES RULE, PRIVACY IN PERIL (New York: Oxford Univ. Press 2007); Julia Angwin, *The Web's New Gold Mine: Your Secrets*, WALL ST. J., July 30, 2010, http:// online.wsj.com/article/SB10001424052748703940904575395073512989404. html.

4. ROSEN, *supra* note 3, at 20, crediting Roger Clarke with coining this term.

5. DANIEL J. SOLOVE, THE DIGITAL PERSON 2 (New York: N.Y. Univ. Press 2004).

6. 31 U.S.C. §§ 5312(a)(2)(A)–(Z). The definition existing at the time of the Patriot Act was expanded by the Intelligence Authorization Act of 2004, but only modestly. Most of the categories of businesses were included in the 1986 enacting law, with all but one other added with the 1988 amendments. Only minor changes have taken place since.

7. Patriot Act § 326; 31 USC § 5318(l); *see* JAY STANLEY & BARRY STEINHARDT, ACLU, THE SURVEILLANCE-INDUSTRIAL COMPLEX: HOW THE AMERICAN GOVERNMENT IS CONSCRIPTING BUSINESSES AND INDIVIDUALS IN THE CONSTRUCTION OF A SURVEILLANCE SOCIETY 18 (2004), http://www.aclu.org/files/FilesPDFs/surveillance_report.pdf [hereinafter SURVEILLANCE INDUSTRIAL COMPLEX].

8. *See, e.g.*, 31 U.S.C. § 5313; 31 C.F.R. § 103.22 (requiring reports of cash transactions above $10,000).

9. Patriot Act § 325; 31 U.S.C. § 5318(h).

10. Patriot Act § 314.

11. *Watchdog Pro—OFAC & PATRIOT Act Compliance Software*, ATTUS, http://www.attustech.com/watchdogpro-ofac-patriot-act-compliance-software. aspx.

12. Tamara Loomis, *The Rising Costs of Patriot Act Compliance*, N.Y.L.J., May 9, 2003, http://www.law.com/jsp/law/LawArticleFriendly.jsp?id=900005535313.

13. Press Release and Consent Decree, State of N.Y. Banking Dep't, *Banking Department Fines Western Union $8 Million for Violating Bank Secrecy, USA Patriot, New York Banking Laws* (Dec. 18, 2002), http://www.banking.state.ny.us/ ea021218.htm.

14. Glenn Simpson, *Easy Money: Expanding in an Age of Terror, Western Union Faces Scrutiny*, WALL ST. J., Oct. 20, 2004, http://online.wsj.com/article/0, SB109823529279550190,00.html.

15. Kathleen Pender, *PATRIOT Act Halts Would-be Investor*, SEATTLE POST-INTELLIGENCER, Sept. 6, 2003, http://www.seattlepi.com/money/138317_patriotact06. html.

16. Daniel J. Solove, *Data Mining and the Security-Liberty Debate*, 75 U. CHI. L. REV. 343, 358 (2008).

17. Leela Jacinto, *Is a Muslim Name Bad for Business?* ABC NEWS (June 11, 2003), http://abcnews.go.com/US/story?id=90212&page=1.

18. *Id.*

19. SURVEILLANCE-INDUSTRIAL COMPLEX, *supra* note 7, at 3–4.

20. *See* MARY FULBROOK, THE PEOPLE'S STATE 241–42 (London: Yale Univ. Press 2008).

21. Olmstead v. United States, 277 U.S. 438, 478 (1928) (Brandeis, J., dissenting).

22. *Eagle Eyes: Watch.Report.Protect*, U.S. AIR FORCE, OFFICE OF SPECIAL INVES-TIGATIONS, http://www.osi.andrews.af.mil/eagleeyes/index.asp.

23. *See Specially Designated Nationals and Blocked Persons*, OFFICE OF FOREIGN ASSETS CONTROL, U.S. DEP'T OF THE TREAS. (Mar. 17, 2011), http://www.treasury.gov/ofac/downloads/t11sdn.pdf.

24. Patriot Act § 326(l)(C) gives the Treasury Secretary the authority to require list-checking.

25. *See Frequently Asked Questions and Answers*, OFFICE OF FOREIGN ASSETS CONTROL, U.S. DEP'T OF THE TREAS., http://www.treasury.gov/resource-center/faqs/Sanctions/Pages/answer.aspx.

26. Ellen Nakashima, *Ordinary Customers Flagged as Terrorists*, WASH. POST, Mar. 27, 2007, http://www.washingtonpost.com/wp-dyn/content/article/2007/03/26/AR2007032602088.html.

27. *Facts for Consumers: Your Access to Free Credit Reports*, FED. TRADE COMM'N (March 2008), http://www.ftc.gov/bcp/edu/pubs/consumer/credit/cre34.shtm.

28. *See* Jon D. Michaels, *All the President's Spies: Private-Public Intelligence Partnerships in the War on Terror*, 96 CAL. L. REV. 901 (2008) (advocating procedural reform).

29. Brian Braiker, *Buying a Home and the Patriot Act*, MSNBC (June 9, 2004), http://msnbc.msn.com/id/5131685/site/newsweek/38534293.

30. Tara K. Gorman, Esq., *PATRIOT Act and Anti-Terrorism Laws: Real Estate Industry Stand Up and Take Notice*, AU2WARE, http://www.au2ware.com/patriot-act-businesses.php.

31. James H. Freis, Jr., *Remarks of James H. Freis, Jr., Director, Financial Crimes Enforcement Network, U.S. Dep't of the Treas. Delivered at the Institute of Internat'l Bankers 2010 AML Conference* (May 20, 2010), http://www.fincen.gov/news_room/speech/pdf/20071022.pdf, at 9–10.

32. Adam Liptak, *A.C.L.U. Board Is Split over Watchlists*, N.Y. TIMES, July 31, 2004, http://www.nytimes.com/2004/07/31/us/aclu-board-is-split-over-terror-watch-lists.html.

33. *ACLU Letter on Combined Federal Campaign "Black List,"* ACLU (July 30, 2004), http://www.aclu.org/national-security/aclu-letter-combined-federal-campaign-black-list; *see* Adam Liptak, *A.C.L.U. to Withdraw from Charity Drive*, N.Y. TIMES, Aug. 1, 2004, http://www.nytimes.com/2004/08/01/us/aclu-to-withdraw-from-charity-drive.html.

34. Stephanie Strom, *Requirement on Watch Lists Is Dropped*, N.Y. TIMES, Nov. 10, 2005, http://query.nytimes.com/gst/fullpage.html?res=9F05E3DF123EF933A25752C1A9639C8B63.

35. *Anti-Terrorist Financing Guidelines: Voluntary Best Practices for U.S.-Based Charities*, U.S. DEP'T OF THE TREASURY (Dec. 9, 2010), http://www.treasury.gov/resource-center/terrorist-illicit-finance/Documents/guidelines_charities.pdf.

36. OMB WATCH AND GRANTMAKERS WITHOUT BORDERS, COLLATERAL DAMAGE: HOW THE WAR ON TERRORISM HURTS CHARITIES, FOUNDATIONS, AND THE PEOPLE THEY SERVE 4, 39–49 (2008).

37. *Id.* at 43.

38. *Insurance Providers Lend Hand in Search*, MICH. DAILY, Nov. 17, 2003, http://www.michigandaily.com/content/insurance-providers-lend-hand-search.

39. Braiker, *supra* note 29.

40. JOHN ROTH, DOUGLAS GREENBURG, & SERENA WILLE, NAT'L COMM'N ON TERRORIST ATTACKS UPON THE UNITED STATES, STAFF REPORT TO THE COMMISSION: MONOGRAPH ON TERRORIST FINANCING 52–57 (2004).

41. *Id.* at 56.

42. *Id.*

43. *Report of the Congress'l Comm's Investigating the Iran Contra Affair*, H.R. REP. NO. 100–433, at 141 (1987).

44. John Markoff, *Chief Takes over at Agency to Thwart Attacks on U.S.*, N.Y. TIMES, Feb. 13, 2002, http://select.nytimes.com/gst/abstract.html?res=F20A11F734 580C708DDDAB0894DA404482.

45. Jay Stanley, *Is the Threat from "Total Information Awareness" Overblown?* ACLU (Dec. 18, 2002), http://www.aclu.org/technology-and-liberty/threat-total-information-awareness-overblown.

46. Speech by Ted Senator, spokesperson for DARPA at DARPATech 2002 Conference in Anaheim, Cal. (2002), http://www.darpa.mil/DARPATech2002/presentations/iao_pdf/speeches/SENATOR.pdf; *see also* Speech by John Poindexter, *Overview of the Information Awareness Office*, at DAPRATech 2002 Conference in Anaheim, Cal. (2002), http://www.fas.org/irp/agency/dod/poindexter.html.

47. William Safire, *You Are a Suspect*, N.Y. TIMES, Nov. 14, 2002, http://www.nytimes.com/2002/11/14/opinion/14SAFI.html.

48. Department of Defense Appropriations Act, 2004, Pub. L. No. 108–187 § 8131, 117 Stat. 1054, 1102 (2003); *see also* 149 CONG. REC. H8755—H8771 (Sept. 24, 2003). *See generally* GINA MARIE STEVENS, CONG. RESEARCH SERV., RL 31730, PRIVACY: TOTAL INFORMATION AWARENESS PROGRAMS AND RELATED INFORMATION ACCESS, COLLECTION, AND PROTECTION LAWS (2003).

49. NATIONAL RESEARCH COUNCIL OF THE NATIONAL ACADEMY OF SCIENCES, PROTECTING INDIVIDUAL PRIVACY IN THE STRUGGLE AGAINST TERRORISM 243 (Washington, DC: National Academies Press 2008), http://books.nap.edu/openbook.php?record_id=12452&;page=7 [hereinafter NATIONAL RESEARCH COUNCIL].

50. ERIC LICHTBLAU, BUSH'S LAW 114 (New York: Pantheon 2008).

51. *See* JAMES BAMFORD, THE PUZZLE PALACE 236–50 (Boston: Houghton Mifflin 1982).

52. John Schwartz & Micheline Maynard, *Airlines Gave F.B.I. Millions of Records on Travelers After 9/11*, N.Y. TIMES, May 1, 2004, http://www.nytimes.com/2004/05/01/politics/01AIRL.html.

53. Eric Lichtblau & James Risen, *Bank Data Sifted in Secret by U.S. to Block Terror*, N.Y. TIMES, June 23, 2006, http://select.nytimes.com/gst/abstract.html?res=F 40F1FFE3D540C708EDDAF0894DE404482.

54. Kim Zetter, *Feds "Pinged" Sprint GPS Data 8 Million Times over a Year*, WIRED (Dec. 1, 2009), http://www.wired.com/threatlevel/2009/12/gps-data/; Sandra Fulton, *You Are Being Tracked*, ACLU (June 28, 2010, 3:02 P.M.), http://www.aclu.org/blog/technology-and-liberty/you-are-being-tracked.

55. Joshua L. Simmons, *Buying You: The Government's Use of Fourth-Parties to Launder Data about "the People,"* 2009 COLUM. BUS. L. REV. 950, 990–97 (2009).

56. *Id.* at 991 n.151; SOLOVE, *supra* note 5, at 22.

57. Glenn R. Simpson, *Big Brother-in-Law: If the FBI Hopes to Get the Goods on You, It May Ask ChoicePoint*, WALL ST. J., Apr. 13, 2001, at A1. According to the Electronic Privacy Information Center, which tracks such information, "One group of documents obtained from the Immigration and Naturalization Service (INS) shows that ChoicePoint offered a contract for unlimited direct access to international databases for a $1 million fee. Other documents obtained from the Department of Justice Management Division show that the agency entered into an $11 million contract with ChoicePoint for fiscal year 2002." *ChoicePoint*, ELECTRONIC PRIVACY INFORMATION CENTER, http://epic.org/privacy/choicepoint/#news.

58. Robert O'Harrow, Jr., *In Age of Security, Firm Mines Wealth of Personal Data*, WASH. POST, Jan. 20, 2005, http://www.washingtonpost.com/wp-dyn/articles/A22269-2005Jan19.html.

59. Simmons, *supra* note 55.

60. SURVEILLANCE-INDUSTRIAL COMPLEX, *supra* note 7, at 33; Robert M. Gellman, *Can Privacy Be Regulated Effectively on a National Level? Thoughts on the Possible Need for International Privacy Rules*, 41 VILL. L. REV. 129, 130 (1996) (arguing that the United States is now significantly behind much of the Western industrialized world in addressing private sector privacy issues).

61. *See, e.g.*, U.S. DEP'T OF JUSTICE, OFFICE OF THE INSPECTOR GEN., UNCLASSIFIED REPORT ON THE PRESIDENT'S SURVEILLANCE PROGRAM 31–32, 77 (2009).

62. NATIONAL RESEARCH COUNCIL, *supra* note 49, at 4.

63. *Id.* at 2, 77–78, 213 (App. H.11).

64. *See* Dana Priest & William M. Arkin, *Top Secret America*, WASH. POST, July 18–21, 2010, http://projects.washingtonpost.com/top-secret-america/.

65. NATIONAL RESEARCH COUNCIL, *supra* note 49, at 71.

66. ALAN WESTIN, PRIVACY AND FREEDOM 57 (New York: Atheneum 1967).

67. ROSEN, *supra* note 3, at 19–21.

68. One blogger, Joelle Pearson, wrote of Facebook: "For starters, you didn't know the first thing about respecting my privacy. You told everyone everything. You sold my secrets to every fatcat company—the music I liked, the places I shopped—you even showed my chats and pictures to anyone who asked . . . I don't care how much you apologize. To me, or anyone else. We're through." *See Blogs Poke Facebook*, PEW RESEARCH CENTER (June 3, 2010), http://pewresearch.org/pubs/1613/facebook-and-privacy-blogs-twitter-apple.

69. MICHEL FOUCAULT, DISCIPLINE AND PUNISH 200–09 (New York: Vintage 1979).

70. RULE, *supra* note 3, at 12.

71. *Id.* at 61.

72. NATIONAL RESEARCH COUNCIL, *supra* note 49, at 167.

73. RULE, *supra* note 3, at 6; NATIONAL RESEARCH COUNCIL, *supra* note 49, at 167.

74. WHITFIELD DIFFIE & SUSAN E. LANDAU, PRIVACY ON THE LINE 143, 170 (2d ed. Cambridge, MA: MIT Press 2007); Kathleen Sullivan, *Under a Watchful Eye: Incursions on Personal Privacy, in* THE WAR ON OUR FREEDOMS 128 (Richard C. Leone & Greg Anrig, Jr. eds., New York: Public Affairs 2003).

75. *See* Albert M. Bendich, *Privacy, Poverty, and the Constitution*, 54 CALIF. L. REV. 407, 408–13 (1966).

76. *See* PHILIPPA STRUM, PRIVACY: THE DEBATE IN THE UNITED STATES SINCE 1945, at 4–7 (Fort Worth, TX: Harcourt Brace 1998).

77. HANNAH ARENDT, THE HUMAN CONDITION 70–71 (2d ed. Chicago: Univ. of Chicago Press 1998).

78. Daniel J. Solove, *Privacy and Power: Computer Databases and Metaphors for Information Privacy*, 53 STAN. L. REV. 1393, 1396–98 (2001).

79. *See generally* MARY MADDEN & AARON SMITH, PEW RESEARCH CENTER, REPUTATION MANAGEMENT AND SOCIAL MEDIA (2010), http://pewinternet.org/~/media//Files/Reports/2010/PIP_Reputation_Management_with_topline.pdf (poll results).

80. NATIONAL RESEARCH COUNCIL, *supra* note 49, at 69.

81. RULE, *supra* note 3, at 19, 63–64.

82. *See generally* James X. Dempsey & Lara M. Flint, *Commercial Data and National Security*, 72 GEO. WASH. L. REV. 1459 (2004).

83. *See* GARRETT HATCH, CONG. RESEARCH SERV., PRIVACY AND CIVIL LIBERTIES OVERSIGHT BOARD: NEW INDEPENDENT AGENCY STATUS (2009), http://www.fas.org/sgp/crs/misc/RL34385.pdf (analyzing the patchwork of laws that govern access to private information).

84. Balkin, *supra* note 2, at 3–4.

Chapter 6

1. JANE MAYER, THE DARK SIDE 46 (New York: Anchor Books 2009) (citing Sept. 21, 2001, Office of Legal Counsel memo); *see* Tim Golden, *A Secret Rewriting of Military Law*, N.Y. TIMES, Oct. 24, 2004, http://www.nytimes.com/2004/10/24/international/worldspecial2/24gitmo.html?_r=3&pagewanted=print&position=&oref=slogin&oref=slogin.

2. My account is based on court papers and descriptions of the case, on a voluminous Inspector General Report, OFFICE OF INSPECTOR GEN., SPECIAL REPORT, A REVIEW OF THE FBI'S HANDLING OF THE BRANDON MAYFIELD CASE (2006), http://www.justice.gov/oig/special/s0601/Chapter7.pdf [hereinafter INSPECTOR GEN. REPORT, MAYFIELD], on press interviews with Brandon Mayfield, and on input from Brandon Mayfield himself.

3. INSPECTOR GEN. REPORT, MAYFIELD, *supra* note 2, at 127–94; *see also* Stipulation for Compromise Settlement and Release at 2, Mayfield v. Gonzales, 504 F. Supp. 2d 1023, *rev'd*, 599 F.3d 964 (9th Cir.), *cert. denied*, ___ U.S. ___, 131 S. Ct. 503 (2010) (No. CV-04-1427AA), http://www.washingtonpost.com/wp-srv/nation/documents/Mayfield_settlement.pdf.

4. INSPECTOR GEN. REPORT, MAYFIELD, *supra* note 2, at 243–52.

5. *Id.* at 243–52.

6. *Id.* at 252–53.

7. *See* Stipulation for Compromise Settlement and Release, *Mayfield*, 504 F. Supp. 2d 1023, *supra* note 3, for the terms of the unsigned and undated settlement.

8. *Apology Note*, WASH. POST, Nov. 29, 2006, http://www.washingtonpost.com/wp-dyn/content/article/2006/11/29/AR2006112901155.html.

9. *Mayfield*, 504 F. Supp. 2d at 1042.

10. *See* NELSON B. LASSON, THE HISTORY AND DEVELOPMENT OF THE FOURTH AMENDMENT TO THE UNITED STATES CONSTITUTION 51–78 (Baltimore, MD: Johns Hopkins Univ. Press 1937).

11. Thomas Y. Davies, *Recovering the Original Fourth Amendment*, 98 MICH. L. REV. 547, 601–11 (1999).

12. The Supreme Court has interpreted the Fourth Amendment as setting a default requirement of search warrants based on probable cause. *See, e.g.*, Chimel v. California, 395 U.S. 752 (1969).

13. Brinegar v. United States, 338 U.S. 160, 180 (1949).

14. 50 U.S.C. § 1801(i).

15. *See* FREDERICK A. O. SCHWARZ, JR., & AZIZ A. HUQ, UNCHECKED AND UNBALANCED 21–23 (New York: New Press 2008).

16. *See* 50 U.S.C. § 1803(a), (b), & (d) (The Chief Justice designates eleven federal district court judges—the number under the original FISA statute was seven—to serve on the Foreign Intelligence Surveillance Court for seven-year terms, and three court of appeals judges to serve on the Court of Review).

17. The FISA court recently proposed revisions to its rules that could allow more frequent publication of its opinions, *see Comments on Proposed Rules of Procedure*, Oct. 4, 2010, http://www.aclu.org/files/assets/2010-10-4_-_ACLU_FISC_Rule_Comments.pdf.

18. *Transcript: Day Two of the Roberts Confirmation Hearings*, WASH. POST, Sept. 13, 2005, http://www.washingtonpost.com/wp-dyn/content/article/2005/09/13/AR2005091301469.html (quoting Roberts as saying, "When I first learned about the FISA court, I was surprised. It's not what we usually think of when we think of a court"). *See* Judith Resnik & Lane Dilg, *Responding to a Democratic Deficit: Limiting the Powers and the Term of the Chief Justice of the United States*, 154 U. PA. L. REV. 1575 (2006).

19. Theodore W. Ruger, *Chief Justice Rehnquist's Appointments to the FISA Court: An Empirical Perspective*, 101 NW. U.L. REV. 239, 257 (2007).

20. *See* OFFICE OF THE ASST. ATT'Y GEN., FISA REPORTS TO CONGRESS, http://www.fas.org/irp/agency/doj/fisa/; *see also Foreign Intelligence Surveillance Act Court Orders 1979–2009*, ELECTRONIC PRIVACY INFORMATION CENTER, http://epic.org/privacy/wiretap/stats/fisa_stats.html (listing link to FISA reports and summarizing FISA requests and orders between 1979 and 2009).

21. 50 U.S.C. §§ 1801(a)(4), (b)(2)(C) & (E), & 1801(c).

22. *See* Wilson v. Arkansas, 514 U.S. 927, 929 (1995); Richards v. Wisconsin, 520 U.S. 385 (1997); Groh v. Ramirez, 540 U.S. 551 (2004).

23. City of West Covina v. Perkins, 525 U.S. 234, 240 (1999).

24. 18 U.S.C. § 2518(8)(d) provides that within ninety days after termination of surveillance, the court will disclose to the target of the wiretap and other parties to intercepted communications an inventory describing the surveillance. The government may seek to delay notification under 18 U.S.C. § 1303a.

25. Patriot Act § 212 (codified at 18 U.S.C. § 3103a(b) & (c)).

26. *See id.*

27. A 2009 Administrative Office Report shows that during fiscal year 2008, only three of 763 sneak and peek warrants were issued in terrorism investigations, *see* DIR. OF THE ADMIN. OFFICE OF THE UNITED STATES COURTS, REPORT ON APPLICATIONS FOR DELAYED-NOTICE SEARCH WARRANTS AND EXTENSIONS (2009), http://big.assets.huffingtonpost.com/SneakAndPeakReport.pdf.

28. City of Indianapolis v. Edmond, 531 U.S. 32 (2000).

29. *Mayfield*, 504 F. Supp. 2d at 1037.

30. The FISA court is to accept the government's certifications on these issues unless they are found "clearly erroneous," 50 U.S.C. §§ 1804(a)(6)(A)–(E) & 1805(a)(4) (eavesdropping); *id.* at §§ 1823(a)(6)(A)–(E) & 1824(a)(4) (physical searches).

31. *Mayfield*, 504 F. Supp. 2d at 1034.

32. FISA delegates to the Attorney General the responsibility for developing guidelines for retention and dissemination of information obtained by electronic surveillance, *see* 50 U.S.C. § 1801(h).

33. *Mayfield*, 504 F. Supp. 2d at 1034.

34. *Mayfield*, 599 F.3d 964, 972 (9th Cir. 2006), *cert. denied*, ___ U.S. ___, 131 S. Ct. 503 (2010).

35. In re All Matters Submitted, 218 F. Supp. 2d 611 (FISC 2002), *rev'd sub nom.* In re Sealed Case, 310 F.3d 717 (FISA Ct. Rev. 2002).

36. Ann Beeson, *On the Home Front: A Lawyer's Struggle to Defend Rights After 9/11*, *in* THE WAR ON OUR FREEDOMS 295 (Richard C. Leone & Greg Anrig, Jr. eds., New York: Century Foundation 2003).

37. Ruger, *supra* note 19, at 255.

38. In re Sealed Case, 310 F.3d 717, 746 (FISA Ct. Rev. 2002).

39. *Id.*

40. ACLU v. United States, 538 U.S. 920 (2003).

41. 50 U.S.C. §§ 1806(c)–(d), 1825(d)–(e).

42. *See* United States v. Hassan Abu-Jihaad, 531 F. Supp. 2d 299, 310 (D. Ct. 2008).

43. *Id.* at 305 n.6.

44. Post 9/11 cases ruling against Fourth Amendment claims: City of Ontario v. Quon, ___ U.S. ___, 130 S. Ct. 2619 (2010); Arizona v. Johnson, ___ U.S. ___, 129 S. Ct. 781 (2009); Herring v. United States, 555 U.S. 135 (2009); Michigan v. Fisher, ___ U.S. ___, 130 S. Ct. 546 (2009); Pearson v. Callahan, 555 U.S. 223 (2009); Virginia v. Moore, 553 U.S. 164 (2008); Scott v. Harris, 550 U.S. 372 (2007); Los Angeles County v. Rettele, 550 U.S. 609 (2007); Wallace v. Kato, 549 U.S. 384 (2007); Hudson v. Michigan, 547 U.S. 586 (2006); Brigham City v. Stuart, 547 U.S. 398 (2006); Samson v. California, 547 U.S. 843 (2006); United States v. Grubbs, 547 U.S. 90 (2006); Muehler v. Mena, 544 U.S. 93 (2005); Illinois v. Caballes, 543 U.S. 405 (2005); Devenpeck v. Alford, 543 U.S. 146 (2004); Hiibel v. Sixth Judicial Dist. Court of Nev., 542 U.S. 177 (2004); Thornton v. United States, 541 U.S. 615 (2004); United States v. Flores Montano, 541 U.S. 149 (2004); Illinois v. Lidster, 540 U.S. 419 (2004); Maryland v. Pringle, 540 U.S. 366 (2003); United States v. Banks, 540 U.S. 31 (2003); Bd. of Educ. of Indep. Sch. Dist. No. 92 v. Earls, 536 U.S. 822 (2002); United States v. Drayton, 536 U.S. 194 (2002); United States v. Arvizu, 534 U.S. 266 (2002); United States v. Knights, 534 U.S. 112 (2001). Cases ruling in favor of Fourth Amendment claims: Safford Unified School Dist. v. Redding, ___ U.S. ___, 129 S. Ct. 2633 (2009); Arizona v. Gant, ___ U.S. ___, 129 S. Ct. 1710 (2009); Brendlin v. California, 551 U.S. 249 (2007); Georgia v. Randolph, 547 U.S. 103 (2006); Groh v. Ramirez, 540 U.S. 551 (2004).

45. Transcript of Oral Argument at 32, United States v. Arvizu, 534 U.S. 266 (2002) (No. 00–1519).

46. *Mayfield*, 504 F. Supp. 2d at 1042.

47. Berger v. New York, 388 U.S. 41 (1967).

48. Lopez v. United States, 373 U.S. 427, 466 (1963) (Brennan, J., dissenting).

49. Matthew R. Hall, *Constitutional Regulation of National Security Investigation: Minimizing the Use of Unrelated Evidence*, 41 WAKE FOREST L. REV. 61 (2006) (proposing a judicially created use restriction); Seth Kreimer, *Watching the Watchers*: 7 U. PA. J. CONST. L. 133, 181 (2004).

Chapter 7

1. United States v. Rumely, 345 U.S. 41, 58 (1953) (Douglas, J., concurring).

2. *Overview*, LIBR. CO. OF PHILADELPHIA, http://www.librarycompany.org/about/index.htm.

3. *History of the Franklin Public Library*, TOWN OF FRANKLIN, MASS., http://www.town.franklin.ma.us/Pages/FranklinMA_Library/libraryhistory.

4. *Jefferson's Library*, LIBR. OF CONG., http://www.loc.gov/exhibits/jefferson/jefflib.html.

5. *Resolution on the USA Patriot Act and Related Measures That Infringe on the Rights of Library Users*, AM. LIBR. ASS'N, http://www.ala.org/Template.cfm?Section=ifresolutions&Template=/ContentManagement/ContentDisplay.cfm&ContentID=11891.

6. American Library Association, Policy 53.4, adopted Feb. 2, 1973, http://www.ala.org/ala/mgrps/rts/godort/godortresolutions/19880713153.cfm.

7. 50 U.S.C. § 1861(a)(1).

8. Nancy Kranich, *The Impact of the USA PATRIOT Act on Free Expression*, FREE EXPRESSION POL'Y PROJECT (May 5, 2003), http://www.fepproject.org/commentaries/patriotact.html.

9. Attorney Gen. John Ashcroft, Proven Tactics in the Fight Against Crime, Address before the Nat'l Restaurant Ass'n (Sept. 15, 2003), http://www.justice.gov/archive/ag/speeches/2003/091503nationalrestaurant.htm.

10. Michele Orecklin, Jeffrey Ressner, & David Thigpen, *Civil Liberties: Checking What You Check Out*, TIME, May 12, 2003, http://www.time.com/time/magazine/article/0,9171,1004797,00.html.

11. Eric Lichtblau, *U.S. Says It Has Not Used New Library Records Law*, N.Y. TIMES, Sept. 19, 2003, http://www.nytimes.com/2003/09/19/us/us-says-it-has-not-used-new-library-records-law.html.

12. Robert D. McFadden, *F.B.I. in New York Asks Librarians' Aid in Reporting on Spies*, N.Y. TIMES, Sept. 18, 1987, http://query.nytimes.com/gst/fullpage.html?res=9B0DE7D6163FF93BA2575AC0A961948260&scp=3&sq=fbi%20spies%20librarys&st=cse.

13. *See* Sidney Koenigsburg, *Library Records Open to Parental Scrutiny: A New Set of Internet Access Controls for Minors?* 29 COLUM. J.L. & ARTS 361, 364 (2006), and Scott Seaman & Ann Miller, *State Statutes on Confidentiality of Library Circulation Records* 13(2) LIBR. & ARCHIVAL SEC. 33, 33 (1996). The other two states, Hawaii and Kentucky, have Attorney General opinions stating that library records deserve more protection than other business records, *see State Privacy Laws Regarding Library Records*, AM. LIBR. ASS'N, http://www.ala.org/ala/aboutala/offices/oif/ifgroups/stateifcchairs/stateifcinaction/stateprivacy.cfm.

14. Connecticut law, for example, provides: "Reports by libraries. Confidentiality of records. (b)(1) . . . records maintained by libraries that can be used to identify any library user, or link any user to a library transaction, regardless of format, shall be kept confidential, except that the records may be disclosed to officers, employees and agents of the library, as necessary for operation of the library. (2) Information contained in such records shall not be released to any third party, except (A) pursuant to a court order, or (B) with the written permission of the library user whose personal information is contained in the records." Conn. Gen. Stat. §§ 11–25 (2004).

15. U.S. Const. art. VI.

16. *See* Olmstead v. United States, 277 U.S. 438 (1928).

17. *See* Beryl A. Howell, *Seven Weeks: The Making of the USA PATRIOT ACT*, 72 GEO. WASH. L. REV. 1145, 1171 (2004).

18. H.R. 1157, 108th Cong. (2003).

19. H.R. 2862, 109th Cong., 151 Cong. Rec. H4494, 4534–43, 4551 (2005) (amendment 280, unenacted).

20. *See, e.g.*, Family Educational and Privacy Rights Act, 20 U.S.C. § 1232g (2006) (codified as subsequently amended by Patriot Act § 507).

21. Health Insurance Portability and Accountability Act of 1996, Pub. L. No. 104–191 §§ 261–64, 10 Stat. 1936, 2021–34 (1996) (codified as subsequently amended in scattered sections of 18, 26, 29 & 42 U.S.C.); *see* 45 C.F.R. §§ 160 & 164 (2002) (codified as amended).

22. Electronic Communications Privacy Act of 1986, Pub. L. No. 99–508, 100 Stat. 1848 (1986) (codified as subsequently amended in scattered sections of 18 U.S.C.).

23. *Statement of Homam Albaroudi, Member, Muslim Community Association of Ann Arbor*, ACLU (July 30, 2003), http://www.aclu.org/national-security/statement-homam-albaroudi-member-muslim-community-association-ann-arbor.

24. The original gag order read: "No person shall disclose to any other person (other than those persons necessary to produce the tangible things under this section) that the Federal Bureau of Investigation has sought or obtained tangible things under this section." Patriot Act § 215 (codified as subsequently amended at 50 U.S.C. § 1861(d)).

25. Declaration of Mary Lieberman, Muslim Cmty. Ass'n of Ann Arbor v. Ashcroft, No. 03–72913 (E.D. Mich., Nov. 3, 2003), http://www.aclu.org/files/FilesPDFs/affidavit_lieberman.pdf.

26. Declaration of John Doe, Muslim Cmty. Ass'n of Ann Arbor v. Ashcroft, No. 03–72913 (E.D. Mich., Nov. 3, 2003), http://www.aclu.org/files/FilesPDFs/affidavit_doe.pdf.

27. *See* David Pozen, *The Mosaic Theory, National Security, and the Freedom of Information Act*, 115 YALE L.J. 628 (2005) (describing and critiquing the mosaic theory).

28. *See* Jameel Jaffer, *The Mosaic Theory*, SOCIAL RESEARCH (Sept. 22, 2010) (discussing the difference between the mosaic theory as a statement of fact as opposed to an argument justifying secrecy). For examples of two very different judicial reactions to the government's assertion of this doctrine to defend secrecy practices, *compare* Detroit Free Press v. Ashcroft, 303 F.3d 681, 709–10 (6th Cir. 2002) ("[T]here seems to be no limit to the Government's [mosaic] argument. . . . The government could operate in virtual secrecy in all matters dealing, even remotely, with 'national security,' resulting in a wholesale suspension of First Amendment rights") *with* Center for Nat'l Sec. Stud. v. Dep't of Justice, 331 F.3d 918, 928 (D.C. Cir. 2003), *cert. denied*, 540 U.S. 1104 (2004) ("We . . . reject any attempt to artificially limit the long-recognized deference to the executive on national security issues. . . . What may seem trivial to the uninformed, may appear of great moment to one who has a broad view of the scene and may put the questioned item of information in its proper context") (internal quotation marks omitted).

29. ACLU v. U.S. Dep't of Justice, 265 F. Supp. 2d 20, 34 (D.D.C. 2003).

30. ACLU v. U.S. Dep't of Justice, 321 F. Supp. 2d 24, 32–33 (D.D.C. 2004).

31. *Oversight of the USA Patriot Act: Hearings Before the S. Comm. on the Judiciary*, 109th Cong. 6 (2005) (statement of Alberto R. Gonzales, Att'y Gen. of the United States), http://www.access.gpo.gov/congress/senate/pdf/109hrg/24293. pdf; *see also* U.S. DEP'T OF JUSTICE, FACT SHEET: USA PATRIOT ACT PROVISIONS SET FOR REAUTHORIZATION (2005), http://www.fas.org/irp/news/2005/04/doj040505b. html.

32. Muslim Cmty. Ass'n v. Ashcroft, 459 F. Supp. 2d 592 (E.D. Mich. 2006). A list of amicus curiae briefs can be found at: *PATRIOT Act Fears Are Stifling Free Speech, ACLU Says in Challenge to Law*, ACLU, http://www.aclu.org/national-security/patri-ot-act-fears-are-stifling-free-speech-aclu-says-challenge-law.

33. *See* Doe v. Ashcroft, 334 F. Supp. 2d 471, 494 n.118 (S.D.N.Y. 2004), *vacated sub nom.* Doe v. Gonzales 449 F. 3d 415 (2d Cir. 2006).

34. United States v. Miller, 425 U.S. 435 (1976).

35. Smith v. Maryland, 442 U.S. 735 (1979).

36. 12 U.S.C. §§ 3401–22 (codified as amended).

37. H.R. Rep. No. 95–1383, at 28 (1978).

38. Electronic Communications Privacy Act of 1986, *supra* note 22, § 201 (codified at 18 U.S.C. § 2703(c)(1)(B).

39. *See, e.g.*, GEOFFREY R. STONE, WAR AND LIBERTY 142 (New York: W.W. Norton 2007); WAYNE R. LAFAVE, SEARCH AND SEIZURE 2.7(b)–(c) at 736, 737 (4th ed. 2004) (influential treatise characterizing the third-party doctrine as "dead wrong"); Sherry Colb, *What Is a Search? Two Conceptual Flaws in Fourth Amendment Doctrine and Some Hints of a Remedy*, 55 STAN. L. REV. 119 (2002); Kathleen Sullivan, *Under a Watchful Eye: Incursions on Personal Privacy, in* THE WAR ON OUR FREEDOMS 128–46 (Richard C. Leone & Greg Anrig, Jr. eds., New York: Public Affairs 2003).

40. *See, e.g.*, Patricia Bellia, *Surveillance Law Through Cyberlaw's Lens*, 72 GEO. WASH. L. REV. 1375, 1397–1403 (2004); Deirdre Mulligan, *Reasonable Expectations in Electronic Communications: A Critical Perspective on the Electronic Communications Privacy Act*, 72 GEO. WASH. L. REV. 1557, 1577–82 (2004).

41. Kyllo v. United States, 533 U.S. 27 (2001) (the Fourth Amendment prohibited federal agents from using a thermal imaging device to detect a marijuana-growing enterprise in the defendant's home).

42. Stanley v. Georgia, 394 U.S. 557 (1969) (the First Amendment protected the defendant against prosecution for private possession of obscene films in his home).

43. *See* Jay Stanley, *The Crisis in Fourth Amendment Jurisprudence*, 4 ADVANCE [Journal of the ACS Issues Groups] 91, 96–97 (2010).

44. In my article, *The USA Patriot Act and the Submajoritarian Fourth Amendment*, 41 HARV. C.R.-C.L. L. REV. 67 (2006), I argue that the Court has inappropriately underinterpreted the Fourth Amendment. I agree with Thurgood Marshall, who dissented in both *Miller* and *Smith*, that the courts have an important role to play in checking dragnet searches, even for information in the hands of third parties, and that it is unfortunate that the Supreme Court has essentially abdicated that role. There is reason to believe that it is not only expert commentators who find the Supreme Court's third-party assumption of risk doctrine unsatisfactory. An empirical study, for example, found that respondents thought the Supreme Court was underprotecting privacy in a number of areas, including protection of business records, *see* Christopher Slobogin & Joseph E. Schumacher, *Reasonable Expectations of Privacy and Autonomy in Fourth Amendment Cases: An Empirical Look at "Understandings Recognized and Permitted by Society,"* 42 DUKE L.J. 727 (1993).

45. OFFICE OF INSPECTOR GEN., U.S. DEP'T OF JUSTICE, A REVIEW OF THE F.B.I.'S USE OF SECTION 215 ORDERS FOR BUSINESS RECORDS IN 2006 ix–xi (2007).

46. Richard S. Dunham, *The Patriot Act: Business Balks*, BUSINESSWEEK, Nov. 10, 2005, http://www.businessweek.com/bwdaily/dnflash/nov2005/nf20051110_9709_db016.htm.

47. *Id.*

48. *See* Michelle Kisluk & Wendy Gross, *Canada's Privacy Laws v. The USA PATRIOT ACT: How Information-Sharing with U.S.-linked Companies May Breach Canada's Laws*, FINDLAW (May 10, 2005), http://library.findlaw.com/2005/May/10/245866.html.

49. *See, e.g.*, Letter to Sen. Arlen Specter from Ass'n of Corp. Counsel, Bus. Civil Liberties, Inc., The Fin. Servs. Roundtable, Nat'l Ass'n of Mfrs., Nat'l Ass'n of Realtors, & U.S. Chamber of Commerce (Oct. 4, 2005) (on file with ACLU), http://www.aclu.org/files/FilesPDFs/business%20patriot%20letter.pdf.

50. Susan Crabtree, *Obama Stares Down Patriot Act Criticism*, THE HILL (Nov. 12, 2009, 7:00 a.m.), http://thehill.com/homenews/administration/67459-administration-stares-down-patriot-act-criticism.

51. After Section 215 was renewed in January 2011, Senator Leahy, Chair of the Senate Judiciary Committee, wrote to Attorney General Holder asking his help in implementing the agreed-upon changes even though they had not become law. Letter from Sen. Patrick Leahy, Chairman, S. Comm. on Judiciary, to Eric Holder, Att'y Gen of the United States, (Mar. 17, 2010), http://judiciary.senate.gov/resources/documents/111thCongress/upload/031710LeahyToHolder.pdf.

52. *See* Charlie Savage, Senators Say Patriot Act Is Being Misinterpreted, N.Y. TIMES, May 27, 2011.

Chapter 8

1. Elaine Scarry, *Resolving to Resist*, BOSTON REV. (February/March 2004), http://bostonreview.net/BR29.1/scarry.html.

2. Alison Leigh Cowan, *Four Librarians Finally Break Silence in Records Case*, N.Y. TIMES, May 31, 2006, http://www.nytimes.com/2006/05/31/nyregion/31library.html?_r=1.

3. Nancy Kranich, *Commentary: The Impact of the USA PATRIOT Act on Free Expression*, FREE EXPRESSION POL'Y PROJECT (May 5, 2003), http://www.fepproject.org/commentaries/patriotact.html.

4. Requests for Information under the Electronic Communications Privacy Act: Memorandum Opinion from the White House Office of Legal Counsel to the Gen. Counsel for the FBI (Nov. 5, 2008), http://www.fas.org/irp/agency/doj/olc/ecpa.pdf.

5. Memorandum in Opposition to Government's Emergency Motion to Stay Pending Expedited Appeal at 3, Doe v. Gonzales, No. 05–4896 (D. Conn. Sept. 19, 2005), http://action.aclu.org/nsl/legal/aclu_memo_vacate_stay_092205.pdf.

6. *History and Application of the USA PATRIOT ACT and the Importance of the Foreign Intelligence Surveillance Act of 1978 (FISA), Hearing Before the S. Select Comm. on Intelligence*, 109th Cong. 98 (2005) (testimony of Alberto R. Gonzales), http://www.fas.org/irp/congress/2005_hr/shrg109-341.pdf.

7. Doe v. Ashcroft, 334 F. Supp. 2d 471 (S.D.N.Y. 2004), *vacated sub nom.* Doe v. Gonzales 449 F. 3d 415 (2d Cir. 2006). The history and subsequent history of this decision will be explained in chapter 9.

8. *Gagged for Six Years, Nick Merrill Speaks Out on Landmark Court Struggle over FBI's National Security Letters*, DEMOCRACY NOW (Aug. 11, 2010), http://www.democracynow.org/2010/8/11/gagged_for_6_years_nick_merrill (interview with George Christian). The story of the Library Connection Four is also told in AMY GOODMAN & DAVID GOODMAN, STANDING UP TO THE MADNESS 52–70 (New York: Hyperion 2008).

9. *See* Doe v. Gonzales, 546 U.S. 1301, 1305–06 (Ginsburg, Cir. J., 2d Cir. 2005).

10. *See* Julie M. Spanbauer, *The First Amendment Right to Petition Government for Redress of Grievances: Cut from a Different Cloth, in* FREEDOM OF ASSEMBLY AND PETITION (THE FIRST AMENDMENT) 85–93 (Margaret M. Russell ed., New York: Prometheus 2010). The courts have not encouraged distinct claims raised under this part of the First Amendment, *see* Michael J. Wishnie, *Immigrants and the Right to Petition*, in *id.*, 174–79 (advocating more stringent judicial review of denials of right to petition).

11. *See, e.g.*, Richmond Newspapers, Inc. v. Virginia, 448 U.S. 555 (1980). The issue of access to the courts will be discussed in chapter 11. Doe v. Gonzales, 386 F. Supp. 2d 66, 73 (D. Conn. 2005).

12. Doe v. Gonzales, 386 F. Supp. 2d 66, 73 (D. Conn. 2005).

13. Alison Leigh Cowan, *Librarians Must Stay Silent in Patriot Act Suit, Court Says*, N.Y. TIMES, Sept. 21, 2005, http://www.nytimes.com/2005/09/21/nyregion/21library.html.

14. Doe Memorandum in Opposition to Pl.'s Emergency Mot. to Vacate Stay at 4, Doe v. Gonzales, No. 05–4896 (2d Cir. Sept. 26, 2005), http://action.aclu.org/nsl/legal/govt_opp_mot_vacate_stay_092605.pdf.

15. *See* Gov't's Memorandum in Support of Mot. for Emergency Closure of Hearing at 1, Doe v. Gonzales, No. 05–4896 (2d Cir. Sept. 27, 2005), http://action.aclu.org/nsl/legal/govt_emerg_mot_close_092705.pdf.

16. Doe v. Gonzales, 449 F.3d 415, 422 (2d Cir. 2006).

17. Doe v. Gonzales, 546 U.S. 1301 (Ginsburg, Cir. J., 2d Cir. 2005).

18. Alison Leigh Cowan, *A Court Fights to Keep a Secret That's Long Been Revealed*, N.Y. TIMES, Nov. 18, 2005, http://query.nytimes.com/gst/fullpage.html?res=9D01E6D7113EF93BA25752C1A9639C8B63&sec=&spon=&pagewanted=1.

19. Barton Gellman, *The FBI's Secret Scrutiny: In Hunt for Terrorists Bureau Examines Records of Ordinary Americans*, WASH. POST, Nov. 6, 2005, http://www.washingtonpost.com/wp-dyn/content/article/2005/11/05/AR2005110501366.html.

20. *Id.*; *see also* Letter from William Moschella to Arlen Specter, Chair, S. Judiciary Comm. (Nov. 23, 2005), http://www.washingtonpost.com/wp-srv/nation/documents/dojletter112305.pdf (response to Gellman article).

21. U.S. DEP'T OF JUSTICE, OFFICE OF INSPECTOR GEN., A REVIEW OF THE FBI'S USE OF NATIONAL SECURITY LETTERS 37 (2007), http://www.usdoj.gov/oig/special/s0703b/final.pdf.

22. George Christian, *Doe v. Gonzales: Fighting the FBI's Demand for Library Records*, ACLU (May 30, 2006), http://www.aclu.org/national-security/idoe-v-gonzalesi-fighting-fbis-demand-library-records-statement-george-christian.

23. *Tuesday Keynote: Meet Two of the Jane Does from Doe v. Gonzales*, N.J. LIBR. ASS'N BLOG (Apr. 25, 2007), http://blog.njla.org/archives/2007/04/tuesday_keynote_meet_two_of_th.html.

24. Abby Goodrum & Velma Rogers Graham, *Impact and Analysis of Law Enforcement Activities on Public and Academic Libraries* 36, AM. LIBR. ASS'N (Aug. 25, 2005), http://www.ala.org/ala/aboutala/offices/oitp/publications/booksstudies/LawRptFinal.pdf.

25. Editorial, *Breaking a Promise on Surveillance*, N.Y. TIMES, July 29, 2010, http://www.nytimes.com/2010/07/30/opinion/30fri1.html?_r=1&ref=usa_patriot_act.

26. Joan Airoldi, *Librarian's Brush with FBI Shapes Her View of the Patriot Act*, USA TODAY, May 17, 2005, http://www.usatoday.com/news/opinion/editorials/2005-05-17-librarian-edit_x.htm.

27. George Eberhart, *Carol Brey-Casiano Tells a Patriot Act Story*, AM. LIBR. (June 29, 2010), http://americanlibrariesmagazine.org/print/4390.

28. Rachel Myers, *Gag Lifted, Brewster Speaks!* ACLU BLOG OF RIGHTS (May 9, 2008, 10:27 A.M.), http://www.aclu.org/2008/05/09/gag-lifted-brewster-speaks.

29. *Anti-Terrorism Investigations and the Fourth Amendment After September 11, 2001, Hearing Before the Subcomm. on the Const. of the H. Comm. on the Judiciary*, 108th Cong. 38 (2003) (testimony of Viet D. Dinh, former Assistant Att'y Gen., U.S. Dept. of Justice), http://frwebgate.access.gpo.gov/cgi-bin/getdoc.cgi?dbname=108_house_hearings&;docid=f:87238.pdf.

30. *Oversight of the FBI: Hearing Before the S. Comm. on the Judiciary*, 110th Cong. 10 (2007) (testimony of Robert S. Mueller, Dir., FBI), http://frwebgate.access.gpo.gov/cgi-bin/getdoc.cgi?dbname=110_senate_hearings&docid=f:38189.pdf.

31. *FBI Won't Publicly Disclose Number of NSLs Used at Libraries*, LIBR. J. (Mar. 3, 2007), http://www.libraryjournal.com/article/CA6430178.html.

32. USA PATRIOT ACT Additional Reauthorizing Amendments Act of 2006, Pub. L. No. 109–78 § 5, 120 Stat. 278, 281 (2006).

33. *See* 18 U.S.C. § 2709(f) (2006).

34. James H. Klinger, *Responses of the FBI Based upon the May 2, 2006 Hearing Before the S. Comm. on the Judiciary Regarding FBI Oversight*, at 122 (Nov. 30, 2006), http://www.ala.org/ala/issuesadvocacy/advocacy/federallegislation/theusapatriotact/Muellerresponses050206.pdf.

35. *See generally* Comm. on Technical and Privacy Dimensions of Info. for Terrorism Prevention and Other Nat'l Goals, Nat'l Research Council, *Public Opinion Data on U.S. Attitudes Toward Government Counterterrorism Efforts*, PROTECTING INDIVIDUAL PRIVACY IN THE STRUGGLE AGAINST TERRORISTS: A FRAMEWORK FOR PROGRAM ASSESSMENT, at 281–334 (Washington, DC: Academy of Sciences 2008), http://books.nap.edu/openbook.php?record_id=12452&page=281. *See* Lydia Saad, *Americans Reject Extreme Anti-Privacy Measures*, Gallup (Aug. 8, 2005) (citing a July 2005 Gallup poll indicating 60 percent of Americans polled opposed permitting the government to search a list of books they have checked out of the library, and only 46 percent of even the most "security minded" of those polled favored government access to library records); ALA Straw Poll (Mar. 8, 2006) (Out of 145 participants, 80 percent of respondents answered "No" and 14 percent answered "Yes," to the question: "Do you think the modifications in the Senate compromise bill (S. 2271) on the Patriot Act offer adequate civil-liberties protections to libraries and their patrons?"), http://www.ala.org/ala/alonline/aldirect/2006pollresults/2006polls.cfm.

36. Scarry, *supra* note 1.

Chapter 9

1. Anonymous, *My National Security Letter Gag Order*, WASH. POST, Mar. 23, 2007, http://www.washingtonpost.com/wp-dyn/content/article/2007/03/22/AR2007032201882.html.

2. AMY GOODMAN & DAVID GOODMAN, STANDING UP TO THE MADNESS 70–71 (New York: Hyperion 2008).

3. *Gagged for Six Years, Nick Merrill Speaks Out on Landmark Court Struggle over FBI's National Security Letters*, DEMOCRACY NOW (Aug. 11, 2010), http://www.democracynow.org/2010/8/11/gagged_for_6_years_nick_merrill.

4. ACLU v. Dep't of Justice, 321 F. Supp. 2d 24 (D.D.C. 2004); ACLU v. Dep't of Justice, 265 F. Supp. 2d 20 (D.D.C. 2003).

5. U.S. DEP'T OF JUSTICE, OFFICE OF INSPECTOR GEN., *A Review of the FBI's Use of National Security Letters* 17 (2007) [hereinafter *Inspector Gen. Report on NSLs*], http://www.usdoj.gov/oig/special/s0703b/final.pdf.

6. *See* Charlie Savage, *White House Seeks to Clarify F.B.I. Powers* VIS-À-VIS *E-mail*, N.Y. TIMES, July 29, 2010, http://www.nytimes.com/2010/07/30/us/30fbi.html; Pete Yost, *FBI Access to E-mail, Web Data Raises Privacy Fear*, GUARDIAN, July 29, 2010, http://www.guardian.co.uk/world/feedarticle/9201265.

7. *See* 12 U.S.C. § 3414(a).

8. *See* Andrew E. Nieland, Note, *National Security Letters and the Amended Patriot Act*, 92 CORNELL L. REV. 1201, 1207–11 (2007); Doe v. Ashcroft, 334 F. Supp. 2d 480, 480–83 (S.D.N.Y. 2004).

9. Congress changed this provision in 1986 to compel financial institutions to comply. *See* Nieland, *supra* note 8, at 1208 n. 45.

10. 18 U.S.C. §§ 2709(a) & (b)(1).

11. Other statutes allow the FBI to use NSLs to collect information from "financial institutions," *see* 12 U.S.C. §§ 3414(a)(5)(A) & (d), to force consumer reporting agencies to turn over all of the information in a consumer's file, *see* 15 U.S.C. §§ 1681(u) & (v), or to compel financial institutions and consumer reporting agencies to disclose records concerning agency employees, 50 U.S.C. § 436.

12. *See* Julian Sanchez, *Obama's Surveillance Power Grab*, AM. PROSPECT (July 29, 2010), http://www.prospect.org/cs/articles?article=obamas_surveillance_power_grab.

13. Pub. L. No. 99–508 § 201, 100 Stat 1848 (1986) (codified as amended in 1993, 1996, 2001, 2006, and 2009 at 18 U.S.C. § 2709). *See* Foreign Intelligence Surveillance Act of 1978, 50 U.S.C. § 1801 for definitions. *See* Nieland, *supra* note 8, at 1208 n. 43 & 1209 n. 65.

14. Pub. L. 103–142 § 1, 107 Stat. 1491, 1491 (1993).

15. Like Section 215, this section also provides that investigations of United States persons could not be conducted "solely on the basis of activities protected by the first amendment to the Constitution of the United States." *See* Pub. L. No. 107–156 § 505, 115 Stat 252, 365 (2001).

16. Barton Gellman, *The FBI's Secret Scrutiny: In Hunt for Terrorists Bureau Examines Records of Ordinary Americans*, WASH. POST, Nov. 6, 2005, http://www.washingtonpost.com/wp-dyn/content/article/2005/11/05/AR2005110501366.html.

17. *See* chapter 8, note 21 and accompanying text.

18. *Inspector Gen. Report on NSLs*, *supra* note 5, at 17.

19. *See* Memorandum from John A. Ashcroft, Att'y Gen. of the United States, to Robert S. Mueller et al., *Intelligence Sharing Procedures for Foreign Intelligence and Foreign Counterintelligence Investigations Conducted by the FBI* (May 6, 2002), http://www.fas.org/irp/agency/doj/fisa/ag030602.html; *see also* Dep't of Justice, *The Attorney General's Guidelines for FBI National Security Investigations and Foreign Intelligence Collection* (Oct. 31, 2003), http://www.fas.org/irp/agency/doj/fbi/nsiguidelines.pdf. In 18 U.S.C. § 2709(d) Congress delegated this job to the Attorney General.

20. Eric Lichtblau, *FBI Data Mining Reached Beyond Initial Targets*, N.Y. TIMES, Sept. 9, 2007, http://www.nytimes.com/2007/09/09/washington/09fbi.html.

21. *See, e.g.*, 18 U.S.C. § 2709.

22. Decision and Order, Doe v. Ashcroft, No. 04 Civ. 2614 (VM) (S.D.N.Y. May 12, 2004), http://www.aclu.org/files/FilesPDFs/decision.pdf; *see also* Dan Eggen, *ACLU Was Forced to Revise Release on PATRIOT ACT Suit: Justice Dept. Cited Secrecy Rules*, WASH. POST, May 13, 2004, http://www.washingtonpost.com/wp-dyn/articles/A22404-2004May12.html.

23. *See Government Gag Exposed*, ACLU (Aug. 19, 2004), http://www.aclu.org/national-security/government-gag-exposed (providing a list of documents that were subjects of redaction battles).

24. Doe v. Ashcroft, 334 F. Supp. 2d 471, 524 (S.D.N.Y. 2004).

25. *Id.* at 519.

26. *Id.* at 520.

27. *Id.* at 515.

28. *Material Witness Provisions of the Criminal Code, and the Implementation of the USA Patriot Act: Section 505 That Addresses National Security Letters, and Section 804 That Addresses Jurisdiction over Crimes Committed at U.S. Facilities Abroad: Hearing Before the Subcomm. on Crime, Terrorism, and Homeland Security of the H. Comm. on the Judiciary*, 109th Cong. 1, 23, 64–66, 72 (2005).

29. 18 U.S.C. §§ 3511(b)(2) & (3).

30. USA PATRIOT Improvement and Reauthorization Act of 2005, Pub. L. No. 109–177 § 117, 120 Stat. 192, 217 (2006) (codified at 18 U.S.C. § 1510(e) (2006)). It is remarkable that the question of what would happen if someone violated a gag order—even by talking to a lawyer—had never come up. The Department of Justice had never prosecuted anyone for noncompliance with an NSL or with the gag order and had never brought an action to compel compliance, so far as we know, because they evidently never had occasion to do so. *See* Letter from William Moschella, Assistant Att'y Gen. of the United States, to Arlen Specter, Chair, S. Judiciary Comm. (Nov. 23, 2005), http://www.washingtonpost.com/wp-srv/nation/documents/dojletter112305.pdf.

31. Doe v. Gonzales, 500 F. Supp. 2d 379 (S.D.N.Y. 2007), *aff'd* by Doe v. Mukasey, 549 F.3d 861 (2d Cir. 2008).

32. Doe v. Gonzales, 500 F. Supp. 2d. at 396–97.

33. *Id.* at 413.

34. U.S. DEP'T OF JUSTICE, OFFICE OF THE INSPECTOR GEN., A REVIEW OF THE FBI'S USE OF NATIONAL SECURITY LETTERS: ASSESSMENT OF CORRECTIVE ACTIONS AND EXAMINATION OF NSL USAGE IN 2006 12 (2008).

35. Press Release, *National Security Letters: Frequently Asked Questions*, FBI (2007), http://www.fbi.gov/pressrel/pressrel07/nsl_faqs030907.htm; *The Use and*

Purpose of National Security Letters, Headline Archive, FBI, http://www.fbi.gov/page2/natsecurityletters.htm; Statement of Valerie E. Caproni, Gen. Counsel, FBI, Before the H. Comm. on the Judiciary, Subcomm. on the Constitution, Civil Rights and Civil Liberties (Apr. 15, 2008), http://www.fbi.gov/congress/congress08/caproni041508.htm; Ellen Nakashima, *Plaintiff Who Challenged FBI's National Security Letters Reveals Concerns,* WASH. POST, Aug. 10, 2010, http://www.washingtonpost.com/wpdyn/content/article/2010/08/09/AR2010080906252.html.

36. Doe v. Ashcroft, 334 F. Supp. 2d 471, 494 n.118, 508 n.171.

37. Id. at 494–506.

38. USA PATRIOT Improvement and Reauthorization Act of 2005, S. 1389, 109th Cong. § 8 (2005) (codified at 18 U.S.C. § 3511(a)).

39. Doe v. Gonzales, 449 F. 3d 415 (2d Cir. 2006).

40. Doe v. Gonzales, 500 F. Supp. 2d at 386 n.3.

41. Doe v. Gonzales, 449 F. 3d at 507.

42. Requests for Information Under the Electronic Communications Privacy Act: Memorandum Opinion from the White House Office of Legal Counsel to the General Counsel for the Federal Bureau of Investigation (Nov. 5, 2008), www.fas.org/irp/agency/doj/olc/ecpa.pdf.

43. Doe v. Gonzales, 449 F.3d at 510 n.175, quoting Daniel J. Solove, *Digital Dossiers and the Dissipation of Fourth Amendment Privacy,* 75 S. CAL. L. REV. 1083, 1084 (2002).

44. *See* Sanchez, *supra* note 12.

45. *See Oversight of the USA Patriot Act, Hearings Before S. Comm. on the Judiciary,* 109th Cong. 17 (2005), http://www.access.gpo.gov/congress/senate/senate14ch109.html.

46. *See* 28 USC § 2709(e).

47. *Inspector Gen. Report on NSLs, supra* note 5, at xvi.

48. *Id.*

49. *Id.* at 118.

50. *See* Michael German, *ACLU Roadmap of Justice Department Inspector General's Review of the FBI's Use of National Security Letters* (Mar. 19, 2007), http://www.aclu.org/national-security/aclu-roadmap-justice-department-inspector-general-s-review-fbi-s-use-national-secu.

51. *Inspector Gen. Report on NSLs, supra* note 5, at 60–64.

52. R. Jeffrey Smith, *FBI Violations May Number 3,000, Official Says,* WASH. POST, Mar. 21, 2007, http://www.washingtonpost.com/wp-dyn/content/article/2007/03/20/AR2007032000921.html.

53. *Hearing Before the H. Comm. on the Judiciary, The Inspector General's Independent Report on the FBI's Use of National Security Letters,* 110th Cong. (2007) (testimony of Valerie Caproni, Gen. Counsel, FBI), http://frwebgate.access.gpo.gov/cgi-bin/getdoc.cgi?dbname=110_house_hearings&docid=f:34175.wais.

54. *Inspector Gen. Report on NSLs, supra* note 5, at xxxv–xxxviii.

55. U.S. DEP'T OF JUSTICE, OFFICE OF THE INSPECTOR GEN., A REVIEW OF THE FBI'S USE OF EXIGENT LETTERS AND OTHER INFORMATIONAL REQUESTS FOR TELEPHONE RECORDS 251 (2010), http://www.justice.gov/oig/special/s1001r.pdf.

56. *See* Doe v. Gonzales, 500 F. Supp. 2d at 420 (S.D.N.Y. 2007) (expressing concern about the FBI's assertions of secrecy chilling free expression and association, especially statements critical of the way the government uses NSLs).

57. *Inspector Gen. Report on NSLs, supra* note 5, at 264. The opinion itself is classified and most of the discussion about it in the IG Report is redacted.

58. *See Hundreds of New Documents Reveal Expanded Military Role in Domestic Surveillance,* ACLU (Oct. 14, 2007), http://www.aclu.org/national-security/hundreds-new-documents-reveal-expanded-military-role-domestic-surveillance.

59. *See, e.g.,* National Security Letter Reform Act of 2009, H.R. 1800, 111st Cong. (2009) (bill proposed by Jerrold Nadler, D-NY, "[t]o establish reasonable procedural protections [including judicial review] for the use of national security letters, and for other purposes" with twenty-seven co-sponsors including Jeff Flake, R-AZ, and Jane Harman, D-CA).

60. Nakashima, *supra* note 35; *see also Gagged for Six Years, supra,* note 3.

Chapter 10

1. Leslie Cauley, *NSA Has Massive Database of Americans' Phone Calls,* USA TO-DAY, May 11, 2006, http://www.usatoday.com/news/washington/2006-05-10-nsa_x.htm.

2. Many commentators reached this conclusion, including the Congressional Research Service, *see* Memorandum from Elizabeth B. Bazan & Jennifer K. Elsea, Legislative Attorneys, CRS, *Presidential Authority to Conduct Warrantless Electronic Surveillance to Gather Foreign Intelligence Information* (Jan. 5, 2006), http://fas.org/sgp/crs/intel/m010506.pdf.

3. James Risen & Eric Lichtblau, *Bush Lets U.S. Spy on Callers Without Courts,* N.Y. TIMES, Dec. 16, 2005, http://www.nytimes.com/2005/12/16/politics/16program.html.

4. U.S. DEP'T OF JUSTICE, OFFICE OF THE INSPECTOR GEN., UNCLASSIFIED REPORT ON THE PRESIDENT'S SURVEILLANCE PROGRAM 31 (2009) [hereinafter *Inspector Gen. Report, NSA*]; *see also* Protect America Act of 2007, Pub. L. No. 110–155, 121 Stat. 552 (2007) (codified at 50 U.S.C. §§ 1801, 1803, & 1805).

5. Cauley, *supra* note 1.

6. Declaration of Mark Klein in Support of Plaintiff's Motion for Preliminary Injunction, Hepting v. AT&T Corp., No. C-06-0672-VRW (N.D. Cal. June 8, 2006), http://www.eff.org/files/filenode/att/Mark%20Klein%20Unredacted%20Decl-Including%20Exhibits.PDF.

7. Cauley, *supra* note 1.

8. FISA Amendments Act of 2008, Pub. L. No. 101-261, 122 Stat. 2436 (2008) (codified at 50 U.S.C. § 1881a). Section 702(h)(3) exempts telecommunications providers from liability.

9. Government Defendants' Notice of Motion and Motion to Dismiss for Summary Judgment at 3–7, 14–15, Jewel v. Nat'l Sec. Agency, 2010 WL 235075 (N.D. Cal. Jan. 21, 2010), (No. C 06–1791 VRW), http://www.eff.org/files/filenode/jewel/jewelmtdobama.pdf; *see* Jones, *infra* note 49, for analysis.

10. *Jewel v. Nat'l Sec. Agency,* 2010 WL 235075 at *1.

11. Al-Haramain Islamic Found. v. Bush, 507 F.3d 1190, 1193 (9th Cir. 2007).

12. Amnesty Int'l USA v. McConnell, 646 F. Supp. 2d 633, 645 (S.D.N.Y. 2009), *rev'd sub nom.* Amnesty Int'l USA v. Clapper, ___ F.3d ___, 2011 U.S. App. LEXIS 5699 (2d Cir. 2011).

13. My sources for the story of events within the DOJ include the 2009 *Inspector General's Report, NSA, supra* note 4; James Comey's testimony before the Senate Judiciary Committee: *Preserving Prosecutorial Independence: Is the Dep't of Justice Politicizing the Hiring and Firing of U.S. Attorneys?—Part IV: Hearing Before the S. Comm. on the Judiciary*, 110th Cong. 213–53 (2007), http://frwebgate. access.gpo.gov/cgi-bin/getdoc.cgi?dbname=110_senate_hearings&docid=f:35800. pdf; and JACK GOLDSMITH, THE TERROR PRESIDENCY (New York: W.W. Norton 2009).

14. GOLDSMITH, *supra* note 13; *see also* JANE MAYER, THE DARK SIDE (New York: Anchor Books 2009); ERIC LICHTBLAU, BUSH'S LAW (New York: Pantheon 2008).

15. GOLDSMITH, *supra* note 13, at 24.

16. *Id.* at 167; Cauley, *supra* note 1; Risen & Lichtblau, *supra* note 3.

17. *Inspector Gen. Report, NSA, supra* note 4, at 23; *see also* David D. Kirkpatrick & Scott Shane, *G.O.P. Senators Say Accord Is Set on Wiretapping*, N.Y. TIMES, Mar. 8, 2006, http://www.nytimes.com/2006/03/08/politics/08nsa. html; Scott Shane & Eric Lichtblau, *Full House Committee Gets Briefing on Eavesdropping*, N.Y. TIMES, Feb. 9, 2006, http://www.nytimes.com/2006/02/09/ politics/09nsa.html.

18. Elec. Privacy Info. Ctr. v. Dep't of Justice, 584 F. Supp. 2d 65 (D.D.C. 2008).

19. *Inspector Gen. Report, NSA, supra* note 4, at 21; Testimony by Comey, *supra* note 13, *at* 226–27.

20. *Inspector Gen. Report, NSA, supra* note 4.

21. *See* 28 U.S.C. § 508(a) (specifying procedures for filling a vacancy of the Attorney General's office).

22. Memorandum from Elizabeth B. Bazan & Jennifer K. Elsea, *supra* note 2, at 36–44.

23. *See* 50 U.S.C. § 1811 (allowing an exception to FISA for fifteen days following a declaration of war); Memorandum from Elizabeth B. Bazan & Jennifer K. Elsea, *supra* note 2, at 37.

24. GOLDSMITH, *supra* note 13, at 206, 227.

25. *Id.* at 206.

26. *See* MAYER, *supra* note 14, at 66–70.

27. *Id.* at 167, 182; *see Inspector Gen. Report, NSA, supra* note 4, at 31.

28. Cauley, *supra* note 1.

29. For an example of a blanket Cheney statement contending, without specific examples or documentation, that our antiterrorism strategies have saved thousands of lives, *see Cheney Says Interrogations Saved Thousands of Lives*, ABC (May 11, 2009, 8:00 A.M.), http://www.abc.net.au/news/stories/2009/05/11/2566040.htm.

30. LAWRENCE WRIGHT, THE LOOMING TOWER (New York: Alfred A. Knopf 2006).

31. *FISA Hearing: Hearing Before the Perm. Select Comm. on Intelligence*, 110th Cong. 76–79 (2007), http://www.fas.org/irp/congress/2007_hr/fisa092007. pdf, at 76–79; *Warrantless Surveillance and the Foreign Intelligence Surveillance Act: The Role of Checks and Balances in Protecting Americans' Privacy Rights (Part II): Hearing Before the H. Comm. on the Judiciary*, 110th Cong. 95 (2007), http:// www.fas.org/irp/congress/2007_hr/warrantless2.pdf.

32. Lawrence Wright, *The Spymaster: Can Mike McConnell Fix America's Intelligence Community?* THE NEW YORKER (Jan. 21, 2008), http://www.newyorker.com/

reporting/2008/01/21/080121fa_fact_wright; *see also FISA Hearing, supra* note 31, at 76–79.

33. Wright, *supra* note 32.

34. *Confronting the Terrorist Threat to the Homeland: Six Years After 9/11, Hearing Before S. Comm, on Homeland Security and Gov't'l Affairs*, 110th Cong. 20 (2007), http://www.dni.gov/testimonies/20070910_transcript.pdf.

35. *See* Dan Eggen, *Wiretap Delay Not Quite as Presented*, WASH. POST, Sept. 29, 2007, http://www.washingtonpost.com/wp-dyn/content/article/2007/09/28/AR2007092801858.html?nav=rss_politics.

36. *Inspector Gen. Report, NSA, supra* note 4, at 31–32.

37. JAMES BAMFORD, BODY OF SECRETS 647 (New York: Anchor Books 2002).

38. Ellen Nakashima & Dan Eggen, *Former CEO Says U.S. Punished Phone Firm*, WASH. POST, Oct. 13, 2007, http://www.washingtonpost.com/wp-dyn/content/article/2007/10/12/AR2007101202485.html.

39. Amy Schatz, *Paul Camp, Liberals Unite On Spy Bill*, WALL ST. J., June 26, 2008, http://online.wsj.com/article/SB121443403835305037.html?mod=googlenews_wsj.

40. ACLU v. Nat'l Sec. Agency, 438 F. Supp. 2d 754 (E.D. Mich. 2006), *rev'd*, 493 F.3d 644 (6th Cir. 2007), *cert. denied* 552 U.S. 1179 (2008).

41. ACLU v. Nat'l Sec. Agency, 493 F.3d 644 (6th Cir. 2007), *cert. denied* 552 U.S. 1179 (2008).

42. ACLU v. Nat'l Sec. Agency, 493 F. 3d 644 (6th Cir. 2007) *cert. denied* 552 U.S. 1179 (2008).

43. Amnesty Int'l USA v. McConnell, 646 F. Supp. 2d 633 (S.D.N.Y. 2009), *rev'd sub nom.* Amnesty Int'l USA v. Clapper, ___ F.3d ___, 2011 U.S. App. LEXIS 5699 (2d Cir. 2011).

44. Amnesty Int'l USA v. Clapper, ___ F.3d ___, 2011 U.S. App. LEXIS 5699 (2d Cir. 2011).

45. Times Topics: People, *Vaughn R. Walker*, N.Y. TIMES, Aug. 6, 2010, http://topics.nytimes.com/topics/reference/timestopics/people/w/vaughn_r_walker/index.html.

46. Senator Arlen Specter, for example, proposed a bill to indemnify the telecoms by making the government responsible instead. S. Amend. 5059 to H.R. 6404, 110th Cong. (2008) (withdrawn on July 9, 2008, having failed to achieve sixty votes in the affirmative); *see* Eric Lichtblau, *Democrats Delay a Vote on Immunity for Wiretaps*, N.Y. TIMES, Dec. 18, 2007, http://www.nytimes.com/2007/12/18/washington/18nsa.html?_r=2.

47. *Jewel v. Nat'l Sec. Agency*, 2010 WL 235075.

48. *Id.*; *see also* Government Defendants' Notice of Motion and Motion to Dismiss for Summary Judgment, *supra* note 9.

49. Tim Jones, *In Warrantless Wiretapping Case, Obama DOJ's New Arguments Are Worse Than Bush's*, DEEPLINKS BLOG (Apr. 7, 2009), http://www.eff.org/deeplinks/2009/04/obama-doj-worse-than-bush.

50. Carol D. Leonnig & Mary Beth Sheridan, *Saudi Group Alleges Wiretapping by U.S.*, WASH. POST, Mar. 2, 2006, http://www.washingtonpost.com/wp-dyn/content/article/2006/03/01/AR2006030102585.html?nav=most_emailed.

51. *See* Philip Shenon, *Lawyers Fear Monitoring in Cases on Terrorism*, N.Y. TIMES, Apr. 28, 2008, http://www.nytimes.com/2008/04/28/us/28lawyers.html.

52. In re Nat'l Sec. Agency Telecomms. Records Litig., 700 F. Supp. 2d 1182, 1189 (N.D. Cal. 2010) (referencing Defendants' Third Motion to Dismiss, or in the Alternative, for Summary Judgment, at 20–23).

53. Memorandum from United States Att'y Gen. Eric Holder to Heads of Executive Dep'ts, Agencies, and Heads of Dep't Components, on Policies and Procedures Governing Invocation of the State Secrets Privilege (Sept. 23, 2009), http://www.justice.gov/opa/documents/state-secret-privileges.pdf; *see also* Press Release, *U.S. Dep't of Justice, Office of Public Affairs, Attorney General Establishes New State Secrets Policies and Procedures*, U.S. DEP'T OF JUSTICE (Sept. 23, 2009), http://www.justice.gov/opa/pr/2009/September/09-ag-1013.html.

54. In re Nat'l Sec. Agency Telecomms. Records Litig., 700 F. Supp. 2d at 1196.

55. *Id.* at 1191.

56. *See* Daphne Eviatar, *Obama DOJ Defies Federal Judge*, WASH. INDEPENDENT, Mar. 2, 2009, http://washingtonindependent.com/31944/obama-doj-defies-federal-judge.

57. Michael Isikoff, *Holder's Dilemma: Will Justice Have to Pay Money to a Terrorist Organization?* NEWSWEEK (Apr. 21, 2010), http://www.newsweek.com/blogs/declassified/2010/04/21/holder-s-dilemma-will-justice-have-to-pay-money-to-a-terrorist-organization.html.

58. Eric Lichtblau & James Risen, *Officials Say U.S. Wiretaps Exceeded Law*, N.Y. TIMES, Apr. 16, 2009, http://www.nytimes.com/2009/04/16/us/16nsa.html?pagewanted=2&_r=1.

59. FREDERICK A. O. SCHWARZ, JR. & AZIZ Z. HUQ, UNCHECKED AND UNBALANCED (New York: The New Press 2008); *see also* Seth Kreimer, *Watching the Watchers: Surveillance, Transparency, and Political Freedom in the War on Terror*, 7 U. PA. J. CONST. L. 133 (2004).

60. *See* 50 U.S.C. §§ 1805b(h)(1)(A) & 1805b(i); In re Directives [redacted text]* Pursuant to Section 105B of the Foreign Intelligence Surveillance Act, 551 F.3d 1004, 1009 (FISA Ct. Rev. 2008).

61. Theodore W. Ruger, *Chief Justice Rehnquist's Appointments to the FISA Court: An Empirical Perspective*, 101 NW. U.L. REV. 239, 257 (2007).

62. In re Directives [redacted text], 551 F.3d at 1014.

63. Motion of the ACLU for Release of Court Records, In re Motion for Release of Court Records (FISA Ct. Aug. 8, 2007) (MISC. 07-01), http://www.aclu.org/files/images/asset_upload_file968_31228.pdf; *see also ACLU Asks Special Intelligence Court to Release Orders That Led to "Emergency" Wiretapping Legislation*, ACLU (Aug. 8, 2007), http://www.aclu.org/national-security/aclu-asks-secret-intelligence-court-release-orders-led-emergency-wiretapping-legis.

64. Matthew R. Hall, *Constitutional Regulation of National Security Investigation: Minimizing the Use of Unrelated Evidence*, 41 WAKE FOREST L. REV. 61 (2006); Kreimer, *supra* note 59, at 171–81.

65. Complaint, ACLU v. Office of the Dir. of Nat'l Intelligence, No. 10-cv-4419, (S.D.N.Y. June 3, 2010), http://www.aclu.org/files/assets/2010-6-3-FAAComplaint_1.pdf.

66. See *Summary of FISA Amendments Act FOIA Documents Released on November 29, 2010*, ACLU, http://www.aclu.org/files/pdfs/natsec/faafoia20101129/20101129Summary.pdf. The documents themselves are available at http://www.aclu.org/national-security/faa-foia-documents.

Chapter 11

1. 9/11 COMMISSION REPORT: FINAL REPORT OF THE NATIONAL COMMISSION ON TERRORIST ATTACKS UPON THE UNITED STATES 365 (Washington, DC: USGPO, 2004), http://www.gpoaccess.gov/911/pdf/fullreport.pdf [hereinafter *9/11 Commission Report*].

2. President Barack H. Obama, Remarks by the President on National Security at the National Archives (May 21, 2009), http://www.whitehouse.gov/the_press_office/Remarks-by-the-President-On-National-Security-5-21-09/.

3. *Transcript of Obama-Sotomayor Nomination*, CNN (May 26, 2009), http://articles.cnn.com/2009-05-26/politics/obama.sotomayor.transcript_1_justice-souter-supreme-court-highest-court?_s=PM:POLITICS.

4. President Obama, Remarks at the National Archives, *supra* note 2.

5. Clinton's decisions were made in January 2010. The Second Circuit Court of Appeals had held in July 2009 that the government had not shown sufficient reason for excluding Ramadan to overcome the First Amendment rights of the American Academy of Religion, the American Association of University Professors, and the PEN American Center to hear his ideas. Am. Acad. of Religion v. Napolitano, 573 F.3d 115 (2d Cir. 2009).

6. Speech by Senator Barack H. Obama, *The War We Need to Win*, Woodrow Wilson Center (Aug. 1, 2007), http://www.barackobama.com/2007/08/01/remarks_of_senator_obama_the_w_1.php.

7. Patriot Act § 102.

8. Peter Baker, *Obama's War over Terror*, N.Y. TIMES, Jan. 17, 2010, http://www.nytimes.com/2010/01/17/magazine/17Terror-t.html.

9. JACK GOLDSMITH, THE TERROR PRESIDENCY 71 (New York: W.W. Norton 2009).

10. Baker, *supra* note 8; JONATHAN ALTER, THE PROMISE 101–03 (New York: Simon & Schuster 2010).

11. GOLDSMITH, *supra* note 9, at 189–90.

12. Presidential Memorandum on the Freedom of Information Act, 74 Fed. Reg. 4,683 (Jan. 21, 2010).

13. *See Justice Department Releases Bush Administration Torture Memos*, ACLU (Apr. 16, 2009), http://www.aclu.org/national-security/justice-department-releases-bush-administration-torture-memos; *see also Selected Opinions of the Office of Legal Counsel (OLC), Department of Justice*, FEDERATION OF AM. SCIENTISTS, http://www.fas.org/irp/agency/doj/olc/index.html (listing released OLC memos and Obama Administration disavowal of OLC opinions).

14. Dep't of Def. v. ACLU, 543 F.3d 59 (2d Cir. 2009), *vacated and cert. granted*, ___ U.S. ___, 130 S. Ct. 777 (2009).

15. Protected National Security Documents Act of 2009, Pub. L. No. 111–83, § 565, 123 Stat. 2142, 2184–86 (2009)

16. President Obama, Remarks at the National Archives, *supra* note 2.

17. President Obama, Remarks at the National Archives, *supra* note 2.

18. OFFICE OF THE INSPECTOR GEN., U.S. DEPT. OF JUSTICE, THE FEDERAL BUREAU OF INVESTIGATION'S TERRORIST WATCHLIST NOMINATION PRACTICES (2009), http://www.justice.gov/oig/reports/FBI/a0925/final.pdf [hereinafter *Inspector Gen. Report, Watchlist Practices*].

19. *Hearing before the S. Comm. on the Judiciary on Reauthorization of the USA PATRIOT ACT*, 111st Cong. (2009) (statement of Glenn Fine, Inspector Gen., U.S. Dep't of Justice).

20. *9/11 Commission Report*, *supra* note 1, at 418–20.

21. *E.g.*, National Security Letters Reform Act of 2007, H.R. 3189, 110th Cong. (2007).

22. Glenn Greenwald, *Obama and the Myth of the Public Opinion Excuse*, SA-LON.COM, (May 18, 2020, 6:19 A.M.), http://www.salon.com/news/opinion/glenn_greenwald/2010/05/18/public_opinion.

23. *Establishing a New Normal: National Security, Civil Liberties and Human Rights Under the Obama Administration*, ACLU (July 22, 2010), http://www.aclu.org/files/assets/EstablishingNewNormal.pdf.

24. For a moving account of the personal impact of the global War on Terror on Muslims, *see* AMITAVA KUMAR, A FOREIGNER CARRYING IN THE CROOK OF HIS ARM A TINY BOMB (Durham, NC: Duke Univ. Press 2010).

25. Committee on Technical and Privacy Dimensions of Information for Terrorism Prevention and Other National Goals, National Research Council, *Public Opinion Data on U.S. Attitudes Toward Government Counterterrorism Efforts*, *in* PROTECTING INDIVIDUAL PRIVACY IN THE STRUGGLE AGAINST TERRORISTS: A FRAME-WORK FOR PROGRAM ASSESSMENT 283–84 (Washington, DC: Academy of Sciences 2008), http://books.nap.edu/openbook.php?rcord_id=12452&page=283.

26. Adam Nagourney & Janet Elder, *New Poll Finds Mixed Support for Wire-taps*, N.Y. TIMES, Jan. 27, 2006, http://www.nytimes.com/2006/01/27/politics/27poll.html?pagewanted=1&ref=newyorktimes-poll-watch.

27. Lydia Saad, *Americans Reject Extreme Anti-Privacy Security Measures*, GAL-LUP (Aug. 8, 2005), http://www.gallup.com/poll/17686/Americans-Reject-Extreme-AntiPrivacy-Security-Measures.aspx.

28. *Terrorism in the United States*, GALLUP (Jan. 8, 2010), http://www.gallup.com/poll/4909/Terrorism-United-States.aspx.

29. JOHN HART ELY, DEMOCRACY AND DISTRUST (Cambridge, MA: Harvard Univ. Press 1980).

30. The other case is Totten v. United States, 92 U.S. 105 (1875), reaffirmed by Tenet v. Doe, 544 U.S. 1 (2005).

31. United States v. Reynolds, 345 U.S. 1 (1953).

32. BARRY SIEGEL, CLAIM OF PRIVILEGE (New York: HarperCollins 2008).

33. Dan Christensen, *Secrecy Appealed*, MIAMI DAILY BUS. REV., Sept. 25, 2003.

34. Dan Christensen, *Secrecy Within*, MIAMI DAILY BUS. REV., Mar. 12, 2003.

35. Warren Richey, *Secret 9/11 Case Before High Court*, CHRISTIAN SCI. MONI-TOR, Oct. 30, 2003, http://www.csmonitor.com/2003/1030/p.01s02-usju.html.

36. Brief Amici Curiae of the Reporters Committee for Freedom of the Press in Support of the Petitioner, M.K.B. v. Warden, 540 U.S. 1213 (2004), http://www.rcfp.org/news/documents/20031103-mkbvwarden.pdf.

37. *M.K.B.*, 540 U.S. 1213.

38. *See* SUSAN N. HERMAN, THE RIGHT TO A SPEEDY AND PUBLIC TRIAL 22–30 (Westport, CT: Praeger 2006).

39. Detroit Free Press v. Ashcroft, 195 F. Supp. 2d 937, 940 (E.D. Mich. Apr. 3, 2002), *reh'g and reh'g en banc denied*, 303 F.3d 681 (6th Cir. 2002).

40. Detroit Free Press v. Ashcroft, 303 F.3d 681, 683 (6th Cir. 2002).

41. *Id.* at 709.

42. *See* David Pozen, *The Mosaic Theory, National Security, and the Freedom of Information Act*, 115 YALE L.J. 628 (2005).

43. North Jersey Media Grp. v. Ashcroft, 308 F.3d 198 (3d Cir. 2002), *cert. denied*, 538 U.S. 1056 (2003).

44. Center for Nat'l Sec. Stud. v. Dep't of Justice, 331 F.3d 918, 928 (D.C. Cir. 2003), *cert. denied*, 540 U.S. 1104 (2004).

45. *North Jersey Media*, 308 F.3d 198.

46. *Detroit Free Press*, 303 F.3d 681.

47. ACLU v. United States, 538 U.S. 920 (2003). Because there was only one party to this case—the government—and the government had won below, no one had the right to file a petition for certiorari, so the Court had an easy out, as described in chapter 6.

48. *M.K.B.*, 540 U.S. 1213.

49. Center for Nat'l Sec. Stud. v. Dep't of Justice, 331 F.3d at 928.

50. United States v. Awadallah, 349 F.3d 42 (2d Cir. 2003), *cert. denied*, 543 U.S. 1056 (2005).

51. ACLU v. Nat'l Sec. Agency, 493 F.3d 644 (6th Cir. 2007), *cert. denied*, 552 U.S. 1179 (2008).

52. United States v. Afshari, 426 F.3d 1150 (9th Cir. 2005), *cert. denied sub nom.* Rahmani v. United States, 549 U.S. 1110 (2007).

53. Mayfield v. United States, 599 F.3d 964 (9th Cir. 2010), *cert. denied*, ___ U.S. ___, 131 S. Ct. 503 (2010).

54. El-Masri v. United States, 479 F.3d 296 (4th Cir. 2007), *cert. denied*, 552 U.S. 947 (2007).

55. *See* Khaled El-Masri, *I Am Not a State Secret*, L.A. TIMES, Mar. 3, 2007, http://articles.latimes.com/2007/mar/03/opinion/oe-elmasri3.

56. *See, e.g.,* James Meek, *Khaled el-Masri Describes America's Secret Offshore Prison Network*, GUARDIAN, Jan. 14, 2005, http://www.guardian.co.uk/world/2005/jan/14/usa.germany.

57. Arar v. Ashcroft, 585 F.3d 559 (2d Cir. 2009) (*en banc*), *cert. denied*, ___ U.S. ___, 130 S. Ct. 3409 (2010).

58. *See Harper's Apology "Means the World": Arar*, BROADCAST NEWS, Jan. 26, 2007, http://www.cbc.ca/canada/story/2007/01/26/harper-apology.html.

59. ACLU v. Nat'l Sec. Agency, 493 F.3d 664; Amnesty Int'l USA v. McConnell, 646 F. Supp. 2d 633 (S.D.N.Y. 2009), *rev'd sub nom.* Amnesty Int'l USA v. Clapper, ___ F.3d ___, 2011 U.S. App. LEXIS 5699 (2d Cir. 2011).

60. Jewel v. Nat'l Sec. Agency, No. C 06–1791 VRW, 2010 WL 235075, at *1 (N.D. Cal. Jan. 21, 2010).

61. Al-Haramain Islamic Found., Inc. v. Bush, 507 F.3d 1190, 1193 (9th Cir. 2007), *remanded sub nom.* In re Nat'l Sec. Agency Telecomms. Records Litig., 700 F. Supp. 2d 1182, 1189 (N.D. Cal. 2010).

62. *Jewel*, 2010 WL 235075, at *1.

63. Al-Kidd v. Ashcroft, 580 F.3d 949 (9th Cir. 2009), *reh'g en banc denied*, 598 F.3d 1129 (9th Cir. 2010), *cert. granted,* Ashcroft v. al-Kidd, ___ U.S. ___, 131 S. Ct. 415 (2010).

64. *See* Jane Mayer, *Outsourcing: The C.I.A.'s Travel Agent*, NEW YORKER (Oct. 30, 2006), http://www.newyorker.com/archive/2006/10/30/061030ta_talk_mayer.

65. John Schwartz, *Obama Backs Off a Reversal on Secrets*, N.Y. TIMES, Feb. 9, 2009, http://www.nytimes.com/2009/02/10/us/10torture.html?_r=2&hp.

66. Mohamed v. Jeppesen Dataplan, 579 F.3d 943, 950 (9th Cir. 2009), *rev'd*, 614 F.3d 1070 (9th Cir. 2010), *cert. denied*, 563 U.S. ___ (May 16, 2011).

67. Ashcroft v. Iqbal, ___ U.S. ___, 129 S. Ct. 1937 (2009).

68. OFFICE OF THE INSPECTOR GEN., U.S. DEP'T OF JUSTICE, THE SEPTEMBER 11 DETAINEES: A REVIEW OF THE TREATMENT OF ALIENS HELD ON IMMIGRATION CHARGES IN CONNECTION WITH THE INVESTIGATION OF THE SEPTEMBER 11 ATTACKS (2003), http://www.usdoj.gov/oig/special/0306/full.pdf.

69. For critiques of *Iqbal, see, e.g.*, Richard G. Bone, *Plausibility Pleading Revising and Revised: A Comment on Ashcroft v. Iqbal,* 85 NOTRE DAME L. REV. 849 (March 2010); Elizabeth M. Schneider, *The Changing Shape of Federal Civil Pretrial Practice: The Disparate Impact on Civil Rights and Employment Discrimination Cases,* 158 U. PA. L. REV. 517 (2010).

70. ERWIN CHEMERINSKY, THE CONSERVATIVE ASSAULT ON THE CONSTITUTION (New York: Simon & Schuster 2010).

71. There are, of course, deep and ardent differences of opinion about the proper role of the judiciary. For one vigorous argument that the courts should defer to the elected branches on antiterrorism policy, *see* ERIC A. POSNER & ADRIAN VERMEULE, TERROR IN THE BALANCE (New York: Oxford Univ. Press 2007).

72. Norman Dorsen, *Foreign Affairs and Civil Liberties,* 83 AM. J. INT'L L. 840 (1989); *see also* WILLIAM H. REHNQUIST, ALL THE LAWS BUT ONE 224–25 (New York: Alfred A. Knopf 1998) ("It is neither desirable nor is it remotely likely that civil liberty will occupy as favored a position in wartime as it does in peacetime").

73. Korematsu v. United States, 323 U.S. 214 (1944).

74. *See* Korematsu v. United States, 584 F. Supp. 106 (N.D. Cal. 1984) (*coram nobis* petition); Peter Irons, JUSTICE AT WAR 206–18 (New York: Univ. Press Oxford 1983).

75. Hirabayashi v. United States, 828 F.2d 591, 598 (9th Cir. 1987).

76. GEOFFREY R. STONE, PERILOUS TIMES 180 (New York: W.W. Norton, 2004). *See* Lee Epstein, Daniel E. Ho, Gary King, & Jeffrey A. Segal, *The Supreme Court During Crisis: How War Affects Only Non-War Cases,* 80 N.Y.U. L. REV. 1 (2005) (attempt at empirical study of Supreme Court behavior during wartime, concluding that "when crises threaten the nation's security, the justices are substantially more likely to curtail rights and liberties than when peace prevails," but that cases not concerning the war itself are most affected).

77. W. Va. State Bd. of Educ. v. Barnette, 319 U.S. 624 (1943).

78. For a fascinating exploration of whether the Supreme Court actually reflects popular will, *see* BARRY FRIEDMAN, THE WILL OF THE PEOPLE (New York: Farrar, Straus & Giroux 2009).

79. *See, e.g.*, JEFFREY ROSEN, THE NAKED CROWD 132–47 (New York: Random House 2005); JAMES B. RULE, PRIVACY IN PERIL 195 (New York: Oxford Univ. Press 2007); Epstein et al., *supra* note 76, at 110–11.

Conclusion

1. ANTHONY D. ROMERO & DINA TEMPLE-RASTON, IN DEFENSE OF OUR AMERICA 205–06 (New York: HarperCollins 2007).

2. THE DOUGLAS LETTERS 16 (Melvin I. Urofsky & Philip E. Urofsky eds., Bethesda, MD: Adler & Adler 1987).

3. Jason Mazzone, *The Security Constitution,* 53 UCLA L. REV. 29, 38 (2005).

4. THE FEDERALIST NO. 41, at 275 (James Madison) (Jacob E. Cooke ed., Middletown, CT: Wesleyan Univ. Press 1961).

5. INTERNATIONAL COMMISSION OF JURISTS, ASSESSING DAMAGE, URGING ACTION: REPORT OF THE EMINENT JURISTS PANEL ON TERRORISM, COUNTER-TERRORISM AND HUMAN RIGHTS 159 (2009), http://ejp.icj.org/IMG/EJP-Report.pdf.

6. Harold Hongju Koh, *The Spirit of the Laws*, 43 HARV. INT'L L.J. 23, 23 (2002).

7. ASSESSING DAMAGE, *supra* note 5, at 164.

8. 9/11 COMMISSION REPORT: FINAL REPORT OF THE NATIONAL COMMISSION ON TERRORIST ATTACKS UPON THE UNITED STATES 394–95 (Washington, DC: USGPO, 2004), http://www.gpoaccess.gov/911/pdf/fullreport.pdf.

9. TERRORISM, GOVERNMENT, AND LAW (Susan N. Herman & Paul Finkelman eds., New York: Praeger 2008).

10. THE FEDERALIST NO. 51, at 351 (James Madison) (Jacob E. Cooke ed., Middletown, CT: Wesleyan Univ. Press 1961).

11. *See* Susan N. Herman, *Collapsing Spheres: Joint Terrorism Task Forces, Federalism, and the War on Terror*, 41 WILLAMETTE L. REV. 941, 947 (2005).

12. Burt Neuborne, *Toward Procedural Parity in Constitutional Litigation*, 22 WM. & MARY L. REV. 725, 731 (1981).

13. *See* Alien and Sedition Acts, Va. Res. (1789), http://avalon.law.yale.edu/18th_century/virres.asp; Alien and Sedition Acts, Ky. Res. (1799), http://avalon.law.yale.edu/18th_century/kenres.asp.

14. *See Resolutions Passed*, BILL OF RIGHTS DEFENSE COMMITTEE (Mar. 27, 2009, 11:55 A.M.), http://www.bordc.org/resources/alphalist.pdf.

15. *See* Herman, *Collapsing Spheres*, *supra* note 11, at 950–55.

16. *See* Heather Gerken, *Foreword: Federalism All the Way Down*, 124 HARV. L. REV. 1, 60–71 (2010) (describing the interplay of dissent by local decision-makers and national policy).

17. *See* FOX BUTTERFIELD, A NATION CHALLENGED: THE INTERVIEWS; *Police Are Split on Questioning of Mideast Men*, N.Y. TIMES, Nov. 22, 2001, http://www.nytimes.com/2001/11/22/national/22POLI.html.

18. Printz v. United States, 521 U.S. 898 (1997); *see* Ann Althouse, *The Vigor of Anti-Commandeering Doctrine in Times of Terror*, *in* TERRORISM, GOVERNMENT, AND LAW, *supra* note 9, at 25.

19. For a critique of the operation of the Fusion Centers, *see* Michael German & Jay Stanley, *What's Wrong with Fusion Centers*, http://www.aclu.org/files/pdfs/privacy/fusioncenter_20071212.pdf, updated in 2008, and in *More About Fusion Centers*, ACLU (June 25, 2010), http://www.aclu.org/spy-files/more-about-fusion-centers. For an academic perspective, *see* Danielle Keats Citron & Frank Pasquale, *Network Accountability for the Domestic Intelligence Apparatus*, 62 HASTINGS L.J. ___ (2011) (critiquing Fusion Centers as eroding civil liberties and overreaching in a manner that has resulted in "wasted resources without concomitant gains in security").

20. *See, e.g.*, *The ACLU Fights Illegal Phone Spying in Colorado*, ACLU (Jan. 16, 2007), http://www.aclu.org/national-security/aclu-fights-illegal-phone-spying-colorado.

21. FISA Amendments Act of 2008, Pub. L. No. 110–261 § 801, 122 Stat. 2436, 2467 (2008).

22. GEOFFREY R. STONE, WAR AND LIBERTY 155 (New York: W.W. Norton 2007).

23. *See, e.g.,* Jack Goldsmith & Cass R. Sunstein, *Military Tribunals and Legal Culture: What a Difference Sixty Years Makes,* 19 CONST. COMMENT. 261, 285 (2002); Mark Tushnet, *Defending Korematsu? Reflections on Civil Liberties in Wartime,* 2003 WISC. L. REV. 273, 294–95 (2003); David Cole, *The New McCarthyism: Repeating History in the War on Terrorism,* 38 HARV. C.R.-C.L.L. REV. 1 (2003).

24. *See* GEOFFREY R. STONE, PERILOUS TIMES 33–41 (New York: W.W. Norton 2004).

25. *Id.* at 71–73.

26. Japanese-American Evacuation Claims Act of 1948, ch. 814, 62 Stat. 1231 (1948) (codified in scattered sections of 50 U.S.C. app.).

27. 18 U.S.C. § 4001.

28. Civil Liberties Act of 1988, Pub. L. No. 100–383, 102 Stat. 903, 903 (codified at 50 U.S.C. app. § 1989).

29. COMMISSION ON THE WARTIME RELOCATION AND INTERNMENT OF CIVILIANS, PERSONAL JUSTICE DENIED 5–8 (Washington, DC: USGPO 1983).

30. Korematsu v. United States, 584 F. Supp. 1406 (C.D. Cal. 1984); Hirabayashi v. United States, 828 F.2d 591 (9th Cir. 1987).

31. Brandenburg v. Ohio, 395 U.S. 444 (1969). *See* JOHN HART ELY, DEMOCRACY AND DISTRUST, 105–16 (Cambridge, MA: Harv. Univ. Press 1980); Geoffrey R. Stone, *Free Speech in the Twenty-First Century: Ten Lessons from the Twentieth Century,* 36 PEPP. L. REV. 273 (2009) (evaluating the line of decisions from Schenck v. United States, 249 U.S. 47 (1919), in 1919, to *Brandenburg* in 1969).

32. FREDERICK A. O. SCHWARZ, JR. & AZIZ Z. HUQ, UNCHECKED AND UNBALANCED 21–56 (New York: New Press 2007).

33. HAROLD C. RELYEA, SPECIAL S. COMM. ON NAT'L EMERGENCIES AND DELEGATED EMERGENCY POWERS, A BRIEF HISTORY OF EMERGENCY POWERS IN THE UNITED STATES (Washington, DC: USGPO 1974).

34. SCHWARZ & HUQ, *supra* note 32, at 59–61.

Further Reading

Bruce Ackerman, *Before the Next Attack: Preserving Civil Liberties in an Age of Terrorism* (New Haven, CT: Yale University Press, 2006).

ACLU Reports: *America Unrestored* (2010); *The New Normal* (2010); *Blocking Faith, Freezing Charity* (2009); *What's Wrong with Fusion Centers?* (2007); *The Surveillance-Industrial Complex* (2004); *Bigger Monster, Weaker Chains: The Growth of an American Surveillance Society* (2003); *Unpatriotic Acts: The FBI's Power to Rifle Through Your Personal Belongings and Records Without Telling You* (2003); *Insatiable Appetite: The Government's Demand for New and Unnecessary Powers After September 11* (2002)—available at http://www.aclu.org.

Jonathan Alter, *The Promise: President Obama, Year One* (New York: Simon & Schuster, 2010).

Hannah Arendt, *The Human Condition* (2d ed. Chicago: University of Chicago Press, 1998).

Andrew Bacevich, *The Limits of Power: The End of American Exceptionalism* (New York: Holt, 2009).

Stewart A. Baker and John Kavanagh, eds., *Patriot Debates: Experts Debate the USA PATRIOT Act* (Chicago: American Bar Assn., 2005).

James Bamford, *Body of Secrets* (New York: Anchor Books, 2002).

James Bamford, *The Puzzle Palace* (Boston: Houghton Mifflin, 1982).

Phillip Bobbitt, *Terror and Consent: The Wars for the Twenty-First Century* (New York: Alfred A. Knopf, 2008).

Erwin Chemerinsky, *The Conservative Assault on the Constitution* (New York: Simon & Schuster, 2010).

Richard A. Clarke, *Against All Enemies: Inside America's War on Terror* (New York: Free Press, 2004).

David Cole, *Enemy Aliens: Double Standards and Constitutional Freedoms in the War on Terrorism* (2d ed. New York: New Press, 2005).

David Cole and Jules Lobel, *Less Safe, Less Free: Why America Is Losing the War on Terror* (New York: New Press, 2007).

Whitfield Diffie and Susan E. Landau, *Privacy on the Line* (2d ed. Cambridge, MA: MIT Press, 2007).

Laura K. Donohue, *The Cost of Counterterrorism: Power, Politics, and Liberty* (New York: Cambridge University Press, 2008).

John Hart Ely, *Democracy and Distrust: A Theory of Judicial Review* (Cambridge, MA: Harvard University Press, 1980).

Eminent Jurists Panel on Terrorism, Counterterrorism, and Human Rights (Geneva: International Commission of Jurists, 2009).

Susan Faludi, *The Terror Dream: Fear and Fantasy in Post-9/11 America* (New York: Metropolitan, 2007).

Bruce Fein, *Constitutional Peril: The Life and Death Struggle for Our Constitution and Democracy* (New York: Palgrave Macmillan, 2009).

Michel Foucault, *Discipline and Punish: The Birth of the Prison* (New York: Vintage, 1979).

Barry Friedman, *The Will of the People: How Public Opinion Has Influenced the Supreme Court and Shaped the Meaning of the Constitution* (New York: Farrar, Straus & Giroux, 2009).

Benjamin H. Friedman, Jim Harper, and Christopher A. Preble, eds., *Terrorizing Ourselves: Why U.S. Counterterrorism Policy Is Failing and How to Fix It* (Washington, DC: Cato, 2010).

Mary Fulbrook, *The People's State: East German Society from Hitler to Honecker* (London: Yale University Press, 2008).

Jack Goldsmith, *The Terror Presidency: Law and Judgment Inside the Bush Administration* (New York: W.W. Norton, 2009).

Amy Goodman and David Goodman, *Standing Up to the Madness: Ordinary Heroes in Extraordinary Times* (New York: Hyperion, 2008).

Bernard Harcourt, *Against Prediction* (Chicago: University of Chicago Press, 2007).

Susan N. Herman, *The Right to a Speedy and Public Trial* (Westport, CT: Praeger, 2006).

Susan N. Herman and Paul Finkelman, eds., *Terrorism, Government, and Law* (New York: Praeger, 2008).

Peter Irons, *Justice at War* (New York: Oxford University Press, 1983).

Amitava Kumar, *A Foreigner Carrying in the Crook of His Arm a Tiny Bomb* (Durham, NC: Duke University Press, 2010).

George Lakoff, *Don't Think of an Elephant!* (White River Junction, VT: Chelsea Green, 2004).

Nelson Lasson, *The History and Development of the Fourth Amendment to the United States Constitution* (New York: Da Capo, 1970).

Richard C. Leone and Greg Anrig, Jr., eds., *The War on Our Freedoms: Civil Liberties in an Age of Terrorism* (New York: Public Affairs, 2003).

Eric Lichtblau, *Bush's Law: The Remaking of American Law* (New York: Pantheon, 2008).

John P. MacKenzie, *Absolute Power: How the Unitary Executive Theory Is Undermining the Constitution* (New York: Century Foundation, 2008).

Jane Mayer, *The Dark Side* (New York: Anchor Books, 2009).

National Commission on Terrorist Attacks upon the United States, The 9/11 Commission Report (Washington, DC: USGPO, 2004).

National Research Council of the National Academy of Science, *Protecting Individual Privacy in the Struggle Against Terrorism* (Washington, DC: National Academies Press, 2008).

Barack Obama, *The Audacity of Hope: Thoughts on Reclaiming the American Dream* (New York: Vintage, 2008).

Christian Parenti, *The Soft Cage: Surveillance in America from Slave Passes to the War on Terror* (New York: Basic Books, 2003).

Eric A. Posner and Adrian Vermeule, *Terror in the Balance: Security, Liberty, and the Courts* (New York: Oxford University Press, 2007).

Richard Posner, *Not a Suicide Pact: The Constitution in a Time of National Emergency* (New York: Oxford University Press, 2006).

William H. Rehnquist, *All the Laws But One* (New York: Alfred A. Knopf, 1998).

David Remnick, *The Bridge: The Life and Rise of Barack Obama* (New York: Alfred A. Knopf, 2010).

Anthony D. Romero and Dina Temple-Raston, *In Defense of Our America: The Fight for Civil Liberties in the Age of Terror* (New York: HarperCollins, 2007).

Jeffrey Rosen, *The Naked Crowd: Reclaiming Security and Freedom in an Anxious Age* (New York: Random House, 2005).

James B. Rule, *Privacy in Peril: How We Are Sacrificing a Fundamental Right in Exchange for Security and Convenience* (New York: Oxford University Press, 2007).

Austin Sarat, ed., *Dissent in Dangerous Times* (Ann Arbor: University of Michigan Press, 2005).

Frederick Schauer, *Profiles, Probabilities, and Stereotypes* (Cambridge, MA: Belknap/Harvard, 2003).

Bruce Schneier, *Beyond Fear: Thinking Sensibly About Security in an Uncertain World* (New York: Copernicus, 2003).

Stephen J. Schulhofer, *Rethinking the Patriot Act: Ideas for Reform* (New York: Century Foundation, 2005).

Frederick A. O. Schwarz, Jr. and Aziz Z. Huq, *Unchecked and Unbalanced: Presidential Power in a Time of Terror* (New York: New Press, 2007).

Barry Siegel, *Claim of Privilege* (New York: HarperCollins, 2008).

Daniel J. Solove, *The Digital Person* (New York: New York University Press, 2004).

Jessica Stern, *Terror in the Name of God* (New York: HarperCollins, 2003).

Geoffrey R. Stone, *Perilous Times: Free Speech in Wartime from the Sedition Act of 1798 to the War on Terrorism* (New York: W.W. Norton, 2004).

Geoffrey R. Stone, *War and Liberty: An American Dilemma: 1790 to the Present* (New York: W.W. Norton, 2007).

Philippa Strum, *Privacy: The Debate in the United States Since 1945* (Fort Worth, TX: Harcourt Brace, 1998).

Cass Sunstein, *The Laws of Fear: Beyond the Precautionary Principle* (New York: Cambridge University Press, 2005).

Ron Suskind, *The One Percent Doctrine* (New York: Simon & Schuster, 2006).

Charles J. Sykes, *The End of Privacy: The Attack on Personal Rights at Home, at Work, On-Line, and in Court* (New York: St. Martin's Press, 1999).

Alexis de Tocqueville, *Democracy in America* (J. P. Mayer ed., George Lawrence trans., New York: HarperCollins, 1988).

W. Kip Viscusi, *The Risks of Terrorism* (New York: Kluwer, 2004).

Ibrahim Warde, *The Price of Fear* (Berkeley: University of California Press, 2007).

Alan Westin, *Privacy and Freedom* (New York: Atheneum, 1967).

Benjamin Wittes, ed., *Legislating the War on Terror: An Agenda for Reform* (Washington, DC: Brookings, 2009).

Lawrence Wright, *The Looming Tower* (New York: Alfred A. Knopf, 2006).

John Yoo, *War by Any Other Means: An Insider's Account of the War on Terror* (New York: Atlantic Monthly Press, 2006).

Photo Credits

Index